T0323813

Heterodox Macroeconomics

The global financial crisis of 2008 is rooted in the contradictory macroeconomic dynamics of the current variant of globalization. The gradual evolution of such a crisis inevitably pushes macroeconomic theory, particularly critical/heterodox theory, in new directions. A subset of these theoretical developments has resulted in a much improved integrated heterodox approach based on the original contributions of Keynes, Marx and early institutionalists. An integrated theory that is more coherent, logically consistent, realistic, flexible and capable of explaining modern macrodynamics in historical time has emerged.

Heterodox Macroeconomics offers a detailed understanding of the foundations of the recent global financial crisis. The chapters, from a selection of leading academics in the field of heterodox macroeconomics, carry out a synthesis of heterodox ideas that place financial instability, macroeconomic crisis, rising global inequality and a grasp of the perverse and pernicious qualities of global and domestic macroeconomic policy making since 1980 into a coherent perspective. It familiarizes the reader with the emerging unified theory of heterodox macroeconomics and its applications.

The book is divided into four key parts:

I   heterodox macroeconomics and the Keynes–Marx synthesis;
II   accumulation, crisis and instability;
III the macrodynamics of the neoliberal regime; and
IV   heterodox macroeconomic policy.

The chapters include theoretical, international, historical and country perspectives on financial fragility and macroeconomic instability.

This book will be of interest to students and researchers in macroeconomics, heterodox economics, political economy, Marxian economics, post Keynesian economics, crisis theory, globalization and financialization.

Jonathan P. Goldstein is Professor of Economics at Bowdoin College, Brunswick, Maine. His fields of specialization include political economy, macroeconomics and applied econometrics. **Michael G. Hillard** is Professor of Economics at the University of Southern Maine, Portland, Maine. He has written widely on labor relations, labor history and the political economy of labor.

Routledge advances in heterodox economics
Edited by Frederic S. Lee
University of Missouri-Kansas City

Over the past two decades, the intellectual agendas of heterodox economists have taken a decidedly pluralist turn. Leading thinkers have begun to move beyond the established paradigms of Austrian, feminist, Institutional-evolutionary, Marxian, Post Keynesian, radical, social, and Sraffian economics – opening up new lines of analysis, criticism, and dialogue among dissenting schools of thought. This cross-fertilization of ideas is creating a new generation of scholarship in which novel combinations of heterodox ideas are being brought to bear on important contemporary and historical problems.

Routledge Advances in Heterodox Economics aims to promote this new scholarship by publishing innovative books in heterodox economic theory, policy, philosophy, intellectual history, institutional history, and pedagogy. Syntheses or critical engagement of two or more heterodox traditions are especially encouraged.

This series was previously published by The University of Michigan Press and the following books are available (please contact UMP for more information):

Economics in Real Time
A theoretical reconstruction
John McDermott

Liberating Economics
Feminist perspectives on families, work, and globalization
Drucilla K. Barker and Susan F. Feiner

Socialism After Hayek
Theodore A. Burczak

Future Directions for Heterodox Economics
Edited by John T. Harvey and Robert F. Garnett, Jr.

Heterodox Macroeconomics

Keynes, Marx and globalization

**Edited by Jonathan P. Goldstein and
Michael G. Hillard**

Routledge
Taylor & Francis Group

LONDON AND NEW YORK

First published 2009
by Routledge
2 Park Square, Milton Park, Abingdon, Oxon, OX14 4RN

Simultaneously published in the USA and Canada
by Routledge
711 Third Avenue, New York, NY 10017

Routledge is an imprint of the Taylor & Francis Group, an informa business

First issued in paperback 2011

Typeset in Times by Wearset Ltd, Boldon, Tyne and Wear

British Library Cataloguing in Publication Data
A catalogue record for this book is available from the British Library

Library of Congress Cataloging in Publication Data
Heterodox macroeconomics: Keynes, Marx and globalization/edited by
Jonathan P. Goldstein and Michael G. Hillard.
p. cm.
Includes bibliographical references and index.
1. Macroeconomics. I. Goldstein, Jonathan P. II. Hillard, Michael G.
HB172.5.H48 2009
339–dc22   2008050954

ISBN10: 0-415-77808-5 (hbk)
ISBN10: 0-415-66597-3 (pbk)
ISBN10: 0-203-87670-9 (ebk)

ISBN13: 978-0-415-77808-4 (hbk)
ISBN13: 978-0-415-66597-1 (pbk)
ISBN13: 978-0-203-87670-1 (ebk)

To Jim Crotty, who inspired generations of graduate students and colleagues and who has done more than any scholar to advance and apply a synthesis of Keynes and Marx to the contemporary era.

Contents

PART II
Accumulation, crisis and instability

PART III
The macrodynamics of the neoliberal regime

Illustrations

Figures

Tables

Contributors

Raford (Ray) Boddy is Emeritus Professor of Economics at San Diego State University. He also taught at the State University of New York, Buffalo, American University and as Exchange Professor in the Department of Economic History, University of Exeter. His PhD is from the University of Michigan.

Gary A. Dymski is the founding Director of the University of California Center, Sacramento (UCCS). He came to UCCS from the University of California, Riverside, where he holds the rank of professor of economics. Gary received his PhD in economics from the University of Massachusetts, Amherst in 1987. Gary has been an invited lecturer in 14 nations, and has been a visiting scholar at Tokyo University, the Bangladesh Institute for Development Studies, the Federal University of Rio de Janeiro and the University of Sao Paulo. He has written about banking and bank mergers, financial fragility, urban development, credit-market discrimination, the Latin American and Asian financial crises, the subprime crisis, economic exploitation and housing finance.

Gerald Epstein is Professor of Economics and a founding Co-Director of the Political Economy Research Institute (PERI) at the University of Massachusetts, Amherst. He received his PhD in Economics from Princeton University in 1981. Epstein has written articles on numerous topics including trade agreements and human development, alternative approaches to central banking for employment generation and poverty reduction, capital management techniques, international credit relations and multinational corporations. Epstein's current research focuses on employment oriented and poverty reducing macroeconomic and trade policies. He is the editor of *Financialization and the World Economy* (Edward Elgar, 2005). He is currently a Visiting Scholar at the University of Paris.

Steven M. Fazzari is Professor of Economics and Associate Director of the Weidenbaum Center on the Economy, Government, and Public Policy at Washington University in St. Louis. Fazzari's research explores two main areas: the financial determinants of investment and R&D spending by US firms and the foundations of Keynesian macroeconomics. His published articles appear in a wide variety of academic journals including the *Brookings Papers on Economic Activity*, the *Journal of Finance* and the *Review of Economics and Statistics*.

Bill Gibson is John Converse Professor of Economics at the University of Vermont. His research has centered on computable general equilibrium models and agent-based modeling.

Jonathan P. Goldstein is Professor of Economics at Bowdoin College. His fields of specialization are political economy, macroeconomics and applied econometrics. He has published journal articles on the following subjects: Marxian crisis theory, Marxian microfoundations, heterodox macroeconomics, pricing and distribution, and labor relations in and labor history of the logging industry.

Ilene Grabel is a Professor and Director of the Graduate Program in Global Trade, Finance and Economic Integration at the Korbel School of International Studies at the University of Denver. Grabel has lectured at the Cambridge University Advanced Programme on Rethinking Development Economics since its founding. She has worked as a consultant to the United Nations Development Programme (UNDP)/International Poverty Centre, the United Nations Conference on Trade and Economic Development (UNCTAD)/Group of 24, the UN University's World Institute for Development Economics Research, and with ActionAid and the coalition, "New Rules for Global Finance." She has published widely on financial policy and crises, international capital flows and central banks and currency boards. Grabel is co-author (with Ha-Joon Chang) of *Reclaiming Development: An Alternative Policy Manual* (Zed Books, 2004).

Michael G. Hillard is Professor of Economics at the University of Southern Maine. He has published widely in the fields of labor relations, labor history and the political economy of labor in academic journals including *Labor: Studies in the Working Class Histories of the Americas, Labor History, Review of Radical Political Economics, Advances in Industrial and Labor Relations, Journal of Economic Issues, Historical Studies in Industrial Relations* and *Rethinking Marxism.* He is currently researching and writing a book on the labor history of Maine paper and logging workers, with a special focus on the S. D. Warren Company. His essay, "Labor at Mother Warren," won *Labor History*'s "Best Essay, US Topic" prize for 2004.

Makoto Itoh, born in 1936, is Professor of Economics, Kokushikan University, in Tokyo, Emeritus Professor of the University of Tokyo, and a member of the Japan Academy. He has also taught at the New School for Social Research, New York University, and the Universities of London, Manitoba, Sydney and Greenwich among others. His books in English are: *Value and Crisis* (Monthly Review Press and Pluto Press, 1980); *The Basic Theory of*

Capitalism (Macmillan, 1988); *The World Economic Crisis and Japanese Capitalism* (Macmillan, 1990); *Political Economy for Socialism*, (Macmillan, 1995); *Political Economy of Money and Finance* (with Costas Lapavitsas, Macmillan, 1999) and *The Japanese Economy Reconsidered* (Palgrave, 2000).

Soo Haeng Kim is a Distinguished Professor at SungKongHoe University, Hang-dong, Guro-gu, Seoul, Korea, after retiring from Seoul National University. He received his PhD with a thesis on Marxist theories of economic crises from Birkbeck College, University of London. He has translated three volumes of Marx's *Capital* into Korean.

David M. Kotz is Professor of Economics at the University of Massachusetts, Amherst. He is the co-editor of *Understanding Contemporary Capitalism: Social Structure of Accumulation Theory for the Twenty-First Century* (with Terrence McDonough and Michael Reich, Cambridge University Press, forthcoming 2009). His articles have appeared in *Monthly Review*, *Science and Society*, *The Review of Radical Political Economics*, *Rethinking Marxism* and in several Russian and Chinese journals. He is a Vice-President of the World Association for Political Economy.

Kang-Kook Lee is Associate Professor, College of Economics, Ritsumeikan University where he is currently teaching in a graduate program on economic development, funded by the Japanese government and international organizations. He received his PhD from the University of Massachusetts in 2004. He specializes in international finance, development economics and East Asia. His recent research interests include financial globalization, financial crises and restructuring, and the East Asian economy.

Richard McIntyre is Director of the University Honors Program and Professor of Economics at the University of Rhode Island. He edits the "New Political Economy" book series for Routledge. His book, *Are Worker Rights Human Rights?*, was published in 2008 by the University of Michigan Press.

Fred Moseley is Professor of Economics at Mount Holyoke College and is the author of *The Falling Rate of Profit in the Postwar United States Economy* (1992) and numerous articles on Marxian crisis theory and the US economy.

Michele I. Naples is Associate Professor of Economics in the School of Business at The College of New Jersey. She received her A.B. from Princeton University and PhD from the University of Massachusetts at Amherst. Her work transverses the interface between macroeconomics and labor economics. She has published award-winning research on the productivity slowdown, and empirically explored quit rates, industrial accidents, strike activity and business failures. She has also studied the determination of the profit rate and debates about its causes, as well as the historical development of the neoclassical theory of costs, price and output. In the last 10 years she has been developing an alternative microfoundations of macro, Strategic Competition, based on more realistic assumptions than the stylized neoclassical model.

Özgür Orhangazi is Assistant Professor of Economics at Roosevelt University in Chicago. His research focuses on the origins and consequences of the financialization of the global economy. He is the author of *Financialization and the U.S. Economy* (Edward Elgar, 2008).

Malcolm Sawyer is Professor of Economics, University of Leeds, UK, and formerly Pro-Dean for Learning and Teaching for the Faculty of Business. He is managing editor of *International Review of Applied Economics* and the editor of the series "New Directions in Modern Economics" published by Edward Elgar. He is the author of 11 books, has edited 22 books and published 90 papers in refereed journals and contributed chapters to over 100 books. His research interests are in macroeconomics, fiscal and monetary policy, the political economy of the European Monetary Union, nature of money, causes and concepts of unemployment and the economics of Michal Kalecki.

Martin H. Wolfson teaches economics at the University of Notre Dame, where he is also the Director of the Higgins Labor Studies Program. Before coming to Notre Dame, he was an economist at the Federal Reserve Board in Washington, DC.

Preface

As we put the finishing touches on our manuscript (November, 2008), the global economy is in the midst of a financial crisis that may rival the Great Depression. The vast majority of commentaries/analyses of the current crisis are myopic in nature. They focus on the interconnection between financial deregulation and financial innovation and view the current situation as if it was an isolated financial crisis. While all the chapters in this volume, with the exception of the Conclusion (Chapter 20), were written just prior to the onset of the immediate turmoil in August of 2007, their common purpose of developing an integrated heterodox macroeconomic theory and applying it to the current Neoliberal era serves as the foundation for understanding the structural and deep-seated nature of current macroeconomic events.

The integrated Keynes–Marx framework developed here provides a deeper understanding of the macrodynamics of the world economy. The current crisis combines the development of under-consumption, over-investment and financial fragility tendencies built up over the last 25 years and associated with a finance-led accumulation regime. As the distribution of income in advanced capitalist economies shifted from labor to industrial capitalists and finance capitalists, an under-consumption problem emerged. The realization of this problem was first deferred via the emergence of a two-earner household, is later propped up via copious amounts of debt, and finally via wealth effect producing asset bubbles. At the same time, the Neoliberal policies of free trade and financial liberalization created more competition between industrial capitalists and also among finance capitalists. As a result, industrial capitalists were forced to protect their illiquid capital through cost-cutting investment that exacerbated an already developing excess capacity problem. In an effort to shore up profits, these industrial capitalists pursued low-road labor strategies that reinforced the tendency to under-consumption. This contradictory and self-reinforcing chain of under-consumption and over-investment is known as the "Neoliberal paradox."

At the same time, competition among financial capitalists led to unregulated financial innovation that resulted in increased financial fragility and asset bubbles. Asset bubbles served a reproductive function by sustaining consumption with additional credit and via a wealth effect. Of course, the glaring contradiction of this growth mechanism is that the level of debt-supported consumption is unsustainable. The extent and bursting of the housing bubble and the extent of toxic asset holdings brings to the forefront the under-consumption problems that lie at the heart of Neoliberal macrodynamics.

The chapters in this book lay out an integrated heterodox theoretical framework and apply that framework to develop a detailed foundation for understanding the current crisis of globalization.

The final chapter, written in January 2009, serves as an epilogue that ties together the integrated heterodox macrofoundations to explain the current crisis.

Jonathan P. Goldstein and Michael G. Hillard

Acknowledgments

This book was inspired by a growing heterodox macroeconomic literature that integrates the ideas of Keynes, Marx and institutionalism to better understand the evolution of the global economy. But inspirations by themselves do not produce finished manuscripts.

First, we must thank those who guided our nascent ideas for a book into a workable product. In this realm, Gary Mongiovi, Jerry Epstein, Fred Lee and Rob Garnett shared their experiences with the process of book publishing. In addition, Fred Lee as editor of Routledge's Political Economy Series, championed and helped promote our ideas.

Second, Bob Pollin and Jerry Epstein, as co-directors of the Political Economy Research Institute (PERI) at the University of Massachusetts at Amherst, helped to disseminate the ideas found in this volume well beyond the print medium. They graciously hosted and financed a conference on Rebellious Macroeconomics held at PERI on October 19–20, 2007, where the papers within were presented. Without the able assistance and coordination skills of Judy Fogg of PERI, this conference would never have gone beyond the planning stages. The conference was a huge success with over 100 people in attendance.

Third, we are grateful to the *Review of Radical Political Economics* for allowing us to use a slightly modified and expanded version of the first two sections of "Heterodox Crisis Theory and the Current Global Financial Crisis," *Review of Radical Political Economics*, 41:4, 2009, as the basis for Chapter 20.

Finally, we are indebted to Elizabeth Palmer and Elizabeth Weston of Bowdoin College for their careful attention to the details of manuscript preparation and formatting. Without their hard and dedicated work, this manuscript would have only slowly seen the light of day.

Part I

Heterodox macroeconomics and the Keynes–Marx synthesis

1 Introduction

A second-generation synthesis of heterodox macroeconomic principles

Jonathan P. Goldstein and Michael G. Hillard

Over the years, both internal and external challenges to heterodox macro-economic theory have pushed that theory in new directions. A subset of these developments, in response to some of the more serious challenges, has resulted in a much improved integrated heterodox approach based on the original contri-butions of Keynes, Marx and early institutionalists. The result is an integrated theory that is more coherent, logically consistent, realistic, flexible and capable of explaining modern macrodynamics in historical time. This new integrated approach is the subject matter of this book.

We call this unification of alternative macro perspectives the "second-generation integration." The first integration occurred shortly after Keynes' seminal work and lasted into the early 1970s. Since the end of that period, a richer and more complete integration has gradually emerged with many import-ant innovations not appearing until the 1990s and later. Given these recent exten-sions and the lack of a volume that reflects on those innovations, the purpose of the original papers in this book is to familiarize the reader with the emerging unified theory of heterodox macroeconomics and its applications.

The second-generation integration overcomes the stagnation that occurred in the unification of heterodox perspectives as a direct result of divisions that emerged from the first integration (internal challenge). In retrospect, the earlier integration merely generated a set of core heterodox general principles (Sawyer (Chapter 2)) and a critique of mainstream theory, but was incapable of gendering consensus concerning key behavioral relations that explain macroeconomic evolution.

While the goal of this book has not been to develop a fully agreed upon model, the chapters within reconsider core principles and make some important progress on developing core behavioral micro and macro relations. The funda-mental distinction between this second integration and the earlier one is the transition from common core principles to common behavioral relations.

It is often and understandably stated that it is easier to know what heterodox macroeconomics is not than to know what that doctrine is. This book helps to resolve this problem by overcoming previous impediments to an identifiable unified body of heterodox macroeconomics and by further branding/extending that unified theory.

The macro theory developed also responds to external challenges, particularly the long dominance of macroeconomics by New Classical economics, the effective demise of viable orthodox alternatives and the failure/crises associated with Neoliberal development strategies/policies.

In the remainder of this introduction, we briefly address the well-known external challenges, focus more on the lesser-known internal challenges and in so doing, briefly introduce the reader to second-generation ideas. We consider different variants of an integrated analysis and finally, we assess how the chapters in this volume contribute to the overall theme of a unified heterodox approach.

External challenges

As stated, it is well known what heterodox economics is not. Thus, what is external to alternative approaches is well defined. Additionally, the heterodoxy has advanced, early on, well-developed critiques of mainstream economics (Davidson (1983, 1992, 2001), Harcourt (2001), Robinson (1962, 1971), Taylor (2004a: Chapter 7, 2004b), McLeod (1997), Lee and Keen (2004), Cohn (2007), Pasinetti (2000) and Seidman (2005) to mention a few). The goal of this book is to highlight and unify the positive/alternative aspects of heterodox thought and is not to harp on criticism. Yet, the failures of traditional theory and policy partially underlie the direction in which heterodox theory evolves.

In particular, there is the current Neoliberal stage of capitalist development where free market economics/ideology and the associated doctrines of free trade and financial liberalization have guided the economic development of an integrated world economy. Here, the challenge is to explain the failures of that guidance – increasing inequality, financial crises, slow demand growth, destructive competition, and a tendency to global excess capacity and unemployment – and to offer alternatives. These failures cry out for a viable and unified alternative perspective, particularly one that can understand the macrodynamics of the Neoliberal regime and provide sound policy recommendations (both sub-themes of this book).

On the theoretical plane, the dominance of New Classical economics within the profession and the convergence of the neoclassical synthesis in its New Keynesian form to be virtually indistinguishable from New Classical analysis have made the orthodoxy less receptive to alternative ideas. These shifts in theory and lack of tolerance respectively require an extended critique (Crotty (1996), Davidson (1992), and Rotheim (1998)) and a renewed strengthening of alternative perspectives.

Challenges from within

The origins of modern-day challenges to orthodox macroeconomic theory (monetarism, New Classical and New Keynesian economics) are rooted in classical economics, particularly the works of Marx and Ricardo, early institutionalist perspectives such as the treatises of Veblen, Mitchell, Means and Schumpeter, and Keynes' pioneering contributions. The seminal ideas in these three traditions were synthesized into a coherent alternative. This first generation synthesis of heterodox ideas, also referred to as the reconstruction of political economy (Kregel (1973)), has dominated the development of heterodox macroeconomics for around 50 years. Yet, this particular synthesis now faces a crisis of practical, political and theoretical proportions.

The first-generation synthesis is best represented by the contributions of Robinson, Sraffa, Kalecki,[1] Kaldor, Baran and Sweezy, and Steindl. These authors developed the general principles that underlie much of heterodox macroeconomic theory. Sawyer (Chapter 2) elaborates these central core propositions. These authors extended or integrated from the original works the concepts of monopolistic market structure, effective demand, under-consumption and even stagnation, the accumulation of capital, decision-making under true uncertainty, historical time, and the importance of social relations. In addition, much attention was given to extending macroeconomics to consider a long period analysis. For many contributors, Marx's reproduction schemes along with the classical form of competition, expressed by the process of the equalization of profit rates, served as a departure point for discussions of growth and sometimes crisis. The long period analysis that developed consisted primarily of studies of balanced growth with a focus on the link between profit, the distribution of income and growth and innovation and its relation to growth.

Despite the best intentions of the early synthesizers, the initial integration treated many core elements of a unified heterodox framework in a superficial manner, focused on what turned out to be less useful/relevant aspects of the originating approaches and generated the conditions for a division in the future development of the heterodox agenda. After this seminal integration, heterodox macro theories – post Keynesian, institutionalist and Marxian – have developed in near isolation from one another with only minimal interaction and further integration.[2] As a result, the preliminary integration has stagnated. The isolated development of constituent traditions has further cemented existing divisions and impeded future integration. Thus, there is fertile ground to pursue a second unification in hopes of developing a more potent and realistic approach.

The problematic/controversial and/or less useful aspects of the first synthesis includes the concept of equilibrium and the simple concept of competition both embodied in reproduction schemes and the associated notion of balanced growth. The latter, discussed below, is most responsible for creating divergent paths in heterodox theoretical development.[3]

In addition, many elements of the first synthesis were superficially developed. The consideration of fundamental uncertainty has eluded a tractable treatment and the integration of real and financial sectors, in both Keynes' and Marx's work, was never effectively included in the early integration.[4] The treatment of social relations has been restricted to the capital–labor relation and within that realm limited to a conflict theory of inflation and a justification of the classical assumption on savings and consumption. A richer analysis of this relation can be used to underpin cyclical fluctuations, both under-consumption and profit squeeze variants, by bringing the critical role of the profit rate to the fore in the theory of effective demand. This relation can also justify underemployment as a normal condition of capitalism.[5] Additionally, other social relations such as the relation among industrial capitalists (competition) and the relation between industrial capitalists and finance capitalists, particularly during the current period of financial liberalization, have important implications for macroeconomic dynamics.

Second-generation integrationists have more centrally placed the profit rate in the theory of effective demand (Goldstein (1985 and Chapter 3), Crotty (2003, 2005) and Moseley (Chapter 10), have extended the Marxian concept of competition) and have analyzed the relationship between industrial and finance capitalists (Epstein (2005), Crotty (2005) and Orhangazi (Chapter 9)) in order to produce a better understanding of macrodynamics under the Neoliberal regime.

The development most responsible for the stagnation in the integration of heterodox economics, over the past quarter century or more, is the pursuit of theories of balanced growth by a significant subset of first-generation economists. This generated a split in the long period analysis between growth theorists and crisis theorists. Given Marx's well-developed theory of economic crises, this division tended to run along Marxian and post-Keynesian lines.[6] The crucial issue of whether a unified heterodox theory should incorporate a crisis theory is affirmatively addressed by Dymski (Chapter 5).

Coming off of Marx's expanded reproduction schemes,[7] the early integration economists such as Robinson and Kaldor developed growth models to establish the "rules of the game"/"tranquility assumptions" necessary to keep the system expanding. While methodologically, this was perceived as a first step for analyzing why balanced growth may not be attained (Kregel (1973: 41)), most post-Keynesians following in this tradition never implemented the crucial second step.[8] Thus, a theory of balanced growth emerges. Later followers, such as Eichner (1973, 1987), extend this approach by developing a microfounded theory of pricing consistent with balanced growth. In this approach, the mark-up and thus the profit rate are subservient to the dictates of accumulation. The mark-up rises to generate the internal funds necessary to finance new investment.[9]

This approach significantly deviates from heterodox fundamental principles (Sawyer (Chapter 2)). It establishes an a priori compatibility between micro decisions and macro stability, it implies that expectations are usually justified, it violates the fundamental uncertainty associated with both expectation formation and the determination of the profit rate, it diminishes/restricts the innovative integration of monopoly (mark-up) pricing particularly in an environment of class struggle over the distribution of income and it employs an equilibrium methodology.

These developments derailed the integration of the various strands of heterodox macroeconomics. The fundamental uncertainty of the profit rate and its impact on effective demand has long been a mainstay of heterodox economics including the historical determination of the relative strength of capital vis-à-vis labor with respect to wage bargaining.[10] In addition, there is the need for a realistic microeconomic approach that considers the potentially contradictory nature of micro decisions on the macro level. This issue is addressed by Goldstein (1986, 2006, Chapter 3) and Gibson (Chapter 6). Finally, the pioneers of alternative macroeconomics, despite confusing indications to the contrary, rejected equilibrium analysis in favor of a dynamic non-equilibrium methodology.[11]

Thus, it is time to follow through on the intentions of the founders and first-generation followers to analyze the impediments to balanced growth. Is it a necessary step to first refine the theory of balanced growth to achieve this goal? Probably not, analyses of crisis clearly identify the impediments to continued growth. In the unified framework advanced here (Goldstein (Chapter 3), Orhangazi (Chapter 9), Moseley (Chapter 10), Boddy (Chapter 12) and Kotz (Chapter 13)) provide an alternative long period analysis, basically indistinguishable from a series of short period outcomes.

This long period approach integrates the analyses of crisis and regulation/reproduction. It recognizes the fundamental role played by institutions, ideologies, politics and potential tendencies to economic crisis and their interactions. It also analyzes the numerous dichotomies in both microeconomic behavior and macroeconomic outcomes (Goldstein (Chapter 3)) to develop a theory of macro-dynamics based on the resulting micro and macro regime shifts or stages of development.[12] This approach explains both long waves/stages of economic development and interim dynamics within a stage to produce a convincing theory of capitalist development.

Strands of unification

Over the years, some authors have overcome divisions between heterodox traditions to lay the foundations of a unified approach. The associated works can be classified into five traditions – the social structure of accumulation (SSA) framework, structuralist macroeconomics (SM), financial integrationists/Minskians, Kaleckians and Crottians. SSA authors (Bowles *et al.* (1986, 1990), Kotz (2001, 2003), Kotz *et al.* (1994), McDonough (2003, 2006) and O'Hara (2000, 2002)) have integrated social relations, and the institutional foundations of growth with short-run crisis theory and long wave analysis. SM economists (Taylor (2004a), Dutt (2002) and Gibson (2003, 2005)) place emphasis on how a particular economy's unique structure – institutions and social relations – shapes aggregate economic behavior. These structural elements are placed within realistic macro models that combine the insights of Keynes and Kalecki on effective demand, mark-up pricing and the distribution of income. Kaleckians (Sawyer (1985, 1999, 2001a), Mott (2002), Lopez and Mott (1999), Fazarri and Mott (1987) and Trigg (2002, 2004)) have advanced Kalecki's integration of effective demand, monopoly microfoundations, the distribution of income and business cycle analysis. Financial integrationists/Minskians (Wray (2002), Fazzari (1992), Wolfson (2000, 2001, 2002), Dymski (2003, 2005), Dymski and Pollin (1994), Pollin

(1997), Epstein (1992, 2005), Sawyer (2001b) and Dufour and Orhangazi (2007)) have furthered Minsky's (1975, 1982) seminal unification of real and financial sector interactions that result in crisis/instability. Additionally, some of these authors have wedded the social relations between industrial and financial capitalists within a theory of financial instability. Finally, Crottians (Crotty and Goldstein (1992), Crotty and Dymski (2001), Crotty and Lee (2006), Goldstein (1985, 1986, Chapter 8), Dymski (Chapter 5) and Boddy (Chapter 12)) have extended the contributions made by Crotty (1985, 1993, 1994, 2003, 2005) that integrate real and financial sectors within a Keynes–Marx theory of effective demand, expand the Marxian concept of competition and the theory of accumulation, advance a tractable treatment of fundamental uncertainty based on institutions as a stabilizing mechanism, and consider the relevance of profit squeeze, under-consumption and over-investment crises for post-World War II capitalist development.

While these different groups of integrationists have often worked in isolation, many of their salient ideas are brought together in this volume with the theme of unifying their contributions.

A unified heterodox macroeconomic approach

The chapters in this volume articulate a unified heterodox macroeconomic approach in the following four areas corresponding to the section divisions of this book:

1   heterodox macroeconomics and the Keynes–Marx synthesis;
2   accumulation, crisis and instability;
3   the macrodynamics of the neoliberal regime; and
4   heterodox macroeconomic policy.

Besides the general themes of this volume – the integration of heterodox ideas, a more realistic theory of macrodynamics, flexible macro modeling, and an analysis of macro regime shifts – subsets of chapters share common subthemes. Goldstein, Gibson, Fazzari, Goldstein and Naples, in Chapters 3, 6–8 and 11, emphasize a role for heterodox microfoundations. Goldstein, Dymski, Orhangazi, Boddy and Kotz, in Chapters 3, 5, 9, 12 and 13, consider macroeconomic regime shifts, while these same authors in addition to Goldstein, Moseley and Naples, in Chapters 8, 10 and 11, analyze specific crisis mechanisms. Dymski and Moseley, in Chapters 5 and 10, consider the integration of Minsky's work with Marx's theory. Finally, Dymski, Boddy, Kotz, Hillard and McIntyre, Itoh, Lee, Epstein, and Grabel, in Chapters 5, 12–16 and 18–19, address macrodynamics under the Neoliberal regime.

Heterodox macroeconomics and the Keynes–Marx synthesis

The five chapters in Part I, excluding this introduction, focus on the central principles, core behavioral relations and methodology of a Keynes–Marx–

Institutionalist heterodox synthesis. In order to quickly familiarize the reader with this integrated macroeconomic approach, we start with the two chapters – Sawyer (Chapter 2) and Goldstein (Chapter 3) – that provide good overviews of this brand of macroeconomics. After the reader is given an introduction to the integrated framework, we next turn to broader methodological issues that underlie the integrated approach. Goldstein addresses the importance of unification, microfoundations and regime shifts, while Wolfson (Chapter 4) considers general methodological principles and Dymski (Chapter 5), more narrowly, focuses on the importance of crisis theory in general and an integrated real and financial sector crisis mechanism. Finally, Gibson (Chapter 6) addresses not only the relevance of microfoundations, but their form.

Sawyer's chapter acts as a bridge between first- and second-generation integrations. He establishes the core general principles that serve as the basis for a modern integration. These principles define the "boundaries" of heterodox macroeconomics.

Sawyer views the macro economy as a fully integrated system of real and financial sectors embedded in a real environment – institutions and social arrangements – characterized by fundamental uncertainty. He recognizes eight key heterodox features of that economy. First, aggregate demand determines output in both the short and long runs. This implies that there is no steady state for the macro economy. Second, the distribution of income, rather than relative prices, is a key determinant of aggregate demand. The resulting distribution is closely linked to a mark-up pricing mechanism. Third, within the theory of effective demand, investment plays a critical role as an uncertain activity that exhibits volatile behavior. Fourth, the demand and supply sides of the economy are interdependent and follow an evolutionary path – a series of short-run equilibriums – influenced by institutions and social interactions. Fifth, financial factors are fully integrated, particularly via an endogenous money supply and the possibility of financial fragility.

The next two principles are related to wage and price determination and inflation. Wages and prices are not set in the labor market. Instead, they are based on mark-up pricing and the relative bargaining power of labor and capital. In turn, wage and price determination affects the profit rate which has feedback effects to aggregate demand. Inflation is primarily the result of unresolved conflicts over income shares. It is not a monetary phenomenon. Finally, an open economy analysis is fundamental particularly given the integrated nature of the world economy.

A secondary theme of the chapter concerns heterodox macroeconomic policy. Sawyer argues that demand management policies, the establishment of an inflation barrier through the equation of wage and productivity increases and the recognition that money/credit matters, particularly for sustaining investment, are important policy prescriptions. While Sawyer does not consider policies related to the open nature of most economies – capital flows, trade and financial liberalization, development strategies etc. – subsequent chapters (Grabel (Chapter 19) and Epstein (Chapter 18)) address these issues.

Goldstein (Chapter 3) advances a unified heterodox theory by suggesting key behavioral components. The synthesis includes the Keynesian concepts of fundamental uncertainty, endogenous money/credit, endogenous expectations/preferences, financial innovation, financial fragility and effective demand. From the Marxian literature, crisis theory, class relations, a conflict-determined distribution of income linked to effective demand, the centrality of accumulation, the Marxian concept of competition and a long-run analysis associated with the SSA framework and endogenous dichotomies/regime shifts in micro behavior and macro outcomes are incorporated. From the institutional approach, the role of institutions in securing a profitable environment for accumulation, providing an environment that supports stable expectations and confidence formation and is responsible for the constitution of economic agents and thus their choice of micro behavior is employed.[13]

The framework developed starts with macrofoundations. The macro environment consists of the class structure including the competition among capitalists and the institutional structure and non-ergodic nature of the environment underlying the class structure. This environment is characterized as a hostile, threatening, coercive and unforgiving arena. Underlying this characterization is the Marxian concept of competition as distinct from the classical/neoclassical notion that underlies harmonious and reproduction outcomes. Coercive competition instead supports frenzied micro survival strategies that may be contradictory at the macro level. The environment also exhibits fundamental uncertainty and a tractable method for integrating it into macro analysis is discussed.

Next, a priority and rationale is established for microfoundations of individual and/or class behavior in a broadly defined manner. Micro behavior is constrained by the macrofoundations of the economy. Thus, micro analysis allows for a foundation to be established for potentially contradictory macro outcomes via a micro–macro interaction.

A basic heterodox model of effective demand is also incorporated where both the consumption and investment functions depend on the distribution of income. In addition, an extension of the standard heterodox investment function with the profit rate and capacity utilization as determinants is incorporated from Goldstein's (Chapter 8) microfounded investment theory. In this approach, investment depends on the profit rate, the degree of competition, the financial condition of the firm and the interactions between these factors. This extended theory better allows real and financial sector impediments to accumulation to be incorporated and also permits coercive competitive constraints to override those impediments potentially resulting in more serious future challenges to growth.

A microfoundation for the determination of the distribution of income is also incorporated in the form of a variable mark-up theory of pricing. Here, the firm optimally determines its mark-up by negotiating a tradeoff between its mark-up and its market share. Thus, the critical role of competition is used to potentially restrict and make mark-up determination less certain.

Financial elements are fully integrated in this framework as is evidenced by the description of the investment relation above. Beyond this, the endogenous role of money/credit and the financial instability hypothesis are employed. The latter is extended, via Crotty (1990), to include the interaction between real and financial sectors in the determination of fragility. In addition, the class relation between industrial capitalists and financial capitalists is incorporated. The potential for financial capitalists to redistribute industrial profits to themselves raises the possibility of a financial profit squeeze.

In this approach, the likelihood of balanced growth is found to be tenuous. Five forms of crisis mechanisms are identified. The economy has no steady state and is viewed as a non-equilibrium process. The long-run is analyzed by considering the impact of changing institutional structures and regime shifts in micro behavior and macro outcomes on crisis and growth. This framework also identifies five crucial dichotomies that underlie regime shifts. Institutional change and the interacting nature of these dichotomies offer many possible outcomes for the dynamic path of the macroeconomy. Thus a rich long-period analysis, dependent on historical and institutional conditions, replaces the first generation focus on balanced growth.

Turning to methodological foundations, Wolfson (Chapter 4) addresses the underlying core methodology for heterodox macroeconomics based on the contributions of Keynes, Marx and early institutionalists. He identifies four methodological principles:

1   contradictions, particularly as a result of class interactions, underlie endogenous change and the business cycle;
2   decision-making under fundamental uncertainty results in real and financial sector interactions that can result in financial crisis;
3   alternative institutional arrangements define different stages of capitalism and their dynamics; and
4   the interactions between contradictions/crises and the institutional structure lead to changing institutions and thus historical change.

Wolfson identifies the work of Crotty (1985, 1990, 1993, 1994) as important for integrating these methodological principles that have their origin in different strands of heterodox approaches.

Dymski's chapter (Chapter 5) serves a dual purpose with respect to the themes of this volume. First, he examines, in more detail, one of the methodology pillars identified by Wolfson – contradictory behavior that can potentially result in economic crises. This analysis takes place on an abstract level. Second, he considers a concrete form of crisis, Minsky's financial instability hypothesis, and argues, contrary to Minsky, that the likelihood of such a crisis has increased in recent times. This analysis is primarily based on empirical evidence, particularly concerning structural changes that have occurred in the Neoliberal era. In this sense, Dymski's chapter is similar to the chapters in Part II by Kotz and Boddy that examine regime shifts associated with crisis mechanisms.

Given the split among heterodox theorists over balanced growth versus crisis, Dymski makes a methodological case for including crisis theory in a unified framework. Dymski argues that balanced growth is only a means to an end. That end being an examination of the impediments to growth.

Dymski then critically analyzes the assumptions of neoclassical models that support Say's Law. He strengthens the methodological status of crisis analysis by rejecting these assumptions and by considering Marx's concept of abstract forms of crisis – Marx's general analysis of crisis possibilities in exchange economies. He establishes that any critique of Say's Law effectively recognizes the possibility for economic crisis. Given that all heterodox economists reject Say's Law, a consideration of crises is central to heterodox analysis.

Dymski then turns to the debate over a concrete form of crisis theory – Minsky's financial instability theory. He argues for extending Minsky's approach to fully integrate real sector influences on financial crises and to be adapted to the new macro realities, including major changes in financial markets, associated with the Neoliberal era. He outlines the nature of such extensions.

Gibson (Chapter 6) addresses a controversial methodological issue for heterodox macroeconomics – a primacy for a microeconomic base.[14] Not only are microfoundations a general methodological issue, but they are intimately linked to Dymski's call for crisis analysis. A major aspect of crisis mechanisms is the idea that individual reproductive/survival strategies may not be consistent with the reproduction of a broader class of similar agents and thus macro stability.

Gibson strongly supports the incorporation of micro analysis into macro theory. He also addresses a perennial and thus far intractable problem associated with micro-based macro analysis – the aggregation problem. An analysis of this problem leads him to abandon representative agent-based microfoundations in favor of multi agent-based models that avoid *ex ante* aggregation and alternatively aggregate heterogenous individuals *ex post*. In this view, macro outcomes are the emergent properties of agent-based models.

While the call for microfoundations has become less controversial over the years as the class of useful micro analyses has broadened, Gibson's call for a particular type of, although flexible, micro modeling may renew part of the microfoundation debate.

Accumulation, crisis and instability

In Part II, we turn from general sketches of behavioral principles, behavioral relations and methodological precepts, to the detailed building blocks of behavioral relations and macroeconomic outcomes. A Crottian theory of the active firm, rather than passive neoclassical firm, is advanced by Fazzari in Chapter 7. Fazzarri uses two applications, production and investment decisions, to illustrate this concept of the firm. He establishes the centrality of the firm's investment decision as the cornerstone of the theory of effective demand. Goldstein, in Chapter 8, expands upon Fazzari's last application by developing a full-fledged microfoundation of the investment decision of a firm with Keynesian–Marxian attributes. The end result is the extended theory of investment described earlier. Goldstein applies this theory of investment to the macrodynamics of the Neoliberal regime and isolates specific crisis tendencies. In Chapters 9 and 10, Orhangazi and Moseley pick up on the crisis theme by respectively considering other recent crisis tendencies and the increased likelihood of financial instability in the current period. Naples (Chapter 11) develops a microeconomic rationale for the cyclically complex relationship between labor demand and the real wage – a relation with asymmetric responses in different cycle phases – advanced by the cyclical profit squeeze theory of crisis.

Fazzari defines an active firm as considering principal-agent problems (social relations), making decisions under fundamental uncertainty and assessing demand fluctuations via expectations formed under uncertainty. The dynamic characteristics of the firm include a changing system of agent relations, preferences, expectations and the influence of institutions. The firm is thus a complex social institution exhibiting rich behaviors and making strategic decisions. Its behavior deviates from the standard theory of the firm. For example, this firm makes production decisions on the basis of an uncertain demand constraint requiring active management decisions that deviate from the typical cost minimization calculus. Investment decisions are also strategic due to the impact of uncertainty and the irreversible nature of investment. In this environment, the firm's decision will deviate from the typical equation of the marginal productivity of capital with the user cost of capital plus marginal adjustment costs.

Goldstein (Chapter 8), develops a microfoundation for an active firm's investment decision. The firm is situated in a Keynes–Marx environment. As a result, the model employs a unique and realistic objective function where the manager must negotiate a profit-financial security (likelihood of default/financial problems) tradeoff in determining the optimal investment strategy. The model includes a Marxian competitive environment via a constraint on the firm's market share and Keynesian fundamental uncertainty and the possibility of fragile financial outcomes.[15] Other Keynesian elements include endogenous expectations and preferences. Additionally, the structure includes the Marxian imperative to accumulate capital and two different forms of investment – offensive and defensive investment. Only defensive investment can be used to increase the firm's market share, but such investment comes with large reorganization costs. Both forms of investment are considered to be irreversible. The manager's preferences for each of the sub-objectives are endogenously determined by the firm's changing financial situation. Thus, the model is both flexible and realistic with respect to both the objective function and the model structure.

The optimal investment decision serves as a foundation for a variety of macro investment behaviors. The model can capture macro transitions from an offensive investment strategy to one dominated by defensive investment and vice versa. A binding competitive constraint in conjunction with a declining mark-up (exogenous) generates the result of forced massive investment in an already financially precarious environment (low profits/cash flow) resulting in the potential for financial crisis. In addition, a binding competitive constraint with a rising mark-up can result in an over-investment situation along with the possibility of under-consumption.

Goldstein applies the Keynes–Marx theory of investment to the Neoliberal period in order to explain the tendency to global excess capacity/over-invest as a result of slower aggregate demand growth, increased international competition and destructive price competition within an industry. While Goldstein does not address increased financial fragility in this environment, Orhangazi develops a complementary perspective that focuses on this element of the crisis in the next chapter.

Orhanganzi (Chapter 9) examines the changing relationship between industrial capitalists and finance capitalists/financial markets during the Neoliberal era. Orhangazi documents alterations in the firm's strategy/behavior and a resulting financial squeeze of industrial profits that occurs through the mechanism of "coupon capitalism." The chapter provides an excellent consolidation of the burgeoning financialization literature. Orhangazi then makes the link between financialization and macroeconomic instability concluding that the changing nature of relations between firms and financial markets has resulted in more unstable investment, increased financial fragility and less transparent financial dealings.

Moseley (Chapter 10) proposes an alternative crisis mechanism to explain current economic conditions. In particular, he explores the integration of Minsky's financial instability hypothesis with Marx's real sector crisis theories. He argues that previous integrations have been restrictive with respect to incorporating Marx's theory and as a result less effective in explaining current economic conditions. In particular, Moseley argues that previous integrations have focused on Marx's profit squeeze theory and have ignored the relevance of the falling rate of profit mechanism and other determinants of profits.[16] He argues that this exclusion matters for the mechanism/policy that can result in recovery from crisis. In particular, to restore the full employment profit rate resulting from a falling rate of profit mechanism requires that capital be significantly devalued.[17] He doubts that stabilization policies will wipe out enough debt, reduce the value of capital by enough and thus restore the profit rate to its full employment level. Thus, the primary mechanism to restore recovery is the devaluation of capital through bankruptcies as a result of the restorative properties of a full recession/depression.

Moseley concludes that the use of misdirected government stabilization policies over the past 30 years has resulted in stagnation by placing a floor under the profit rate[18] that does not allow enough capital devaluation to return the profit rate to its full employment value – the necessary condition for growth. This nexus of crisis and policy mechanisms offers an alternative perspective on slow growth than the theories that examine a tendency to global excess capacity associated with the Neoliberal era.

Naples further strengthens the cyclical profit squeeze argument by developing a microeconomic rationale for the complex cyclical relationship between labor demand and the real wage.[19] Naples starts from a active/flexible/strategic firm, such as those discussed by Fazzari and Goldstein (Chapters 7–8), characterized by constant short-run returns to labor and strategic decision-making in pursuit of satisfying behavior/long-run profit strategies.[20] These assumptions motivate the relative autonomy of wage-setting with respect to firm employment decisions. In particular, wages are partially set institutionally on the basis of company and industry specific factors. Using these factors and the above assumption set, Naples is able to justify the positive relation between labor demand and the real wage in the early expansion and a negative relation in the late expansion.

The macrodynamics of the Neoliberal regime

The five chapters in Part III all focus on regime shifts in economic performance and institutional structures associated with the transition to the Neoliberal era. The chapters by Boddy (Chapter 12) and Kotz (Chapter 13) consider qualitative changes in the crisis mechanisms operating during the Golden Age (Keynesian/regulated regime) and Neoliberal capitalism. Hillard and McIntyre (Chapter 14) analyze how labor movements have influenced different institutional regimes. Itoh (Chapter 15) considers changes in the social structure of accumulation and uses the theory of unequal exchange to explain the further polarization in wealth and power during the current period. Finally, Lee (Chapter 16) explains a different transition, particularly the transition from growth to crisis in the Korean economy as a result of Neoliberal-induced policy shifts from capital controls to financial liberalization.

Boddy empirically tests the cyclical income share implications of one of the most common behavioral relations used in heterodox models – mark-up pricing. Boddy develops a unified theory of the determinants of labor share of income over the business cycle by integrating competing heterodox theories of mark-up pricing. Those determinants are unemployment, capacity utilization and a threshold level of unemployment. He econometrically tests his specification and shows that the relation between labor share and capacity utilization and the degree of unemployment has shifted/weakened between the Keynesian period and the Neoliberal era. The weakening of the profit squeeze mechanism has occurred despite lower unemployment rates over the last two Neoliberal cycles. This outcome reflects the weakened economic and political position of labor.[21]

Boddy's findings on the weakening of the profit squeeze mechanism over time, indirectly supports the increased likelihood of either under-consumption and/or over-investment problems.[22] Kotz (Chapter 13) picks up where Boddy's analysis leaves off by empirically testing the relative strength of alternative crisis mechanisms across the regulated and Neoliberal macro regimes. Kotz uses an accounting decomposition of the profit rate, in the tradition of Weisskopf (1979), to analyze the link between institutional structure and crisis. In his analysis he isolates four crisis tendencies – profit squeeze, under-consumption, over-investment and asset bubbles. The inclusion of speculative bubbles is an important extension of the profit rate decomposition methodology. He concludes that during the regulated Keynesian era, the profit squeeze was prevalent in all five cycle expansions, while in the two cycles associated with the Neoliberal era over-investment problems occur and in the latter cycle a bubble is present. These findings are consistent with other authors (Crotty (2003, 2005), and Orhangazi

(Chapter 9)) who have combined over-investment and financial instability explanations of crisis during the Neoliberal period.

Historical contingency and institutional specificity of particular national economies are central heterodox macroeconomic methodological assumptions. Using this approach, Hillard and McIntyre (Chapter 14) focus on the capital–labor dynamics that have emerged in advanced economies in the Neoliberal era. They address what accounts for the somewhat diverging patterns of inequality and erosion of social insurance in many economies since 1970, with emphasis on the US experience. Their answer lies in uncovering historically developed distinctions in the institutional and class formation in the countries considered. Through their historical-institutional analysis, they account for the specifically intense deterioration of working conditions in the USA, identifying how the class forces and even political dynamics of particular economies can account for secular and cyclical macroeconomic developments, particular the deleterious ones of the Neoliberal era.

Itoh (Chapter 15) revisits an important methodological question in heterodox theory – what theoretical alternatives exist for underpinning an analysis of wealth and income inequalities generated in the international economic system. After a review of the history of thought for the doctrine of unequal exchange, he observes:

> the wide gap in wages between the central and the peripheral countries is an essential source of international unequal exchange and exploitation, thus differences in social structures and institutions for capital accumulation ... between the center and the periphery of the world capitalism must be important in this context.

Based on his institutional analysis, he identifies three distinct groups of peripheral countries' experience with the Neoliberal regime – the oil-producing countries that have generally prospered because of huge ground rents collected on oil; a second group of "least among the less developed countries" (LLDC), such as sub-Saharan African nations deeply poor to begin with and recently battered by debt and high energy costs; and the prospering East Asian economies that have deployed national industrial policy models and financial controls that permitted development. Despite these distinct experiences, he concludes that there is "common pressure and difficulties of working people ... under dominant neo-liberal globalization of world capitalism" and a "common need ... to amend the neo-liberal globalization policy tide for the sake of the great majority of working people in the world."

Kang-Kook Lee (Chapter 16) presents a case study for the Korean economy that forcefully argues that national industrial policy, supported by extensive capital controls on international financial flows, can succeed, contra the Neoliberal model, in promoting impressive macroeconomic strength; and that, conversely, liberalizing international capital controls can, and in South Korea's case did, result in dramatic volatility and macroeconomic reversals, despite the optimistic ideology of Neoliberal policy proponents. He supports this conclusion via a detailed depiction of *how* capital controls dovetailed with a national economic development policy to create sustained macroeconomic stability and prosperity (what Epstein (Chapter 18) refers to as the technical aspects of controls); how the circumstances and fallout of capital control liberalization in the mid-1990s contributed to a massive financial crisis; and how the subsequent embrace of expanded liberalization by South Korea led to an attendant loss of control over the domestic economy, general economic stagnation, a significant deterioration in the economic standing of Korean working people and a persistent susceptibility to continued macroeconomic volatility.

Lee demonstrates the main policy themes of heterodox macroeconomics, namely that a highly regulated financial system, particularly with respect to international finance, is a precondition for stability, not a source of instability, as Neoliberal policy advocates have maintained. In this regard, this chapter antici-pates the chapters by Epstein and Grabel in Part IV.

Heterodox macroeconomic policy

In Part IV, alternative macroeconomic policies are considered. Kim (Chapter 17) argues from a methodological perspective that a unified heterodox policy per-spective requires that Keynesian policy principles need to be enhanced through the consideration of the class implications of policies and the class nature of policy formation and implementation. Epstein (Chapter 18) reconsiders the case for capital controls and Grabel (Chapter 19) examines the failure of IMF policy prescriptions and argues for alternative policies based on capital controls, gradual liberalization and national and greater regional macro policy autonomy.

Soohaeng Kim (Chapter 17) presents a Marxian critique of Keynes's analysis of macroeconomic crisis and his policy orientation that serves as the basis for unifying Keynesian and more radical policy perspectives. Kim's central point elucidates a well-defined fissure between Keynesians and Marxians going back to the first generation integrationists, namely, whether capital–labor relations are an equal object of policy transformation along with state and investment rela-tions, with Keynesians historically focusing on just the latter. Kim argues that it is necessary for the contemporary "second generation" heterodox macro synthe-sis to surmount this fissure by recognizing the class nature of policies and policy formation. In this vein, Kim also argues that Keynes' vision of an impartial state is blind to powerful class forces that shape macroeconomic policies. Kim also identifies and contrasts Keynes' vision of the socialization of investment with that of Marx's, showing how Keynes' formulation relied on an underspecified view of capitalist behavior. These methodological suggestions serve as the basis for the policy formulations related to current macrodynamics discussed in the remainder of Part IV.

Epstein (Chapter 18) makes the case for both the technical and transformative aspects of capital controls in the era of Neoliberalism by synthesizing the differ-ent perspectives of Keynes and Marx on the topic. With respect to the technical characteristics, he considers how capital controls can facilitate desirable policies pertaining to employment, growth and an equitable distribution of income. On the transformative side, he argues that controls can facilitate progressive political and economic transformations even in the current macro environment.

Grabel (Chapter 19) examines the detrimental and unintended consequences of the global Neoliberal regime on developing countries. She takes a broader view of the very same questions examined by Lee by focusing on IMF policies. Those policies have subjected world policy makers to conform because of "the new commitment to policy coherence and by interlocking commitments to liberalization that are embodied in bi- and multi-lateral trade and investment agreements." This new policy regime has contributed directly to a chronic and widespread series of financial/currency crises in Asia and Latin America that commenced with the Mexican peso collapse of 1994–1995. Grabel's analysis employs the financial instability thesis and argues that such modern cyclical asset dynamics are accelerated and accentuated by Neoliberal policy structures. She finds that "neoliberal financial reform heightens the stagnationist tendencies and inequalities of wealth, income, and power that are an inherent feature of developing, and, indeed all capitalist economies."

Grabel provides a crucial analytical foundation for explaining *why* Neoliberal policies and institutional frameworks have created systematic tendencies towards crisis. She then provides clear policy alternatives that include capital controls, gradual financial integration and liberalization, the protection of national and regional policy space and the dramatic examples of many Latin American and Asian nations pulling back or outright withdrawing from the Neoliberal policy apparatuses. Beyond the USA, if not inside it, the insights and recommendations of heterodox macroeconomists are beginning to find a new saliency.

Conclusion

In the final chapter, Goldstein applies the integrated heterodox macroeconomic framework, developed throughout this volume, to explain the causes of the current global financial crisis. He argues that the source of the crisis is deep rooted and goes well beyond the readily visible financial aspects. In particular, the crisis is seen as involving the nexus of under-consumption, over-investment and financial crises. The origins of the crisis are associated with structural and institutional changes that begin around 1980 with the Neoliberal regime. Goldstein concludes that in order to restore balanced growth, the corporate form of globalization with its finance-led accumulation regime must be dismantled and replaced with a bounded wage-led accumulation regime combined with fair trade and financial regulation.

Notes

1 Given Kalecki's anticipation of many of Keynes' major contributions, published in Polish, he could easily be incorporated into the group of founding, rather than synthesizing, economists. See Feiwel (1975: 27–86) and Sawyer (1985: Chapter 9).

2 Goldstein (Chapter 3) confronts the contention of certain heterodox economists that a convergence within heterodox thought has taken place.

3 The theories of stagnation based on rising monopoly profits and under-consumption (Baran and Sweezy (1966) and Steindl (1952)) also were less useful for the analysis of the first phase of post-World War II economic development. There is a direct lineage from the under-consumption arguments of Marx to Luxemburg to Kalecki to Baran and Sweezy and Steindl. Boddy and Crotty (1975) were responsible for changing the focus of theories of the Golden Age from under-consumption to profit squeeze dynamics by reviving the reserve army crisis theory of Marx. This is not to say that under-consumption crises have not become relevant again in the Neoliberal era.

4 Minsky (1975, 1982), who we consider as an early second-generation theorist, developed, via his financial instability hypothesis, an integration of the real and financial sectors. Also, Crotty (1985) argues that Marx fully integrated these two sectors and Crotty (1986, 1990) calls for a richer interaction of these sectors than the one established in Minsky's work.

5 Kalecki (1943) analyzed the political aspects of full employment. Bowles (1985) extends Kalecki's notion in a formal model of contested exchange. Additionally, Marx's (1967: Chapter 25) analysis of the reserve army serves as an alternative justification for unemployment as a condition of existence of capitalism. These two explanations of unemployment stand in contrast to New Keynesian theories of underemployment equilibrium based on asymmetric information and monopolistic competition, although some similarities exist between contested exchange and efficiency wages.

6 The tension within first generation heterodox economists is evident in Kalecki's criticism of growth theory (Feiwel (1975: 9, 48, 56)) and his pursuit of business cycle models and Baran and Sweezy's and Steindl's development of crisis theories.

7 An obvious tension exists in Marx between balanced growth analysis (reproduction) and crisis dynamics. This same tension underlies Marx's alternative use of equilibrium concepts and non-equilibrium arguments.

8 Goodwin's (1967) growth cycle is an exception.

9 See Shapiro and Sawyer (2003) for a review of post-Keynesian approaches to pricing.

10 Goldstein (1985) offers an alternative theory of dynamic mark-up pricing that serves as the basis for a theory of price in an integrated heterodox framework (Goldstein (Chapter 3)).

11 Despite their fundamental objections, Keynes, Marx, Robinson and Kalecki all flirted with and used the concept of equilibrium.

12 Kalecki (1968) integrated trend and cycle and Baran and Sweezy (1966) considered the monopoly stage of capitalism as a qualitatively distinct period.

13 This last point identifies a preference for microfoundations in Goldstein's approach that may not be accepted by all second-generation economists. While Sawyer (Chapter 2) does not rule out the possible productiveness of micro analysis, he does not place a priority on it. Additionally, SM economists do not use microfoundations in their structuralist models. In contrast, Goldstein (Chapter 3), Gibson (Chapter 6) and Fazzari (Chapter 7) emphasize their importance.

14 As Goldstein (2006) argues, this controversy has been overblown by the reaction of heterodox economists to an extreme form of micro methodology purported by the methodological individualist wing of Analytical Marxists. Goldstein (2006) develops a moderate, rather than fundamentalist, justification for heterodox microfoundations and identifies various forms of micro analysis outside of rational choice models that can satisfy this methodological priority.

15 In some sense, the model can be considered a microfoundation for Minsky's financial fragility hypothesis.

16 Such as increases in unproductive labor, decreases in the length of the working day and decreases in the intensity of labor.

17 It should be noted that a major difference between Moseley and other crisis theorists in this volume is his reliance on the restoration of the full employment profit rate, rather than a recovery in the general profit rate, as the necessary condition for a recovery.

18 This floor is established as stagnant growth hurts labor and reduces the real wage.

19 Goldstein (1985) developed a microfoundation for the non-labor market aspects of the profit squeeze.

20 Short-run profit maximization is not consistent with constant returns.

21 Boddy shows that the last Neoliberal cycle (ending in 2001) does exhibit some more pronounced profit squeeze characteristics, but he dismisses the revival of this crisis mechanism by arguing that monetary policy mistakenly allowed the expansion to continue for too long a period.

22 The shift in the balance of power from labor to capital is either associated with corporate responses to increased competitive pressures and/or a weakening of labor independently of competitive pressures. In the former case, over-investment is likely to emerge while in the latter under-consumption could occur.

References

Baran, P. A. and Sweezy, P. M. (1966) *Monopoly Capital: An Essay on the American Economic and Social Order*. New York: Monthly Review Press.

Boddy, R. and Crotty, J. R. (1975) "Class Conflict and Macro-Policy: The Political Business Cycle," *Review of Radical Political Economics*, 7(1): 1–19.

Bowles, S. (1985) "The Production Process in a Competitive Economy: Walrasian, Neo-Hobbesian, and Marxian Models," *American Economic Review*, 75(1): 16–36.

Bowles, S., Gordon, D. M. and Weisskopf, T. E. (1986) "Power and Profits: The Social Structure of Accumulation and the Profitability of the Postwar U.S. Economy," *Review of Radical Political Economics*, 18(1/2): 132–67.

—— (1990) *After the Waste Land: A Democratic Economics for the Year 2000*. Armonk and London.

Cohn, S. M. (2007) *Reintroducing Macroeconomics: A Critical Approach*. Armonk and London.

Crotty, J. (1985) "The Centrality of Money, Credit, and Financial Intermediation in Marx's Crisis Theory: An Interpretation of Marx's Methodology," in *Rethinking Marxism: Struggles in Marxist Theory. Essays for Harry Magdoff and Paul Sweezy*, 45–81, Brooklyn.

—— (1986) "Marx, Keynes, and Minsky on the Instability of the Capitalist Growth Process and the Nature of Government Economic Policy," in *Marx, Schumpeter, Keynes: A Centenary Celebration of Dissent*, 297–324, Armonk and London.

—— (1990) "Owner-Manager Conflict and Financial Theories of Investment Instability: A Critical Assessment of Keynes, Tobin, and Minsky," *Journal of Post Keynesian Economics*, 12(4): 519–42.

—— (1993) "Rethinking Marxian Investment Theory: Keynes–Minsky Instability, Competitive Regime Shifts and Coerced Investment," *Review of Radical Political Economics*, 25(1): 1–26.

—— (1994) "Are Keynesian Uncertainty and Macrotheory Compatible? Conventional Decision Making, Institutional Structures, and Conditional Stability in Keynesian Macromodels," in *New Perspectives in Monetary Macroeconomics: Explorations in the Tradition of Hyman P. Minsky*, 105–39, Ann Arbor.

—— (1996) "Is New Keynesian Investment Theory Really 'Keynesian'? Reflections on Fazzari and Variato," *Journal of Post Keynesian Economics*, 18(3): 333–57.

—— (2003) "The Neoliberal Paradox: The Impact of Destructive Product Market Competition and Impatient Finance on Nonfinancial Corporations in the Neoliberal Era," *Review of Radical Political Economics*, 35(3): 271–9.

—— (2005) "The Neoliberal Paradox: The Impact of Destructive Product Market Competition and 'Modern' Financial Markets on Nonfinancial Corporation Performance in the Neoliberal Era," in *Financialization and the World Economy*, 77–110, Cheltenham, UK and Northampton, MA.

Crotty, J. and Dymski, G. (2001) "Can the Global Neoliberal Regime Survive Victory in Asia? The Political Economy of the Asian Crisis," in *Money, Finance and Capitalist Development*, 53–100, Cheltenham, UK and Northampton, MA.

Crotty, J. and Goldstein, J. P. (1992) "A Marxian–Keynesian Theory of Investment Demand: Empirical Evidence," in *International Perspectives on Profitability and Accumulation*, 197–234, Aldershot: Edward Elgar.

Crotty, J. and Lee, K.-K. (2006) "The Effects of Neoliberal 'Reforms' on the Post-crisis Korean Economy," *Review of Radical Political Economics*, 38(4): 669–75.

Davidson, P. (1983) "Rational Expectations: A Fallacious Foundation for Studying Crucial Decision-Making Processes," *Journal of Post Keynesian Economics*, 5(2): 182–98.

—— (1992) "Would Keynes Be a New Keynesian?" *Eastern Economic Journal*, 18(4): 449–63.

—— (2001) "If Markets Are Efficient, Why Have There Been So Many International Financial Market Crises since the 1970s?" in *What Global Economic Crisis?* 12–34, Houndmills and New York.

Dufour, M. and Orhangazi, O. (2007) "International Financial Crises: Scourge or Blessings in Disguise?" *Review of Radical Political Economics*, 39(3): 342–50.

Dutt, A. (2002) "Structuralist and Institutionalist Approaches to Development Political Economy," *International Journal of Development Issues*, 1(1): 1–26.

Dymski, G. A. (2003) "The International Debt Crisis," in *The Handbook of Globalisation*, 90–103, Cheltenham, UK and Northampton, MA.

—— (2005) "Financial Globalization, Social Exclusion and Financial Crisis," *International Review of Applied Economics*, 19(4): 439–57.

Dymski, G. A. and Pollin, R. (eds.) (1994) *New Perspectives in Monetary Macroeconomics: Explorations in the Tradition of Hyman P. Minsky*. Ann Arbor.

Eichner, A. S. (1973) "A Theory of the Determination of the Mark-up Under Oligopoly," *Economic Journal*, 83(332): 1184–200.

—— (1987) *The Macrodynamics of Advanced Market Economies*. Armonk: M. E. Sharpe.

Epstein, G. (1992) "Political Economy and Comparative Central Banking," *Review of Radical Political Economics*, 24(1): 1–30.

—— (ed.) (2005) *Financialization and the World Economy*. Cheltenham, UK and Northampton, MA.

Fazzari, S. M. (1992) "Introduction: Conversations with Hyman Minsky," in *Financial Conditions and Macroeconomic Performance: Essays in Honor of Hyman P. Minsky*, 3–12. Armonk, NY and London.

Fazzari, S. M. and Mott, T. L. (1987) "The Investment Theories of Kalecki and Keynes: An Empirical Study of Firm Data, 1970–1982," *Journal of Post Keynesian Economics*, 9(2): 171–87.

Feiwel, G. R. (1975) *The Intellectual Capital of Michal Kalecki: A Study in Economic Theory and Policy*. Knoxville: University of Tennessee Press.

Gibson, B. (2003) "An Essay on Late Structuralism," in *Development Economics and Structuralist Macroeconomics: Essays in Honour of Lance Taylor*, 52–76, Cheltenham, UK and Northampton, MA.

—— (2005) "The Transition to a Globalized Economy: Poverty, Human Capital and the Informal Sector in a Structuralist CGE Model," *Journal of Development Economics*, 78(1): 60–94.

Goldstein, J. P. (1985) "The Cyclical Profit Squeeze: A Marxian Microfoundation," *Review of Radical Political Economics*, 17(1–2): 103–28.

—— (1986) "The Micro–Macro Dialectic: A Concept of a Marxian Microfoundation," in *Research in Political Economy. Volume 9*, 127–55, Greenwich: JAI Press.

—— (2006) "Marxian Microfoundations: Contribution or Detour?" *Review of Radical Political Economics*, 38(4): 569–94.

Goodwin, R. (1967) "A Growth Cycle," in C. H. Feinstein (ed.) *Capitalism and Economic Growth*. Cambridge: Cambridge University Press.

Harcourt, G. C. (2001) "Theoretical Controversy and Social Significance: An Evaluation of the Cambridge Controversies," in *Selected Essays on Economic Policy*, 23–47. Houndmills and New York.

Kalecki, M. (1943) "Political Aspects of Full Employment," *Political Quarterly*, 4: 322–31.

—— (1968) "Trend and Cycle Reconsidered," *Economic Journal*: 263–76.

Kregel, J. A. (1973) *The Reconstruction of Political Economy: An Introduction to Post-Keynesian Economics*. London: Macmillan.

Kotz, D. M. (2001) "The State, Globalization and Phases of Capitalist Development," in *Phases of Capitalist Development: Booms, Crises and Globalizations*, 93–109. Houndmills, and New York.

—— (2003) "Neoliberalism and the Social Structure of Accumulation Theory of Long-Run Capital Accumulation," *Review of Radical Political Economics*, 35(3): 263–70.

Kotz, D. M., McDonough, T. and Reich, M. (eds.) (1994) *Social Structures of Accumulation: The Political Economy of Growth and Crisis*. Cambridge, New York and Melbourne.

Lee, F. S. and Keen, S. (2004) "The Incoherent Emperor: A Heterodox Critique of Neoclassical Microeconomic Theory," *Review of Social Economy*, 62(2): 169–99.

Lopez, J. and Mott, T. (1999) "Kalecki versus Keynes on the Determinants of Investment," *Review of Political Economy*, 11(3): 291–301.

McDonough, T. (2003) "What Does Long Wave Theory Have to Contribute to the Debate on Globalization?" *Review of Radical Political Economics*, 35(3): 280–6.

McDonough, T. and McDonough, N. E. (2006) "Social Structures of Accumulation, the Regulation Approach and the European Union," *Competition and Change*, 10(2): 200–12.

McLeod, A. N. (1997) "A Critique of Neoclassicism and New Keynesianism," *Eastern Economic Journal*, 23(1): 101–12.

Marx, K. (1967) *Capital; Volume 1*. New York: International Publishers.

Minsky, H. P. (1975) *John Maynard Keynes*. New York: Columbia University Press.

—— (1982) *Can it Happen Again?* Armonk: M. E. Sharpe.

Mott, T. (2002) "Longer-Run Aspects of Kaleckian Macroeconomics," in *The Economics of Demand-led Growth: Challenging the Supply-side Vision of the Long Run*, 153–71, Cheltenham, UK and Northampton, MA.

O'Hara, P. A. (2000) "The Evolution of a New 'Neoliberal, Balanced Budget' Social Structure of Accumulation? Emerging Prospects for the United States and World Economies," in *The Economics of Public Spending: Debts, Deficits and Economic Performance*, 30–56, Cheltenham, UK and Northampton, MA.

—— (2002) "A New Financial Social Structure of Accumulation in the United States for Long Wave Upswing?" *Review of Radical Political Economics*, 34(3): 295–301.

Pasinetti, L. L. (2000) "Critique of the Neoclassical Theory of Growth and Distribution," *Banca Nazionale del Lavoro Quarterly Review*, 53(215): 383–431.

Pollin, R. (1997) "The Relevance of Hyman Minsky," *Challenge*, 40(2): 75–94.

Robinson, J. (1962) "Review of H. Johnson, *Money, Trade and Economic Growth*," *Economic Journal*, 72: 690–2.

—— (1971) *Economic Heresies*. New York: Basic Books.

Rotheim, R. J. (ed.) (1998) *New Keynesian Economics/Post Keynesian Alternatives*. London and New York: Routledge.

Sawyer, M. (1985) *The Economics of Michal Kalecki*. London: Macmillan.

—— (1999) "The Kaleckian Analysis and the New Millennium," *Review of Political Economy*, 11(3): 303–19.

—— (2001a) "Kalecki on Imperfect Competition, Inflation and Money: Review Article," *Cambridge Journal of Economics*, 25(2): 245–61.

—— (2001b) "Kalecki on Money and Finance," *European Journal of the History of Economic Thought*, 8(4): 487–508.

Seidman, L. S. (2005) "The New Classical Counter-Revolution: A False Path for Macroeconomics," *Eastern Economic Journal*, 31(1): 131–40.

Shapiro, N. and Sawyer, M. (2003) "Post Keynesian Price Theory," *Journal of Post Keynesian Economics*, 25(3): 355–65.

Steindl, J. (1952) *Maturity and Stagnation in American Capitalism*. Oxford: Blackwell.

Taylor, L. (2004a) *Reconstructing Macroeconomics: Structuralist Proposals and Critiques of the Mainstream*. Cambridge and London.

—— (2004b) "Structuralist Economics: Challenge to the Mainstream: Interview with Lance Taylor," *Challenge*, 47(5): 104–15.

Trigg, A. B. (2002) "Surplus Value and the Kalecki Principle in Marx's Reproduction Schema," *History of Economics Review*, 35: 104–14.

—— (2004) "Kalecki and the Grossmann Model of Economic Breakdown," *Science and Society*, 68(2): 187–205.

Weisskopf, T. E. (1979) "Marxian Crisis Theory and the Rate of Profit in the Postwar U.S. Economy," *Cambridge Journal of Economics*, 3(4): 341–78.

Wolfson, M. H. (2000) "Neoliberalism and International Financial Instability," *Review of Radical Political Economics*, 32(3): 369–78.

—— (2001) "Institutional Analysis of Financial Crises," in *Crossing the Mainstream: Ethical and Methodological Issues in Economics*, 332–52, Notre Dame.

—— (2002) "Minsky's Theory of Financial Crises in a Global Context," *Journal of Economic Issues*, 36(2): 393–400.

Wray, L. R. (2002) "What Happened to Goldilocks? A Minskian Framework," *Journal of Economic Issues*, 36(2): 383–91.

2 The central core of heterodox macroeconomics

Malcolm Sawyer[1]

Introduction

This chapter is firmly based on the idea that there is a common core of heterodox macroeconomics. It seeks to sketch the contents of that core, and to briefly consider some of the implications of the heterodox analysis particularly in the policy direction. In this chapter I have avoided using the term post-Keynesian (rather than heterodox) as many of the propositions advanced below either do not make an appearance in Keynes' writings or run counter to his analysis (and it enables me to side-step the issue of what is post-Keynesian, though leaving the question of what are the boundaries of heterodox macroeconomics). Although we do not seek to ascribe the origins of the ideas sketched here, many of them come from the works of Kaldor, Kalecki and Robinson.

The chapter outlines what are considered to be the eight key features of a heterodox macroeconomic analysis. The following section draws out three sets of implications from those features. Whilst we would argue that the eight features listed are the central ones, the three sets of implications are intended to be illustrative rather than exhaustive.

The key features of heterodox macroeconomics

Heterodox macroeconomics is macroeconomics in the sense described by Pasinetti that it is

> not "macro-economic" in the sense of representing a first simplified rough step towards a more detailed and disaggregated analysis. It is macroeconomic because it could not be otherwise. Only problems have been discussed which are of a macro-economic nature; an accurate investigation of them has nothing to do with disaggregation. They would remain the same – i.e. they would still arise at a macro-economic level – even if we were to break down the model into a disaggregated analysis.
>
> (Pasinetti, 1974)

But it is also the case that heterodox macroeconomic analysis has always involved microeconomics in the obvious sense that the behaviors of households, workers, social classes and firms are analyzed and modeled. The ways in which that microeconomic analysis is undertaken varies considerably between authors: this is particularly noticeable with respect to the behavior of firms and the nature of competition. Whereas there is a uniformity in the mainstream approach with utility and profit maximization widely applied, there is no attempt to apply the same mode of behavior to all, and any notion of methodological individualism is rejected. The institutional and social arrangements in an economy have to be reflected in the ways in which economic behavior is analyzed.

Heterodox macroeconomics analysis is clearly intended to be that of a monetary capitalist economy in which the monetary and financial sectors play a central role (in contrast to the passive monetary sector as envisaged in most mainstream macroeconomics). The decision-making of individuals and firms, the interactions of those decisions and the evolution of the economy have to be analyzed in the context of fundamental uncertainty (in the sense of Keynes) where the future is unknown and unknowable, and the evolution of the economy must depend on the collective decisions which are made.

There are, we suggest, eight key features in heterodox macroeconomic analysis, and it is to these we now turn.

Aggregate demand

A central element in heterodox macroeconomics is that the level of demand is always important for the level of economic activity, that is in the long run (however that is defined) as well as the short run. There is thereby a denial of the validity of approach of the neoclassical synthesis portraying the long run as characterized by supply-side equilibrium (at full employment). Whilst some other approaches to macroeconomics recognize the role of demand in the short run but not in the long run, the heterodox approach views the role of demand as pervasive. There are then no market forces which could be relied on to propel the level of aggregate demand towards any supply-side equilibrium (or towards any other desired level of economic activity). There is a denial of the operation of relative prices to clear markets or of the real balance effect (in an endogenous money world) as the instrument of adjustment. Indeed, as illustrated in the paper of Hein and Stockhammer (2007), how private aggregate demand changes in the face of unemployment depends on the reactions of wages and prices, the change in the distribution of income and the impact which that has on the level of demand, and those changes may lead aggregate demand towards a supply-side equilibrium, or may lead demand away. There are numerous ways in which the level of demand impacts on supply and the evolution of supply potential, and this is outlined below (pp. 27–8).

Role of investment

There has long been agreement in heterodox macroeconomic analysis on the key and dual roles played by investment as a relative volatile component of aggregate demand and the driving force in the savings–investment relationship, and as involving the creation of productive potential. Investment by its nature is forward-looking and firms are looking for rewards from their investment over a long future time horizon. But the future is inherently uncertain and unknowable, and investment decisions cannot come from or be modeled by precise optimization.

Investment is undertaken by firms, and hence the amount of investment undertaken depends on the objectives of the firms, their organization structure and goals as well as the market structure and competitive framework within which they operate. Heterodox macroeconomists have provided many analyses of investment, based on different approaches to firms' organization and behavior (see, for example, Crotty, 1990). Limitations of space preclude any significant discussion of those analyses, except to say that the analysis of investment behavior has to be institutional specific. A significant development in the past two decades or so has been that of financialization (e.g. Epstein, 2005) and the changing relationship between industry and finance. In macroeconomic terms a key aspect of that has been the impact on rate of investment and capital accumulation (there are, of course, many other important aspects). The pace of investment at any time has also to be understood in the context of the prevailing technological paradigm.

In terms of the macroeconomic variables which influence investment, there is broad agreement, notably profitability as a source of finance and as a spur to capital accumulation, and the level and change in capacity utilization through some form of accelerator mechanism. Investment in effect fuses together the demand and supply side in that it is a component of demand but adds to productive potential. The particular significant aspect of the heterodox approach is that investment responds to ongoing events including those impacted by the level of demand (most obviously capacity utilization) rather than being the way in which the capital stock adjusts to the pre-determined growth path of the economy. "The long-run trend is but a slowly changing component of a chain of short-period situations; it has no independent entity" (Kalecki, 1968, p. 263). Further, "technical progress is infused into the economic system through the creation of new equipment, which depends on current (gross) investment expenditure" (Kaldor and Mirrlees, 1962, p. 174).

Income distribution

Distributions of income, personal and functional, are, of course, of considerable interest and concern in their own right. Heterodox macroeconomics has viewed the functional distribution of income as determined within the macroeconomic analysis, and that the distribution of income impacts on the level of demand. It is a basic proposition from Kaldor (1956) and Kalecki that the propensity to save out of wages is small (or zero) and out of profits substantial. Kaldor (1956) clearly indicates the relevance of that proposition for the distribution of income between wages and profits, though his analysis is based a full employment assumption. The Kaleckian approach views the distribution of income as set by the degree of monopoly, leading to the view that the volume of profits is determined by the spending decisions of capitalists; the well-known aphorism that "workers spend what they earn, capitalists earn what they spend" summarizes this view.[2]

The view that the propensity to spend out of wages was much larger than that out of profits led to a stagnationist view, namely that low demand and hence stagnation could result from wage share being relatively low thereby depressing consumption demand. The incorporation of the idea that investment depends on profitability and capacity utilization by Bhaduri and Marglin (1990) along with the differential propensities led to the distinction which they drew between a stagnationist regime and an exhilirationist regime, now more usually referred to as wage-led or profit-led regimes. The significance of this approach is that it brings income distribution into a central role in the determination of aggregate demand and the level of economic activity. It also serves as a reminder that shifts in behavior or in structure – in this case in the differential in propensity to consume and the influence of profitability on investment – can have marked effects on approach to policy. The particular important element of this approach is the view that in a wage-led regime application of the orthodox medicine for unemployment – that is restraint of real wages – becomes counterproductive. The establishment of whether an economy is in a wage-led or profit-led regime then becomes a matter of some importance.

Interdependence of demand and supply and path dependency

The independence of demand and supply has been a (perhaps the) central proposition in mainstream economics, whether at the microeconomic level where the demand and supply curves only interact through the price mechanism with a separation of the factors influencing demand and those influencing supply or at the macroeconomic level. The AD-AS analysis rather replicates the microeconomic demand and supply analysis. The separation of the real and monetary sides of the economy, reflected in the classical dichotomy and the use of the term "natural" "to try to separate the real forces from monetary forces" (Friedman, 1968, following Wicksell). The way in which the growth process has been modeled as converging on the "natural rate of growth" is a further illustration.

The interdependence of demand and supply is closely related with path dependency. The term path dependency is used to emphasize two features. First, the path of the economy is not pre-determined as in neoclassical growth theory (including endogenous growth theory) but rather the path emerges in an evolutionary manner. Second, it is used rather than the term hysteresis which tends to suggest a movement from one equilibrium to another, albeit that the equilibrium toward which there is movement is influenced by the path taken.

The mechanisms by which there is path dependency and by which the path of demand opens up future supply are various, but three are generally to the fore. The first one, already discussed in the context of investment, where it is clear that current demand influences investment which thereby adds to the capital stock. This general idea can readily be extended to a range of investment including that in education and health provision. The second is the way in which people are drawn into or pushed out of the effective labor supply through demand. Participation rates vary, ages of entry into and exit from the labor force change and there is regional and international migration. Clearly not all of such changes can be ascribed to pressures of demand as demographics, changes in social attitudes etc. are involved. But the evolution of the labor force cannot be understood without reference to demand. The third comes from the operation of a Verdoorn law type effect and "learning by doing" (and a variety of other forms of learning, e.g. "learning by exporting"). The rate of productivity change is then linked with the level of activity in the economy, which itself is determined by the level of demand.

Bhaduri (2006) provides an example of a growth model which fuses together the demand and supply sides. His model is one in which "both investment and savings decisions exert their influences on the long-run equilibrium growth of output." While this result is a natural outcome of introducing aggregate demand in the analysis by separating investment from savings decisions, it is the endogeneity of labor productivity growth with increasing returns that provides the main impetus to the growth process on the supply side. A novel aspect of this model is to view the growth in both the real wage rate and in labor productivity "as being driven simultaneously by the forces of intra-class competition among capitalist firms over market shares, as well as by inter-class conflict over income shares" (p. 80). Dutt (2006) is a further example with "a simple model with endogenous technological change in which aggregate demand and aggregate supply both have a role to play and in which long-run growth can be affected by aggregate demand" (p. 331).

Money and credit

The role of money created through the credit system and now labeled endogenous money has been a central element in heterodox macroeconomics for the past quarter of a century, though ideas on endogenous money and the development of the circuitist approach go much further back. Moore (1988) was a major contribution which marked out the way for post-Keynesian analysis, and ensured an emphasis was given to the money creation processes.[3] Kalecki (as argued in Sawyer, 2001), Kaldor (1970), Robinson (1956) and others had incorporated an essentially endogenous money approach. Keynesian analysis (in the form of IS-LM) had, of course, proceeded with exogenous money and all that entailed, and it was perhaps only the onslaught of monetarism which required more serious attention be given to the nature and role of money (Kaldor, 1970).

Endogenous money is important for macroeconomic analysis in a number of ways. First, an adjustment process which relies on some idea of real balance effect is no longer viable since endogenous money does not constitute net worth; the orthodoxy (in the form of the new consensus in macroeconomics, NCM: see

Arestis and Sawyer, 2008) has now adopted some aspects of endogenous money but rely on the wisdom of the Central Bank in the setting of interest rates (at the "natural rate of interest"). The adjustment process becomes a matter of administrative decision rather than market mechanism. Second, the manner in which loans are provided by the bank system becomes a central question. It is not only that banks hold the key to expansion since any refusal on their part to provide loans would limit any expansion of expenditure. The way in which the inevitable credit rationing occurs in terms of who are "awarded" loans and who are not reflects a wide range of discrimination (gender, ethnicity etc.). The type of sectors (e.g. large vs. small business, high tech vs. low tech) favored which influence the evolution of the economy in a path dependent world. The terms and conditions on which loans are supplied can also interact with the analysis of financial liberalization. Instead of the "loanable funds'"approach of McKinnon (1973) and Shaw (1973) in which banks act as intermediaries between savings and investment, the banks provide credit "off their own bat."

Third, monetary policy becomes more closely identified with interest rate policy, though interest rate policy has always been the key element in monetary policy even in the heyday of monetarism. But the heterodox analysis suggests that interest rate movements have relatively small effects and points to the need for a broader concept of monetary policy (see Arestis and Sawyer, 2006a).

Fourth, the behavior of banks and related credit institutions become important for the economy. Their willingness or otherwise to provide loans and the terms on which they are provided impact on the level and structure of demand. Further, the financial sector is prone to act in ways which generate bubbles and crises: "instability is determined by mechanisms within the system, not outside it; our economy is not unstable because it is shocked by oil, wars or monetary surprises, but because of its nature" (Minsky, 1986, p. 172).

Finally, any notion of the non-neutrality of money disappears. It is difficult to even envisage what a non-monetary economy would look like in order to judge the neutrality or otherwise of money. But since money comes into existence via the credit process, the ways in which credit is created impacts on investment, and thereby the productive potential of the economy.

Price and wage determination and the supply-side of the economy in the short run

There have been many contributions by heterodox economists to the analysis of price determination and of wage determination. Here we can only sketch some aspects.[4] Firms make interrelated decisions on price, output supply and employment offers in light of the demand conditions which they face and their own productive capacity. In doing so, firms set the relationship between price and wage, and their pricing decisions bear on profit determination. The determination of wages is represented by a wage curve as a positive relationship between real wages and employment and based on efficiency wage considerations and/or on collective bargaining. From the interaction of these price and wage determinations a form of supply-side equilibrium can be derived, which can be seen as forming an inflation barrier. This could be seen as akin to a non-accelerating inflation rate of unemployment (NAIRU). But this inflation barrier differs from the NAIRU in (at least) two major respects. First, it is presented in a manner which seeks to emphasize that the interaction of prices and wages do not take place in what may be described as "the labor market," and hence the supply-side equilibrium is not set by the features of the labor market. Instead the emphasis is placed on the role of productive capacity. Second, there is no presumption that the inflation barrier acts as a strong (or even weak) attractor for the actual level of economic activity. There are no market forces which lead the level of aggregate demand to adjust to the inflation barrier.

Inflation

Inflation is a non-monetary phenomenon in the sense that changes in the stock of money do not determine the rate of inflation in any causal sense, but rather the rate of change of the stock of money (endogenously) adjusts to the pace of inflation. There are a range of factors which impact on the rate of inflation including a struggle over income shares, the level of and rate of changes of the level of aggregate demand and cost-push factors coming notably from the foreign sector (change in import prices and the exchange rate).

A heterodox approach (which we labeled a structuralist approach, Arestis and Sawyer, 2005) concentrates on three key elements in the inflationary process. One set of inflationary pressures comes from the level of demand relative to the size of productive capacity. There is no presumption that there is adequate capacity in an economy to support the full employment of labor, and hence enterprises may be operating at or even above normal capacity with substantial levels of unemployment.

A second and related set of inflationary pressures comes from the inherent conflict over the distribution of income. The ability of the economy to reconcile the conflict depends, *inter alia*, on the productive capacity of the economy. The determination of an inflation barrier (as indeed in the literature on the NAIRU and on the "natural rate of unemployment") involves the notion that wages and prices rise together with the difference in the rate of increase of wages and that of prices being equal to the rate of labor productivity growth. In other words, the distribution of income between wages and profits would remain constant. This serves as a reminder that there are basic conflicts over the distribution of income. If all groups and classes in society were in effect content with the existing distribution of income, then it could be expected that there would not be a problem of inflation: at a minimum it would mean that the rate of inflation was constant. An increase in the rate of inflation can be viewed as arising from some combination of intention of some groups to increase their share of income and enhanced opportunity to do so. A higher level of demand for labor may, for example, be seen as enhanced opportunity for workers to increase their share. But a related higher level of demand for output would allow firms to increase their profits. The "conflict theory" of inflation can be seen as based on this insight.

Third, the level of economic activity depends on the level of aggregate demand, and there is no presumption that the level of demand will generate full employment of labor and/or full capacity utilization. Investment has a crucial dual role to play through its impact on aggregate demand and through its enhancing impact on capital stock. Further, there is no automatic mechanism, which takes the level of aggregate demand to any supply-side equilibrium. Mechanisms such as adjustment of real wages to clear the labor market, or the operation of the real balance effect, are explicitly rejected.

Open economy considerations

The openness of an economy means that the domestic economy is buffeted by events in the rest of the world. There is no reason to think that the domestic economy can be insulated from the rest of the world through smooth adjustments in the exchange rate: hence inflation in the rest of the world impacts on domestic inflation in that it cannot be assumed that some form of purchasing power parity holds under which the nominal exchange rate would move to offset any inflation differential.

It would be generally agreed that there has been considerable volatility of exchange rates (both nominal and real) under the floating exchange rate regime, and that capital related flows, rather than trade related flows, across the exchanges are the dominant factor influencing movements in the exchange rate. It has not been possible to understand the movements in the exchange rate, perhaps other than to say that uncovered interest rate parity does not apply. Whilst the real exchange rate has some mean reverting properties, these do not prevent movements of the order of +/–25 to 30 percent in the real exchange rate (and also in the nominal exchange rate given the similarities of inflationary experience across industrialized countries).

Orthodox economics makes much of "inter temporal budget constraints" and the limitations which they place on the behavior of individuals and of government. Yet the most significant of those type of constraints, namely that on the country as a whole, has played little role.[5] In heterodox economics by contrast a variant of such constraints has played a considerable role, notably in the form of balance of payments constrained growth as developed by Thirlwall (e.g. Thirlwall, 1979). The argument is straightforward: as a country cannot borrow more and more on its capital account, this places a constraint on its current account and trade position. Imports and exports of goods and services have to grow at much the same rate, and putting continuous real devaluation to one side, this leads to growth of domestic income equal to the income elasticity of demand for exports multiplied by growth of world income divided by income elasticity of demand for imports.

Some implications

In this section we briefly draw out three sets of implications from the heterodox analysis to indicate the importance and relevance of that analysis for our understanding of the world.

Demand management policies

In the heterodox approach, securing a high level of aggregate demand and of economic activity retains a high priority for the usual reasons (including the low-ering of unemployment) but also for the longer term effects. There is clearly no presumption that the level of demand will be consistent with a high level of eco-nomic activity (nor that there is sufficient productive capacity to employ the available labor). Nor is there any clear market mechanism which would secure the required level of demand. The heterodox approach would tend to view fiscal policy as a much more potent means of securing the high level of demand than monetary policy (Arestis and Sawyer, 2003). The arguments which have been advanced against the use of fiscal policy are based on the assumption that there is no issue over the lack of aggregate demand (Arestis and Sawyer, 2006b): for example crowding out arguments assume there is something to be crowded out.

The nature of inflation barriers and policy implications

A key aspect of the prevailing orthodoxy can be summarized in the terms "natural rate of unemployment" (NRU) and "non-accelerating inflation rate of unemployment" (NAIRU).[6] The significance of those terms is that the emphasis is placed on the labor market (if such exists) as the arena in which the level of unemployment is effectively determined. It is a supply-side concept with the (often implicit) assumption that the level of economic activity will gravitate to that level of unemployment. Further, there is the suggestion that a relatively high level of unemployment is a consequence of poorly functioning, over-regulated, inflexible labor markets.

The heterodox approach has often been viewed in terms that money wages may be settled in the labor market (whether through collective bargaining or not) but real wages are effectively set in the product market through the pricing decisions of firms. This type of view is evident in Keynes (1936) and Kalecki's analysis of the degree of monopoly which not only is seen to set the distribution of income but also the level of real wages. Whilst accepting that the setting of wages must necessarily be in money terms, and that pricing decisions of firms are significant for real wages, we bring in the effects of workers' aspirations and bargaining power into the determination of any inflation barrier. There is a con-flict over the distribution of income, and the inflation barrier represents the posi-tion where there is some "reconciliation" of that conflict.

In market economies, there is often a mismatch between available productive capacity and the labor force and its geographical distribution. Specifically, the zero output gap (where output equals trend output) and the full employment of labor cannot be used interchangeably. Higher levels of employment require more productive capacity. The aligning of productive capacity with the size and distri-bution of the work force is a major task, which is rarely accomplished. There are generally supply-side (as well as demand-side) constraints on the achievement of full employment of labor. But the nature of those constraints comes from the lack of productive capacity rather than any notion of them arising from inflexible or rigid labor markets. Industrial and regional policies are required to ensure that any inflation barrier is compatible with the full employment of labor. Public expenditure, particularly investment, can also be structured to ease supply constraints. It then follows that policies which may be described as industrial and regional policies are required to address these issues of lack of productive capacity.

The non-neutrality of money and finance

"Money matters" is a rather bizarre way of summarizing monetarism in the sense that while money supply was viewed as a causal factor in inflation, it had no effect on the level of or composition of output and employment. The neutrality of money and the classical dichotomy were central to monetarism and related approaches. In a similar vein the Wicksellian based new consensus in macroeconomics retains a sense of neutrality in that it is based around a "natural rate of interest" which

> is neutral in respect to commodity prices, and tend neither to raise nor to lower them. This is necessarily the same as the rate of interest which would be determined by supply and demand if no use were made of money and all lending were effected in the form of real capital goods. It comes to much the same thing to describe it as the current value of the natural rate of interest on capital.
>
> (Wicksell, 1965, p. 102)

It is difficult (impossible) to envisage how a sophisticated market economy would operate without money or finance, and hence the "benchmark" of a real economy against which the neutrality of money and finance would be assessed is not available. It is clearly possible to write down macroeconomic models without explicit mention of money or finance, as is done in many Kaleckian models. But there is an implicit (and sometimes explicit) view of the banking system to the effect that loans will be forthcoming to enable investment to be financed and that if loans were not provided then the investment could not occur.

Conclusions

The belief which lies behind this chapter is that there is a set of propositions which are broadly shared by heterodox macroeconomists. We have sought to sketch out those propositions and to illustrate their significance, and to look at some of the implications of this heterodox approach.

Notes

1 I am grateful to Philip Arestis and John King for comments on an earlier draft, and to the participants at the Rebellious Macroeconomics conference held at the Political

Economy Research Institute of the University of Massachusetts for general discussion and comments.

2 Ascribed by Joan Robinson to Kalecki, but not actually to be found in his writings (see Robinson, 1966, p. 341).

3 See Arestis and Sawyer (2006c) for a wide range of essays on heterodox approaches to money and finance.

4 This section is heavily influenced by Sawyer (2002).

5 It is well-known that a deficit (of whatever kind) of d relative to income will lead to a debt ratio which would stabilize at $b = d(g - r)$; this requires $g > r$, which may hold for governments (who can borrow at the risk free rate of interest and in effect pay the post-tax rate of interest) but is unlikely to hold in general for individuals or for countries.

6 The terms are often used synonymously though we would associate the "natural rate of unemployment" with the market-clearing position of a competitive labor market, and hence akin to full employment, and the "non-accelerating rate of unemployment" with imperfectly competitive markets (e.g. Layard *et al.*, 1991).

References

Arestis, P. and Sawyer, M. (2003) "On the effectiveness of monetary and fiscal policy," *Review of Social Economics*, 62(4): 441–63.

—— (2005) "Aggregate demand, conflict and capacity in the inflationary process," *Cambridge Journal of Economics*, 29(6): 959–74.

—— (2006a) "The nature and role of monetary policy when money is endogenous," *Cambridge Journal of Economics*, 30(6): 847–60.

—— (2006b) "Fiscal policy matters," *Public Finance*, 54: 133–53.

—— (eds.) (2006c) *A Handbook Of Alternative Monetary Economics*, Cheltenham: Edward Elgar.

—— (2008) "A critical reconsideration of the foundations of monetary policy in the new consensus macroeconomics framework," *Cambridge Journal of Economics*, 32(5): 761–79.

Bhaduri, A. (2006) "Endogenous economic growth: a new approach," *Cambridge Journal of Economics*, 30: 85–103.

Bhaduri, A. and Marglin, S. (1990) "Unemployment and the real wage: the economic basis for contesting political ideologies," *Cambridge Journal of Economics*, 14: 375–93.

Crotty, J. (1990) "Owner-manager conflict and financial theories of investment demand: a critical assessment of Keynes, Tobin and Minsky," *Journal of Post Keynesian Economics*, 12(4): 519–42.

Dutt, A. K. (2006) "Aggregate demand, aggregate supply and economic growth," *International Review of Applied Economics*, 20(3): 319–36.

Epstein, G. (ed.) (2005) *Financialization and the World Economy*, Cheltenham, UK and Northampton, MA: Edward Elgar.

Friedman, M. (1968) "The role of monetary policy," *American Economic Review*, 58(1): 1–17.

Hein, E. and Stockhammer, E. (2007) "Macroeconomic policy mix, employment and inflation in a post-Keynesian alternative to the New Consensus Model" (mimeo).

Kaldor, N. (1956) "Alternative theories of distribution," *Review of Economic Studies*, 23.

—— (1970) "The new monetarism," *Lloyds Bank Review*, no. 97.

Kaldor, N. and Mirrlees, J. (1962) "A new model of economic growth," *Review of Economic Studies*, 29: 174–92.

Kalecki, M. (1968) "Trend and the business cycle," *Economic Journal*, 78: 263–76.

Keynes, J. M. (1936) *The General Theory of Employment, Interest and Money*, London: Macmillan.

Layard, R., Nickell, S. and Jackman, R. (1991) *Unemployment: Macroeconomic Performance and the Labour Market*, Oxford: Oxford University Press.

McKinnon, R. I. (1973) *Money and Capital in Economic Development*, Washington, DC: Brookings Institution.

Minsky, H. P. (1986) *Stabilizing an Unstable Economy*, New Haven: Yale University Press.

Moore, B. (1988) *Horizontalists and Verticalists: the Macroeconomics of Credit Money*, Cambridge: Cambridge University Press.

Pasinetti, L. (1974) *Growth and Income Distribution*, Cambridge: Cambridge University Press.

Robinson, J. (1956) *The Accumulation of Capital*, London: Macmillan.

—— (1966) "Kalecki and Keynes," in P. A. Baran (ed.) *Problems of Economic Dynamics and Planning: Essays in Honour of Michal Kalecki*, 335–41. Oxford: Pergamon.

Sawyer, M. (2001) "Kalecki on money and finance," *The European Journal of the History of Economic Thought*, 8(4): 487–508.

—— (2002) "The NAIRU, aggregate demand and investment," *Metroeconomica*, 53(1): 66–94.

Shaw, E. S. (1973) *Financial Deepening in Economic Development*, New York: Oxford University Press.

Thirlwall, A. P. (1979) "The balance of payments constraint as an explanation of international growth rate differences," *Banca Nazionale del Lavoro Quarterly Review*, March.

Wicksell, K. (1965 [1898]) *Interest and Prices*, Cranbury: Scholars Bookshelf.

3 An introduction to a unified heterodox macroeconomic theory

Jonathan P. Goldstein

An introduction to a unified heterodox macroeconomic theory

In the Neoliberal era, free market economics/ideology and the associated doctrines of free trade and financial liberalization have guided the economic development of an integrated world economy. The resulting development path has been marred by increasing income inequality, financial crises, slow aggregate demand growth, destructive competition and a tendency to global excess capacity and unemployment. These outcomes arise from the anarchy and inherent contradictions of global free markets and the accompanying complement of Neoliberal policies. The benefits of this Neoliberal regime have primarily accrued to financial capitalists and, to a lesser extent, to international industrial capitalists at the expense of other social groups.

Despite this poor track record, the economic foundations that underlie this development strategy – neoclassical microeconomics and new classical macroeconomics – have dominated the economics profession for over 25 years. The drawback of this method, based on its unrealistic set of assumptions, is its real world irrelevance for a global economic system far removed from perfect competition and dominated by coercive decisions influenced by an endogenous distribution of income and made under fundamental uncertainty. Despite this fundamental irrelevance, neoclassical practitioners have readily enlisted policymakers and power/class brokers to adopt free market policies purely on ideological and self-interested grounds.

The one orthodox alternative, the new Keynesian new neoclassical synthesis (Goodfriend (2004)), attempts to integrate Keynes' critique of neoclassical economics within the neoclassical general equilibrium framework. This alternative subsumes Keynes within neoclassical economics and thus is disappointing (Davidson (2003), Crotty (1992, 1996)). Besides the derivation of an underemployment equilibrium as an alternative center of gravity for the economy, a strong faith in the effectiveness of policy is all that is needed to bring the new Keynesian alternative equilibrium in line with the new classical full employment solution and thus establish an uncomfortable convergence of the two approaches.[1]

On the other hand, heterodox economics, particularly post-Keynesian, institutionalist and Marxian analyses, have developed flexible models based on realistic assumptions that help us to better understand the contradictory evolution of the global economy and the detrimental impact of Neoliberal policies. Unfortunately as Goldstein and Hillard (Chapter 1) argue, the full potential of heterodox alternatives has not been realized. Despite some authors' insistence that heterodox theories have followed a convergence path (Lavoie *et al.* (2004), Lavoie (2006), and Tymoigne and Lee (2003: 284)), the convergence has been superficial at best and an integration of heterodox ideas into a more potent theory has not occurred (Fontana (2005: 412)). Basically, fundamentalists' positions on both the post-Keynesian and Marxian sides and a self-preserving reluctance among post-Keynesians to associate with the more systematic (radical) Marxian critiques of capitalism have created barriers to such an integration. Despite these impediments, numerous authors (referenced in Chapter 1) have laid a foundation for integrating Keynesian, Marxian and institutionalist approaches.

The goal of such an integration is a flexible and realistic theory of the evolution of the capitalist global economy achieved by combining the best complementary aspects of alternative left theories, rejecting problematic and unrealistic aspects of those approaches and by resolving contradictory competing claims of those theories. In this chapter, I focus on the integration of Marxian and Keynesian ideas.

This synthesis adapts from post-Keynesian economics   true/fundamental uncertainty, endogenous money/credit, endogenous expectations, financial innovation, financial fragility and effective demand. These elements are integrated with Marxian crisis theory, adversarial class relations, a conflict-determined distribution of income and its impact on effective demand, the imperative to accumulate and the Marxian concept of competition as distinct from the classical/neoclassical concept of competition. In addition, the social structure of accumulation (SSA) approach and its associated long wave theory is used to establish the institutional mechanisms and change that underlie long-term growth/accumulation. From both approaches, the role of institutions is integrated, particularly with respect to the constitution of the individual economic agent, the formation of expectations and confidence in expectations and as a support system for profitable long-term accumulation.

Also, problematic positions/theories in both camps, discussed in Chapter 1, that act as barriers to a synthesis, are set aside for the pragmatic purpose of developing a unified theory.

Integrating Keynesian and Marxian economics: the nexus of Marxian competition, irreversible investment, crisis theory, financial fragility and fundamental uncertainty

In this section, I sketch an integrated Keynes–Marx approach to macroeconomics. The hallmarks of this method are a flexible and realistic approach to macroeconomics that is capable of explaining the dynamics of the macroeconomy including key regime shifts/transitions. While many of the basic concepts are rooted both in Keynes' and Marx's writings, many of the integrative ideas and extensions come from the work of Crotty (1980, 1983, 1985, 1986, 1989, 1990a, 1990b, 1992, 1993, 1994, 1996, 2000, 2002, 2003a, 2003b, 2005). I start by considering the class and uncertain nature of the macro environment. The resulting environment is argued to be a hostile/threatening, coercive and unknowable one with the potential for contradictory outcomes. Next, I consider the theory of effective demand where the accumulation of capital plays a central role and the demand side is integrally linked to the supply-side of the economy. I outline a Keynes–Marx theory of investment that goes beyond simple Keynesian and Marxian variants of the determinants of investment. Next, I consider pricing and profit rate determination then crisis mechanisms, the illusive nature of balanced growth, long-run adjustments through institutional change and long-run dynamics via regime shifts.

Macrofoundations: a hostile, forbidding and unforgiving arena

While I argue below that microeconomic behavior is integrally linked to the macro environment, I start with macrofoundations because they characterize the environment that determines/constraints the menu of individual actions that can be pursued. Macrofoundations encompass the existing class structure and the competitive, institutional and non-ergodic nature of the environment that underlies that class structure. While the elements of macrofoundations have a historic-specific character,[2] I only focus on a general theoretical framework in this chapter.

The starting point is a well developed set of capitalist class relations where the Marxian concept of class interactions is employed. From that perspective, class relations relate to the production, appropriation and distribution of surplus value/profits in a capitalist economy. While many different forms of class relations exists, the central ones are between capital and labor (K–L), capital and other capitals (K–K) or capitalist competition and finance capital and capital (FK–K). Given that many Marxists focus on the capital–labor relation, the capital–capital and finance capital–capital relations have been under-analyzed.

It is the historically contingent and institutionally-specific determination of the balance of power between classes that is central to how class interactions affect the economy. Changes in the balance of power have significant impacts on the distribution of income with important feedbacks to effective demand, supply decisions and the role played by financial markets. Additionally, the balance of power significantly and endogenously shapes/constrains the preferences, objectives and behavior of individual agents.

Marxian competition as the antithesis of classical competition is brought to life in Crotty (1993, 2003a). Here, Marxian competition takes on a fundamentally uncertain, warlike nature where "capitalists eat other capitalists." On the micro level, individual capitalist reproductive behavior must consider this type of competition. This competitive relation neither produces a harmonious outcome nor a stable set of class relations. In fact, it underlies potentially coercive and frenzied microeconomic survival behavior that may be inconsistent with the reproduction of all capitalists – a micro–macro dialectic exists (Goldstein (1986a)). Thus, it serves as the basis for crisis tendencies, particularly a direct tendency to over-investment and an indirect tendency to under-consumption as attempts are made to extract more profit at the expense of labor in order to finance the accumulation process.

It is this nature of competitive relations that serves as the basis for the centrality and volatility of investment in a theory of effective demand. In such a belligerent environment, a competitive criteria may dominate the typical optimality criteria, such as the maximization of profits, when it comes to individual behavior.[3] Crotty (1993) discusses an "invest or die" strategy that fulfills a competitive criteria. Here, significant amounts of defensive investment may become an imperative despite the current profit and financial status of the firm. In addition, the qualitative and innovative nature of investments geared at securing the competitive survival of the firm are likely to generate significant costs of adjustment within the structure/operation of the firm.

Crotty (1993: 4–8, 2003a) in developing and systemizing the concept of the Marxian competition locates two forms of competition: fraternal or corespective competition and fratricidal or coercive competition.[4]

In a corespective competitive regime, competing firms coordinate their activities in a manner that bounds the intensity of competition among them. In this competitive regime, competition is restricted to competition over market share through advertising and more effective marketing and distribution. Price wars, especially in a sluggish demand growth environment, are avoided. Price-cost mark-ups are maintained, and investment activity is coordinated to avoid unwanted excess capacity. High profits support a moderate pace of innovation that increases productivity.

In contrast, coercive competition has as its mainstay destructive price competition. The primary tool is cost-cutting technological innovation. Given the irreversible nature of investment that creates an inability for firms to freely exist the industry, firms face an invest-or-die defensive strategy. Due to fundamental uncertainty over which firms will survive the next competitive onslaught, there is an overall tendency for firms to over-invest in this situation. This strategy is typically coupled with low road labor strategies – cutting wages and benefits and using layoffs – to increase competitiveness. Thus, tendencies to under-consumption and excess capacity emerge. This represents another example of the micro–macro dialectic at work.

These competitive regime distinctions add a first layer of numerous dichotomies in the heterodox macroeconomic framework developed here. These dichotomies/regimes add a historic and institutional flexibility to the method that allows it to explain fluidity in the evolution of capitalist economies.

These alternative competitive regimes also have important implications for microeconomic behavior as they impact the objective function of the firm. Shaikh (1978) and Goldstein (1985a) were the first to establish these microeconomic effects. Shaikh conceptually established a competitive criteria as distinct from profit maximization (Goldstein (2006: 581, fn. 12)), while Goldstein

(1985a, 1985b) developed a formal model where the firm's profit maximization objective is constrained by a competitive market share constraint. Crotty and Goldstein (1992a, 1992b) and Goldstein (Chapter 8) use a competitive market share constraint to effect changes in investment strategy from offensive to defensive investment that effectively amount to a shift from profit maximization to meeting a competitive criteria.

Fundamental or Keynesian uncertainty lies at the core of the macro environment.[5] True uncertainty affects the most crucial decisions and responses of the firm. When exist from an industry is costly, the firm's competitive survival/investment strategy is fraught with uncertainty. Also, the profit rate as a heuristic for the general health of the economy as well as its individual determinants are inherently uncertain. The fallout from declining profit rates, both in the real (declining demand) and financial sectors (bankruptcies and diminished cash flow) and the taking on of financial obligations when cash flows are unknown are all uncertain activities. Despite the centrality of uncertainty, a tractable method for incorporating it into an integrated framework has been elusive. True uncertainty seems to imply theoretical chaos.

Crotty (1994) offers a methodological approach that both bounds the unsettling aspects of uncertainty, while preserving the volatile and contradictory aspects of decision-making under uncertainty. His suggestions allow Keynesian uncertainty to be successfully integrated into a heterodox macroeconomic framework. His solution is based on the stabilizing aspects of institutions and the dialectical interaction of individual decision-making with the institutional structure.

In particular, institutions form a macroeconomic foundation of conditional stability for decision-making under true uncertainty. The institutional structure or SSA under normal circumstances bounds the overall behavior of the economy and underlies a process of conventional expectation formation and confidence formation. Given that agents are socially constituted and have a deep psychological need to create the illusion of order and continuity, they rely on conventional expectations and confidence levels based on rules and heuristics. Yet, they also know that the conventional wisdom periodically makes large forecast errors. Thus, expectations are fragile and subject to sudden change; particularly when social conventions are challenged by recent events. Such challenges are inevitable given the contradictory nature of microeconomic behavior that are at the core of the integrated theory's microeconomic foundations.

This treatment of uncertainty adds a second dichotomy, for micro behavior and macro outcomes, between stable expectations and a crisis of confidence.

In sum, the existing power relations between classes, the intense competitive and uncertain environment serve as the macroeconomic basis for a rich heterodox theory of capitalist evolution.

Microfoundations

The approach developed here places a priority for reducing the underlying mechanisms for economic and social outcomes to a basis in human agency. Goldstein

(2006) develops a rationale for microeconomic reduction based on a rejection of fallacy of composition (holism) critiques of microfoundations and the use of flexible and realistic objective functions and model structures that capture critical social interactions and potentially contradictory behavior.[6]

In such models, individual behavior is conditionally/conjuncturally determined by the macrofoundations discussed above. In turn, individual or group behavior alters the social and economic environment with important feedback effects to micro behavior. Goldstein (1986a, 2006) refers to this micro–macro interaction as the micro–macro dialectic, while Crotty (1990a, 1994, 2003a) recognizes the mutual determination of both spheres.

It should be made clear that while a preference exists for rational choice models to achieve micro reductions, in no way is this an absolute priority. Such micro reductions simply may not be feasible. The non-existence and lack of uniqueness of optimizing behavior make it necessary to adopt different methods for achieving micro reduction. In particular, rules of thumb, bounded rationality, the use of habits, norms, conventional wisdom and rituals can all underlie microeconomic behavior. The incorporation of such foundations for individual behavior is perfectly acceptable. Thus, the call for microfoundations in an integrated approach is to use micro reductions when they are feasible.

The prevalence of microfoundations in the components of an integrated heterodox macro theory will be obvious in the subsequent presentation (see Chapter 7). In particular, formal micrfoundations for pricing and the related distribution of income (Goldstein (1985a, 1985b)) and of the investment function (Crotty and Goldstein (1992a, 1992b) and Goldstein (Chapter 8)) are developed. In addition, much of Crotty's integrative contributions use informal microfoundations. In particular, Crotty (1994) relies on conventional wisdom to explain the stability and potential volatility of the expectation formation process and to understand the inter-firm interactions associated with destructive competition (Crotty (2003a, 2003b)).

Effective demand and the distribution of income

The Marxian competitive environment, even in its fraternal form, places the distribution of income, particularly the generation of profits, at the center of the theory of effective demand. While profits can be affected in numerous ways, conflictual struggles over the distribution of income, especially when competitive pressures intensify, play an important role. Alterations in the distribution of income can have important and potentially offsetting impacts on the level of effective demand. These mechanisms are captured through the consumption and investment functions used in heterodox macroeconomics. The consumption function derives from the classical analysis of consumption and savings. In particular, an income share-weighted Keynesian consumption function is employed where in a simple two-class world

$$C = \beta_0 + \beta_L \frac{1}{\alpha} Y + \beta_K \left(1 - \frac{1}{\alpha}\right) Y$$

and β_L is the marginal propensity to consume of labor, $\frac{1}{\alpha}$ is labor's share of income, β_K is the marginal propensity to consume of capital, $\left(1 - \frac{1}{\alpha}\right)$ is profits share of income, C is consumption, Y is income, β_0 is a constant and $\beta_L > \beta_K$. The simplest investment function can be expressed as $I = f(\pi_R)$ where π_R is the profit rate. The current profit rate, or weighted past values, serves as a heuristic for the uncertain future profitability of investment. The profit rate in turn depends on the profit share of income and the capital-output ratio; $\pi_R = \dfrac{\left(1 - \frac{1}{\alpha}\right)}{\frac{K}{Y}}$. It should be noted that the typical Keynesian emphasis on the role of capacity utilization on investment is captured within the $\frac{K}{Y}$ term of the profit rate.

In this effective demand system, the distribution of income has competing effects on aggregate demand. Decreases (increases) in the profit share of income reduces (increases) investment, while increasing (decreasing) consumption. The integrated approach developed here, takes the responsiveness of investment to short-run changes in the distribution of income to outweigh consumption responses. This crucial aspect of the relation between aggregate demand and the distribution of income is based on more than the centrality of investment to the theory of aggregate demand. It is supported by larger cyclical swings in the profit share then in the capital-output ratio, evidence in favor of slow changes in consumption patterns and the centrality of future expected long-run profits, in contrast to transitory demand-induced changes on the expected profit rate. Yet, in the long-run a larger response of consumption to decreases in labor's share may dominate.

While many heterodox theories of investment never go beyond the profit rate and/or capacity utilization as the key determinants of investment, important extensions of the simple theory of investment have been developed by Crotty (1993), Crotty and Goldstein (1992a, 1992b) and Goldstein (Chapter 8). These authors developed a microfounded Keynes–Marx theory of investment that further incorporates the external financing of investment based upon uncertain future profit flows, the irreversibility of investment and the coercive role of competition on investment. In this approach, the investment function is extended to depend on the profit rate, long-term and short-term heuristics for the firm's financial robustness and the intensity of competition. It is the interaction of these factors that fundamentally alters the nature of the investment function, particularly the typical role assigned to capacity utilization. The main dynamic of the model is an investment-induced growth-financial safety tradeoff facing the firm. Using this approach, a *ceteris paribus* increase in the financial fragility of the firm reduces investment and can be used to explain autonomous financial crises. In addition, the typical behavior of the profit rate, particularly changes in income shares, is preserved in this theory. Along these lines, the interaction of the profit rate and financial determinants allows for real sector sources of financial fragility to be incorporated into a macro model. Here, a profit squeeze that shifts expectations of future profits forces firms and lenders to alter their perceptions on short-term and long-term levels of acceptable debt. The responses of these agents can produce a cycle based on increases in financial fragility.

Finally, it is the role of competition that brings out other contradictory possibilities in the model. As in Goldstein (1985a), competition is treated via a competitive share constraint that alters the objective function of the firm. The binding/non-binding nature of the constraint is respectively analogous to Crotty's (1993) coercive/co-respective forms of competition and the firm's investment strategies respectively takes two forms: defensive/offensive investment. Defensive investment is a form of coercive investment where firms are forced to implement cost-cutting technology that dramatically disrupts the organizational culture of the firm in order to ensure its survival by recapturing its market share. In other words, when the constraint is binding, firms face a fundamentally uncertain invest-or-die situation. Given the irreversibility of investment, exit from the industry is typically not a viable option. There is always the uncertain hope that the firm can be one of the survivors in the shakeout and reorganization of the industry that drives the decision to invest and that underlies a tendency for all firms to over-invest.

When the constraint does not bind, investment behaves as described above via the navigation of a growth–financial safety tradeoff. In the coercive (binding) competitive case, competition forces the firm to invest irrespective of the tradeoff. If the constraint binds when the profit rate is low, firms are forced to invest and take on more debt when their financial position is already compromised. If the constraint binds when excess capacity is prevalent, the firm is forced to take on more capacity as its survival strategy. In this case, capacity utilization is no longer a good indicator of investment behavior. Finally, in the case where both the profit rate is low and excess capacity exists, further investment leads to both financial and capacity (over-investment) crises.

This extended theory of investment integrates both real and financial determinants of investment and includes the coercive role that competition plays. The competitive effect and the dominance of investment sensitivity to changes in the distribution of income squarely place investment at the center of an integrated theory of effective demand. The coercive nature of competition underlies Marx's imperative to accumulate capital – "accumulate, accumulate is Moses and the prophets."

This integrated theory of effective demand that considers conflict over the distribution of income, coercive competitive relations, irreversible investment, the fundamental uncertainty of the profit rate, the financial condition of the firm and competitive survival at its core produces a richer theory of effective demand than pre-existing strands of heterodox theory. This approach moves investment, profitability, financial robustness/fragility and expectation formation to the center of the theory of effective demand.

The microfoundations of the distribution of income

The distribution of income is essential to the theory of effective demand. The heterodox tradition has linked macro distribution issues to the pricing decisions of the firm, particularly mark-up pricing. While various mark-up pricing hypothesis exist (Shapiro and Sawyer (2003), Lee (1984), Lavoie (2001)), I argue that the theory of price most consistent with an integrated approach is one that respects the fundamental uncertainty of the profit rate and one that considers the firm's strategic/survival responses that may alter/constraint the ability to maximize profits. Goldstein (1985a, 1985b) developed a microfoundation for a variable mark-up on prime costs, rather than full cost, with these characteristics. While the model serves as a microfoundation for a cyclical profit squeeze crisis, it has broader implications for pricing, the distribution of income, and crisis.

In the model, the firm faces a tradeoff between its mark-up (price and profit) and its market share. This tradeoff is consistent with the Marxian concept of competition, which includes a competitive criterion or emphasis on defensive actions geared at reproducing the firm by maintaining its market share in the long run. One of the model's optimal conditions that marginal revenue is less than marginal cost captures the key role played by competition. The price leader gives up some of its monopoly profits in order to preserve its market share.

The optimal solution demonstrates that a rational pricing strategy includes a reduction in the firm's mark-up during the crucial mid-expansion phase of the cycle. This is the result of the nexus of class relations impinging on the firm. The decline in the markup is understood as the result of an organic whole – a dual shift in the balance of power between capital and labor during different phases of the cycle rather than the one-sided portrayal of labor as the predator of profits in Goodwin (1967).

The necessary conditions for the profit squeeze are an effective competitive constraint on demand and a set of adversarial industrial relations. Thus, bounded competition and/or bounded industrial relations can offset a profit squeeze.

The model has broader implications. Goldstein (1986b) showed that the optimal cyclical mark-up-pricing trajectory is consistent with the actual behavior of mark-ups/profit margins.

Given criticism of Marx's labor theory of value as a theory of price, this result suggests that mark-up pricing may be a suitable substitute for the labor theory of value in this context (Goldstein (1985a: 107–9, 2000)).

The necessary conditions of the profit squeeze can be extended in a secular sense to the occurrence of both under-consumption crises and long-term oscillations between secular profit squeeze crises and under-consumption crises. An intense competitive environment can underlie a tendency to an over-investment crisis as exhibited in the theory of investment developed above. Additionally adversarial industrial relations can result in long periods of erosion of labor's share of income and a tendency to under-consumption when capital has the upper hand.[7] When the balance of power shifts secularly toward labor, both of these factors can generate a long-term profit squeeze crisis. Goldstein (2000) and Bowles *et al.* (1990: 28–9) recognized this tendency for long-run swings between profit squeeze and under-consumption crises. In this same vein, these conditions suggest that stable economic growth is likely to be illusive for advanced capitalist economies unless a regime of bounded competition and bounded industrial relations can be maintained. Gordon (1980: 13) recognized the importance of moderation in competition for stability.

Thus, the theory of variable mark-up pricing serves as a bridge between the distribution of income and the theories of effective demand and crisis. This part of an integrated theory adds another layer of interacting dichotomies ultimately used to explain transitions in economic evolution. Here, shifts in the balance of power between labor and capital underlie different potential crisis mechanisms: under-consumption verses profit squeeze.

Finally, in light of Crotty's (2000, 2002, 2003a, 2005) identification of destructive product market competition in the form of price wars, the above mark-up model should be extended to include alternatives to the price leader relationship in domestic industries. This extension will not change the qualitative aspects of the variable mark-up theory because it merely adds further competitive intensity already handled in the model.

Financial elements: financial fragility and impatient finance

The full integration of financial and real sectors is a major element of a united heterodox macroeconomic approach. Yet, impediments exist to such an integration. Keynes' (1936) integration of these sectors through his treatment of liquidity preference did not consider the key role played by financial intermediation. The Modigliani–Miller (1958) theorem that argued that the financial structure of the firm, internal versus external financing, had no macroeconomic relevance diverted neoclassical Keynesians from a consideration of financial factors and debt-deflation mechanisms.[8] Marxian economics had its equilvalent of the Mogdigliani–Miller theorem that the sphere of circulation was thought to be methodologically subordinate to the sphere of production.

Despite these impediments, important breakthroughs emerged that allowed for a monetary/credit sector to play an integrative role in heterodox analysis. Minsky (1975, 1982) developed the financial instability hypothesis (FIH), New Keynesians applied asymmetric information to credit markets to develop a theory of credit rationing,[9] and Crotty (1985) argued that Marx fully integrated the spheres of circulation and production through his concept of abstract forms of crisis. In addition, Crotty (1985) flushes out Marx's conception of financial crisis to reveal that this mechanism shares a lot in common with Minsky's financial instability hypothesis.

Minsky's FIH serves to integrate financial markets. In brief, Minsky's theory of endogenous money supply/credit linked to endogenous expectations about the buoyancy of real and financial markets, particularly changes in perceptions about the acceptably of short-run indebtedness levels, lubricates an expansion through the provision of credit. When traditional forms of credit expansion hit constraints, financial innovation, feeding off of buoyant expectations, takes over. This system of interdependent financial obligations is all supported by a fundamentally uncertain distribution of profit flows used to meet financial commitments. This endogenous money supply/credit mechanism bolstered by illusionary and over-optimistic expectations, as the conventional wisdom enables higher debt levels, underlies a potential over-investment crisis by facilitating investment as a survival mechanism for an uncertain competitive process. It also serves as a financial crisis mechanism by founding investment on fragile financial supports. A crisis can evolve in different ways: either endogenous credit avenues dry up and the interest rate rises resulting in decreased investment, or a major firm or bank fails resulting in a reversal of expectations, or profit-taking triggers a reversal of expectations. In all cases, the financial bubble bursts and debtors are forced to sell financial assets to cover debt obligations and the downturn is exacerbated by Keynes' debt-deflation mechanism.

Crotty (1986, 1990a) critiques the pure financial nature of such a crisis and Crotty and Goldstein (1992a, 1992b) and Goldstein (Chapter 8) integrate real sector influences into a financial theory of investment. Crotty (1986, 1990a) rightfully recongnizes that the fundamental uncertainty of the profit rate and its real sector determinants, from both the supply and demand side, is an important impulse mechanism for a financial fragility crisis. Crotty and Goldstein (1992a, 1992b) and Goldstein (Chapter 8) show how changes in the mark-up/distribution of income can result in financial fragility-induced declines in investment and how competition-coerced investment can result in financial instability.

Besides finance-related crisis mechanisms based on endogenous credit and expectations and investment behavior, there are the class and distributional aspects of the financial sector. The rise to power of rentiers/finance capitalists in the Neoliberal era has generated important distributional and competitive effects that have adversely impacted both industrial capitalists and labor. Crotty (2005), Dumenil and Levy (2005) and Epstein and Jayadev (2005) have empirically documented the impact that finance capitalists have had in lowering the profitability of non-financial corporations. The complementary policies of free trade and financial liberalization, embraced by finance capitalists, have intensified competitive pressures on industrial capitalists, while rentiers' impatient desire for short-term financial returns have penetrated corporate governance structures and have shortened managerial planning horizons and diverted some funds to speculative financial investments away from investment in physical capital.[10] The rise to power of finance capitalists has resulted in a financial squeeze of profits. On one side, financial markets extract higher payments from industrial capitalists, while on the other side, increased competition restricts those costs from being passed on. One contradictory response by firms is a regime of wage and benefit cutting that slows aggregate demand growth and further intensifies product market competition.[11]

The full integration of financial markets adds additional layers of interacting dichotomies that are ultimately used to explain dynamic changes in the course of capitalist development. In particular, the distinctions between financially fragile and financially stable environments and profit-led and finance-led accumulation regimes add further flexibility to a heterodox theory of capital development.

Crisis mechanisms and the illusive nature of balanced growth

The integrated framework developed here has at its roots antagonistic class relations, coercive competitive relations, the potential for contradictory micro behavior and a notion of economic evolution without a steady state. These attributes establish a set of conditions for the attainment of balanced growth that are unlikely to be met. Thus, the potential for economic crises and for crisis-free, but potentially future crisis-producing growth are given equal weight. Prolonged periods of crisis-free growth are possible, but they require offsetting/postponing possible crisis through policy intervention and/or institutional change and/or modified micro behavior. The potential contradictory impact of such changes suggests that periods of smooth growth can be interrupted at any time.

Within the integrated theory developed here, the interaction of effective demand with pricing/distribution of income mechanisms and financial markets generates tendencies to five forms of crisis: traditional profit squeeze, under-consumption, over-investment, financial profit squeeze and financial fragility crises. Each crisis has both cyclical and secular variants although the conditions that underlie a cyclical variant of under-consumption are unlikely to develop. In addition, some crises have alternative impulse mechanisms. Over-investment can be induced by coercive investment or through endogenous credit based on over-optimistic expectations. Under-consumption crises can be set off via a redistribution of income from labor to capital or by macro policies that slow aggregate growth and profit crises can be influenced by different forms of coercive competition acting either as a competitive pricing constraint, a market share constraint and/or price wars associated with insufficient aggregate demand when shares remain constant.

While the occurrence of crises are merely possibilities until the conditions that underlie these crisis tendencies obtain, the conditions for a profit squeeze, established in Goldstein (1985a, 1985b) and by extension the conditions for under-consumption crises when considered together suggest that a profit squeeze or an under-consumption crisis are likely to exist under a broad set of realistic circumstances and that the economy may sequentially experience these two forms of crisis over longer periods of time. In particular, when adversarial K–L relations exist and the balance of power favors labor and a viable competitive constraint on prices exists then a profit squeeze is likely to occur. In contrast, when the balance of power shifts to capitalists and competition is coercive, a tendency to an under-consumption and over-investment crisis exists. It is only when both competition and adversarial industrial relations, including the K–FK relation, are bounded that balanced growth is likely to be achieved. Even in this situation, it may be necessary for state policies to bolster consumption demand. In addition, this scenario is further complicated by financial market conditions/ stability which can have their own autonomous influences.

Thus, the integrated Keynes–Marx theory suggested here does not support the notion that balanced economic growth is the long-run tendency for advanced capitalist economies. While potent offsetting tendencies to economic crises exist, particularly for an under-consumption crisis, these are not equilibrium mechanisms for balanced growth. Rather they displace or postpone current contradictions with future exacerbated variants of the same crisis mechanism or new or compounded future crisis mechanisms.[12] Thus, the evolution of the economy more closely resembles a disequilibrium process without a steady state.

Part and parcel of this long-run adjustment process are changes in institutions, ideologies and policies initiated by capitalist class interests in an attempt to maintain or restore a profitable environment for the accumulation of capital. This SSA approach to long-run dynamics was initially developed by Bowles *et al.* (1986). This method has been used to analyze the rise and fall of the Golden Age (1945–1980) and recent extensions (Kotz (2003) and McDonough (2003)) have focused on the Neoliberal period. These studies have paid particular attention to the instability of the current regime.[13]

Crotty (2002, 2003a, 2003b, 2005) has combined the crisis theory associated with the short to medium analysis of the integrated Keynes–Marx approach with the institutional and macrofoundation changes associated with the long-run analysis to develop a theory of the contradictory dynamics of the world economy under the Neoliberal regime.

Crotty uncovered a global excess capacity crisis rooted in under-consumption, over-investment and financial profit squeeze tendencies that he refers to as the Neoliberal Paradox. These crises were brought on by shifts in the balance of power from labor to capital, capital to finance capital and a shift to a coercive competitive regime. In particular, slow aggregate demand growth as a result of Neoliberal policies, shifts in the distribution of income away from labor, and intensified coercive international competition, as a result of slow demand growth, free trade policies and the industrialization of developing nations, and a financial squeeze of industrial profits have resulted in an over-investment and under-consumption crisis with self-perpetuating tendencies. The significant cost of existing in an industry where investment is substantially irreversible and the uncertain outcome of the competitive struggles compel firms to defend their substantial sunk capital by investing in cost-cutting technology. This expansion of capacity, particularly by marginal firms hoping to survive the competitive shake-out, in a period of slow demand growth leads to over-investment, excess capacity, in turn, can lead to destructive price wars that further reduce profits. Additionally, the rise to power of impatient finance capitalists siphons off more profits from the firms and pressures firms to achieve ever-expanding earnings on a quarterly basis. This forces managers, egged-on by corporate financial officers, to improve earnings by further cutting wages and benefits, thus resulting in further slower demand growth, intensified competition and further defensive investment. Thus, a vicious cycle that perpetuates the over-investment and under-consumption tendencies exists.

In addition, this crisis tendency underlies a financially fragile environment. Consumer spending is bolstered by unsafe levels of debt and in a coercive competitive regime with a financial squeeze of profits and price wars that further reduce industrial profits, corporations become more debt dependent in an environment with more uncertain profit flows.

Dichotomies, regime shifts, institutional change and long-run capitalist development

The flexible, realistic, historically contingent and institutionally specific aspects of the integrated heterodox macro framework developed here make it well suited for explaining long-run capitalist development, particularly fundamental transitions in that development path. Key layers of interacting dichotomies and trichotomies in the integrated framework facilitate this long-run analysis.

Key distinctions between conditions that support profit squeeze and underconsumption crises, coercive and corespective competitive regimes and the associated defensive and offensive investment strategies, fragile versus stable financial structures, stable expectations versus a crisis in confidence and profit-led, wage-led and finance-led accumulation regimes underlie this flexible theory of capitalist development. These dichotomies are integrally linked to the balance of power and effective competitive conditions for balanced/unbalanced growth. The conditions for balanced/sustainable growth require bounded competition and bounded/cooperative K–L relations along with a cooperative/supportive K–FK relation and macro policies that bolster consumption and investment expenditures. These conditions were met during the Golden Age when a wage-led growth regime and Keynesian macro policy flourished.

The dynamics of the Neoliberal regime are readily understood in this framework as described above

Conclusion

The unified heterodox macroeconomic framework discussed here integrates Keynesian uncertainty, Minskian financial fragility, volatile effective demand, Marxian class conflict, particularly over the distribution of income, Marxian competition, Marxian crisis theory and an institutional theory of macrofoundations supportive of profitable accumulation. This realistic and flexible framework sheds problematic aspects of existing theories and unifies the significant contributions of those theories into a potent approach capable of explaining the contradictory path of capitalist development across different historical eras.

Notes

1 Crotty (1989) has examined the limits of Keyesian macropolicy in the Neoliberal era.
2 Crotty (1990b, 1994, 2000, 2003a) emphasizes the institutionally specific and historically contingent nature of this environment.
3 See Shaikh (1978) and Goldstein (2006: 581, fn. 12). Coercive competition may force a survival investment strategy that otherwise would not be undertaken.
4 Crotty adapts corespective competition from Schumpeter (1976 [1943]).

5 The concept of fundamental uncertainty is well defined. Thus I do not elaborate on it here. For discussions of the concept see Davidson (2003), Shackle (1955), Rosser (2001) and Crotty (1994).
6 Goldstein (2006) argues that the flexibility and realism of microeconomic models allows holism and reductionism to be reconciled.
7 See Crotty (2002, 2003a, 2003b) and Goldstein (2000) on recent tendencies to over-investment and under-consumption.
8 As Tobin (1975) points out, Keynes lost the under-employment equilibrium debate with Pigou, by not considering the dynamics of debt-deflation.
9 Given that new Keynesian credit rationing theories mischaracterize the objectives of the managerial firm, treat uncertainty in an erodic fashion and result in an exogenous theory of cyclical fluctuation, they are not further considered here. Second-generation new Keynesian financial theories based on bankruptcy costs resolve the first problem, but not the remaining ones. For a critique of new Keynesian theories, see Crotty (1996).
10 Crotty (2003a, 2005) discusses the implications of institutional changes in financial markets on the accumulation/growth process.
11 Crotty (2002, 2003b, 2005) analyzes these contradictory tendencies under the title of the "Neoliberal Paradox."
12 For example, the extension of credit may temporarily offset an under-consumption problem, but in turn generates both a future compounded under-consumption and financial crisis.
13 See Chapters 12 and 13 in this volume.

References

Boddy, R. and Crotty, J. (1975) "Class Conflict and Macro-Policy: The Political Business Cycle," *Review of Radical Political Economics*, 7(1): 1–19.

Bowles, S., Gordon, D. and Weisskopf, T. (1986) "Power and Profits: The Social Structure of Accumulation and the Profitability of the Postwar U.S. Economy," *Review of Radical Political Economics*, 18(1/2): 132–67.

—— (1990) *After the Waste Land: A Democratic Economics for the Year 2000.* Armonk and London: M. E. Sharpe.

Crotty, J. (1980) "Post Keynesian Theory: A Sympathetic Critique," *American Economic Review*, 70(2): 20–5.

—— (1983) "On Keynes and Capital Flight," *Journal of Economic Literature*, March, 59–65.

—— (1985) "The Centrality of Money, Credit, and Financial Intermediation in Marx's Crisis Theory: An Interpretation of Marx's Methodology," in S. Resnick and R. Wolff (eds.) *Rethinking Marxism: Struggles in Marxist Theory. Essays for Harry Magdoff and Paul Sweezy*, 45–81, Brooklyn: Autonomedia.

—— (1986) "Marx, Keynes and Minsky on the Instability of the Capitalist Growth Process and the Nature of Government Economic Policy," in D. Bramhall and S. Helburn (eds.) *Marx, Keynes and Schumpeter: A Centenary Celebration of Dissent*, 297–326, Armonk: M. E. Sharpe.

—— (1989) "The Limits of Keynesian Macroeconomic Policy in the Age of the Global Marketplace," in A. MacEwan and W. Tabb (eds.) *Instability and Change in the World Economy*, 82–100, New York: Monthly Review Press.

—— (1990a) "Owner–Manager Conflict and Financial Theories of Investment Instability:

A Critical Assessment of Keynes, Tobin, and Minsky," *Journal of Post Keynesian Economics*, 12(4): 519–42.

—— (1990b) "Keynes on the Stages of Development of the Capitalist Economy: The Institutional Foundation of Keynes's Methodology," *Journal of Economic Issues*, 24(3): 761–80.

—— (1992) "Neoclassical and Keynesian Approaches to the Theory of Investment," *Journal of Post Keynesian Economics*, 14(4): 483–96.

—— (1993) "Rethinking Marxian Investment Theory: Keynes–Minsky Instability, Competitive Regime Shifts and Coerced Investment," *Review of Radical Political Economics*, 25(1): 1–26.

—— (1994) "Are Keynesian Uncertainty and Macrotheory Compatible? Conventional Decision Making, Institutional Structures, and Conditional Stability in Keynesian Macromodels," in G. Dymski and R. Pollin (eds.) *New Perspectives in Monetary Macroeconomics: Explorations in the Tradition of Hyman P. Minsky*, 105–39, Ann Arbor: University of Michigan Press.

—— (1996) "Is New Keynesian Investment Theory Really 'Keynesian'? Reflections on Fazzari and Variato," *Journal of Post Keynesian Economics*, 18(3): 333–57.

—— (2000) "Structural Contradictions of the Global Neoliberal Regime," *Review of Radical Political Economics*, 32(3): 361–8.

—— (2002) "Why There Is Chronic Excess Capacity," *Challenge*, 45(6): 21–44.

—— (2003a) "Core Industries, Coercive Competition and the Structural Contradictions of Global Neoliberalism," in N. Phelps and P. Raines (eds.) *The New Competition for Inward Investment: Companies, Institutions and Territorial Development*, 9–37, Northampton: Edward Elgar.

—— (2003b) "The Neoliberal Paradox: The Impact of Destructive Product Market Competition and Impatient Finance on Nonfinancial Corporations in the Neoliberal Era," *Review of Radical Political Economics*, 35(3): 271–9.

—— (2005) "The Neoliberal Paradox: The Impact of Destructive Product Market Competition and 'Modern' Financial Markets on Nonfinancial Corporation Performance in the Neoliberal Era," in G. Epstein (ed.) *Financialization and the World Economy*, 77–110, Cheltenham, UK and Northampton, MA: Edward Elgar.

Crotty, J. and Goldstein, J. (1992a) "A Marxian–Keynesian Theory of Investment Demand: Empirical Evidence," in F. Moseley and E. Wolff (eds.) *International Perspectives on Profitability and Accumulation*, 197–234, Brookfield: Edward Elgar.

—— (1992b) "The Impact of Profitability, Financial Fragility and Competitive Regime Shifts on Investment Demand: Empirical Evidence," Levy Economics Institute of Bard College, Working paper No. 81 (September).

Davidson, P. (2003) "Setting the Record Straight on A History of Post Keynesian Economics," *Journal of Post Keynesian Economics*, 26(2): 245–72.

Dumenil, G. and Levy, D. (2005) "Costs and Benefits of Neoliberalism: A Class Analysis," in G. Epstein (ed.) *Financialization and the World Economy*, 17–45, Cheltenham, UK and Northampton, MA: Edward Elgar.

Epstein, G. and Jayadev, A. (2005) "The Rise of Rentier Incomes in OECD Countries: Financialization, Central Bank Policy and Labor Solidarity," in G. Epstein (ed.) *Financialization and the World Economy*, 46–74, Cheltenham, UK and Northampton, MA: Edward Elgar.

Fontana, G. (2005) "A History of Post Keynesian Economics Since 1936: Some Hard (and Not so Hard) Questions for the Future," *Journal of Post Keynesian Economics*, 27(3): 409–21.

Goldstein, J.P. (1985a) "The Cyclical Profit Squeeze: A Marxian Microfoundation," *Review of Radical Political Economics*, 17(1–2): 103–28.

—— (1985b) "Pricing, Accumulation, and Crisis in Post Keynesian Theory," *Journal of Post Keynesian Economics*, 8(1): 121–34.

—— (1986a) "The Micro–Macro Dialectic: A Concept of a Marxian Microfoundation," in P. Zarembka (ed.) *Research in Political Economy. Volume 9*, 127–55, A Research Annual. Greenwich: JAI Press.

—— (1986b) "Mark-up Variability and Flexibility: Theory and Empirical Evidence," *Journal of Business*, October.

—— (2000) "The Global Relevance of Marxian Crisis Theory," in R. Baiman, H. Boushey and D. Sanders (eds.) *Political Economy and Contemporary Capitalism: Radical Perspectives on Economic Theory and Policy*, 68–77, Armonk and London: M. E. Sharpe.

—— (2006) "Marxian Microfoundations: Contribution or Detour?" *Review of Radical Political Economics*, 38(4): 569–94.

Goodfriend, M. (2004) "Monetary Policy in the New Neoclassical Synthesis: A Primer," *Federal Reserve Bank of Richmond Economic Quarterly*, 90(3): 21–45.

Goodwin, R. (1967) "A Growth Cycle," in C. H. Feinstein (ed.) *Capitalism and Economic Growth*. Cambridge: Cambridge University Press.

Gordon, D. (1980) "Stages of Accumulation and Long Economics Cycles," in T. Hopkins and I. Wallerstein (eds.) *Processes of the World-System*, 9–45, Beverly Hills: Sage Publications.

Keynes, J. (1936) *The General Theory of Employment Interest and Money*. New York: Harcourt Brace and World.

Kotz, D. (2003) "Neoliberalism and the Social Structure of Accumulation Theory of Long-Run Capital Accumulation," *Review of Radical Political Economics*, 35(3): 263–70.

Lavoie, M. (2001) "Pricing," in R. Holt and S. Pressman (eds.) *A New Guide to Post Keynesian Economics*, 21–31, Florence: Routledge.

—— (2006) "Do Heterodox Theories Have Anything in Common? A Post-Keynesian Point of View," *Intervention. Journal of Economics*, 3(1): 87–112.

Lavoie, M., Rodriguez, G. and Seccareccia, M. (2004) "Similitudes and Discrepancies in Post-Keynesian and Marxist Theories of Investment: A Theoretical and Empirical Investigation," *International Review of Applied Economics*, 18(2): 127–49.

Lee, F. (1984) "Full Cost Pricing: A New Wine in a New Bottle," *Australian Economic Papers*, 23(42): 151–66.

McDonough, T. (2003) "What Does Long Wave Theory Have to Contribute to the Debate on Globalization?" *Review of Radical Political Economics*, 35(3): 280–6.

Minsky, H. (1975) *John Maynard Keynes*. New York: Columbia University Press

—— (1982) *Can "it" Happen Again*. Armonk: M. E. Sharpe.

Modigliani, F. and Miller, M. (1958) "The Cost of Capital, Corporation Finance, and the Theory of Investment," *American Economic Review*, June: 261–97.

Rosser Jr., J. (2001) "Uncertainty and Expectations," in R. Holt and S. Pressman (eds.) *A New Guide to Post Keynesian Economics*, 52–64, Florence: Routledge.

Schumpeter, J. (1976) *Capitalism, Socialism and Democracy*, 4th edition. London: George Allen & Unwin.

Shackle, G. (1955) *Uncertainty in Economics*. Cambridge: Cambridge University Press.

Shaikh, A. (1978) "Political Economy and Capitalism: Notes on Dobb's Theory of Crisis," *Cambridge Journal of Economics*, 2(2): 233–51.

Shapiro, N. and Sawyer, M. (2003) "Post Keynesian Price Theory," *Journal of Post Keynesian Economics*, 25(3): 355–65.

Tobin, J. (1975) "Keynesian Models of Recession and Depression," *American Economic Review*, 65(2): 195–202.

Tymoigne, E. and Lee, F. (2003) "Post Keynesian Economics since 1936: A History of a Promise That Bounced?" *Journal of Post Keynesian Economics*, 26(2): 273–87.

4 Methodology and heterodox economics

Martin H. Wolfson

Introduction

Heterodox economics has always encompassed a wide variety of economic theories and perspectives. In fact, printed in each issue of the *Review of Radical
Political Economics* is the following statement:

> As the journal of the Union for Radical Political Economics, the Review
> publishes innovative research in political economy broadly defined as
> including, but not confined to, Marxian economics, post-Keynesian eco-
> nomics, Sraffian economics, feminist economics, and radical institutional
> economics.

Given the broad purview of heterodox economics, the question arises: do the
various theories that make up the subject have some methodological coherence,
or are they disjoint – united in their opposition to neoclassical economics, but
with theoretical assumptions, principles and methods, i.e. methodologies, that
are incompatible with each other?

The argument of this chapter is that there is coherence.[1] In particular, there is
an emerging heterodox macroeconomic framework that builds upon the perspectives of Karl Marx, John Maynard Keynes and institutionalists like Wesley Clair
Mitchell.[2]

In the next section of the chapter, key assumptions and principles of the
Marxian, Keynesian and institutional perspectives, which form the building
blocks for the new framework, will be discussed. In the third section, the contributions of heterodox macroeconomist James Crotty to combining, deepening, and
extending these perspectives into a new framework will be addressed. Finally, the
fourth section concludes with a statement of the new methodological framework.

Building blocks: Marx, Keynes and Mitchell

Below are the building blocks, or starting points, for the new heterodox macroeconomic framework. They are basic methodological assumptions and principles
from Marx, Keynes and Mitchell. They are often taken to be representative of
three separate theories, with little or no convergence.

Karl Marx

Historical materialism

This basic philosophical perspective of Marx's has been the subject of numerous books, articles and treatises. At the risk of oversimplification, I take it to mean two basic concepts. First, people's "material conditions," especially the social relations of production (the relationships people enter into in the process of production), have an important influence on the ideas, culture, religion, politics and other aspects of the "superstructure" of society. This materialist point of view should be distinguished from determinism, which claims that the material conditions *determine* the superstructure, and from the view that the superstructure has no effect or influence on the material conditions. An important implication of Marx's materialist philosophy is that one needs to make a "concrete analysis of concrete conditions," i.e. thoroughly investigate the reality one is trying to explain.

Second, historical analysis is an essential component of the Marxian perspective. One cannot understand current reality without analyzing the historical forces that have brought the present into being.

Dialectical contradiction

The process that propels history forward is the working out of the contradictory relationship between two opposing forces. These opposing forces have different interests and are always in struggle with each other. This perspective has two important and related implications.

First, the change that results from contradictions is endogenous. It is internal to the contradictory relationship being analyzed. Second, there is no permanent equilibrium. The two opposing forces within a contradiction can arrive at a temporary equilibrium, which is best understood as stabilization at a moment in time. But because the two forces continue to be in contradiction with one another, struggle will continue that will eventually disrupt that temporary equilibrium.

This is not to say that exogenous events cannot play a role in Marxian analysis. But Marx's concept of dialectical contradiction rules out the neoclassical view of equilibrium as a permanent end point that can be disrupted only by exogenous "shocks."

Class conflict

In Marx's analysis, the fundamental contradiction in capitalist society is between capital and labor. The historical working out of the contradiction between these two opposing forces is the key to understanding the dynamics of a capitalist economy.

Also important are intra-class conflicts, such as those between industrial and financial capital, among capitalist firms competing with each other, and also among segments of the working class.

Theory of the state

In capitalist society the dominant class, i.e. the capitalist class, has a dominant influence on the "state," taken to be the apparatus of government broadly conceived: the legislative and executive branches, the courts, police, military, etc. Many Marxists view the state as a "contested terrain," in which labor can vie for influence, but in which the capitalist class usually dominates because of instrumental and structural influences.

Because of its income and wealth, the capitalist class can influence the levers, or "instruments" of state power. For example, representatives of the capitalist class can be appointed or elected to positions of power, and their lobbyists can influence decisions.

Also, capitalists hold a central structural position within a capitalist economy. They hire and fire workers and make decisions about the expansion of production and investment. Even governments sympathetic to labor are influenced by the powerful role capitalists play in a capitalist economy.

Evolution of economic systems

Marx analyzed a progression of economic systems, from simple commodity production, slavery, feudalism, to capitalism. He predicted that capitalism would be replaced by socialism. In the contradiction between capital and labor, labor would become dominant and would change the institutional structures defining capitalism to those compatible with a socialist system. Aiding this transition would be the contradiction between the forces of production (such as plant and equipment, technology, and human skills and abilities) and the social relations of production. Marx thought that capitalist social relations would increasingly become obstacles to further growth of the forces of production, and would be transformed.

Despite continuing controversies about Marx's prediction of socialism, his theory that class struggle, and the contradiction between the forces and social relations of production, would lead to a new institutional structure is a key building block of the new macroeconomic framework, as discussed below.

John Maynard Keynes

Fundamental uncertainty

Nobel laureate Niels Bohr said "it is difficult to make predictions, especially about the future." As Keynes stressed, about much of the future, we simply do not know. Note that this is much different from the neoclassical concept of risk, which enables one to know all possible future events and establish a probability for each.

Financial crises and speculation

Because of fundamental uncertainty, financial markets are subject to crises and speculation. Herd behavior leads to euphoric booms and sudden panic, when the optimistic expectations that fueled the boom are not fulfilled.

Wesley Clair Mitchell

Endogenous business cycle

Mitchell, the founder of the National Bureau of Economic Research, was a leading institutional economist of the early twentieth century. He pioneered quantitative research on the business cycle. Based on his research, he hypothesized an endogenous business cycle with various stages, such as recovery, expansion, crisis, panic and depression. Mitchell's business cycle is endogenous in the sense that it traces a process of cumulative change in which one stage of the cycle is transformed into the next.

Institutional methods

Mitchell's methods were both quantitative and institutional. He accumulated data on hundreds of data series and then analyzed the data inductively to create his theoretical concepts. He focused on quantitative data. Other institutionalists have used other methods, such as surveys, participant–observer techniques, pattern models, historical analysis, etc. But like all institutionalists, he understood that a concrete, detailed investigation of institutional conditions was a necessary element to the understanding of social reality.

Crotty's contributions

James R. Crotty starts with the basic building blocks from Marx, Keynes and Mitchell, but extends them by combining, deepening and extending the basic theories.

Combining Mitchell and Marx: class conflict and the business cycle

Crotty, with co-author Raford Boddy (1974, 1975), viewed Mitchell's endogenous business cycle through the lens of class conflict. Mitchell, using data from business cycles in the early twentieth century, observed an increase in labor costs and a decline in labor productivity toward the end of the business-cycle expansion, with a resultant negative effect on profits and investment. Boddy and Crotty, analyzing the business cycles of the early post-World War II period, observed similar trends but interpreted them in the context of Marx's "wage-squeeze" crisis theory.

In Marx's theory (1967, Chapter 25), the wage squeeze is due to a depletion of the industrial reserve army (the unemployed) and thus an increase in the bargaining power of labor. Boddy and Crotty extend Marx's theory by viewing capital's reaction in the context of macroeconomic policy and Marx's theory of the state. In the business cycles that Boddy and Crotty investigated, the Federal Reserve raised interest rates, which slowed economic activity and helped to replenish the reserve army. It thus intervened on the side of capital to reduce the power of labor and the wage squeeze on profits.

In addition, in their analysis Boddy and Crotty employed the approach of both Marx and Mitchell: the institutional investigation of concrete conditions.

Adding Keynes: financial crises and speculation

Boddy and Crotty's analysis of the business cycle, carried out in the 1970s, focused primarily on real variables. As time went on, it became clear that the financial system played a significant role in the dynamics of the business cycle and needed to be incorporated into the macroeconomic framework.

Post-Keynesians had stressed the neglect by neoclassical economists of Keynes' theory of fundamental uncertainty. But if the future was unknowable, how could decisions that implied knowledge of the future be made? By incorporating Keynes' ideas about conventions, herd behavior and conditional stability, Crotty (1994) demonstrated how fundamental uncertainty could be an essential part of a coherent macrotheory and an integral part of business-cycle analysis.

Those who need to make a decision, but who do not know the future, would fall back on "conventional wisdom," what most people thought most other people thought. Often the conventional wisdom was that the future would be like the past. Speculative booms could develop, as financial market participants projected an optimistic scenario far into the future. Even market professionals would invest because they thought everyone else would be investing.

But because these conventions were not based on any firm knowledge of the future (which was impossible), they were liable to be quickly rejected at the first sign of trouble. Financial market participants could quickly head for the exits and initiate a financial crisis.

Deepening our understanding of Marx: finance and the business cycle

Most discussions by radical political economists in the 1970s of Marxian crisis theory considered only real variables. The assumption was that Marx saw crises originating in the real sector, in the sphere of production. So if one wanted to combine the real and financial sectors of the economy in a more comprehensive business-cycle theory, it would be necessary to go beyond Marx by incorporating insights from Keynes.

However, in an insightful analysis in the mid-1980s, Crotty (1985, 1987) argued that the limitation of Marx's crisis theory to the sphere of production was a misunderstanding of Marx's methodology. Crotty's argument was that Marx treated production and circulation as a unified whole and did not give production a logical priority over circulation.

Crotty's interpretation of Marx's argument is that a crisis comes about as a result of the interaction of both the real and financial sectors. Once money is used as a means of payment (to repay debts), contractual commitments on debt can escalate over the course of the business-cycle expansion. Problems with profitability make it difficult to repay these debts. It is the interaction of profitability problems with the high level debt repayment commitments that causes the crisis.

Thus Crotty's analysis shows that Marx analyzed both the real and financial sectors, and that a heterodox macroeconomic framework is strengthened by incorporating the analyses of both Marx and Keynes on financial crises and instability.

Extending institutional analysis: stages of capitalism

The increased attention to financial variables in the 1980s was not a coincidence. More attention was paid to these variables because financial problems and crises became more prominent. Radical political economics, and others, devoted increasing attention to changes in the US and global economies over the course of the post-World War II period. It became clear that institutional changes had occurred that had led to a qualitatively different stage of capitalism.

These qualitatively different stages of capitalism were characterized by changes in how the macroeconomy operated and how macrotheory was to be interpreted (more on that below). Thus radical political economists had to adopt an institutional methodology if they were to comprehend the changes in the economy and adopt a relevant macrotheory.

A number of theories of stages of capitalism exist. Baran and Sweezy's *Monopoly Capital* (1966) is one; the social structure of accumulation theory by David Gordon and his co-authors (Gordon *et al.*, 1982) is another. But Crotty (2002) is a leader in analyzing the post-World War II stages of capitalism as a transition from a "Golden Age" to a stage characterized as "Global Neoliberalism."

Deepening our understanding of Keynes: Keynes' institutional methodology

Neoclassical economics views Keynes' *General Theory* (1936) as a timeless analysis of capitalism as an economic system. Even some radical political economists view it in this way. But, as Crotty (1990) demonstrates, Keynes' analysis in the *General Theory* applied only to the specific institutional structures that existed in early twentieth-century capitalism. Keynes thought that the different institutional conditions of the nineteenth century constituted a different stage of capitalism with different economic characteristics.

Keynes, according to Crotty, saw a "heroic" entrepreneur in the nineteenth century, one who viewed investing as a way of life and plowed back the firm's profits into investment without regard to cost–benefit analysis. Accompanying the heroic entrepreneur was the Victorian rentier class that was content to put its savings into long-term bonds and preferred stock (not common stock) for long-term income rather than short-term capital gains. Under these conditions, long-term real investment was encouraged.

In contrast, in the twentieth century institutional conditions were significantly different. Inflation following World War I undermined the rentier class, firms began to rely much more on external equity financing, and owners became increasingly distinct from managers. Under these conditions, the speculation and instability of investment described by Keynes in the *General Theory* became the norm.

The important points to note, at this point, are the centrality of institutional analysis to the emergent heterodox macroeconomic framework, and the ease with which Keynes' analysis falls within the institutionalist perspective.

Extending institutional analysis: macrotheory differs across stages of capitalism

The significance of stages of capitalism for a heterodox macroeconomic framework is that the behavior of economic actors and the nature of macro policy differ across different stages, and thus the relevant macrotheory does as well. In a series of articles, Crotty has systematically investigated this process. In particular, he has explored the behavior of industrial and financial corporations, the nature of macro policy, and the characteristics of economic and financial crises.

The behavior of industrial and financial corporations

Crotty (1993) cites Marx's distinction between "fraternal" and "fratricidal" modes of competition. Under these two modes of competition, investment behavior by industrial corporations differs. Fraternal competition leads to "corespective" behavior and investment that is primarily capital widening (expanding the scale of investment incorporating current technology). In contrast, fratricidal competition leads to "coercive" investment that emphasizes capital deepening (investment incorporating new technology that has the potential to undermine the value of the existing capital stock).

Crotty applies this analysis to the corespective Golden Age and the competitive neoliberal era. He describes some additional characteristics of corporate behavior under neoliberalism: "Disrupting organizational structure and routine, firing workers, slashing wages, closing (or slaughtering) nonamortized plants, attacking unions, taking on debt levels previously considered to be intolerably dangerous" (Crotty, 1993: 19). He notes that these behaviors are risky tactics. They did not characterize corporate behavior during the corespective Golden Age; they are adopted in the neoliberal era only because of the pressure of fratricidal competition.

The changed corporate behavior has important implications for the global economy. Crotty (2000, 2003a) concludes that this behavior (coercive investment, attacking labor etc.) under neoliberalism has led to *both* chronic excess aggregate supply and chronically inadequate global aggregate demand. This inability of aggregate demand and supply to equilibrate, an impossibility in neoclassical analysis, is explained by Crotty (2000: 367) as the interaction of demand and supply effects in a vicious cycle:

> The more competitive pressures develop, the more they force firms to cut wages, smash unions, substitute low for high wage labor, and pressure governments to cut spending and generate budget surpluses. But these actions constrain global aggregate demand even more tightly, creating yet stronger competitive intensity.

Deregulated financial markets in the neoliberal era have also been subject to increased competitive pressures. This has led them to become increasingly speculative and to take on increasing risk, a process that thus far has enabled financial corporations to report increased profits (Crotty, 2007).

However, financial markets have put additional pressure on non-financial corporations. Crotty (2003b) analyzes the shift in financial markets from "patient" finance to impatient financial markets. He points out that financial markets under neoliberalism have forced a portfolio conception onto non-financial corporate behavior: corporate assets must continually be restructured to maximize the corporation's stock price. Moreover, the pay structure of corporate management has shifted: instead of being rewarded according to the long-term success of the firm, corporate manager compensation is now much more firmly tied to the corporate short-term stock price.

This has led to what Crotty (2003b: 271) calls the "'neoliberal paradox': financial markets demand that corporations achieve ever higher profits, while product markets make this result impossible to achieve." He concludes that this impossible situation led to the increase in financial accounting fraud that was observed in the late 1990s.

The nature of macro policy

The change from the Golden Age to the neoliberal stages of capitalism has had implications for the nature of macroeconomic policies. Crotty (2003a) describes a number of changes in macro policy under neoliberalism, all of which have contributed to the problem of chronically inadequate aggregate demand growth.

Monetary policy has become decidedly more oriented to an anti-inflation stance. The deregulation of financial markets has enabled financial corporations to use capital flight to punish countries that do not adopt the corporations' preferred high interest-rate, low-inflation monetary policies.

Fiscal policy has also become increasingly restrictive. Crotty notes that large cuts in the social safety net and an aversion to fiscal deficits have characterized fiscal policy under neoliberalism.

Restrictive monetary and fiscal policies have been enforced on many countries by the International Monetary Fund's austerity policies. Crotty estimates that 40 percent of the world's population, living in 55 countries, has been subject to such policies. Also, financial deregulation and liberalization, and the IMF's dominant role, have forced many countries to abandon policies that regulated the macroeconomy, such as capital controls and state regulation of credit allocation.

The character of economic and financial crises

In a series of articles on the Asian financial crisis (such as Crotty and Dymski, 1998), Crotty and his co-authors explain the connection between increasing international financial crises and the neoliberal model. The defining elements of the neoliberal model – deregulation, privatization, and liberalization – have led to heightened capital mobility, widespread speculation and increasing financial crises.

It is perhaps no accident that we observe both increasing financial crises and chronically inadequate aggregate demand in the neoliberal era. Both likely can be linked to some of the corporate behavior discussed earlier: firing workers, slashing wages and attacking unions. These strategies, along with tax cuts that favor the wealthy, and a whole host of government and corporate policies, have dramatically increased income and wealth inequality. And as John Kenneth Galbraith (1988: xiv) so colorfully reminds us, "what well-rewarded people regularly do with extra cash" is to "sluice funds into the stock market" and other financial investments.

Falling wages and weakened unions, along with increasing inequality and financial capital mobility, have resulted in chronic under-consumption problems and increasing financial speculation and financial crises. The conditions that led to the wage-squeeze economic crises in the Golden Age have changed, and so have the nature of economic and financial crises in the neoliberal era.[2] Although Crotty has not yet revisited this issue in the context of his 1970s papers with Raford Boddy, it may well be on his agenda.

Extending Marx: historical change in the capitalist global economy

The idea of stages of capitalism obviously raises the issue: how does one stage of capitalism transform into the next? What is the process of historical change?

Here is where Marx's concepts of class struggle and contradiction between the forces of production and the social relations of production come into play. Crotty (2002) shows that a similar analysis can be used to analyze the transition from the Golden Age to neoliberalism.

Although the Golden Age constituted a settled institutional structure, the ongoing contradictions of a capitalist society (between capital and labor, between industrial and financial capital, among capitalist firms, etc.) changed the economic environment. Crotty (2002) discusses rising inflation, increased trade competition, balance of payments deficits, etc. These changes in the economic environment put pressure on the existing institutional structure of the Golden Age, such as the Bretton Woods monetary system. Eventually the old institutions could no longer function. A crisis ensued, and the old institutions were dismantled.

What would be the new institutional structure to be created? Crotty (2002) explains that the new institutional structure, neoliberalism, was not inevitable. Neoliberal institutions were created because they were the deliberate choice of "elites" (capital) and because the capitalist class had the power to enforce its choice. Here the basic concepts of Marx are extended to apply to the historical change that transforms one stage of capitalism into another.

Methodology and heterodox economics

What, then, are the methodological principles that constitute the emergent heterodox macroeconomic framework? Below is a summary of the main points that emerge from the review of Crotty's contributions.

Contradictions, class conflict, endogenous change and the business cycle

The working out of the main contradictions of capitalism, particularly the class conflict between capital and labor, provide the impetus for endogenous change in the capitalist economy. In particular, class conflict (and intra-class contradictions) strongly influence the dynamics of the business cycle.

Fundamental uncertainty, financial crises and speculation

Macroeconomic activity takes place under conditions of fundamental uncertainty. Speculation and financial crises are an outcome of decision-making under fundamental uncertainty and the interaction of real and financial developments.

Institutional conditions and stages of capitalism

The macroeconomy behaves differently under different institutional conditions, in particular the different institutional conditions that characterize different stages of capitalism. The behavior of industrial and financial corporations, macroeconomic policy, even the dynamics of the business cycle and the nature of economic and financial crises, have changed as the institutional conditions of the Golden Age were replaced by those of neoliberalism.

Historical change and possibilities for the future

Historical change takes place as economic changes, driven by the contradictions of capitalism, erode, or come up against, the institutional structure. A crisis takes place as the old institutional structure is swept away. The new institutional structure that takes its place, whether a new stage of capitalism or a new economic system, depends on the relative balance of power between the economic classes.

The emergent heterodox macroeconomic framework depends on an integration of principles from Marx, Keynes and institutionalists like Mitchell. To that new framework, Jim Crotty's contribution is significant. His analysis is leading the way forward to a new methodology for heterodox macroeconomics.

Notes

1 This chapter concentrates on methodological assumptions and principles. For a discussion of institutional methods, see Wolfson (2001).
2 For more on this issue, see Wolfson (2003) and Kotz (2007).

References

Baran, P. A. and Sweezy, P. S. (1966) *Monopoly Capital*. New York: Monthly Review Press.

Boddy, R. and Crotty, J. R. (1974) "Class Conflict, Keynesian Policies, and the Business Cycle," *Monthly Review*, 26(5): 1–17.

—— (1975) "Class Conflict and Macropolicy: The Political Business Cycle," *Review of Radical Political Economics*, 7(1): 1–19.

Crotty, J. R. (1985) "The Centrality of Money, Credit and Financial Intermediation in Marx's Crisis Theory," in S. Resnick and R. Wolff (eds.) *Rethinking Marxism: Essays in Honor of Harry Magdoff and Paul Sweezy*, 45–82, New York: Autonomedia.

—— (1987) "The Role of Money and Finance in Marx's Crisis Theory," in R. Cherry, F. Moseley, C. D'Onofrio, C. Kurdas, T. Michl and M. I. Naples (eds.) *The Imperiled Economy*, Volume 1. New York: Union for Radical Political Economics.

—— (1990) "Keynes on the Stages of Development of the Capitalist Economy: The Institutionalist Foundation of Keynes's Methodology," *Journal of Economic Issues*, 24(3): 761–80.

—— (1993) "Rethinking Marxian Investment Theory: Keynes–Minsky Instability, Competitive Regime Shifts and Coerced Investment," *Review of Radical Political Economics*, 25(1): 1–26.

—— (1994) "Are Keynesian Uncertainty and Macrotheory Incompatible? Conventional Decision Making, Institutional Structures and Conditional Stability in Keynesian Macromodels," in G. Dymski and R. Pollin (eds.) *New Perspectives in Monetary Macroeconomics: Explorations in the Tradition of Hyman Minsky*, 105–42, Ann Arbor: University of Michigan Press.

—— (2000) "Structural Contradictions of the Global Neoliberal Regime," *Review of Radical Political Economics*, 32(3): 361–8.

—— (2002) "Trading State-Led Prosperity for Market-Led Stagnation: From the Golden Age to Global Neoliberalism," in G. Dymski and D. Isenberg (eds.) *Seeking Shelter on the Pacific Rim: Financial Globalization, Social Change, and the Housing Market*, 21–41, Armonk: M. E. Sharpe.

—— (2003a) "Structural Contradictions of Current Capitalism: A Keynes–Marx–Schumpeter Analysis," in J. Ghosh and C. P. Chandrashekar (eds.) *Work and Well-Being in the Age of Finance*, 24–51, New Delhi: Tulika Books.

—— (2003b) "The Neoliberal Paradox: The Impact of Destructive Product Market Competition and Impatient Finance on Nonfinancial Corporations in the Neoliberal Era," *Review of Radical Political Economics*, 35(3): 271–9.

—— (2007) "If Financial Market Competition is so Intense, Why are Financial Firm Profits so High? Reflections on the Current 'Golden Age' of Finance." A paper prepared for a conference on "Financialization: in Retrospect and Prospect," sponsored by the IWGF, University of Manchester, London, February 12–13.

Crotty, J. R. and Dymski, G. (1998) "Can the Global Neoliberal Regime Survive Victory in Asia? The Political Economy of the Asian Crisis," *International Papers in Political Economy*, 5(2): 1–47.

Galbraith, J. K. (1988) *The Great Crash: 1929*. Boston: Houghton Mifflin.

Gordon, D. M., Edwards, R. and Reich, M. (1982) *Segmented Work: Divided Workers*. New York: Cambridge University Press.

Keynes, J. M. (1936) *The General Theory of Employment, Interest, and Money*. New York: Harcourt, Brace, and World.

Kotz, D. M. (2007) "Crisis Tendencies in Two Regimes: A Comparison of Regulated and Neoliberal Capitalism in the U.S." A paper presented at a panel on "Reconstituted Social Structures of Accumulation: Macroeconomics, Profits, Finance, and Performance" at the Union for Radical Political Economics sessions at the Allied Social Science Associations annual conference in Chicago, January 6, 2007.

Marx, K. (1967) *Capital*, Volume 1. New York: International Publishers.

Wolfson, M. H. (2001) "Institutional Analysis of Financial Crises," in Amitava Krishna Dutt and Kenneth P. Jameson (eds.) *Crossing the Mainstream: Methodological and Ethical Issues in Economics*, 332–52, Notre Dame: University of Notre Dame Press.

—— (2003) "Neoliberalism and the Social Structure of Accumulation," *Review of Radical Political Economics*, 35(3): 255–62.

5 Does heterodox economics need a unified crisis theory?

From profit-squeeze to the global liquidity meltdown

Gary A. Dymski

Introduction

This chapter makes two abstract theoretical arguments and one empirical one. The first theoretical claim advanced here concerns the nature of heterodoxy in economics. All economic theories define both the primary actors and forces that constitute any society's economic relations, and propose some vision of the successful reproduction of these relations. Usually successful reproduction is equated with stable growth. Some theories embed the assumption that if a given set of economic relations can achieve stability or balance, it can, if left undisturbed, sustain stable growth. Other theories embed the assumption that the possible breakdown of stable growth is endogenous: a crisis in reproduction is immanent in the very nature of economic relations. This distinction – the exogeneity or endogeneity of the possibility of crisis – defines the difference between *heterodox* and *orthodox* approaches to economic theory.

The second theoretical claim advanced here is that heterodox theories are more robust when they encompass the possibility that stable growth can be undermined, and crisis can emerge, for different reasons. A multidimensional approach, which encompasses several possible avenues in which economic relations can break down, is contrasted here with unicausal approaches in general and, in particular, Minsky's single factor crisis mechanism.

An empirical argument is then made, using a stylized rendering of aggregate US empirical evidence. Specifically, it is shown that Minsky's ideas about what causes crisis, and about what policy measures can overcome crises, are largely consistent with these data through 1980; but after 1980, his specific theoretical/ policy approach are inconsistent with the data. Minsky remains a protean figure in heterodox theory because he insists so strongly that instability will invariably emerge from stability – a lesson that non-heterodox thinkers never seem to learn. But a multifaceted approach provides a surer framework for understanding the trajectory of lived crises, from the profit-squeeze episodes of the 1960s and 1970s to the global liquidity meltdown of the present day.

What is heterodox economic theory?

Many economists have dissented from the strictures on theorizing implicit in orthodox economic theory since the latter theory took shape in the writings of Walras, Jevons and Marshall. What these economists have shared is dissatisfaction with the critical assertion of the orthodox approach: the insistence that autonomous market forces tend to lead the economy to an equilibrium that cannot be improved by government policy interventions.

A question that has persisted throughout the century or more that heterodox thinking has gathered force is this: what defines or binds those who dissent from the orthodox – the "mainstream"? Heterodoxy and orthodoxy in any theoretical field exist in dialog. Orthodoxy authorizes certain methods and ideas and then polices their boundaries. A heterodoxy develops alternative methods and ideas to reach conclusions that are ruled out under orthodox constraints.

In the field of economics, orthodox macroeconomic theory crafted its vision of smooth, undisturbed economic growth precisely by discarding central ideas of some of its principal historical forebears – Marx, Keynes and Schumpeter. These theorists all build on the idea that emphasize endogenous forces would eventually undermine any period of economic growth. But this is precisely what was abandoned in neoclassical theory. A satisfactory demonstration that a decentralized "general" equilibrium could be achieved by agents interacting in markets – the avatar of the orthodox approach, achieved by Debreu (1959) – was possible only if time and ignorance, as well as power, were eliminated from consideration in advance. Introducing time means allowing both for the fact that some economic processes require the passage of time, and for the fact that everything doesn't happen at once. Ignorance refers to the inability of agents in any economic setting to comprehend what is happening, or what might happen; of special importance is uncertainty – that is, agents' inability to predict future events with complete confidence, no matter how much historical data they possess. Power, in turn, is exerted in an economic setting when one agent can use some advantage – larger size, threat of force or superior liquidity – to extract additional rent or effort from another.

Removing power permits economists to abstract from the social processes that underlie and construct market relations, and from the social consequences of economic processes. Removing time and ignorance eliminates examination of agents whose economic roles require them to make decisions in real time, based on conventional beliefs about their future prospects, which they hold with greater or less degrees of confidence. That is, this step removes any consideration that expectations about future events are fragile, and based on understandings that can change violently when circumstances change.[1]

So once time, ignorance and power are eliminated, one can then build economic models in which well-behaved, fully informed agents make choices based on their own net individual gain from any sequence of transactions. The terrain of orthodox theory has broadened considerably from the timeless, once-and-for-forever market framework that was used to demonstrate the existence of decentralized equilibrium itself. Orthodox theory now incorporates many varieties of game-theoretic and dynamical models, which respectively envision sequences of moves among interacting agents and sequences of choices across time. The equilibria that can be achieved in these more open frameworks are weaker, and often non-unique. However, a distinctive orthodox approach persists, in that the emphasis remains on how sustainable equilibria can be sustained in these thicker interactional or longer-term settings. And while the tools of utility maximization and equilibrium market exchange are being applied to ever more diverse social settings – leading to the creation of a contemporary field of "political economy" that has usurped a term formerly associated exclusively with the classical tradition of Smith, Ricardo and Marx. This new "political economy" remains orthodox in that it explains why the social or political phenomena analyzed – ranging from government policy choices, to election outcomes, to laws about abortion or adoption – can be explained as the result of a well-formed calculation of self-interest by the agents involved, given their information sets, endowments and preferences. That is, emphasis remains on how a given event could arise and persist as a result of a consensual process.[2]

A different type of unifying thread runs through heterodox theory: an insistence that economic systems contain within themselves the possibility of disruptures – of crises of reproduction and growth. The theories embodying this approach have different substantive foci – some center on the impact and consequences of power relations, some on uncertainty, and some on firm strategies. But in every case, these investigations identify structural elements within the economy that create ruptures. These ruptures – that is, serious disruptions in the overall capacity of capitalist economies to increase aggregate income levels and generate profit and interest for owners of firms and of assets – can be described as *crises*.

So whereas orthodox theory seeks to characterize the movement of the capitalist economy through time as a harmonious dynamic of equilibrium market exchanges, heterodox theory centers on the fragility and unsustainability of growth trajectories. Thus, heterodox economics cannot be accurately labeled an anti-doctrine, nor can it be reduced to a curiosum of special-case parameters in equilibrium models.[3] Rather, heterodox macroeconomic theory has arisen and persisted as a terrain of inquiry precisely because of its preoccupation with the problem of crisis. So heterodox economic theory doesn't just *need* a crisis theory: it *is* crisis theory.

One critical flaw or many?

For many years, heterodox economists have divided into schools of thought based on the flaws they have identified in capitalist dynamics and, in turn, in orthodox theory. Some have turned to Keynes and his vision of how uncertainty undermines belief and convention in unstable market settings; some turn to Kalecki and his vision of how conflict over distribution undermines capitalist dynamics; some turn to Marx and his focus on conflict at the point of production, or on secular long-term forces that gradually constrict the rate of profit.

This is where divisions emerge in heterodox economic theory. Capitalist economic growth can rupture in several different ways; and the theoretical basis for these different breakdown mechanisms is associated with different foundational figures – Marx, Keynes, Kalecki, Schumpeter and so on. So heterodox theorists differ over whether there is one primary flaw in economic reproduction mechanisms, or many. Some build on one foundational figure, others on several. This means that there are as many substantive controversies between heterodox theorists as between heterodox and orthodox theorists.

Heterodox economics is best served when it allows for different forms of crisis and is open to the insights of multiple foundational figures. If the point is to understand how crises can arise, then frameworks that encompass more critical dimensions of capitalist dynamics are more likely to capture the various forms of crisis that may occur.

James Crotty's extensive writings (see references) on capitalism take precisely this expansive approach to crisis, and thus provide arguably the best basis for surveying the terrain of heterodox macroeconomic theory.[4] Further, Crotty is without parallel in emphasizing that contemporary heterodox theory is both forward- and backward-looking: forward-looking in that it is based on a critique of orthodox theory, and backward-looking in being built largely on the living ideas of ancestral progenitors. And in addition, as discussed below, Crotty's close reading of Marx led him to introduce the crucial distinction between the possibility and the occurrence of crisis into contemporary discourse. This distinction gave precedence to financial aspects of capitalism just as financial instability became a defining feature of the emerging neoliberal age.

Crotty's critique of orthodoxy centers on four points:

1 it presumes pre-coordination in market exchanges, thus denying the possibility that market outcomes can frustrate participants' intentions;
2 it ignores power;
3 it ignores the role of firm strategy; and
4 it pays no attention to the institutional features of real-world economies.

The first three of these critiques aim squarely at the orthodoxy's approach to theory qua theory. In Crotty's view, an opposition to orthodoxy must be based first and foremost on an analytically coherent counter-approach. To deny any model's conclusions requires clarity about alternative assumptions that can generate other conclusions.

Following in the footsteps of both Marx (Crotty 1985) and Keynes (Crotty 1986), Crotty showed that embracing real time and ignorance means not only acknowledging the importance of fundamental uncertainty, but also discarding the possibility of pre-coordination.[5] Even small failures in agents' abilities to signal their intentions lead to aggregate demand/supply mismatches. That is, a real-time framework is invariably one in which unemployed labor and unsold goods are possible in equilibrium states. This in turn implies that aggregate demand has different determinants than aggregate supply, and may take on different magnitudes.

That is, Crotty's orthodox framework is one in which Say's Law – "supply creates its own demand" – does not hold. Crotty's analysis was based in large part on – and helped to revive interest in – Marx's ideas about the possibilities of crisis in his *Theories of Surplus Value* (especially Chapter 17). Marx, in these passages, not only anticipated Keynes' reflections on the monetary implications of real time and uncertainty; they anticipated Minsky's ideas about financial fragility.[6] Crotty himself, as shown below, extensively studied and debated Minsky.

Drawing on his theoretical reflections on Marx, Keynes and Minsky, Crotty has emphasized that monetary and financial relations become uniquely important, and uniquely fragile when Say's Law is violated. Important, because when everything does not happen at once, and when future outcomes are unknowable, those seeking goods must exchange either money or the promise of monetary payments to obtain them. To speed up the pace of production and exchange – and hence profit-making – capitalist firms will tend to use trade credit and other debt obligations (that is, obligations to provide monetary payment after goods or services are received) more. Fragile, because such latticeworks of credit become more likely to break down, the further they are extended in periods of tranquility or sustained growth. In effect, the very structure of economic transactions – the interpenetration of credit commitments and payments – creates the possibility of crises. Financial and credit relations are consequently a uniquely vulnerable element in capitalist reproduction. In short, any framework that embodies a critique of Say's Law effectively recognizes the possibility for economic crisis. Given that all heterodox economists reject Say's Law, a consideration of crises is central to heterodox analysis.

Another implication of a real-time framework is that the financial sector plays an "active" role in determining the level of employment and output. Insofar as the financial sector transfers funds from net savers to net borrowers, its assessments of real-sector risks and opportunities – not to mention the terms and conditions on which it makes loans – determine how much growth occurs, and how. So financial firms and wealth-owners, in contending with the unknowable, develop conventions in the face of uncertainty, and the confidence to believe their own conventions.

This leads immediately to the idea that financial instability is an inherent tendency in the capitalist economy: competitive pressures among firms and wealth-holders lead them to take on increasing degrees of leverage in search of higher rates of return; so when conditions change, they invariably are overcommitted. These pressures can lead to rapid asset-price shifts; and these shifts in turn undercut confidence further, leading to more instability, and so on.

The second element in Crotty's critique involves orthodoxy's inattention to power. Power in Crotty's conception has both micro and macro dimensions. At the micro level, power is exerted in work-settings over those who must sell their labor to reproduce themselves, and whose labor is exploited by those who hire them. This exploitation is organized by the firms that manage the production processes creating the goods and services needed for human reproduction and consumption. At the macro level, power is asserted at the national or even super-national level. This last point – which places the insights of Boddy and Crotty into the international setting – leads to globalization of labor processes; and this brings the problematic of national power/hegemony into the discussion of economic fluctuations.

Crotty also insists on the importance of firms' strategies, especially those of the large firms that shape market forces. The real-business cycle (and other mainstream) model(s) conceptualizes only the self-consistent behavior of one representative agent. But it is the possibly contradictory interactions of key sectors and key actors that demands our attention.[7] In the financial sector, as noted, instability rests in lenders' dual goals of minimizing their exposure to risks, on one hand, and their desire to maximize returns. Firms in the real sector also undertake self-undermining actions: for example, they expand production to widen their market reach in periods of economic expansion, while seeking to sustain profits by repressing wages. Again, outsourcing and global-factory solutions can mitigate the resulting tension between product-market demand and labor cost, but there is no avoiding a day of reckoning.[8] As Crotty has put it, "in order to be able to explain adequately the dynamics of the capitalist economy, a macrotheory must root instability in both the real and financial sectors" (Crotty 1990: 540)

Finally, Crotty insists on the importance of the institutional context within which cyclical and other economic forces play out. The lynchpin of Crotty's work on Korea and its crisis, for example, is his appreciation of the unique set of institutions that had permitted Korea to grow rapidly for so long prior to the Asian financial crisis (Crotty and Dymski 1998).

From profit-squeeze in the USA to Korea in the grip of neoliberalism

In the realm of macroeconomic dynamics, a crisis occurs when the overall reproduction of social relations and asset values in the economic realm is jeopardized and/or breaks down. What are the links between the theoretical first principles discussed above and real-world crises? Crotty has applied his ideas about crisis principally to two episodes in recent history.[9]

Crotty's celebrated essay with Raymond Boddy (1975) identified a "political business cycle" in the US economy of the 1960s and 1970s, triggered by recurrent profit squeeze. This model drew primarily on Kalecki and Marx to argue that US macro policy protected the interests of capitalists by slowing the economy – and thus deepening the reserve army of labor – when workers' excessive wage demands threatened profit rates. This paper was prescient in pointing out tensions that had arisen amidst the "Golden Age":

> There are contradictions in the application of macroeconomic policy ... First, as evidenced by the Indochina War, domestic cycle relaxation needs can conflict with the requirements of imperialist war. The latter obviously takes precedence, but only at the cost of severe future economic dislocations.

Second, the internal need to discipline labor through the cycle conflicts with the long-term planning which is crucial if the U.S. is to regain undisputed international capitalist hegemony.

(Boddy and Crotty 1975: 16)

Crotty's work with Boddy emphasized the problem of power in capitalist relations. In the early 1980s, Crotty began to develop his ideas about the centrality of financial fragility and business strategy in capitalist crisis. This new approach to crisis came at a crucial time in the trajectory of heterodox macroeconomic theory. It was common, until the mid-1980s, to differentiate between shorter-term or cyclical models, such as the Boddy–Crotty framework, and longer-term of secular models, such as the Cambridge heterodox approach.[10] Mimicking a distinction in neoclassical economics between demand-management and long-term growth models, the former class focused on fluctuations, the latter on longer-run equilibrium states. But by the 1980s, this conventional division collapsed, as the cyclical dynamics of the US economy were undergoing a fundamental shift, as the next two sections show. The US macroeconomy's new empirical patterns challenged this distinction: the US macroeconomy's formerly dependable cyclical patterns dissolved from 1980 onward; the long-run trajectory of the US economy slowed; and ferocious and unrestrained financial crises became a defining feature of the post-1980 world economy.

The age of globalization had arrived. And Crotty's reconceptualization of crises as manifestations of theoretical possibilities of rupture – that unfold in institutionally-specific (and hence ever-changing) ways, and that heterodox theory can consider because of its pre-commitment to the importance of power, inequality, and instability – itself proved prescient.

Minsky on stabilizing instability in the US economy

Crotty's multi-source, multi-influence approach to crisis, set out above (pp. 000–000), can be contrasted with that of Hyman Minsky – a celebrated heterodox macroeconomist who emphasized one progenitor (Keynes) and one root cause of crisis (financial instability). Crotty, while among Minsky's deepest admirers, criticized his inattention to the determinants of investment, and by extension to capital–labor conflict. Crotty's insights into capital–labor conflict can explain why Minsky's policy prescription for capitalist instability falls short in the neoliberal era, and moreover help us to understand the ever-new faces and phases of crisis in the contemporary global economy.

Beginning in the 1970s, Hyman Minsky wrote a series of papers and books arguing that advanced capitalist economies are subject to cyclical variability because of their financial instability.[11] The availability of financing boosts demand, but carries a cost: the economy becomes more financially fragile as financial commitments rise relative to income flows. Minsky argued that expectations, debt-financed expenditures and balance-sheet relationships – and hence financial fragility – evolve systematically during the business cycle, from "robust" to "fragile" to "Ponzi." Eventually, a significant number of borrowers cannot meet repayment demands and cash-flow disruptions spread throughout the economy's balance sheets. As financial instability worsens, asset values fall and a debt-deflation cycle may be unleashed.

Minsky argues that there was a fundamental transformation in the dynamics of capitalism because of Depression-era government policy reforms. In the pre-Depression era of what Minsky called "small-government capitalism," financial instability operated via cataclysmic downward debt-deflation cycles, which wreaked havoc on wealth-owning and asset-owning units. As the 1929 stock market crash and 1933 banking holiday dramatically demonstrated, this was a very socially wasteful method of ridding the economy of unsustainable debt commitments. With the New Deal, in Minsky's account, two crucial new roles for government were embraced: the Federal Reserve accepted its role as "lender of last resort" for the financial system; and the federal government committed to using public spending to stabilize aggregate demand.

These changes defined the initiation of "big-government capitalism." Cyclical dynamics changed fundamentally, in Minsky's characterization. Price deflation was checked by the interventions of the Federal Reserve and by counter-cyclical government expenditures. Consequently, the threat of debt-deflation was replaced by an inflationary bias. The huge increases in business failures, bank failures, and unemployment that had accompanied cyclical downturns were eliminated. Balance sheets are not thoroughly "cleaned" through widespread business failures in the downturn, as in the small-government period; so debt/income ratios build up over time. Investment too is stabilized at a low but positive level. Debt/income levels rise both cyclically and secularly. In effect, a tendency toward price infla-tion was the price of an interventionist state that "stabilized the unstable economy" (Minsky 1986). Minsky asserted that robust economic growth could resume once stable financial conditions were reestablished.[12]

Empirical evidence about Minsky's big-government/small-government claim

Dymski and Pollin (1994) investigated Minsky's claim that capitalism could be divided into "small" and "big" government eras, and that adequate policy tools for stabilizing the economy and assuring prosperity had been found. These authors collected annual US data for the period 1887–1988 for key variables in Minsky's model. Observations in each data series were then grouped, using NBER business-cycle turning-point data. The observation for a given variable in a "peak" year preceding a downturn was denoted that for "year 0;" its value in the following year was termed "year 1," and so on. Typical cyclical trajectories were then computed for these variables by averaging (without permitting any double-counting). The two periods of World War (1913–1918 and 1937–1951) were discarded.

Was Minsky right? Yes – to a point. Several variance-based tests determined that these cyclical patterns did indeed fall naturally into "small government" and "big government" groupings – but only until the arrival of the 1980s. The contrast between these two regimes is clearly seen in the contrasts in their average post-peak cyclical behavior.

As Figure 5.1 shows, average GDP decline in the downturn is substantially larger in the small-government than in the big-government era. Big government puts a higher "floor" under real GDP growth. And while the unemployment rate (Figure 5.2) grew and remained high for a sustained period in the small-government era, in the big-government era its explosive growth was blocked, and it remained at a much lower level than in the previous era.

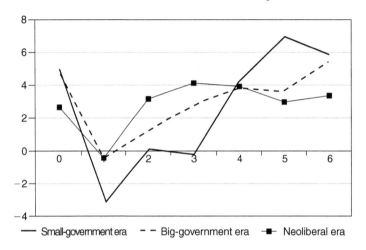

Figure 5.1 Post-peak US real GDP growth: small and big government and neoliberal eras.

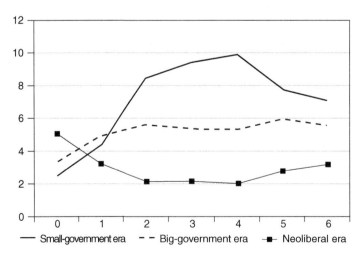

Figure 5.2 Post-peak US unemployment rate: small and big government and neoliberal eras.

The contrast in the behavior of price movements is even sharper. Figure 5.3 shows the contrast between the two eras most dramatically. The cyclical data for the small-government era reveal the sustained deflationary momentum that follows the downturn. The big-government era is characterized instead by mounting inflationary pressure in the downturn, as the monetary authority intervenes and counter-cyclical spending is triggered. Here is evidence that government macro-managers are exploiting the inflation/stability tradeoff in favor of stability. The data for real interest rates in Figure 5.4, not surprisingly, show very similar patterns (since nominal interest rates usually move much less than

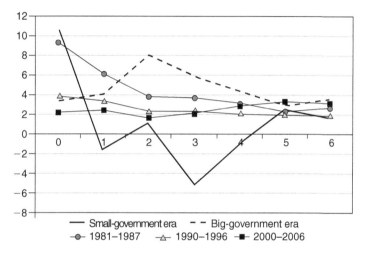

Figure 5.3 Post-peak US price inflation (changes in GDP deflator): small and big government and neoliberal eras.

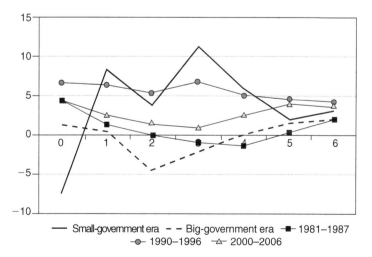

Figure 5.4 Post-peak US real interest rates: small and big government and neoliberal eras.

prices over the cycle). In the small-government era, the real interest rate rises substantially and for a prolonged period after the peak – a pattern related to that era's deflationary bias. By contrast, real interest rates fall after the peak in the big-government era due to Federal Reserve intervention.

There are also strong contrasts between the post-peak behavior of stock market prices and of the bank failure rate.[13] In the small-government era, stock-market prices decline and the bank failure rate climbs post-peak; in the big-government era, by contrast, stock-market prices actually rise in the post-peak period, while the rate of bank failures is low and shows no cyclical momentum.

Financial instability and crisis in the neoliberal era

If US cyclical patterns remained as they were prior to the 1980s, Minsky might have been right that "big government" could tame capitalist instability and assure managed prosperity. But they have not. To the contrary, post-1980 business cycles have followed a new behavioral pattern. Consequently, the idea of aggressive countercyclical government spending has evaporated: the US economy has left the "big government" era and entered the neoliberal age.

Neoliberal-era cyclical patterns

Cyclical dynamics have been transformed in the neoliberal era.[14] As Figure 5.1 demonstrates, GDP growth rates in the neoliberal era show substantial variation. The 1981–1987 cycle is remarkably volatile; however, in the next two cycles, GDP growth rates have shown relatively little variability. In Figure 5.2, which depicts the cyclical dynamics of the unemployment rate, the neoliberal era marks a sharp break with the big-government pattern: in both the 1981–1987 and 1990–1996 periods, the unemployment rate climbs quickly to higher levels than in previous eras, and then drifts steadily downward.

Another sharp difference in the neoliberal era is seen in the price-movement data in Figure 5.3. The patterns for all three post-1970s business cycles are very similar, and utterly different than the big-government pattern. In the 1981–1987 and 1990–1996 data, inflationary pressure is highest at the initial business-cycle peak. This pressure then moderates steadily through the downturn and renewal of expansion. In the 2000–2006 data, there is literally no cyclical inflationary pressure. Similarly, as Figure 5.4 shows, the real interest rate – by contrast with the big-government era – are virtually constant through this period.

Cyclical movements in stock-market prices in the neoliberal era follow no single pattern; but the bank failure rate has varied in a revealing way. As the 1980s unfolded, the first significant wave of bank failures since the Great Depression era gradually gathered force. During the 1990s, this wave dampened; by the turn of the new century, the bank failure rate was again almost nil.

In short, the US economy has entered a new period of cyclical behavior from the 1980s onward. Real interest rates and price inflation no longer vary systematically over the cycle; these variables appear to be responding to forces other than the cyclical momentum of the US economy. Whatever measures are taken by government in the wake of recessions, they do not dampen the upward drift of the unemployment rate in the downturn.

In the USA, the neoliberal era has been defined by fundamental economic transformations: systematic financial deregulation; increasingly globalized financial and consumption markets; steadily declining real wages and unionization rates for workers in many industries; and outsourcing and the use of extended cross-border supply chains in production. The Reagan administration signalled a sea-change in social-welfare government spending, especially for the unemployed and the poor. Counter-cyclical and safety-net policies were rejected in favor of "supply-side" tax cuts. Percentage changes in post-peak per-capita federal outlays on individuals were substantially lower in the neoliberal era than in the big-government era.

Crotty's sympathetic critique of Minsky

So what went wrong? Why all these changes, if the solution was already at hand? An explanation can be found in Crotty's extended argument with Minsky over the nature of economic crisis.

These two thinkers had several face-to-face dialogs over the years. Crotty also reflected on Minsky's financial instability hypothesis in several articles and chapters.[15] On numerous occasions, Crotty praised Minsky's analytical insight and his willness in policy debate to unabashedly advocate "big government" spending to combat stagnation (Crotty 1986: Introduction). But Crotty raised deep objections to Minsky's conceptual apparatus. Crotty had a "thick" approach to crisis, encompassing numerous real- and financial-sector factors; Minsky had a "thin" approach, encompassing only financial factors.

Crotty observed that "Minsky can find no impediment to perpetual balanced growth in the real sector of the economy" (Crotty 1992: 536). Minsky assumed that productive investment would follow passively from stable financial conditions; and while this may have reflected his sympathy for Schumpeter's model of enterpreneurship (see footnote 12), in Minsky's work, "the real sector of the economy has no active, essential role to play in the fundamental behavioral processes of his theory" (Crotty 1986: 10). A further problem was Minsky's inattention to labor-market or capital-labor relations. Crotty observed:

> the constant-mark-up Kalecki model of profit determination used by Minsky ... [is] quite unsatisfactory. This model assumes cyclical and secular constancy in the mark-up and the marginal efficiency of investment, the absence of any tendency for the rate of profit on capital to fall until after the expansion ends, and secular constancy in the rate of profit on capital.
>
> (1986: 6–7)

Not only were these assumptions contradicted by available empirical evidence; building them into the model blinded it to any potential instability in the capital–labor relationship due to wage-related conflicts or struggles over de-industrialization. But this was precisely a problematic aspect of cyclical dynamics in the big-government era. Figure 5.5 shows the problem clearly. Real wage/salary payments rose systematically through the entire post-peak period, in the big-government era. This was the price for maintaining stability by reflating the economy just when it was perched to plunge into what would otherwise be a debt-deflation collapse. This figure also demonstrates that the cyclical behavior of real wage/salary payments was remarkably consistent and very different in the neoliberal era. Real wage/salary levels plunged after cyclical peaks in the neoliberal era.

How about the effect of the neoliberal era on profit rates? Figure 5.6 illustrates the post-peak behavior of profits by depicting year-over-year percentage changes in the manufacturing profit rate (calculated on an after-tax basis relative to owners' equity). In the big-government era, profit rates rise mildly in the first year after the peak, and then fall; in general, their behavior is sluggish. In the neoliberal era, two distinct patterns are found. In the 1981–1987 period, the profit rate falls after the peak year, but then recovers. In the next two cyclical episodes, the profit rate falls after the peak, but then climbs spectacularly for an extended period.

Clearly, Minsky's "hedgehog" model (in Pollin and Dymski's 1993 characterization), which focused only on the need to check financial instability, provided a lens for seeing only a portion of the entire landscape of macroeconomic forces. The very factor that Boddy and Crotty emphasized – the constraints on the profit rate under the institutional conditions of the big-government era – was apparently among those that inclined owners of the US corporate sector to

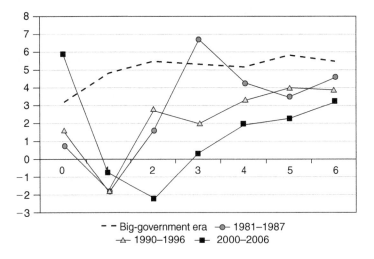

Figure 5.5 Post-peak US real non-government wage and salary payments: big government and neoliberal eras (% change).

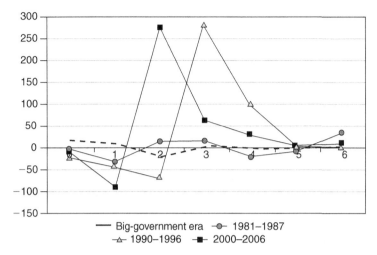

Figure 5.6 Post-peak changes in the manufacturing profit rate: big government and neo-liberal eras (% change).

embrace the dismantling of the social-welfare state that had been built up since the 1930s (and dubbed big-government capitalism by Minsky).

Global instability and stability in the neoliberal era

How did Minsky and Crotty adjust as the neoliberal era deepened? Minsky found that the major dangers in the neoliberal era would arise from the global spread of unchecked, highly-leveraged financial market relations. Even in his last essay, Minsky (1996) wrestled with the implications of what he called "money manager capitalism" and its implications for uncertainty and the problem of coordinating expectations in globalizing financial markets.

Crotty, by contrast, approached neoliberalism as a complex global phenomenon. His thick framework was far better suited to comprehend. His writing examined the global capital–labor struggle as well as the implications of the explosively growing financial markets. With the coming of the Asian financial crisis, Crotty made South Korea the focus of his study of neoliberalism. Korea was an apt choice. Not only had it so quickly changed places from "model of development" to a global site of rent-seeking elites, but Korea's long-term success had proven fragile, masking a cauldron of state violence, class conflict and institutional power plays.

This contrast is not made to show that Minskyian financial crises are obsolete. To the contrary, financial instability is an ever-more-common feature of global dynamics, as the East Asian, Brazilian, Russian, Turkish and subprime-mortgage-based crises attest.[16]

Further, the search for stability – another of Minsky's themes – has remained a key part of the global economy. Indeed, the most recent global crisis is rooted in that search.[17] The roots of the subprime lending crisis are to be found in one of the global economy's distinctive structural features since the mid-1980s – a growing US current-account deficit. This deficit has been balanced by steady financial inflows, many of which have bought mortgage-backed securities (MBSs). The volume of MBSs has grown dramatically, fed by the rapid growth of US mortgage loans – and in turn by some rapid advances in financial intermediaries' capacity to bundle, securitize and sell mortgage debt into the market.

Figure 5.7 shows that except for two years of market disorganization in the early 1980s, real per-adult US mortgage debt has grown steadily. This growth is related, of course, to the US economy's systematically low interest rates in the neoliberal era (Figure 5.4) – and the stagnant Japanese economy's even lower interest rates (Slater, 2006). Further, mortgage debt has been relatively impervious to the business cycle. The willingness of many global funds to hold – and the low apparent risks associated with – MBSs led many lenders to devise fee-based strategies, paying little attention to recourse or default risk. Investors' apparently insatiable demand for MBSs induced lenders to create instruments that teased new buyers into the market. Those previously excluded because of racial discrimination or because of inadequate savings or incomes could now have their housing purchases financed. The higher fees, rates and penalty clauses associated with these subprime mortgages meant both more income up-front for lenders and a steady set of steroid boosts to housing demand.

Ironically, the very fact that US-originated MBSs seemed to offer an island of tranquility in a world of chronic financial crises created incentives for perverse competitive forces. These ultimately have undermined entire portions of the US mortgage market – and threatened financial market stability the world over. The bank run of the 1930s has been transformed into the non-bank bank run – the liquidity black hole – of the new century (Persaud 2007).

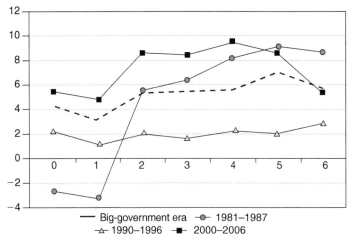

Figure 5.7 Post-peak changes in mortgage debt: big government and neoliberal eras (% change in real per-adult debt).

Certainly, this situation is symptomatic of the transplanting of Minsky's model of the US economy onto the global stage. The current crisis arose when US households' burden of being simultaneously the world's consumers of last resort and its borrowers of first resort, in a world of risk-evading financial intermediaries and shifting currency values, became too great to bear. Localized defaults spread, fed by intermediaries that have forgotten how to bear risk, and that now have the world's economies into a global liquidity meltdown.

Minskyian policy measures have attempted to stabilize this latest instantiation of instability. Several times, the Federal Reserve's "big bank" interventions have attempted to calm the markets and restore order (and liquidity).[18] But these measures have not worked as intended. The Federal Reserve cannot get the cooperation it needs to ease cash-flows in ever more distant corners of the money markets. It is clear that as the neoliberal era goes on and unchained markets and bank strategies have gotten ever bolder, those who are assigned lender-of-last-resort duties are ever farther from knowing how to restore order. They simply do not control enough of the markets in which the players that have taken incalculable risks have made their plays.

So it is not enough to find out (and respond to), as Minsky liked to say, financial market-makers' "model of the model."[19] The challenge is to find the crisis within the crisis. And here all the elements that Jim Crotty has identified for heterodox economics – instability, the active and sometimes destabilizing role of the financial sector, the use and abuse of power, firm strategies and the peculiar institutional framework of the neoliberal order – are there to be unwound.

Conclusion

Heterodox economists have long been united in agreeing that the neoclassical model constitutes a fundamentally flawed approach to understanding real-world economic dynamics. At the same time, they have otherwise constituted a group whose diversity of approach sometimes seems Babel-like: it is not just that followers of Keynes diverge from followers of Marx, but that followers of Keynes and of Marx disagree among themselves about how to construct more representative models of capitalist relations. This creative, if cacophonous, outpouring of insight leads to two central problems: what does define heterodox theory in economics? And how can one choose which approaches in heterodox theory show more promise?

This chapter has argued that the term "heterodox" should apply to all theoretical approaches that build in the assumption that capitalist economic relations are prone to immanent breakdown for endogenous reasons. Heterodox theory is coterminous with approaches that view crises of reproduction as a defining characteristic of capitalist economies. How then to choose which are the more promising approaches to heterodox theory? We have argued here that heterodox economic theory should be thick – sensitive to the possibility that reproduction crises can arise in several different ways – and not thin (focused on one source of breakdown).

The ideas of James Crotty provide an exemplar of the approach to heterodox theory set out here.

Crotty places the problem of crisis – sustained breakdowns in economic reproduction – not evolution, at the center of the heterodox agenda. He is careful to acknowledge and build on ideas handed down from intellectual progenitors. Further, in Crotty's vision, no contributor can or should settle on one source of crisis, or on one solution to crisis. Crises can arise due to asymmetric economic power, the vicissitudes of uncertainty, or inconsistent firm strategies – or due to contradictory interactions among these elements. There is no magic bullet. The analyst should not simplify too quickly, but should continually examine her logic from the multiple points of view that co-exist, however uneasily, within the fire-lit sanctuary of heterodox theory.

To illustrate these two approaches within heterodox theory, Crotty's approach has been contrasted here with Minsky's "hedgehog"-like financial-fragility framework. This chapter has shown that Minsky's model does not hold up as a characterization of economic dynamics in the neoliberal era. This doesn't mean Minsky is wrong; to the contrary, his ideas – as the subprime crisis shows – are more relevant than ever. But his approach should be extended so that it fully integrates real-sector influences on financial crises, and so it accounts for the new macro realities, including shifting financial markets and processes, that have unfolded in the neoliberal era.

What will bring economics out of this neoliberal midnight? None can say. But might not this renewal start with a flickering insight, born in the uneasy reflections of a heterodox imagination? It would not mark the first time that devalued but carefully kept traditions have rekindled our understanding of what has happened, and what must be done next in the world in which we live:

> As I see it, Marx, Keynes, and Minsky might all be embarrassed to be found in bed together, but they are not such strange bedfellows after all. Each has his role to play in constructing a theory of political economy adequate to our needs.
>
> (Crotty 1986: 29)

Notes

1 There is not space here to work through the specific implications of the removal of time, ignorance and power from market-exchange frameworks. For detailed examinations of these relationships, see Crotty (1985), among others.

2 This is not to belittle the usefulness of equilibrium reproduction frameworks as indicative tools and as points of reference within heterodox theory. Understanding how something works is fundamental in understanding how it can break down: the analysis of balanced growth is a useful means to the end of examining impediments to growth. This way of understanding equilibrium growth frameworks, of course, implies that crises are not simply short-run phenomena experienced on the way to long-term steady states; to the contrary, these steady states are reference points for understanding crisis.

3 And it is often misunderstood in the latter way. For example, a *New York Times* reporter (Hayes 2007) wrote that "heterodox" "categorizes people by what they don't

believe … in the case of heterodox economists, what they don't believe is the neo-classical model that anchors the economics profession."

4 We have not emphasized the micro/macro distinction, as it is not important for the larger argument being made in this chapter. Crotty's writings have examined both macroeconomics and paid little attention to explicitly microeconomic frameworks.

5 Also see Dymski (1990).

6 See Crotty (1985, 1986).

7 The inescapability of contradictory relationships among economic agents and structures is one reason why, in Crotty's conception, macroeconomic dynamics lead to recurrent crises, and also why crises involve interactions at a macro-scale; see Crotty (1993b).

8 There is recent evidence that China is beginning to confront labor shortages; see Barboza (2006).

9 Crotty's writings about real-world capitalist crises represent contributions to the broader landscape of heterodox crisis theories. Kotz (2006) sets out a useful typology of heterodox crisis theories.

10 This latter bias is especially evident in Marglin (1984).

11 See especially Minsky (1975). Pollin and Dymski (1993) succinctly summarize his framework.

12 Minsky believed that sustained financial stability would permit Schumpeterian entrepreneurs to obtain financing and create new sources of employment and investment (Minsky 1986; Ferri and Minsky 1992).

13 These data are not shown here, but are available from the author.

14 This argument is developed in Dymski (2002), which extends the Dymski–Pollin method for the first two post-1970s cycles and presents some pertinent comparative data for the three eras.

15 See especially Crotty (1986, 1990, 1993a).

16 See Kregel (1998) and Crotty and Dymski (1998), among others.

17 Two useful discussions of this unfolding crisis are Slater *et al.* (2007) and Ip and Hilsenrath (2007).

18 As Kregel notes, this "big bank" role far outweighs the "big government" role in global financial crises.

19 The phrase was Peter Albin's; it is quoted in Minsky (1996).

References

Barboza, D. (2006) "Labor Shortage in China may lead to Trade Shift," *New York Times*, April 3.

Boddy, R. and Crotty, J. (1975) "Class Conflict and Macro-Policy: The Political Business Cycle," *Review of Radical Political Economics*, 7: 1–19.

Crotty, J. R. (1985) "The Centrality of Money, Credit, and Financial Intermediation in Marx's Crisis Theory: An Interpretation of Marx's Methodology," in S. Resnick and R. Wolff (eds.) *Marxian Political Economy: Essays In Honor of Harry Magdoff and Paul Sweezy*, 45–82, New York: Autonomedia.

—— (1986) "Marx, Keynes, and Minsky on the Instability of the Capitalist Growth Process and the Nature of Government Economic Policy," in David F. Bramhall and Suzanne W. Helburn (eds.) *Marx, Schumpeter, and Keynes: A Centenary Celebration of Dissent*, 297–326, Armonk: M. E. Sharpe.

—— (1990) "Owner-Manager Conflict and Financial Theories of Investment Instability: A Critical Assessment of Keynes, Tobin, and Minsky," *Journal of Post Keynesian Economics*, 12(4): 519–42.

—— (1992) "Neoclassical and Keynesian Approaches to the Theory of Investment," *Journal of Post Keynesian Economics*, 14(4): 483–96.

—— (1993a) "Rethinking Marxian Investment Theory: Keynes–Minsky Instability, Competitive Regime Shifts and Coerced Investment," *Review of Radical Political Economics*, 25(1): 1–26.

—— (1993b) "Structural Contradictions of the Global Neoliberal Regime," *Review of Radical Political Economics*, 32(2): 361–8.

Crotty, J. R. and Dymski, G. A. (1998) "Can the Global Neoliberal Regime Survive Victory in Asia? The Political Economy of the Asian Crisis," *International Papers in Political Economy*, 5(2): 1–47.

Debreu, G. (1959) *Theory of Value*. New York: Wiley.

Dymski, G. A. (1990) "Money and Credit in Radical Political Economy: A Survey of Contemporary Perspectives," *Review of Radical Political Economics*, 22(2/3): 38-65.

—— (2002) "Post-Hegemonic U.S. Economic Hegemony: Minskian and Kaleckian Dynamics in the Neoliberal Era," *Keizai Riron Gakkai Nempo (Journal of the Japanese Society for Political Economy)*, 39(April): 247–64.

Dymski, G. A. and Pollin, R. (1994) "The Costs and Benefits of Financial Instability: Big-Government Capitalism and the Minsky Paradox," in G. Dymski and R. Pollin (eds.) *New Perspectives in Monetary Macroeconomics: Essays in the Tradition of Hyman P. Minsky*, 369–401, Ann Arbor: University of Michigan Press.

Ferri, P. and Minsky, H. P. (1992) "Market Processes and Thwarting Systems," *Structural Change and Economic Dynamics*, 3(1): 79–91.

Hayes, C. (2007) "Hip Heterodoxy," *New York Times*, June 11.

Ingrao, Bruna and Giorgio, I. (1990) *The Invisible Hand: Economic Equilibrium in the Hostory of Science*. Cambridge: MIT Press.

Ip, G. and Hilsenrath, J. E. (2007) "How Credit Got So Easy And Why It's Tightening," *Wall Street Journal*, August 7, A1.

Kotz, D. M. (2006) "Crisis Tendencies in Two Regimes: A Comparison of Regulated and Neoliberal Capitalism in the U.S.," mimeo, Political Economy Research Institute, University of Massachusetts at Amherst, December.

Kregel, J. (1998) "Yes, 'It' Did Happen Again – A Minsky Crisis Happened in Asia," Working Paper No. 234, Jerome Levy Economics Institute of Bard College, April.

Marglin, S. A. (1984) *Growth, Distribution, and Prices*. Cambridge: Harvard University Press.

Minsky, H. P. (1975) *John Maynard Keynes*. New York: Columbia University Press.

—— (1986) "Money and Crisis in Schumpeter and Keynes," in David F. Bramhall and Suzanne W. Helburn (eds.) *Marx, Schumpeter, and Keynes: A Centenary Celebration of Dissent*. Armonk: M. E. Sharpe.

—— (1996) "Uncertainty and the Institutional Structure of Capitalist Economies," Working Paper No. 155, Jerome Levy Economics Institute of Bard College, April.

Persaud, A. (2002) "Liquidity Black Holes," WIDER Discussion Paper No. 2002/31, United Nations University, March.

—— (2007) "The Politics and Micro-economics of Global Imbalances," in A. F. P. Bakker and I. R. Y. van Herpt (eds.) *Central Bank Reserve Management: New Trends from Liquidity to Return*, 37–45, Cheltenham, UK and Northampton, MA: Edward Elgar.

Pollin, R. and Dymski, G. A. (1993) "Hyman Minsky as Hedgehog: The Power of the Wall Street Paradigm," in Steven Fazzari (ed.) *Financial Conditions and Macroeconomic Performance*, 27–62, Armonk: M. E. Sharpe.

Slater, J. (2006) "Dollar's Tumble May Hurt Players In Carry Trade," *Wall Street Journal*, December 13, C1.

Slater, J., Lyons, J., Barta, P. and Davis, A. (2007) "Markets Fear U.S. Woes Will Hit Global Growth," *Wall Street Journal*, August 17, A1.

6 The current crisis in macroeconomic theory

Bill Gibson[1]

Introduction

Since the 1970s, mainstream economics has attacked Keynesian macroeconomics for not being a science in the proper sense of the term. The latter lacks realistic microfoundations, according to the orthodoxy, and is generally inconsistent with the Walrasian system. This chapter argues that the problem lies deeper than the absence of a choice theoretic framework in the Keynesian model. The main problem with macroeconomics of any theoretical flavor is aggregation and because macroeconomics aggregates *ex ante* it arrives at an indefensible position of using aggregates as policy instruments. Aggregation is an intractable problem and is at the root of controversies that run from Marxian value theory to the capital controversy to the negative result of Sonnenschein, Mantel and Debreu (SMD), that no coherent microfoundations for aggregate economics exists.

There have been various responses to the inability to unify macro and micro theories. The rise of "clean identification" methods in econometrics is an effort to restore scientific credibility to economics. Many of the traditional problems central to the discipline, however, were abandoned as the literature focused on "cute and clever" microeconomics.

It is argued here that it is possible that macroeconomics can be rescued by way of agent-based models. These models require no *ex ante* aggregation and provide a platform for policy intervention since the "representative agent" is no longer required. Outcomes can be then be measured by aggregating the heterogeneous individuals *ex post*. Familiar macroeconomic characteristics arise from these complex systems as emergent properties. What is sacrificed as we turn to computer simulations is the elegant formal mathematical analysis that characterized the Walrasian system of the past.

The chapter is organized as follows: the next section reviews the problems of Keynesian economics and the reaction of heterodox economists and asks why the project of the unification of micro and macro has largely been abandoned. The subsequent suggests that agent-based models may be a way to recover realistic microfoundations for macroeconomics. The final section concludes with some comments on the nature of big problems in economics and science generally.

The crisis of Keynesian economics

On a recent trip to the UK, a passport inspector noted that I had listed my profession as Professor of Economics. "Hum..." he said, as he regarded me with the mix of curiosity and suspicion required of his post. "Economics, that is ... like ... Keynesian economics, right?" I nodded affirmatively and after a pregnant pause he asked "What is Keynesian economics?"

The innocence of his question set me thinking: here is a public official, in the land of Keynes and where the Keynesian edifice was constructed, and yet he does not even know what it is. Is this just some form of rational ignorance? A second darker hypothesis is that what we do as economists has little "street value," nothing of worth in a social context. Science generally does have street value, both private and public, as is made clear every day in the press. Breakthroughs are regularly reported in publications such as the *New England Journal of Medicine, Science, Nature*, along with a host of television programs.

Certainly at one stage of the not-too-distant past economics, and especially macroeconomics, possessed a good deal of street value. The golden age of macroeconomics, in the 1960s, was based on the widely accepted notion that the economy was a complex machine that would occasionally get out of sorts with itself and require some adjustment. Government relied on macroeconomists for advice through the Council of Economic Advisors. Most large corporations, and virtually all banks, had large and expensive econometric forecasting teams. Microeconomics was a sideshow with its cost curves, discounting formulas and welfare triangles.

Keynesian theory enjoyed almost complete hegemony, even among the most conservative members of the profession. By the late 1980s, however, micro had staged a dramatic comeback and macroeconomics was almost entirely displaced from graduate curricula across the country. Part of the reason was an inconsistency in advanced general equilibrium theory noticed by Debreu and others.[2]

At the policy level, it was the stagflation of the 1970s that reduced to rubble the simple Keynesian program of "if there is inflation, run a surplus and when there is unemployment, run a deficit." At the center of the controversy was the instability of the Phillips curve:

> the inflationary bias on average of monetary and fiscal policy (in the 1970s) should ... have produced the lowest average unemployment rates for any decade since the 1940s. In fact, as we know, they produced the highest unemployment since the 1930s. This was economic failure on a grand scale.
> (Lucas and Sargent (1978: 277))

As the Phillips curve dissolved into a shapeless scatter diagram, the street value of macroeconomics and its associated macroeconometric models diminished. Lucas identified a fundamental problem in the macroeconometric literature based on the Keynesian structural model, that agents would alter their behavior in reaction to changes in policy (Lucas (1976)) The structural parameters could change in response to policy initiatives and if this were not part of the analysis, it would become impossible to predict the effects of policy. Only self-interest remained invariant to policy change.

Moreover, models that assumed no theory whatsoever, the vector-autoregression models, seemed to do as well as those that traveled with heavy theoretical baggage. As Diebold notes, "the flawed econometrics that Lucas criticized was taken in some circles as an indictment of all econometrics." *New York Times* economic columnist Peter Passell, in an article titled "The model was too rough: why economic forecasting became a sideshow," wrote that "Americans held unrealistic expectations for forecasting in the 1960's – as they did for so many other things in that optimistic age, from space exploration to big government" (*New York Times*, February 1, 1996). Rather than predict interest rates with a staff of the econometricians, firms hired MBAs to hedge against its movements. Public policy, as Keynes himself predicted, is still a few decades behind the curve and references to aggregate demand and other Keynesian motifs can still be heard, whether at the Federal Reserve, Wall Street or the Congressional Budget Office. Theoretical economics, however, has by and large moved on, with the exception of heterodox economists.

The heterodox reaction

Here is a proposition: it could be that none of this talk of science, microfoundations and the like is relevant. Indeed economics, and especially macroeconomics and macroeconomic policy, is just a tool of the rich used to bludgeon the poor into accepting low wages. Economics is not a science and never was, but is rather auxiliary to the broader project of class domination by the rich and powerful. The poor and powerless are the victims of policy designed to shift resources and political power to capital. Economists are implicated in this grand scheme of domination, a band of self-referential (and self-refereeing) pseudo-scientists, who as a subsumed class take a cut of the surplus for themselves. Their main task is thus ideological, rather than scientific, jawboning. The political creed of the orthodoxy in economics is anti-progressive, essentially libertarian on domestic issues and neoliberal internationally. The scientific method is no more central to this project than it is to, say, religion or a backyard barbecue.

Fine, but isn't this proposition contradicted by the evolution of heterodox economics? In the 1960s and 1970s Marxian economics was a professionally viable alternative to orthodox economics. As a result, some of the more broad-minded neoclassical economists, Samuelson and Morishima for example, took up Marxian themes. At the same time, radical economics began to insert itself in graduate programs around the United States and Europe, graduate programs that were training young economists in the standard tools of scientific inquiry. It was in some ways natural that cross-pollination would come about and in the late 1970s a number of non-neoclassical analysts produced work that bore the imprint of their training. Sweezy, Baran and Emmanuel, and Samir Amin, gave way to Marglin, Bowles, Gintis, Gordon, Roemer and others from both sides of the Atlantic. Their work was defined by four essential features:

1   they addressed the decidedly "nonscientific" questions of income distribution, power, racism, sexism, imperialism and inequality as opposed to the traditional efficiency of resource allocation issues;
2   they were unafraid of "bourgeois" tools of analysis, especially mathematics, data analysis and econometrics;
3   they were sensitive to the criticism of dogmatism in their analysis and sought to remove elements that could not be substantiated by logic or fact;
4   they rejected the relativism of emerging post-modernism in favor of methodological individualism (at least to a considerable degree).

These writers were above all eclectic, accepting or rejecting hypotheses on their own terms as opposed to tradition. Although they were unified by themes that had traditionally been of interest to Marxists, the project as a whole was a definitive break from the traditional Marxism of the preceding 150 years.

These analytical Marxists continued to define themselves in opposition to the orthodoxy, often unclear about their positive contributions, but very clear about what they were not: neoclassicals. Ironically, much of neoclassical theory found its way into their work, but piecemeal, one component at a time. Some used the Walrasian system, others growth theory, monetary theory or computable general equilibrium models and, especially, game theory. There was no part of neoclassical theory that was completely off limits and it is probably fair to say that all of it was used one way or another at some point.

Anti-neoclassicism then flowered into many theoretic directions, surveyed by (Colander (2003) and (Gibson (2003)). The term "Marxist," for example, began to fall out fashion, but more for substantive than stylistic reasons. The backdrop was an explicit recognition of the possibility that the scientific method could illuminate the incoherencies and irrationalities of the capitalist system. Many heterodox writers accepted the view that the nature of the analytical tools employed is not constitutive of the conclusions derived. Roemer and his associates expressed the proposition most clearly: if exploitation was a fundamental fact of capitalist society, it should be able to survive the transition to the Walrasian environment. That is, given tastes, technology and the distribution of the endowment, exploitation was logically entailed. This specialized project drew the attention of a specialized audience, certainly, but it was at the same time widely respected.

Walrasian Marxism was subject to the same SMD criticism as the orthodoxy; in short, no more macroeconomics was to come from Walrasian Marxism than from the standard approach. Certainly this feature was of little concern for Roemer, who was primarily interested in the more basic issues of traditional Marxian economic theory, such as exploitation and its relationship to social class. But from the general perspective of microfoundations of macro, the work led to a dead end.

Declare victory and withdraw

Branching out from the work of the early anti-neoclassicals was a wide range of heterodox approaches to problems of growth, distribution, and trade and finance, powered by standard analytical methods of comparative statics, dynamics, econometrics and game theory. Most of the macromodels in the tradition of Dutt, Skott, Semmler, Taylor, Setterfield and many others had no specific microfoundations, but relied instead on a demonstrated correspondence to the object of study, a particular economy at a particular time. Most heterodox economists were simply unconcerned with microfoundations (Dutt 2003). Macromodels were structural in nature and gave content to welfare propositions that hinged essentially on the level of output, employment and inflation.

The traditional problems of preference revelation and preference aggregation were not ceded any space; there was no need to aggregate the utilities of the employed and unemployed since they were incommensurate. It follows that the welfare of the system as a whole was not to be determined by an aggregate of the welfare of individuals.

Macropolicies that improved outcomes for the rich and the rich only, even if there were no change in the well-being of the poor, were not necessarily superior as they would be in standard analysis. Thus social welfare could not be mediated exclusively by private welfare no matter how it was aggregated. The aggregation problem, which dogged the traditional approach since its inception, was solved by critical acclamation. In the process, the unification project was sacrificed.

Naturally the balance of anti-neoclassical micro-oriented economists took an entirely opposite approach. For Bowles, Gintis, Skillman, Roemer and others attracted to game theory it was literally impossible to forego maximizing models with some conception of individual welfare at the core. Imagine, for example, a prisoners' dilemma in which the detainees were indifferent to their own freedom. When it came down to micro foundations versus macroeconomics, they followed the orthodoxy in dismissing the latter. Bowles and Heinz (1996), for example, used industry level data to show that raising wages in South Africa would cause a contraction in employment despite the fact that progressive macroeconomists had compiled data showing that the economy was "stagnationist" in Bhaduri and Marglin's infelicitous terminology (Bhaduri and Marglin (1990); Nattrass (2000)).

Keynesian theory seemed to be abandoned by the orthodoxy not necessarily because it conflicted with empirical observation, but because it was incomplete and at variance with their libertarian, individualist biases. The heterodox à la carte approach never produced a coherent alternative because it could not coalesce around a common theoretical framework. The debate seemed not to be about science and method, but about competing philosophical positions.

Granted, heterodox economists might object that their work is scientific, solid, empirically grounded, objective and replicatable. Heterodox articles are frequently peer-reviewed and this forces objectivity as it does elsewhere in the scientific community. There is certainly something to this argument. It might be possible to feign objectivity individually, but it is very difficult for a crowd of skeptically minded individuals to do so, unless as Surowiecki (2004) notes, the "wisdom" of the crowd is highly correlated. But the view that heterodox economics is not truly heterodox according to the ordinary definition of the term, but rather the name of a broad coalition of anti-capitalist researchers might still be vindicated. Indeed, heterodoxy is far more homogeneous than the economics profession it opposes. There are no personally right-wing economists who are attracted to the field of heterodox economics for purely methodological, technical or other professional reasons. The closely correlated attitudes of the heterodox clan undermines their objectivity in Surowiecki's scheme.

Perhaps, then, macroeconomics is just a logical impossibility, like a failed state, vulnerable to take-over by anti-scientific types. If so, then the options appear to be limited. One can press on with the Keynesian model with its obvious deficiencies. Or one can decamp to something with more scientific content, as much of the profession seems to be doing.

Smart rats and clean identification

One of the greatest problems of aggregation is that one cannot often hold the composition of the aggregated variables constant. Were there a tight lattice structure preventing slippage within society, then we could be more confident about policy recommendations. Competition plays this role in economics but it cannot be relied upon to hold structure entirely constant. But since structure tends to self-organize in response to policy, it becomes ever more difficult to distinguish correlation and causality. This is, of course, an age-old problem and it pervades every branch of science. Feynman (1999) in the classic "Cargo-cult science" describes the attempts of a psychologist, identified only as Young, to hold variables constant in a experiment with rats looking for food:

> The question was, how did the rats know, because the corridor was so beautifully built and so uniform, that this was the same door as before? Obviously there was something about the door that was different from the other doors. So he painted the doors very carefully, arranging the textures on the faces of the doors exactly the same. Still the rats could tell. Then he thought maybe the rats were smelling the food, so he used chemicals to change the smell after each run. Sill the rats could tell … He finally found that they could tell by the way the floor sounded when they ran over it. And he fixed that by putting his corridors in sand. So he covered one after another of all possible clues and finally was able to fool the rats so they would go in the third door. If he relaxed any of his conditions, the rats could tell.
>
> (Feynman (1999: 215))

Feynman goes on to claim that this is "A-number-1 science" because it reveals the efforts one must undertake to hold everything constant. Macroeconomics also seems to have had its smart rats.

In retrospect, it seems clear now that macroeconomics of the 1950s and 1960s was held together by spurious correlation of macro variables driven by time. When time was removed by way of co-integration techniques, much of the supposed causality in macroeconomic theory evaporated. One reason macroeconomics enjoys so little street value now is that it has been so difficult to rebuild it on a solid foundation since. Micro has to some degree risen to the challenge.

Levitt and Dubner (2005) is perhaps the most visible evidence of the restoration of the scientific method in economics, but this has been accompanied by an invasion of social science by methods from chemistry, biology, geology and a wealth of other disciplines. Diamond is another well-known architect of the interdisciplinary approach, but there is also Hoxby's study of competition in schools as demarcated by streams and rivers in urban environments (Diamond (1997, 2005)). More streams implied more schools and better learning outcomes (Hoxby (2000)). Another well-known example is Donohue and Levitt's (2001) claim that the legalization of abortion after Roe vs. Wade resulted in the lowered crime rates in the 1990s. Their work challenged Lott's (2000) assertion that "shall carry" laws were responsible.

These last papers are all based on natural or quasi-experiments, differential applications of policies in an arguably random way.[3] Natural experiments are second only to the gold standard of controlled experiments, such as the well-known Star study of the effect of student teacher ratios on test scores (Mosteller (1995)). But controlled experiments, like professional football, are often expensive and sometimes dangerous and almost always imperfectly controlled.[4] Still, clean identification is an attempt to more closely adhere to Feynman's definition of A-number-1 science in the effort to distinguish correlation from causality.

The quasi-experimental approach, what Heckman has called the "cute and the clever," is an effort to restore credibility to correlations attacked by skeptics (Scheiber (2007)). These studies range from Levitt's "Why drug dealers don't live with their mamas," to point shaving in basketball and sumo wrestling.[5] The methods and datasets used in some of these studies have already found their way into econometrics textbooks and serve to educate future econometricians.

To the heterodox mind, this may just be additional evidence of the complete sell-out of the orthodox establishment, hiding behind methodological refinements to avoid confronting more serious problems.[6]

Traditional economic issues such as poverty, inequality, business cycles, global warming and environmental racism all go unanalyzed for lack of proper instruments or experiments by which confounding factors may be eliminated or controlled for. From this optic, there are too few, not too many, interesting problems amenable to statistical analysis based naturally randomizing treatment effects afforded by quirks of nature or the whim of policymakers.

Big issues, however, almost always arise as outcomes, or *ex post* aggregates. They result from something more fundamental at the ground level, behavior that was not adequately captured in the aggregate models. Thus, even if they were correct, the models would not lead to any clear policy implications because they do not model the diversity of underlying agents. On the other hand, Levitt's studies of criminal behavior does at least show that criminals are partially rational and will therefore likely respond to incentives to obey the law. Most macroeconomic indicators, by contrast, are signals that some underlying behavior in the system might be out of adjustment. What it is and how we are to get it back into sync remains unspecified by the model. This is why studies with clean identification are reviewed in scientific publications such as *Nature*, *Science* and *Scientific American* while macro studies undertaken by heterodox economists never are. The former have street value, clearly understandable methodologies and direct policy implications.

There is one set of macro studies undertaken by heterodox economists that does seem to draw a reaction from outside the heterodox community, agent-based or multi-agent systems models.

Agent-based models

Choi and Bowles (2007), for a recent example, published a study in *Science* using an agent-based framework to study the coevolution of altruism and war. Agent-based models grew out of game theoretic simulations and papers by Fehr, Basu, Axelrod and others have been regularly reviewed in the scientific press.[7] They hold out the promise of separating correlation and causality because they allow experiments to be undertaken in silico, with literally everything else held constant.[8] They are also relatively inexpensive and safe, except for the occasional laptop fire. The catch is convincing the scholarly community that the simulation is realistic and appropriate to the problem.

Might it be possible, then, to have a macro-theoretical framework that relies on individual self-interest, however imperfectly expressed, and at the same time addresses bigger questions than the cute and clever micro literature? Let us first specify what we mean: agent-based models blend structure and agency in a way that emphasizes the individual. This is not to say that "structure does not matter," inasmuch as decisions made by agents in the past confront current agents as ossified structure and is, therefore, ultimately endogenous. The macro features of the model are not imposed, but rather arise out the micro specification as emergent properties (Gatti *et al.* (2008)). Following Jensen and Lesser (2002) for a general definition, a multi-agent system S, is composed of n agents $A = \{a_1, a_2, \ldots, a_n\}$ and an environment E. Each agent is an object with methods that cannot generally be invoked by other agents. Agents operate on state variables and transform them according to the methods each agent employs. State variables are passed to agents and serve to define the spatial distribution of resources, information about other agents and any additions or updates of the methods by which this information is processed. The concept of an agent includes the standard notion of consumer or producer as special cases, but is broader and more general.

Agents in multi-agent systems are best thought of as heterogeneous computational entities who make decisions based in an informationally constrained environment and with limited computational means (Wooldridge (2002); Sandholm and Lesser (1997)). Agents may lack the resources to make the appropriate calculations leading to an optimal allocation and/or may not have the time to complete calculations already begun if the environment E changes. "Social pathologies" studied in the game theoretic literature, various prisoners' dilemmas, suboptimal spending on public goods and ultimatum irrationalities can easily arise in multi-agent systems (Jensen and Lesser (2002)).

Schelling's (1971) neighborhood model is an early example of a multi-agent system. White liberals following simple behavioral rules to generate entirely segregated neighborhoods, despite preferences for more integrated ones. Each agent is unaware of the true nature of its neighbors and only processes information about skin color. Where white neighborhoods will be in the next round is more difficult for the agents to compute, however, and in the simplest version of the model, agents move randomly, away from their current, undesirable location, without thinking about where it will land. An agent might improve the chances that it would not have to move a second time by way of a method that predicts the moves of other white liberals.

Agents are then computational entities or objects and any personality that might or might not evolve is itself an emergent property of these computations. In Gibson (2007), agents make only a decision whether to stay in their current job or leave it and interesting macroeconomic properties arise. Initially technologies, or blueprints, are randomly scattered around a grid. Both a unit of labor (an agent) and a variable amount of finance are required in order to activate the technology of a given cell. Finance is available from wealth accumulated by agents in the past and is distributed back to cells according to profitability with a random error term. Profit is the difference between wages and output and is redistributed to agents in proportion to their wealth plus a random error term.

The key to the dynamics of the model is the wage bargain between agents and the cells on which the agents reside. Cells can compute the marginal product of labor, but agents lack sufficient information. Agents can compute their own reservation wage, based on life-cycle variables as agents age, reproduce and die.

The decision variable is whether the agent is satisfied with her current job. Job satisfaction depends mostly upon whether wealth is increasing or decreasing, but there are also variables that derive from reinforcement learning models (Sutton and Barto (1998)). Agents must learn what the grid as a whole has to offer in terms of consumption possibilities. Unsuccessful agents become "stuck" in relatively low wage jobs either because they do not have the accumulated wealth to finance a move or they lack the education and skills required to take advantage of nearby opportunities.

If agents move, they must then Nash-bargain over the wage payment with the new cell. In the Nash bargain, the surplus is defined as the difference between the marginal product of labor and the agent's reservation wage. The outcome of the bargaining process depends on relative impatience of the agent to the cell. Cells are equally impatient in that they know that unless they are profitable, they will be unable to attract capital and will fall into disuse. Agents realize if they reject the offered wage they must move again, with all its associated costs and

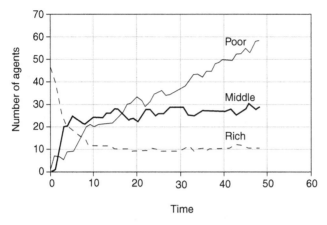

Figure 6.1 Income classes.

uncertainty. If the agent's reservation wage exceeds the marginal product, cells raise their prices, provoking inflation. As a result, they are less able to compete for finance for their operations.

In this simple model the economy grows with less than full employment on a track that underutilizes the available technology. There is very little that is optimal about this model in the tradition sense, but neither is it excessively prone to mass unemployment nor spiraling inflation. A skewed distribution of income is an emergent property of this simple system. Figure 6.1 is drawn from Gibson (2007).

Even if the economy begins with an egalitarian wealth distribution, it will deteriorate over time and eventually follow a power-law distribution of wealth. Educated agents who secure good jobs early and keep them for a long time end up wealthy. Those who move tend to run down their wealth but they may also succeed in finding a better opportunity.

Appeal to heterodoxy

Heterodox economists have to some extent embraced the agent-based methodology discussed here, as the citations above suggest. Foley (2003) makes the strongest case that the method of complex adaptive systems is broadly consistent with the underlying program of classical political economy. Smith, Ricardo, Malthus and Marx all analyzed the capitalist system as an ordered social structure, arising out of the chaos of individual decisions. The system is "self organized" in that no one, not even a Walrasian auctioneer, is directing the outcome. Foley notes that complex systems are "dialectical" in that the components can exhibit features that appear to contradict those of the system as a whole.

Above all, Foley sees multi-agent systems in fundamental opposition to the pseudo-dynamic neoclassical system. The latter is designed for an essentially static world in which a stable equilibrium is the principal theoretical objective.

Time paths converge to a well-defined equilibrium, the characteristics of which have nothing to do with the processes by which they were obtained. He notes that complex adaptive structures are also determinant in that it is at least in principle possible to write down their equations of motion. In practice, however, is not usually possible to obtain a closed form solution that serves as a practical guide to the dynamic properties of the system.

Complex systems are globally stable in the limited sense that they have broad error tolerance and are relatively invulnerable to localized failure. They are not brittle systems subject to catastrophic collapse as some crisis theorists have foretold. On the other hand, they tend to exhibit a wide range of sub-optimalities that can be studied experimentally via computer simulations. Heterodox economists interested in policy formulation, whether in regard to racial segregation, class formation, poverty and income distribution or barriers to growth and technological change might well find agent-based models analytically suitable. It is one thing, for example, to build into a model unintended consequences to some policy or program, consequences foreseen by the analyst. It is quite another when the model itself generates unintended consequences on it own, surprising analyst and reader alike.

Conclusion

As the model of the previous section illustrates, the only way to avoid the problems of aggregation in macroeconomics is to start building the paradigm from the bottom up. Macroeconomics must become an "emergent property" of the micro, not a simple aggregation, but something surprising that was not obvious from inspection of the individual microeconomic elements. The microfoundations afforded by the agent-based approach provides a link between previously disembodied macroeconomic framework of analysis and the underlying heterogeneous and boundedly rational agents that populate the system. This framework can be calibrated empirically to given historical specific economies to ask questions about how policies might affect individual and thus aggregated outcomes.

The return to the scientific foundations of research methodology seems to be less about high theory than about better observations and in this regard, orthodox economics is a very different opponent from what it was in the 1960s and 1970s. A common criticism of the orthodoxy in the past was over-application of over-simplified theory. "Have model will travel," intended to imply that Paladin had no concern for the broader implications. Now the reverse seems to be true: with cleaner observations and more diverse, dare say heterodox theory, the scientific method is showing its true worth, at least when applied to small, well-defined problems. The challenge is to return to the bigger questions and this chapter has provided some suggestions for how that could be done.

The conflict between big and little questions is hardly confined to the arena of economics. There are many scientists who opposed the Superconducting Super Collider which was projected to cost more than 12 billion dollars before it was canceled by Congress in 1993 (Mervis and Seife (2003)). Just as many object to the space program and in particular to the International Space Station (ISS) as a colossal waste of money. The amount of real science that is accomplished on the ISS is minimal and there has been heavy criticism of it since it crowds out smaller projects.

Consider this from Steven Weinberg, a particle physicist at the University of Texas at Austin and a co-recipient of the 1979 Nobel Prize in physics:

> No important science has come out of it. I could almost say no science has come out of it. And I would go beyond that and say that the whole manned spaceflight program, which is so enormously expensive, has produced nothing of scientific value.

This is not just one opinion: in 1991, the American Physical Society issued a policy statement that "potential contribution of a manned space station to the physical sciences have been greatly overstated" (Klerkx (2004: 228)).[9]

Macroeconomics may have in the past escaped the surly bounds of science in order to pretend to answer the big questions. The rest of science, however, remains very dismal. To take a well-known example, string theory, an attempt in physics to reconcile the macro of relativity and micro of quantum theory, has been less than fully successful. An editorial in *Scientific American* recently referred to string theory as "recreational mathematical theology" while Woit (2006) argues that it is Not Even. Now that is failure on a grand scale.

Notes

1 January 2008; John Converse Professor of Economics, University of Vermont, Burlington, VT 045405 and Professor of Public Policy and Economics, University of Massachusetts, Amherst, MA 01003 USA 413–548–9448. wgibson@econs.umass.edu; http://people.umass.edu/wgibson. Thanks to Diane Flaherty and Jon Goldstein for comments on an earlier version of this paper.
2 See Debreu (1974). For an interpretation of SMD theory, see Rizvi (1994, 1997). Except under restrictive conditions, the aggregate excess demand function need not be downward sloping; it could take on any shape whatsoever. The long sought after link between micro and macroeconomics seemed to be permanently out of reach. Some writers barely acknowledged the rift and continued to assert the primacy of macro over micro for a variety of reasons. But for the bulk of the profession, the unification of macro and microeconomics had been mortally wounded by SMD.
3 For the counter-argument see Helland and Tabarrok (2004).
4 And, often unnecessary. See Smith and Pell (2002) for a satirical account of control group methodology.
5 See Levitt and Dubner (2005) and http://ideas.repec.org/e/ple59.html for a more complete list of topics.
6 Clean identification is not based on an assumed superiority of the rational model. Just as often, its studies reveal that fixed costs matter or that there is asymmetry of up- and down-side risk or that individuals contribute to public goods, vote or care about fairness when neoclassical theory suggests that they should not. The rational model is interrogated on many levels, theoretical with multiple-self configurations, experimentally and in numerical simulations of neurotransmission mechanisms and in neuroscience experiments with live subjects.

7 See for example Brock and Durlauf (2005), Durlauf and Young (2001) and Gatti *et al.* (2008).
8 It is appropriate that in silico here only simulates Latin and is not the real thing.
9 Certainly there can be no bigger issues than the sequencing of the human genome, our place in the universe and our ability to colonize other worlds for good or evil, but far more scientific activity is devoted to much smaller questions. Why? Because the small questions are answerable and the big ones may or many not be; and if they are, it will only be the result of the expenditure of vast sums of money, time and possibly careers. Moreover, big questions may in themselves undermine the scientific method in that results that necessarily involve massive expenditure are *ipso facto* difficult to replicate.

References

Bhaduri, A. and Marglin, S. (1990) "Unemployment and the real wage: the economic basis for contesting political ideologies," *Cambridge Journal of Economics*, 14(4): 375–93.

Bowles, S. and Heinz, J. (1996) "Wages and jobs in the South African economy: an econometric investigation." Department of Economics, University of Massachusetts.

Brock, W. A. and Durlauf, S. (2005) "Social interactions and macroeconomics." Available at www.ssc.wisc.edu/econ/archive/wp2005–05.pdf.

Choi, J.-K. and Bowles, S. (2007) "The co-evolution of parochial altruism and war," *Science*, 318(5850): 636–40.

Colander, D. (2003) "Post Walrasian macro policy and the economics of muddling through," *International Journal of Political Economy*, 33(2): 17–35.

Debreu, G. (1974) "Excess demand functions," *Journal of Mathematical Economics*, 1: 15–21.

Diamond, J. (1997) *Guns, Germs, and Steel: The Fates of Human Societies*. New York: W. W. Norton and Company.

—— (2005) *Collapse: How Societies Choose To Fail Or Succeed*. New York: Viking.

Donohue, J. J. and Levitt, S. D. (2001) "The impact of legalized abortion on crime," *The Quarterly Journal of Economics*, 116(2): 379–420.

Durlaf, S. N. and Young, H. P. (2001) *Social Dynamics, Volume 4 of Economic Learning and Social Evolution*. Cambridge, MA: MIT Press for the Brookings Institution.

Dutt, A. (2003) "On post Walrasian economics, macroeconomic policy and heterodox economics," *International Journal of Political Economy*, 33(2): 47–67.

Feynman, R. (1999) *The Pleasure of Finding Things Out*. Cambridge, MA: Perseus Books.

Foley, D. (2003) *Unholy Trinity: Labor, Capital and Land in the New Economy*. London and New York: Routledge.

Gatti, D. D., Gaffeo E., Gallegati, M., Giulioni, G. and Palestrini, A. (2008) *Emergent Macroeconomics*. Frankfurt: Springer.

Gibson, B. (2003) "Thinking outside the Walrasian box," *International Journal of Political Economy*, 33(2): 36–46.

—— (2007) "A multi-agent systems approach to microeconomic foundations of macro." University of Massachusetts, Department of Economics Working Paper series.

Helland, E. and Tabarrok, A. (2004) "Using placebo laws to test more guns, less crime," *Advances in Economic Analysis and Policy*, 4(1): 1–9.

Hoxby, C. (2000) "The effect of class size on student achievement: new evidence from population variation," *Quarterly Journal of Economics*, 115(4): 1239–85.

Jensen, D. and Lesser, V. (2002) "Social pathologies of adaptive agents," in M. Barley and H. Guesgen (eds.) *Safe Learning Agents: Papers from the 2002*. Menlo Park: AAAI Press.

Klerkx, G. (2004) *Lost in Space: The Fall of NASA and the Dream of a New Space Age*. New York: Pantheon.

Levitt, S. D. and Dubner, S. J. (2005) *Freakonomics: A Rogue Economist Explores the Hidden Side of Everything*. New York: HarperCollins.

Lott, J. (2000) *More Guns Less Crime*. Chicago: University of Chicago Press.

Lucas, R. E. (1976) "Econometric policy evaluation: a critique," *Carnegie-Rochester Conference Series on Public Policy*, 1(1): 19–46.

Lucas, R. E. and Sargent, T. J. (1978) "After Keynesian macroeconomics," in *After the Phillips Curve: Persistence of High Inflation and High Unemployment*, 49–72, Boston: Federal Reserve Bank.

Mervis, J. and Seife C. (2003) "10 years after the SSC: lots of reasons, but few lessons," *Science*, 3(October): 38–40.

Mosteller, F. (1995) "The Tennessee study of class size in the early school grades," *The Future of Children: Critical Issues for Children and Youths*, 5(2): 113–27.

Nattrass, N. (2000) *Macroeconomics: Theory and Policy in South Africa* (2nd edn). Cape Town: David Philip.

Rizvi, S. A. T. (1994) "The microfoundations project in general equilibrium theory," *Cambridge Journal of Economics*, 18: 357–77.

—— (1997) "Responses to arbitrariness in contemporary economics," *History of Political Economy*, 29(Supplement): 273–88.

Sandholm, T. W. and Lesser, V. R. (1997) "Coalitions among computationally bounded agents," *Artificial Intelligence*, 94(1–2): 99–137.

Scheiber, N. (2007) "Freaks and geeks: how freakonomics is ruining the dismal science," *The New Republic*: 27–31.

Schelling, T. (1971) "Dynamic models of segregation," *Journal of Mathematical Sociology*, 1(July): 143–86.

Smith, G. C. S. and Pell, J. P. (2003) "Parachute use to prevent death and major trauma related to gravitational challenge: systematic review of randomized controlled trials," *BMJ*, 327(7429): 1459–61.

Surowiecki, J. (2004) *Wisdom of Crowds*. New York: Doubleday.

Sutton, R. S. and Barto, A. G. (1998) *Reinforcement Learning*. Cambridge, MA and London: MIT Press.

Woit, P. (2006) *Not even Wrong: The Failure of String Theory and the Search for Unity in Physical Law*. New York: Basic Books.

Wooldridge, M. (2002) *MultiAgent Systems*. West Sussex: John Wiley and Sons.

Part II

Accumulation, crisis and instability

7 Modern business behavior

The theory of the active firm

Steven M. Fazzari

Suppose one were to ask the typical "person on the street:" which agents or institutions are the movers and shakers in modern capitalist economies? Most likely, business firms, perhaps in the form of the large corporation, would appear at the top of the list. Firms hire and fire. Firms set prices. Firms develop the technologies and invest in the capacity to transform labor into goods. Firms determine what consumers can buy. Yet, mainstream economic models present the firm as a remarkably passive agent. Macroeconomic theory, especially, usually portrays the firm as a technological automaton that mechanically spits out homogeneous final products from simplistic labor and capital inputs to maximize owners' profits.

In sharp contrast, an important part of heterodox research explores the behavior of firms as active economic entities. Firm management has interests and aspirations that exist independently from its anonymous owners. When making production decisions, these firms must assess demand fluctuations. As it makes technological and investment choice, the active firm must confront fundamental uncertainty that cannot be reduced to simplistic, objective probability distributions. The active firm provides the heartbeat of macroeconomic activity.

This chapter does not focus on all heterodox approaches to the active firm. Instead, it considers Crotty's conception of the firm by primarily focusing on two significant pieces of work. In 1990, Crotty published "Owner–Manager Conflict and Financial Theories of Investment: A Critical Assessment of Keynes, Tobin, and Minsky." This paper proposes a fundamental role of management, independent from owners, in the decision-making processes of modern firms. In a remarkable 1994 essay, "Are Keynesian Uncertainty and Macrotheory Compatible? Conventional Decision Making, Institutional Structures, and Conditional Stability in Keynesian Macromodels," Crotty develops the theme of fundamental uncertainty and how firms respond to it. While these papers explore a broad range of issues, this chapter focuses on their contributions to an active theory of the firm as the basis for macroeconomic analysis.

Passive vs. active firms in the microfoundations of macro

It seems obvious that firms are the engine of modern economic activity in developed countries. Virtually all members of the labor force work for a firm.

Large corporate institutions clearly sit at the pinnacle of economic power, and wield enormous influence in the halls of government. But in neoclassical theory, especially in the much-discussed "microfoundations" of macroeconomics, the institutional complexity and behavioral autonomy of the firm is almost completely absent. In the typical model, the perfectly competitive representative firm passively maximizes profits. The firm is a mere repository of the technology for transforming inputs into output, and that technology is usually independent of any action of the firm or its managers.[1]

Why does mainstream theory rely on such a passive concept of the firm? A partial answer comes from the focus of neoclassical theory on the *allocation* of resources rather than the *creation* of economic activity. The competitive general equilibrium model that provides the foundation for neoclassical theory begins from the problem of allocating pre-existing resources to isolated consumers with exogenous preferences. Graduate courses in advanced theory begin (and sometimes end) with models of "exchange economies" with no production at all. While such models are obviously simple abstractions that are just the starting point for theory, their place at the foundation of neoclassical thinking suggests that they capture the essence of the phenomena that the theory is designed to illuminate. That is, we can start our analysis of modern capitalism by abstracting from production completely. When the time comes to introduce production, the objective is to do so with as little additional theoretical structure as possible. Thus, the theory posits the firm as simply a mathematical entity that maps inputs into outputs, maintaining the idea that the primary economic action is allocation of given resources (now in the form of inputs) to satisfy competing consumer preferences. Indeed, in many macro models with production, the firm has disappeared all together. The "Robinson Crusoe" representative consumer is simply endowed with the production technology. Crotty (1992: 483) identifies this approach as "ideological" based on what Schumpeter would call a "pre-analytic Vision" of a "theory of how markets efficiently coordinate the decisions of atomized agents."

Crotty's papers present a strikingly different concept. Writing about Keynes' view of economic agents he says (1994: 111):

> The economic outcomes we observe over time ... are generated by an ever-changing system of agents, agent preferences, expectations, and economic, political, and social institutions, a system of "originative" choice in which future states of the world are in part created by the current agent choice process itself.

This conception contrasts sharply with the mainstream neoclassical approach (p. 119) in which: "agents are ... autonomously constituted, lifeless Walrasian calculating machines."

These observations about agents in general apply especially to firms. Crotty's firms are complex social institutions that actively create economic outcomes. Their behaviors are rich and their decisions fundamentally strategic. Crotty and

Goldstein (1992) lay out several key properties that distinguish modern firms from the passive model usually employed in mainstream macro models:

- Firms operate in an environment of true uncertainty in which the information about key future variables (or their probability distributions) cannot be known.
- Firm managers' objectives differ from those of the firm's owners. Managers make strategic decisions subject to constraints imposed by ownership (dividend payments, for example). Specifically, managers seek the long-term financial viability of the firm.
- The largely irreversible capital investment decision and its financing are critical strategic choices that create the path of the firms' futures.

Although Crotty clearly draws heavily on Keynes, he explicitly distances his theory of the firm from Keynes in the 1990 paper. In Keynes' investment theory, the dominant role of asset markets implies that owners drive investment decisions. Crotty argues, however, that there is no strong basis in Keynes' theory for this assumption. Why should owners' interests in short-term gains in volatile asset markets dominate managers' objective to sustain the firm's long-term viability? Keynes fears that the short-term speculative motives of firm owners will overcome the "enterprise" of managers that reflect a longer horizon. Crotty has more confidence in the ability of management to assert its control: "enterprise management will always have more complete and higher-quality information about those variables that determine the expected profitability of a prospective capital investment than even the best-informed stockholders, never mind Keynes' 'ignorant individuals'" (1990: 535). By imposing its interest in long-run viability, Crotty clearly raises the status of the firm as an autonomous institution, not simply a repository of technology acting as a lapdog for shareholders.

Has the ability of the managerial class to control firm decision-making decreased in recent years? The answer is probably, to some extent, yes. From a theoretical point of view, mainstream finance and industrial organization have encouraged greater shareholder control to overcome so-called "agency problems." Crotty would likely classify these developments as ideological for similar reasons that he attributes this label to the basic passive theory of the firm found in most mainstream macro models. In neoclassical theory, a more owner-responsive firm seems a better profit maximizer and hence seems closer to the neoclassical ideal of efficiency and optimality. But this welfare criterion is exceedingly narrow, and it assumes that the true social role of the firm is as a passive technological repository. Are firms that bend more easily to shareholders' short-term interests really better at promoting social welfare? A detailed answer lies outside the scope of this chapter but there are clearly reasons to doubt that the answer is yes. Excessive catering to the short-term horizon of outside investors may reduce profits in the long run, a reflection of Keynes' speculation versus enterprise insight. Modern corporate strategies designed to please shareholders also threaten employment and long-run connections between workers and employers, with negative social consequences. The evolution of finance, particularly the emergence of the leveraged buyout and private equity strategies have likely reduced managerial control, which, according to the Crotty perspective, likely elevates short-term returns over long-run stability and viability. The result could easily be an industrial structure that serves society less well.[2]

Perhaps an even more important aspect of the Crotty firm is its location in an environment of fundamental uncertainty. This requires an active conception of the firm because it must make strategic decisions when much relevant information is simply unknowable. In Crotty (1994), following Keynes again, he argues "that the future is *unknowable in principle*" (p. 111, emphasis in original). Why should this be the case? It is exactly because economic agents, firms in particular, are indeed active, that is, their decisions and strategies shape the future:

> the economic outcomes we observe over time, [Keynes] argued, are generated by an every-changing system of agents, agent preferences, expectations, and economic, political, and social institutions, a system of "originative" choice in which future states of the world are in part created by the agent choice process itself.
>
> (p. 111)

Some researchers have rejected fundamental uncertainty on the basis that it is a dead-end for economic theory. If agents can't "know" future probability distributions, how can theorists model their behavior in contexts where current actions have future consequences? Crotty rejects this view and proposes a rich theory of expectation formation and decision-making under fundamental uncertainty. His core idea, taken from Keynes but developed significantly, is the concept of convention. Agents know they cannot obtain or infer information about the true probability distributions they face (indeed, these distributions probably do not exist in any meaningful sense), but they assume the future will be more or less like the recent past in the absence of any compelling information to the contrary. One reason is that normal experience supports this behavioral rule much of the time, perhaps as a kind of self-confirming equilibrium: if agents believe the future will be similar to the recent past they will take actions that typically reproduce the conventional outcome. Although this interpretation is not taken directly from Crotty's writing, it has support in his concept of "conditional stability." Crotty (1992: 487) writes that "conventional decision making creates a significant degree of continuity, order, and conditional stability in a Keynesian model in spite of the potential for chaos and perpetual instability seemingly inherent in the assumption of true uncertainty" and (1994: 116) that "history demonstrates that capitalist economies move through time with a substantial degree of order and continuity that is disrupted only on occasion by burst of disorderly and discontinuous change." Most of the time, therefore, conventional expectations are confirmed by experience.

Complementary support for conventional expectations arises from humans' deep-seated desire for control. Uncertainty may be ubiquitous, but it is also discomforting. Although Crotty sharply criticizes the mainstream assumption that firms make decisions with the knowledge of objective probability distributions, he writes (1994: 120), somewhat ironically, that

> people want to believe that they are in the same position in which economists place neoclassical agents, with all the information required to make optimal choices.... Keynes tells us that we have a psychological need to calm our anxieties, to remove the constant stress created by forced decision making under inadequate information, a need that is neither irrational nor socially or economically dysfunctional.

In the context of firms, human managers convince themselves of the relevance of conventional expectations as a kind of defense mechanism against the nagging insecurity of uncertainty. In addition, convention acquires a *social* reinforcement. In the absence of objective information about how to behave, agents refer to others in their social reference groups, a kind of psychological law of large numbers.[3] Such behavior likely imbues convention with more weight of truthfulness than it objectively deserves. Think about the perception of perpetually rising energy prices in the late 1970s or the sense that home prices in the early and mid 2000s could never fall. Rousseau said "the mind decides in one way or another, despite itself, and prefers being mistaken to believing in nothing."[4]

While agents follow convention in forming expectations and experience often confirms them, conventions can and do fail. Such failure may be unusual, but it is among the most significant of macroeconomic events. Conventional expectations are not based on objective reality that is independent of human perception. The very fact that active agents make creative, originative choices implies that things will happen that could not, even in principle, have been forecast ahead of time. While sudden change may occur in either direction, periods of "crisis" receive the most attention for macro purposes. Crotty (1992: 487) writes that "at such times, confidence in the meaningfulness of the forecasting process will shatter, and key behavioral equations may become extremely unstable."

These observations imply the presence of a rich, autonomous set of firm behaviors to navigate a world of uncertainty. Crotty (1994: 119) expresses the idea exceptionally well: "agents are socially and endogenously constituted human beings.... The theory of agent choice, therefore, must reflect both the social constitution of the agent ... as well as the psychological complexity of the human-being-in-society." In this role, firms actively create economic outcomes. These are the firms the person on the street can identify with, not the passive "Walrasian calculating machines." The contrast with a mainstream view comes into sharper focus with an analogy to geology. The earth is a complex system. Interesting, unpredictable, even chaotic phenomena happen as one set of geologic forces raise mountains while others wear them down. But, absent the active intervention of a deity, there is no "will" or "agency" in these forces. The neoclassical approach, with all its formal complexity, can generate a wide variety of outcomes. But the models reduce human agency to the analog of impersonal geologic forces. Crotty's vision of human agency, particularly applied to the locus of production in the modern firm, is qualitatively different. We now apply this conception of the active firm in two contexts: production and capital investment.

The firm and demand: production in a Keynesian economy

Firms choose production levels and firms hire works. Thus, firms make the decisions that, in the most simple and direct sense, provide the microfoundations for macroeconomic outcomes that drive the business cycle. In mainstream macro, the production choices by passive firms are exceedingly dull. Under perfect competition, exogenous technology and the pre-determined capital stock *entirely determine* production and the demand for labor. The sale of output poses no constraint at prices set independently of firm behavior. Given technology and the assumption of profit maximization, there is not much else to say about firm behavior.

This hollow caricature seems an inadequate depiction of the modern firm, especially when it faces the uncertainty identified in Crotty's research. The firm cannot assume that it can sell all it wants at the prevailing price level (with perhaps the exception of corn farmers in Iowa or similarly situated small producers of homogeneous commodities that constitute a trivial portion of modern capitalism in developed countries). The firm must forecast demand and make strategic production, employment and inventory choices (we consider investment in productive capacity in the next section). I argue that expected sales is the most important factor that determines a firm's short-term production choices, dominating the variables that get top billing in neoclassical models, such as the relative price of labor. It seems obvious that the central problem firms face in a deep recession is an involuntary constraint on the ability to sell what they could produce, not that the real wage has risen inducing simplistic "Walrasian calculating machines" to voluntarily reduce output and employment.[5] But to forecast demand, adjust employment strategically, assess the risks of excess inventory in a downturn or stockouts in a boom, etc. requires an active management. Management must form expectations and therefore the willful behavior of real human beings provides the "microfoundation" of production.

These observations suggest an active conception of firm behavior, rooted in managerial choice with fundamental uncertainty, lies behind Keynesian macro. I know of no systematic empirical evidence that is directly relevant to assessing the relevance of active behaviors in contrast to the passive and mechanical technical response of the "representative firm" in most mainstream macro. The absence of tests may reflect the utterly obvious fact that firms adjust production in response to sales expectations. Are firms responding to rapid and uncertain developments in detailed markets or are they mechanically setting the real wage equal to the marginal product of labor? My intuition strongly suggests the former alternative, and I believe that vision of the production decisions flows from Crotty's conception of the firm. But further research should take the radical step of *asking* firms how they make production choices over the business cycle.

Investment with fundamental uncertainty

Crotty (1990: 534) writes that the "capital investment decision will be considered to be of the utmost importance by management because it is the most important, most risky, and least reversible influence on the intermediate and long-term prosperity of the enterprise." Capital investment, including long-term development of technology through R&D, is the foundation for the long-term viability of the firm. With fundamental uncertainty, the active character of firms' investment behavior again contrasts strongly with conventional views. Neoclassical models of investment assume that firms know future probability distributions over all possible outcomes (or that firms have perfect foresight). The resulting theory depicts investment decisions as a mechanical optimization problem of matching dynamic marginal productivity with the "user cost" of capital and (unobservable) marginal adjustment costs. Might firms, for example, adjust investment in response to a new investment tax credit? Perhaps yes, especially the timing of their investment around a tax change. But this kind of decision-making, representative of the typical issue illuminated by neoclassical theory, seems far removed from the strategic decisions taken by firms as conceptualized in Crotty's work.

The active firm facing uncertainty must both imagine a set of strategies it might pursue and then probe the space of imagined possibilities to find, if possible, a configuration of capital that generates profit. Some things work out, others don't. Some things might work for a while in a given environment, and therefore be expanded and copied. But when the environment shifts, the strategy could ultimately fail. Consider for example, investment in energy extraction during the late 1970s when conventional wisdom predicted rising oil prices as far as the eye could see. For a few years, such investments seemed like they "couldn't miss," but the world changed in unforeseen ways, and the expectational convention shattered. As another example, during the years prior to 2007, the conventional expectations in the mortgage lending industry held that home prices would continue to rise and refinancing terms would remain easy. In this environment the lending revolution proceeded, raising household lending until it may well be reaching a breaking point as of this writing. Were the conventional expectations that housing prices would keep rising indefinitely ever realistic? Probably not, but they became convention, and firms making residential construction and mortgage-lending decisions, could not see the systemic problems coming.[6] Crotty writes (1994: 125): "From time to time events take place that will make it impossible to sustain the convention that the future will look like the present extrapolated."

This perspective applies to the link between investment and finance.[7] Neoclassical investment theory through at least the early 1980s, epitomized the passive firm in the realm of capital investment: firms invest when the marginal product of capital exceeds the Jorgensonian user cost. The theory again focuses solely on relative prices and technology. When one considers Crotty's managerial perspective for firm behavior, however, the story changes. External finance raises investment possibilities but threatens managerial autonomy. With fundamental uncertainty, the long-term viability of the firm becomes subject to risks of bankruptcy or shareholder revolt that cannot be known in advance, even probabilistically. For this reason, external finance cannot be a perfect substitute for internal cash flow, as it would be in the Modigliani–Miller world. The financing decision therefore cannot be passive, indeed it is among the most important strategic decisions that management must take. Again, rather than simply mechanistically transforming inputs into outputs with the "optimal" capital structure, the human agency of firm managers actively creates the future as new activities are pursued and financial commitments are established.

The decision to seek and accept external financing confronts management with a significant tradeoff that could easily dominate the technological–relative price tradeoff of neoclassical theory, and that places finance at center stage for the active firm. Crotty and Goldstein write that when

> the firm is in a financially precarious position, management responds to the threat to its decision-making autonomy by placing more weight on financial security relative to growth and, therefore, is less willing to undertake inherently risky investment projects. *Financial fragility constrains investment.*
>
> (1992: 5, emphasis in original)

This perspective obviously applies to firms that face financial setbacks, for example, when a recession curtails funds available to service debt. But the tradeoff also impinges on a successful, growing firm as its managers contemplate the value of growth versus the control that they must sacrifice to lenders or new shareholders to obtain external funds. The way in which firm managers facing fundamental uncertainty navigate the risks of external finance compared to the growth potential new funds provide is far from mechanistic and passive. These choices depend on expectations and confidence that constitute a central and autonomous behavioral component of modern capitalism.

It is not just the decision to take on external finance for investment that poses a challenge to the modern firm. Firms must also confront the terms on which they can obtain finance, if they can get it at all. That is, firms face financing constraints. This idea has become more common in mainstream analysis over the past 25 years, particularly due to the attention given to asymmetric information in credit markets (see Fazzari and Variato 1994). As such, the mainstream has moved some distance away from the passive firm model. When a firm cannot finance all investment projects with positive net present value the firm's internal structure and history, such as its reputation and collateral value, affect its access to finance and the firm becomes more than just a repository of technology. This progress, however, still leaves a big theoretical gap with the active

Crotty firm. The firms modeled in asymmetric information-financing constraint models are more interesting than the technological automatons of earlier neoclassical models. But these models typically assume that firms and lenders know the probability distribution of investment returns. They do not recognize the psychological nuances of human agency, indeed agent behaviors assumed in these models could be programmed into a computer! The mainstream has yet to understand how seeking finance and managing the tradeoff between expansion and threats to viability and control risk is a key creative activity of the active firm.

There is extensive empirical evidence to support the view that finance matters for investment (recent work is summarized by Brown *et al.* (2009)), but this evidence is not particularly useful in distinguishing the channels through which financial effects operate. The widespread evidence that internal cash flow affects investment spending, even controlling for profit expectations, rejects the passive financial neutrality of Modigliani–Miller. In the mainstream, these results are taken to support the presence of external financing constraints due to asymmetric information and agency problems that drive a wedge between the opportunity cost of internal funds and the explicit cost of external finance. But cash flow effects on investment could just as well signal management's drive to maintain control of firm activities.

Another prominent feature of empirical research on investment and finance is "heterogeneity:" financial effects appear to be stronger for firms that are a priori more likely to face external financial constraints. For example, small or young firms have larger cash flow effects on investment than large or mature firms. These findings do not imply the absence of managerial control considerations. It is certainly possible that internal control effects co-exist with external financing constraints. Future research, however, might refine our understanding of this issue. For example, how are investment and finance related across large, mature firms, with supposedly easy access to external finance, that face different degrees of takeover threat? One might also study the effect of uncertainty per se on investment. The Crotty firm should invest less when conventional wisdom is in turmoil and confidence in forecasts is low. It is tricky to measure the degree of uncertainty, but creative research along these lines could deepen our understanding. Crotty and Goldstein (1992) offer an interesting contribution along these lines by showing that greater competitive pressure (measured by the degree of import penetration), which should threaten managerial control and long-term firm viability, increases investment even after controlling for measures of profitability. More work along these lines, particularly with micro data, will be welcome.

The active behavior of firms: a "missing link" in neoclassical theory

In modern capitalism, the firm matters as a human institution, with complex behaviors deriving from the way its managers respond to inherent uncertainty. Crotty (1994: 121) writes:

> In place of the complete information appropriate to the fairy-tale world of neoclassical agent choice, Keynes substitutes an expectations formation and decision-making process based on custom, habit, tradition, instinct, and other socially constituted practices that make sense only in a model of human agency in an environment of genuine uncertainty.

The managers of firms make production and investment decisions in an effort to preserve and expand the institutions that provide their livelihoods. Economists need to understand the nuances of firm behavior by exploring the psychological motivations of "human agents" situated in a fundamentally social and fundamentally uncertain environment. The active behavior of firms cannot be deduced from the simple constrained maximization problems of neoclassical theory. We need empirically based behavioral models to make sense out of firm choices and to lay the foundation for macro-dynamic theory.

Recent contributions to "behavioral economics" have begun to peek into how real people behave in economic settings. This work is interesting, but has not yet offered much to reveal the motivation of modern firms, the central characters in the capitalist economic play. These are the behaviors that create the modern economy and macroeconomics emerges from their aggregation. This style of macroeconomics largely eludes the mainstream, but the research of James Crotty has confronted these issues directly, illuminating a rich perspective on firm behavior, and its macroeconomic implications, long before the recent wave of behavioral ideas became popular in conventional departments of economics. Nearly 15 years ago, Crotty (1994: 131) wrote that:

> Keynes's stress on the humanity of the agent suggests the use of observational and experimental methods for the study of the psychology of individual and group decision-making, and his work on conventional expectations formation calls for the legitimation of institutional, sociological, psychological, historical and survey research methodology as complements to the traditional deductive logic of economic theory.

Crotty was ahead of his time and we hope to see this vision realized.

Notes

1 This description of mainstream theory is admittedly somewhat limited. Industrial organization models, for example, often emphasize "agency problems" and endogenous growth models consider the evolution of technology. Due to space limitations, I will not consider these models further here. Crotty (1990) discusses the relation between his concept of the firm and neoclassical models with agency problems.

2 These comments probably apply primarily to the large corporations of monopoly capitalism. The ability to start small enterprise possibly has been enhanced by the evolution of financial markets, particularly the availability of new sources of external equity finance. See Brown *et al.* (2009) for further discussion.

3 Akerlof (2007) relates firm behavior to social norms. The extensive role of social influence on consumption and household debt is developed by Cynamon and Fazzari (2008) who provide extensive further references.

4 Quoted by Mark Lilla in "The Politics of God," *New York Times Magazine*, August 19, 2007.
5 See Fazzari *et al.* (1998) for a more detailed discussion of this point, albeit in a static setting without fundamental uncertainty.
6 Of course, the same point applies to the borrowing households, see Cynamon and Fazzari (2008).
7 Aspects of this topic were the subject of a published interchange in Crotty (1996) and Fazzari and Variato (1996).

References

Akerlof, G. A. (2007) "The Missing Motivation in Macroeconomics," *The American Economic Review*, 97: 15–36.

Brown, J. R., Fazzari, S. M. and Petersen, B. C. (2009) "Financing Innovation and Growth: Cash Flow, External Equity and the 1990s R&D Boom," *Journal of Finance*, 64: 151–86.

Crotty, J. R. (1990) "Owner-Manager Conflict and Financial Theories of Investment Instability: A Critical Assessment of Keynes, Tobin, and Minsky," *Journal of Post Keynesian Economics*, 12: 519–42.

—— (1992) "Neoclassical and Keynesian Approaches to the Theory of Investment," *Journal of Post Keynesian Economics*, 14: 483–96.

—— (1994) "Are Keynesian Uncertainty and Macrotheory Compatible? Conventional Decision Making, Institutional Structures, and Conditional Stability in Keynesian Macromodels," in G. Dymski and R. Pollin (eds.) *New Perspectives in Monetary Macroeconomics: Explorations in the Tradition of Hyman Minsky*, 105–42, Ann Arbor: University of Michigan Press.

—— (1996) "Is the New Keynesian Theory of Investment Really Keynesian?" *Journal of Post Keynesian Economics*, 18: 335–57.

Crotty, J. R. and Goldstein, J. (1992) "The Impact of Profitability, Financial Fragility and Competitive Regime Shifts on Investment Demand: Empirical Evidence," Working Paper No. 81, Levy Economics Institute.

Cynamon, B. Z. and Fazzari, S. M. (2008) "Household Debt in the Consumer Age: Source of Growth–Risk of Collapse," *Capitalism and Society*, 3: 2, Article 3. Available at: www.bepress.com/cas/vol3/issz/art3.

Fazzari, S. M. and Variato A. M. (1994) "Asymmetric Information and Keynesian Theories of Investment," *Journal of Post Keynesian Economics*, 16: 351–69.

—— (1996) "Varieties of Keynesian Investment Theories: Further Reflections," *Journal of Post Keynesian Economics*, 18: 359–68.

Fazzari, S. M., Ferri, P. E. and Greenberg, E. D. (1998) "Aggregate Demand and Micro Behavior: A New Perspective on Keynesian Macroeconomics," *Journal of Post Keynesian Economics*, 20: 527–58.

8 A Keynes–Marx theory of investment

Jonathan P. Goldstein

Introduction

The theory of investment lies at the center of an integrated heterodox macro model.[1] Yet, heterodox theories of investment have not advanced beyond simplistic expressions of the investment function. In particular, Keynesian investment functions have focused on capacity utilization as the primary determinant of investment, while Marxian approaches have concentrated on the profit rate. These simplistic theories are inadequate for understanding the complex macro-economic dynamics of the capitalist growth process in the era of the Neoliberal regime. Thus, the purpose of this chapter is to extend the basic theory of investment in order to better explain the macro dynamics of the global economy.

Based on the work of Crotty (1993) and Crotty and Goldstein (1992a, 1992b, 1992c), I develop a microfoundation for the firm's investment decision. This theory integrates both Keynesian and Marxian insights in order to produce a more flexible and realistic investment function. In particular, the theory further incorporates the external financing of investment based upon uncertain future profit flows, the irreversibility of investment, and the coercive role of competition on investment. The investment function is extended to depend on the profit rate, long-term and short-term heuristics for the firm's financial robustness and the intensity of competition. The interaction of these factors fundamentally alters the nature of the investment function, particularly the typical role assigned to capacity utilization.[2]

This chapter is organized in the following manner. In the first section, I present an overview of the model. This is followed by sections on the details of the model, the optimal investment strategy, and a constrained version of the model that highlights the crucial Marxian competition effect. The final section elaborates how the theory is useful for understanding the macro dynamics of the Neoliberal regime.

Model overview

In this section, I outline a Keynesian–Marxian theory of the firm's investment decision. The Keynesian aspects of the model include true/Keynesian uncertainty and the possibility of financially fragile outcomes in such an environment, the illiquid nature of capital, endogenous expectations and preferences, and the potential for misaligned interests between firm management and shareholder/owners and creditors. The Marxian attributes include the Marxian competitive environment, as distinct from the neoclassical concept of competition, including critical regime shifts in the form of competition, transitions between different modes of accumulation, the imperative to accumulate capital through the progressive maximization of surplus value/profits and endogenous expectations and preferences.

It is assumed that managers control the firm subject to constraints made on their decision-making autonomy by owners and finance capitalists. Managers pursue the objectives of the growth and financial safety of the firm and in doing so maximize their own goals (utility). Within both of these objectives are constraints imposed by owners and creditors in the form of dividends, interest payments[3] and the expectation of continued credit-worthiness. Failure to meet historically determined marks for these categories can possibly set off stockholder revolts, bankruptcy proceedings or creditor interference[4] with firm decision-making.

The Marxian competitive environment emphasizes the importance of the growth objective of the firm and at times acts as an additional constraint on the firm's investment strategy. For Marx, competition was a coercive force that compelled individual capitalists to continually investment as a survival strategy.[5] Thus, growth is essential to reproduction. Here, competition has anarchic and war-like attributes that force firms to take an offensive position with respect to investment as a means of generating enough profit to ultimately defend the firm from competitive onslaughts in the form of innovation by competitors. Firms that have ineffective investment strategies or do not keep pace with competitors are either marginalized or fail. Thus, competition can create an "invest or die" situation for the firm.[6] When competition intensifies to this point, investment must become defensive by focusing on new cost-cutting production methods as a means of shoring up the firm's market share. In this defensive situation, investment acts as an overarching constraint on the firm that trumps the constraints imposed by shareholders and creditors.[7] In this manner, competition-induced defensive investment can become an imperative that must be undertaken despite its impacts on the financial position of the firm. In this coerced situation, a competitive criteria – the imperative to revive the firm's competitive position irrespective of its consistency with other firm objectives – dominates.[8] In addition, regime shifts between two forms of competition (co-respective and coercive) can be used to explain transitions in investment behavior from an offensive form (widening of capital) to a defensive form (deepening of capital).

While investment in either of its forms is an imperative of the firm, a successful firm in a cyclically unstable environment, predicted by Marxian crisis theory, must also know when not to invest. Profit squeeze or under-consumption crises that periodically result in declining aggregate demand must be forecasted as best as possible in an uncertain environment. New investment mistakenly undertaken in such circumstances is likely to further exacerbate the firm's profit and cash flow positions and increase the likelihood of not meeting debt obligations and earnings expectations. Thus, investment, while necessary, is also risky. In addition, investment can also be mandatory (a competitive criteria dominates) and thus it can induce further reliance on debt at inopportune times or the generation of further excess capacity.

The incorporation of Keynesian uncertainty, irreversible investment and a dependency on external finance adds a new and deeper dimension to the potential financial fragility associated with investment. In such an environment, finance can both enhance and impinge on capital accumulation. With external finance, firms take on certain debt obligations that are to be paid from uncertain future profit flows without the cushion of being able to effectively sell capital assets when profit expectations are disappointed. It is this risk of reductions in the firm's financial security and as a result its decision-making autonomy that underlies an investment-induced growth–safety tradeoff. The severity of the firm's financial difficulties can also lead to a change in management's relative preferences for its growth and safety objectives. In periods of financial crisis, the firm is likely to shift its focus to solving security problems. In the case where the competitive constraint on the firm's behavior is binding, preferences are shifted back to growth based on an investment-induced cost-cutting strategy irrespective of the firm's financial condition.

In light of the model's main attributes and the firm's operating environment, the firm's optimization problem can be specified. Managers maximize a utility function, O, that is a function of the growth, G, and safety, S, objectives of the firm subject to a competitive constraint on the firm's market share, M, by choosing an optimal investment strategy from two forms of investment – offensive investment, I, and defensive investment, I^D. Thus, the firm's optimization problem is

Maximize

$$O[G(I, I^D), S(I, I^D)] \tag{1a}$$

subject to

$$M(I^D) \geq M^* \tag{1b}$$

where M^* is a critical market share level below which the firm must undertake defensive investment in order to shore up its competitive position for long-run survival.[9]

Two aspects of the model require clarification. First, the model is static, while standard investment models are dynamic. Second there exists a dichotomy in the implementation of the two investment strategies. If the competitive constraint is non-binding, the firm only uses I, offensive investment – the expansion of output via investment that replicates the existing technology or makes minor improvements in technology. When the competitive constraint is binding, the firm solely relies on I^D which constitutes investment in new cost-cutting technology.

Under a realistic set of three assumptions that are consistent with the Keynesian–Marxian environment elaborated above and a specification of the S function that includes both short-term and long-term security concerns, it can readily be shown that the firm's dynamic optimization problem reduces to the problem specified in Equations 1a and 1b.[10]

The dichotomy in the implementation of the two forms of investment is justified by the disruptive nature of defensive investment. An I^D strategy is both dangerous and costly. It might entail a disastrous confrontation with labor and tension between management and short-sighted shareholders and has enormous "costs of adjustment" that are proportional to the level of I^D such that it will never appear to be optimal over an intermediate-length investment horizon. However, when competitive pressure threatens long-term survival, the firm has no choice but to adopt an I^D strategy and absorb the costs in the short-run – the competitive criteria dominates the profit or O maximization objective.

Model details

I keep the level of model detail to the minimum necessary to lay bare the fundamental workings of the model. Full details of model components are contained in Crotty and Goldstein (1992c) and in an appendix available upon request from the author.

The growth objectives of the firm depend on the present value of expected future earnings designated as R – expected net revenues. R depends on the pattern of expected future demand and cost conditions and the present value of debt and dividend payments. The firm's price-cost markup, α, is an important index of how demand and cost factors influence R.

A fuller specification of the R function: demand and cost structures, financing mechanisms and the firm's dividend policy is contained in the above referenced appendix. Here, I briefly touch on demand and cost conditions.

I assume a fixed-coefficient, constant variable cost production function and a downward-sloping demand curve: $Q = Q(I, I^D; K, K^D)$, $P = P(Q(I, I^D; K, K^D))$ and $U = \bar{U}$ where Q is output, P is expected output price, U is expected variable cost, $\bar{U}$ is a constant, K and K^D are the initial levels of offensive and defensive capital stocks and the relations between K and I and K^D and I^D are implicitly incorporated.[11] I further assume that $P_Q < 0$ and $P_{QQ} \leq 0$ where subscripts denote partial derivatives. Integrating the firm's price-variable cost markup (α), gross profits, π, can be expressed as $\pi(I, I^D) = \alpha(I, I^D) Q(I, I^D)$ where $\alpha = (P - U)$.[12] This implies that R, which is a function of π, depends on α.

Explicitly considering the role of international competition on market shares, $Q = M(I^D, P; P^F) Q^W(P; P^F, Y^W)$ where P^F is the foreign competitor's price, Q^W is a world demand curve and Y^W is a world demand shift parameter, such as world GDP. Thus, the firm has a share (M) of the world demand curve. The incorporation of international competition in this manner does not necessitate any change in our demand curve assumptions.[13]

In order to capture both the short-term and long-term aspects of the firm's financial security, the S function is comprised of two security sub-goals. In the current period, the firm can lessen impingements on its decision-making autonomy by maintaining a comfortable margin between its expected gross profits, π, and x defined as the interest plus dividend payments necessary to preserve managerial autonomy. Given the uncertain nature of π, there exists an expected probability distribution of π, conditional on the current level of the two distinct capital stocks, defined as f. Thus, the perceived likelihood of an autonomy crisis is given by F, the cumulative probability that $\pi < x$. It should also be recognized that $R \equiv \pi - x$.[14]

Given the static treatment of the investment decision, it is necessary to ensure that the firm also considers its long-run financial position. I define D' as an index of the firm's current perception of its long-term financial vulnerability. In particular, $D' = (D - \hat{D})$, where D is the current level of debt and $\hat{D}$ is the maximum debt level that management is comfortable carrying into its uncertain future based on conjunctional expectations of financial institutions. The inclusion of D' in S forces the firm's current investment decision to be consistent with its long-term safety objective. Both F and $\hat{D}$ reflect managerial optimism or pessimism over short and long periods and both can shift endogenously as optimism and confidence in forecasts ebb and flow. The use of a conventional, rule-of-thumb variable such as $\hat{D}$ constitutes a very Keynesian solution to this long-term aspect of the uncertainty problem (Crotty 1994). Integrating these two security sub-goals, the security function takes the following form: $S(F(I, I^D), D'(I, I^D))$.

Finally, the firm's market share constraint can be written as $M(P^F - \alpha U(I^D)) \geq M^*$ where P^F is the price of competing foreign goods, and $P = \alpha U$. The firm's market share depends on its output price relative to competitors' prices and only the I^D form of investment can lower unit cost.

Key parameters of the model that are revealed in current and more detailed specifications of the above functions include: the firm's mark-up, the initial levels of both types of capital stock, the mean and variance of the firm's subjective probability distribution for π and the form of that distribution, initial debt levels, the maximum acceptable debt level, the price of capital, the price of competing foreign goods, the firm's target market share, the interest rate, the dividend payout rate and a constant rate of depreciation.

Given this partial detail, the firm's optimization problem can be rewritten as:

maximize

$$O[G(R(I, I^D;P^F)), S(F(I, I^D), D'(I, I^D))] \qquad (2a)$$

subject to

$$M(P^F - \alpha U(I^D)) \geq M^* \qquad (2b)$$

Given the dichotomous treatment of I and I^D strategies, I first examine the firm's optimal decision for the case where the market share constraint is not binding.

Thus, I explore the firm's offensive investment strategy. The case where the constraint binds when coercive competition forces a transition to a defensive investment strategy – the Marxian competition effect – is subsequently analyzed.

The optimal investment strategy

At the heart of the unconstrained model is an investment-induced G–S tradeoff. The G–S tradeoff is best understood by examining $G_I = G_R R_I$ and $S_I = S_F F_I + S_{D'} D'_I$ where $G_R > 0$, $S_F < 0$ and $S_{D'} < 0$ are preference weights for the R, F and D' sub-objectives.

The sign indeterminacy of F_I and thus S_I imply that the nature of the G-S tradeoff is undetermined.[15] However, it is shown in an available appendix that the first order conditions for (2) and the assumptions that $P_Q < 0$ and $P_{QQ} \leq 0$, restrict $S_I < 0$ and $G_I > 0$ in the neighborhood of equilibrium: an investment-induced G–S tradeoff is operational. The mechanics of the tradeoff are straightforward. A one unit increase in I increases G, and thus utility, through an increase in net revenues as security concerns force the firm to under-invest in general ($PDV > 0$ compared to conventional solutions where $PDV = 0$). At the same time, marginal I decreases S either through a simultaneous increase in the probability of short-term financial strife ($R_I < 0$) and long-term debt dependency or an increase in long-term debt dependency that outweighs, in utility units, the decline in F ($R_I > 0$).

The dependence of O in Equation (2a) on multiple objectives (G and S) and sub-objectives (R, F and D') requires that management's relative subjective ranking of these objectives and sub-objectives be made explicit. For simplicity, it is assumed that S and G are linear in their arguments: $S_{FF} = S_{D'D'} = S_{FD'} = G_{RR} = 0$. In Keynesian and Marxian traditions, the relative preference ordering for G and S is variable and thus endogenous. It is assumed that $O_{GG} = O_{GS} = 0$, while $O_{SS} < 0$: the firm's imperative to grow is a constant unyielding commitment that is independent of the size of the firm, while the firm's response to financial security, and uncertainty is variable. At lower levels of financial security, management responds by choosing an investment/debt strategy which focuses on restoring financial security even at the expense of maintaining or promoting the firm's growth objective. A financially fragile firm will sacrifice potential growth to lower the probability of crisis. Thus, that the intensity of the G–S tradeoff is variable. *Ceteris paribus*, at higher levels of I (and thus higher levels of G and lower levels of S) the relative preference for security increases.

The first order condition for an interior solution to maximization problem (2) is $O_G G_I = O_S S_I$ or alternatively $O_G [G_R R_I] + O_S [S_F F_I + S_{D'} D'_I] = 0$.

The firm invests to the point where the marginal utility gains (losses) from growth are exactly offset by the marginal utility losses (gains) from financial security/autonomy. In equilibrium $\text{sgn}(-S_I) = \text{sgn}(G_I)$ – the firm faces a G–S tradeoff.

The second order condition for a maximum requires that:

$$O_G G_{II} + G_I O_{GI} + O_S S_{II} + S_I O_{SI} < 0.$$

Recognizing that $O_{SI} = O_{SS} S_I$ and that $O_{GI} = O_{GG} G_I = 0$, the second order condition can be stated as:

$$O_G G_{II} + O_S S_{II} + S_I^2 O_{SS} < 0 \qquad (3)$$

This condition is met under the assumptions that $P_Q < 0$, $P_{QQ} \leq 0$ and additionally that $Q_{II} = 0.$[16]

The managerial firm's optimal I decision is depicted in Figure 8.1. In finding the I^* that ensures $G_I(I) = \dfrac{O_S}{O_G} S_I(I)$, management must resolve the G–S tradeoff. At levels of $I < I_1$, marginal increases in I increase gross profits by enough to:

1 offset the marginal increments in the costs of autonomy and thus ensure that G rises $(G_I > 0)$;
2 ensure that F declines by enough, despite the increase in financial obligations, to offset the increase in D', thus S increases and;
3 increase the relative preference weight, $\dfrac{O_G}{O_S}$ assigned to the G objective as safety increases and thus O_S declines.

Thus for $I < I_1$, $O_1 > 0$: total utility increases with I. For $I_1 < I < I_2$ marginal increases in investment result in smaller increases in gross profits as the firm's profit per unit decreases at higher levels of output. As a result, π_I^g offsets the marginal increments in the costs of autonomy by less – G_I declines – and is no longer capable of reducing F by enough to offset the rise in D' – S_I becomes negative. In addition, $\dfrac{O_G}{O_S}$ declines. Thus G continues to rise but at the expense of

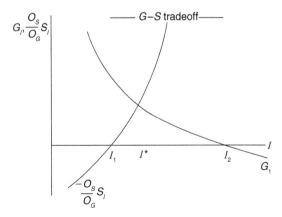

Figure 8.1 The optimal solution and G–S tradeoff.

a decline in $S(S_I < 0)$: the *G-S* tradeoff is operable. As long as $G_I > -\dfrac{O_S}{O_G}S_I$ marginal increments in I will increase O. But, given that $\pi_{II}^g < 0$ (which ensures that $S_{II} < 0$), $G_{II} < 0$, and $O_{SS} < 0$, beyond I^* marginal increments to I will no longer generate enough profits to ensure that the appropriately weighted increase in G offsets the increasingly more heavily weighted declines in S.

Comparative statics

In this section, the comparative static effects of model parameters are discussed for the unconstrained model. These results are used later to establish the macro dynamics of the Neoliberal paradox (Crotty (2003a, 2003b, 2005). Detailed derivations are contained in an available appendix.

In general the effect on I^* and K^* of a one unit change in any parameter, p (with the exception of K^0) can be expressed as

$$\frac{dI}{dp} = -\frac{(O_G G_{Ip} + O_S S_{Ip} + S_I S_p O_{SS})}{|H|}$$

where $O_{GG} = 0$ is invoked, $|H|$ is the second order condition in Equation (3), and O_{Sp} is written as $S_p O_{SS}$. Given that $|H| < 0$, the sign of $\dfrac{dI}{dp}$ depends on the sign of three separate effects: $O_G G_{Ip}$, $O_S S_{Ip}$ and $S_I S_p O_{SS}$. These effects respectively represent:

1   the change in investment-induced increases in growth objectives evaluated in utility terms by O_G;
2   the change in investment-induced reductions in financial security evaluated in utility terms by O_S; and
3   the change in the evaluation of the investment-induced reduction in financial security (S_I) as a result of changes in the preference weight $O_{Sp} = (S_p O_{SS})$ that occur as S changes.

Given that $O_G > 0$, $O_S > 0$, $O_{SS} < 0$ and $S_I < 0$ in the neighborhood of equilibrium, the sign of $\dfrac{dI}{dp}$ depends on the signs of G_{Ip}, S_{Ip} and S_p.

The comparative static results are best understood by recognizing that each of these three effects alters the intensity of the *G-S* tradeoff. Unambiguous increases in the intensity of the tradeoff (any combination of $G_{Ip} < 0$ or $S_{Ip} < 0$ or $S_p < 0$) will result in less I and conversely.

To show how the model works, we consider in detail a change in α, the firm's profit markup. Changes in α are the primary channel through which real sector developments directly affect the pace of accumulation in the model. $dI/d\alpha$ can be expressed as:

$$\frac{dI}{d\alpha} = -\frac{\left[O_G\left(G_R(1-\beta)\pi_{I\alpha}^g\right) + O_S\left(S_F f(\beta-1)\pi_{I\alpha}^g\right) + S_I O_{SS}\left(S_F(\beta-1)Qf\right)\right]}{|H|}$$

where $\pi_{Ia}^g = Q_I(1 + QP_{Qa})$ and β is the divided payout rate. If demand increases such that $P_{Qa} \geq 0$ and $\pi_{Ia}^g > 0$, then $G_{Ia} > 0$, $S_{Ia} > 0$ and $S_a > 0$ implying that $\frac{dI}{da} > 0$.

A rise in α stimulates I in three ways. First, it increases the marginal return to growth – marginal gross profits are increased because the additional output is sold at a higher α, marginal costs remain the same, and the marginal decline in price when Q grows is either unaffected or reduced. Second, it reduces the marginal decline in safety because F is reduced. Third, it increases the level of S through higher gross profits that reduce F, and thereby lower the weight on the investment-induced decline in S. All three effects reduce the intensity of the G-S tradeoff and result in optimal trades of investment-induced reductions in S in favor of investment-induced increases in G. Thus, I increases. As can be seen in Figure 8.2, the first (or demand) effect shifts the G_I curve to the right while the latter effects ($S_{Ia} > 0$ and $S_a > 0$) both shift the $\frac{-O_s}{O_G} S_I$ curve to the right.

This result is important on both the micro and macro levels. On the micro level, it shows how shifts in demand and cost functions (changes in profitability) alter I demand. On the macro level, it provides a feedback mechanism through which macroeconomic variables, including the distribution of income, shift the firm's demand and cost functions and thus influence microeconomic profitability and I.

Other comparative static results are summarized in Table 8.1.

The constrained model: the Marxian competition effect

When coercive competition erodes or is expected to erode the firm's market share below the critical M^* level, the firm faces an invest-or-die situation. The firm must either defend its illiquid capital, be marginalized by the competition or forced to sell off its assets to satisfy the demands of finance capitalists and shareholders. In this situation, investment goes from a necessary, but risky, activity to a required activity. Here, a competitive criteria dominates the maximization of combined growth and safety objectives and as a result financial security

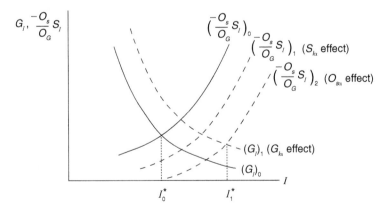

Figure 8.2 The effect of $d\alpha$ on optimal I.

Table 8.1 Comparative static results*

Parameter	O_GG_{IP}	O_SS_{IP}	$S_IS_PO_{SS}$	$\dfrac{dI}{dP}$
α (mark-up)	+	+	+	+
D^0 (initial debt)	N/A	N/A	−	−
$\hat{D}$ (acceptable debt)	N/A	N/A	+	+
σ^2 (variance of gross profits)	N/A		−	**
π^0 (initial cash flow)	N/A	N/A	+	+
P^K (price of capital)	−	−	?	?***
R (interest rate)	−	−	−	−

Notes

*Under the assumption that future profits are distributed uniformly or normally.

**For the special case of an extremely financially fragile firm, $\dfrac{dI}{d\sigma^2} > 0$. Here a firm on the verge of bankruptcy will take an investment gamble hoping to draw one of the marginal extreme positive outcomes added to its distribution by an increase in σ^2.

***An increase in P^K raises the value of the firm assets and thus lowers the firm's debt-equity ratio resulting in the indeterminant sign in S_P.

objectives are abandoned in the intermediate run. The firm can only improve its market share through the implementation of a qualitatively distinct form of investment referred to as defensive investment.

It is important to note that the abandonment of safety concerns can be accompanied by different circumstances that underlie the violation of the market share constraint. Declining market shares can be caused by:

1 rising mark-ups;
2 intensified competition during periods of stagnant demand growth including price wars (destructive competition); and
3 intensified rivalries during periods of normal demand growth.

While these three scenarios produce the same defensive competitive response on the micro level, the particular combination of circumstances have important implications for the resulting macroeconomics environment (discussed below, pp. 123–4).

The Marxian competition effect and the firm's transition from an offensive to a defensive investment strategy are depicted in Figure 8.3 where each curve represents a linearized version of the locus of mark-up (α) – offensive investment (*I*) combinations for a fixed market share (*M*) that maximize the firm's unconstrained *G-S* objective function. Along each curve, only one of the two forms of price competition is operable – the impact of rising prices/mark-ups on the international demand for the firm's product is abstracted from so that it can be properly included as a shift parameter with other changes affecting the firm's market share. The positive relation between α and *I* reflects the $\dfrac{dI}{d\alpha}$ comparative static result discussed above.

Starting from point *A* (I_0, α_0, M_0), a *ceteris paribus* increase in α to α_1 results in an increase in optimal *I* to I_1 when international competition is not considered

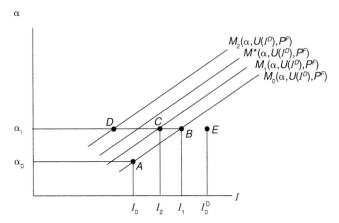

Figure 8.3 The Marxian competition effect.

and more appropriately to a smaller rise in *I* to I_2 due to the reduction in market share to M_1 when all forms of competition are considered.

Any combination of individual increases in α, increases in *U*, or declines in P^F that reduces the firm's market share below *M** such as at point *D*, sets off a transition to a defensive investment strategy. Given that the transition to a production process with a new cost-cutting technology requires significant amounts of defensive investment, investment demand rises significantly to say point *E* with an initial defensive investment level of I_0^D. Point *E* represents both a constrained optimum and a disequilibrium point with respect to the firm's unconstrained *G–S* equilibrium.

In the disequilibrium sense of point *E*, the firm is forced to undertake a level of investment that is far greater and is associated with far more financial risk then it would normally assme at equilibrium point *D*. While a discussion of disequilibrium dynamics from point *E* back to an unconstrained *G–S* equilibrium is beyond the scope of this chapter, particularly due to the potential macro crisis tendencies (discussed below, pp. 123–4) embedded in such micro decisions, some points can be made. Abstracting from crisis generating mechanisms, the I^D strategy, if successful, will improve the firm's market share and after a transition period, the new production techniques become the accepted technology implying that further investment in these methods constitutes the next generation of offensive investment. Thus, the movement from point *E* will be back to an unconstrained *G–S* equilibrium. If we assume for simplicity that I_0^D restores the firm's market share to M_0 and the firm maintains its markup at α, then the movement will be from point *E* to *B*. Of course, other paths are possible depending on how the firm negotiates the tradeoff between its markup and market share (Goldstein 1985)

An I^D strategy can be set off in a variety of ways. Any mechanism that raises the firm's price relative to their competitor's price will lower the firm's market share – increases in competition (lower competitor's prices), or increases in the firm's mark-up. The latter can occur from defending the markup against a profit squeeze (Goldstein 1985) or from increases in the rate of exploitation when capital has the upper hand in the capital–labor relation. In addition, price wars either within the domestic industry or the entire industry can lead to I^D. In this situation, either the market share is expected to decline from this form of destructive competition or if firms resist I^D and match competitor's price declines, then the decline in the profit rate may lead financial capitalists to pressure firms to increase their earnings. In this case, the most viable response would be to use I^D.

When the competitive constraint is binding there are also some situations in which an I^D strategy may not be pursued. The firm can always opt out of the industry – the die option – or finance capitalists with control over the firm can decide to sell off the assets of the firm to maximize the wealth of the stockholders. While these are possible outcome, the more typical response is to defend the firm's illiquid capital. Thus, from a representative agent perspective, the I^D strategy is the dominant outcome.

The Keynes–Marx theory of investment and the Neoliberal paradox

Given that the theory of investment lies at the core of an integrated heterodox macroeconomic theory, the Keynes–Marx theory of investment should be capable of explaining some of the key macro dynamics of the Neoliberal regime. In this section, I use the model to capture the Neoliberal paradox – a tendency to chronic global excess capacity – developed by Crotty (2003a, 2003b, 2005).

In the Neoliberal era, free trade and financial liberalization have led to increases in international competition, particularly as firms in developing nations enter established markets and direct investment across developed nations increases. A decline in market shares for firms in advanced countries reduces their relative demand growth shifting the G curve to the left and the S curve to the left as net revenues are reduced on the margin and simultaneously making the competitive constraint more binding. At the same time, one of the hallmarks of the Neoliberal regime has been macro policies and firm low road labor strategies that shift income away from the working class and slow global aggregate demand growth. This general erosion of demand growth would have the same effects as increased competition on the G and S curves, but would not further tighten the competitive constraint as market share should remain relatively constant from this general decline in demand growth. The impact of these two factors on the firm's optimal investment strategy would be for offensive investment to be reduced. If the described shifts in the G and S curves are large enough, the curves could meet in the northwest quadrant of Figure 8.1 where I is negative implying that the optimal capital stock exceeds the initial capital stock – excess capacity exists. This excess capacity would exist at the same time that the firm's competitive constraint is closer to being violated. If the constraint is not yet violated, then destructive competition in the form of price wars is likely to break out. This represents one strategy by which the firm can defend its illiquid capital with the hopes of emerging as one of the remaining firms after the industry shake-out settles. In addition, international competition from developing areas is likely to increase. Both of these tendencies will result in the tightening or ultimate violation of the market share constraint. In the case of a price war, either the firm's market share is expected to decline if it does not reciprocate with price cuts, or the reduction in profits from successive price declines will trigger finance capitalists and shareholders to demand increased earnings. The firm's best strategy in both of these cases is to engage in defensive investment and to pursue low road labor strategies.

Increases in defensive investment will further exacerbate the excess capacity crisis. While low road labor strategies will further slow aggregate demand growth and reproduce the excess capacity problem that started this dynamic process. Hence the excess capacity problem has a chronic and global dimension.

Notes

1 See Chapter 3 in this volume.
2 Capacity utilization does not explicitly enter as a determinant of investment because it is subsumed in the capital-output ratio component of the profit rate.
3 While not formally addressed, legacy labor (retiree) costs and stock buy backs to buoy the stock price can be readily included.
4 Creditor interference has become more relevant in the current period of a finance-led accumulation regime.
5 See Crotty (1993) on the relation between investment and competition.
6 See Crotty (1993) for a discussion and extension of the Marxian concept of competition, particularly as it relates to the firm's investment decision. Crotty's contribution includes distinguishing forms of Marxian competition, particularly a co-respective form and a coercive form.
7 Unless, these groups decide it is in their best interests to force a sale of the firm's assets.
8 Shaihk (1978) is the first to mention a competitive criteria as distinct from a profit maximization objective. Goldstein (2006) discusses the use of competitive constraints in Marxian microfoundations. Shaihk (1978) discussed a "switch or die" imperative for the firm with respect to a transition to a new cost-cutting technology, while Crotty (1993) considers a similar "invest or die" transition in investment strategy.
9 An alternative constraint could entail reductions in the firm's earnings as a result of destructive competition that sets off finance capitalist demands for improved earnings. These demands can be met through a defensive investment strategy.
10 An appendix that demonstrates the reduction of the firm's dynamic problem to the problem in equations (1a and 1b) is available upon request from the author.
11 Given the dichotomy in the firm's usage of I and I^D, it is assumed that the production function retains these properties separately with respect to both forms of capital. After a transition period associated with a shift to an I^D strategy, the new technology exhibits the assumed production function characteristics. In the remainder of the chapter, the initial values of both types of capital stock is suppressed in the notation. Thus every time I or I^D appears in functional notation, they should respectively be followed by K and K^D.

12 In this model, the firm's mark-up is treated exogenously for a given level of investment. Goldstein (1985) develops a microfoundation for a variable mark-up pricing strategy for the firm. Ideally, the pricing and investment decisions of the firm should be integrated. Given the complexities of the current model, I treat the markup exogenously.

13 PQ is qualitatively the same. Quantitatively, there are now two determinants of the elasticity of demand. *Ceteris paribus*, as the firm raises its price, both domestic and foreign competitors capture a portion of the firm's demand.

14 It is argued, in the available appendix, that the use of such a subjective probability distribution is consistent with the notion of Keynesian uncertainty. In particular, the firm is only able to effective use such a distribution in the current period. Future distributions are not knowable. Thus, long-term financial vulnerability is treated through a separate sub-objective of the firm to ensure that the firm does not make short-run decisions that are inconsistent with its long-run objectives.

15 In this model with the inclusion of S, the firm acts in a risk–averse fashion setting $PDV > 0$. Thus, $R_I > 0$. For F_I, an increase in investment can increase expected gross profit flows by either more or less than the increase in current autonomy payments.

16 All derivations and proofs that are subsequently applied hold for the more general case where $Q_{II} \leq 0$.

References

Crotty, J. (1993) "Rethinking Marxian Investment Theory: Keynes–Minsky Instability, Competitive Regime Shifts and Coerced Investment," *Review of Radical Political Economics*, 25(1): 1–26.

—— (1994) "Are Keynesian Uncertainty and Macrotheory Compatible? Conventional Decision Making, Institutional Structures, and Conditional Stability in Keynesian Macromodels," in G. Dymski and R. Pollin (eds.) *New Perspectives in Monetary Macroeconomics: Explorations in the Tradition of Hyman P. Minsky*, 105–39, Ann Arbor: University of Michigan Press.

—— (2003a) "Core Industries, Coercive Competition and the Structural Contradictions of Global Neoliberalism," in N. Phelps and P. Raines (eds.) *The New Competition for Inward Investment: Companies, Institutions and Territorial Development*, 9–37, Northampton, MA: Edward Elgar.

—— (2003b) "The Neoliberal Paradox: The Impact of Destructive Product Market Competition and Impatient Finance on Nonfinancial Corporations in the Neoliberal Era," *Review of Radical Political Economics*, 35(3): 271–9.

—— (2005) "The Neoliberal Paradox: The Impact of Destructive Product Market Competition and 'Modern' Financial Markets on Nonfinancial Corporation Performance in the Neoliberal Era," in G. Epstein (ed.) *Financialization and the World Economy*, 77–110, Cheltenham, UK and Northampton, MA: Edward Elgar.

Crotty, J., and Goldstein, J. (1992a) "A Marxian–Keynesian Theory of Investment Demand: Empirical Evidence," in F. Moseley and E. Wolff (eds.) *International Perspectives on Profitability and Accumulation*, 197–234, Brookfield: Edward Elgar.

—— (1992b) "The Impact of Profitability, Financial Fragility and Competitive Regime Shifts on Investment Demand: Empirical Evidence," Levy Economics Institute of Bard College, Working Paper No. 81, September.

—— (1992c) "The Investment Decision of the Post-Keynesian Firm: A Suggested Microfoundation for Minsky's Investment Instability Thesis," Levy Economics Institute of Bard College, Working Paper No. 79, September.

Goldstein, J. (1985) "The Cyclical Profit Squeeze: A Marxian Microfoundation," *Review of Radical Political Economics*, 17(1–2): 103–28.

—— (2006) "Marxian Microfoundations: Contribution or Detour?" *Review of Radical Political Economics*, 38(4): 569–94.

Shaikh, A. (1978) "Political Economy and Capitalism: Notes on Dobb's Theory of Crisis," *Cambridge Journal of Economics*, 2(2): 233–51.

9 Did financialization increase macroeconomic fragility?

An analysis of the US nonfinancial corporate sector

Özgür Orhangazi

Introduction

The post-1980 era has been characterized by weak global aggregate demand growth and intensified competition in key product markets, which led to low profits and chronic excess capacity. At the same time, financial markets greatly expanded and put increased pressure on nonfinancial corporations (NFCs) to generate higher earnings and distribute them to the financial markets.[1] Unable to increase their profits due to adverse conditions in the product markets, NFCs were forced to pay an increasing share of their internal funds to financial markets. They responded to this paradox with a change in their corporate strategies and long-term growth orientation left its place to short-term survivalist strategies that prioritized increasing returns to shareholders. The establishment of a market for corporate control with its hostile takeover waves, the rise of the "shareholder value movement," and changes in managerial incentive structures shortened the NFC planning horizons and led the NFC management to change their priorities and increase dividend payments and/or buyback firm's own stocks in an attempt to meet financial market demands. This was accompanied by an increase in NFCs' investments in financial assets and subsidiaries. In a process now commonly referred to as financialization, the relationship between financial markets and the NFCs was fundamentally transformed.[2]

In this chapter, I argue that financialization increases the potential instability and the degree of financial fragility in the nonfinancial corporate sector. First, the dominance of financial markets' short-termist perspective adds to the inherent instability of the investment demand. Second, NFCs' high indebtedness leads to a higher degree of financial fragility. This is further complicated with the earnings pressure of the stock market and with increased involvement of NFCs in financial investments. Third, the "neoliberal paradox" together with the proliferation of new financial instruments heightens the uncertainty in the economy by creating increasingly less transparent financial dealings. Before moving onto the discussion, I should make it clear that my purpose in this chapter is not to develop a formal model of financial fragility and instability in a financialized economy, but rather to outline the potential sources of fragility and instability for the NFCs. Also, while many have pointed out that the financial sector participants now engage in increasingly risky ventures and hence heighten the potential fragility of the system, this chapter will only focus on the NFCs and present a partial analysis in that sense.[3]

Instability of "coupon pool" capitalism

A main feature of twentieth-century US capitalism has been the separation of ownership and management. This ensured that the day-to-day requirements of business were carried out by a professional managerial class, who over time gained autonomy from the financial capitalists that owned the firms. During the "Golden Age," NFC management followed a strategy of retaining their earnings and reinvesting them in projects with long-term growth prospects and long-run profitability. However, starting in 1980s the relationship between the NFCs and the financial markets in the US economy was fundamentally transformed. The corporate strategy has been reconfigured around distributing a higher share of earnings to shareholders; a shift from "retain and reinvest" to "downsize and distribute" (Lazonick and O'Sullivan 2000). With the rise of institutional investors such as mutual funds, pension funds and insurance companies, the takeovers advocated by agency theorists became possible and the shareholders gained collective power to directly influence both the management of NFCs and the returns and prices of corporate shares they held. Financial firms shifted their focus from supporting long-term investment activities of NFCs through long-term financing to trading securities and generating fees and capital gains (Lazonick and O'Sullivan 2000).

This transformation created a "coupon pool capitalism" where corporations first return their earnings to financial markets and then compete to re-acquire these funds. In this configuration the coupons are

> all the different kinds of financial paper (bonds and shares) traded in the capital markets and coupon pool capitalism exists where the financial markets are no longer simple intermediaries between household savers and investing firms but act dynamically to shape the behaviour of both firms and households.
>
> (Froud *et al*. 2002: 120)

"Coupon pool" capitalism increases the potential instability of the system in two ways. First, it exacerbates the fundamental contradiction between the necessity of long lasting investment in production and the demand of absolute free movement of finance capital (Dumenil and Levy 2005: 40). Impatient financial markets of the financialization era demand that NFCs discharge an ever-growing part of their earnings to the financial markets and keep the stock prices rising. This is a reflection of the shift in the beliefs and understanding of finance capital

> from an implicit acceptance of the Chandlerian view of the large NFC as an integrated, coherent combination of relatively illiquid real assets assembled

to pursue long-term growth and innovation, to a "financial" conception in which the NFC is seen as a "portfolio" of liquid sub-units that home-office management must continually restructure to maximize the stock price at every point in time.

(Crotty 2005: 88)

When firms discharge their earnings to the financial markets and then compete to re-acquire them, the planning horizon for investment funding is shortened and the degree of uncertainty is heightened. Unlike the earlier period of "retain and reinvest," managers now cannot be sure of the amount and cost of the funds they will be able to re-acquire. This could especially hamper investments that have longer periods of gestation by creating uncertainty about the ability of the firm to finance the projects in the coming years. The pressure to provide high short-term returns to shareholders can shorten planning horizons for NFCs too, as the attempt to meet the short-term expectations of the financial markets, rather than investment in long-term growth of the firm, becomes the primary objective.[4] This creates a situation in which the vulnerability of NFCs to adverse economic developments is increased as impatient financial markets can withdraw credit at the first sign of weakness. A slowdown in economic growth could quickly be translated into a withdrawal of funds and further deepen the recession. As I discuss below, the situation is complicated by the increased degree of financial fragility the NFCs face today.

The second impact of the "coupon pool" is similar, but in the opposite direction: financial markets can cause rapid overheating of an expansion. Both Keynesian and Marxian approaches to instability stress that finance capital is an important and dominating accelerator of the growth process and a destabilizer at the same time (Crotty 1986). The credit system allows the accumulation process to take place at a faster pace and an expanded scale that otherwise would not be attainable. When the conditions are favorable and investment expands rapidly, the resulting increase in confidence levels leads firms to make use of greater amounts of credit while the creditors make more loans, some of which are increasingly riskier. The pace and the scale of the expansion then depend on the amount of the finance capital thrown into the expansion. However, these expansions prepare their own ends as they endogenously produce either financial or real problems within the economy (Crotty 1986). Financialization makes the allocation of funds across industries and firms largely subject to the volatile expectations of large financial institutions, including institutional investors. These institutions are mostly focused on acquiring high returns on their investment in the short-run. The high-tech boom of the second half of the 1990s provides a good example. In the height of the boom "pension funds and capital market institutions were prepared to throw capital at new economy companies that had no earnings and uncertain prospects of profiting from digital economies" (Feng *et al.* 2001). The result was a rapid expansion in the industry with significant levels of over-investment until the boom came to an end in early 2000s.[5] The new configuration, hence, is likely to exacerbate the role of finance capital in generating speculative expansions or overheating expansions in growing industries.

Debt and fragility

Financial fragility refers to the vulnerability of economic units to adverse economic developments that put their ability to meet payment obligations at risk.[6] In general, an economy is thought to be more financially fragile as financial payment commitments as a ratio of earnings increase and a smaller disturbance in earnings can potentially disrupt the ability of economic units to fulfill their payment commitments. Adverse economic developments in the product markets, such as a decline in profitability, or disturbances in the financial markets, such as rising interest rates or a spectacular failure that leads to the erosion of confidence can then create a larger impact on the system. A fragile "financial system can turn what might have been a mild downturn into a financial panic and depression" (Crotty 1986: 306) and have a significant impact on the participants of the financial system as well as the whole economy.

Compared with the Golden Age, it is clear that financialization brought a spectacular increase in the debt levels in the recent decades. Total credit market debt as a percentage of GDP, which stood below 150 percent in the period of 1952–1973, showed a secular increase and exceeded 300 percent in the 2001–2006 period. Household borrowing in the same period more than doubled and averaged above 80 percent after 2001 (see Figure 9.1). Average NFC credit market debt as a percentage of NFC net worth was around 30 percent during the Golden Age, but exceeded 50 percent in the 1990s, before declining to an average of 46 percent in the 2000s (see Figure 9.2).

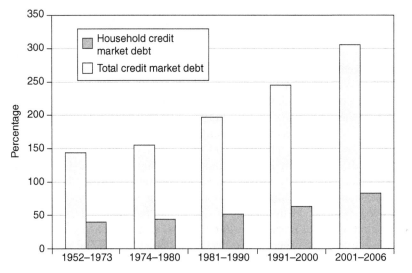

Figure 9.1 Total and household credit market debt as a percentage of GDP (source: Flow of Funds Accounts, Tables L.1 and F.6).

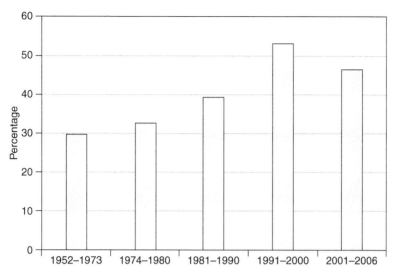

Figure 9.2 NFC credit market debt as a percentage of NFC net worth (market value) (source: Flow of Funds Accounts, Table B.102).

Starting in the late 1960s into the early 1980s, NFCs in the US faced increasing international competition while at the same time facing declining profitability. As a response to increased competition, NFCs undertook coercive (or defensive) investment and shrinking internal funds led firms to finance this investment through increased borrowing. The transformations in financial markets created three additional factors that raised NFC indebtedness. First, faced with a hostile takeover movement in the 1980s during which nearly half of the major corporations in the US received a takeover offer (Mitchell and Mulherin 1996), managers of targeted firms defended their turfs by loading the firm with debt to deter potential raiders (Crotty 2005: 90). At the time, increased indebtedness of firms was also perceived as a good solution to the potential agency problems. Second, especially in the 1990s, managers started using debt-financed stock buybacks and special cash dividends to deter a potential takeover attempt, maximize the value of their stock options, meet shareholder value targets and keep the earnings per share and dividend growth increasing. For example, during the 1990s boom, when the profits peaked in 1997

> companies have compensated for a declining return on total capital employed by leveraging their balance sheets in order to maintain the return on equity. They repurchased shares so that earnings per share and dividend growth increased at the cost of balance sheet deterioration. The resulting shrinkage in stock market equity helped support stock prices, and returns on directors' stock option plans.
>
> (Plender 2001)

Furthermore, as I discuss below, the increased stock buybacks and dividend payments leave NFCs with limited internal funds and hence create an additional force to borrow in order to finance their normal operations. Finally, while NFCs engaged in coercive investment in an attempt to keep their turf in the face of increasing international competition they also found another venue in financial investments and started using part of their borrowing in financing their holding of financial assets.

When NFCs are heavily indebted, even minor increases in the interest rates or minor declines in the profit flows can lead to financial problems for them. This is because high indebtedness implies that an increasing portion of future earnings is now committed to interest payments and debt repayments. The ratio of NFC financial liabilities to internal funds cycled between four and six in the period of 1952–1973, then increased rapidly (see Figure 9.3). Despite a decline in recent years due to a strong recovery in profits, the average ratio still stood above eight in the 2000s. When debt is used to finance profitable investments, as these investments pay off in time the firms can meet their payment obligations. However, an adverse economic development that hurts the earnings of the firm, a decline in the confidence level, or a rise in the interest rates could result in firms with high levels of debt facing problems in meeting their contractual payment obligations. The degree of fragility then depends on the share of firms that constitute, in Minsky's terms, hedge, speculative or Ponzi financing units.[7] At the aggregate level NFCs gross interest payments as a percentage of their internal funds have more than doubled in the era of financialization. In the Golden Age era, less than 20 percent of NFC total internal funds was used to meet gross interest payments. This ratio exceeded 50 percent between 1981 and 1990 and then fell down thanks

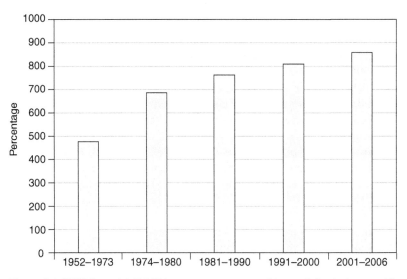

Figure 9.3 NFC financial liabilities as a percentage of internal funds (source: Flow of Funds Accounts, Tables B.102 and F.102).

Note
Internal funds equal to total internal funds with inventory valuation adjustment plus net dividends.

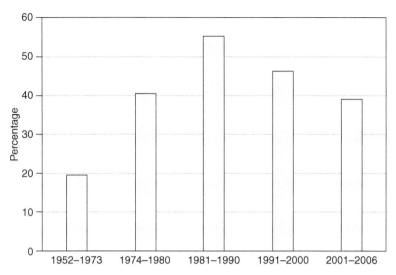

Figure 9.4 NFC gross interest payments as a percentage of internal funds (source: Flow of Funds Accounts, Tables F.102 and National Income and Product Accounts Table 7.11).

Note
Internal funds equal to total internal funds with inventory valuation adjustment plus net dividends.

to lower interest rates in the 1990s and a strong recovery of the profits in the 2000s (Figure 9.4). However, a downturn in profitability or an increase in interest rates could easily reverse this trend. These contractual payment obligations make NFCs less flexible in their use of internal funds. NFCs either have to find ways to keep increasing their profitability or risk not being able to meet their payment obligations in the face of an economic downturn.

Non-contractual financial payments

Rising debt and interest payment ratios constitute only one side of the financialization story. On the other side, a significant chunk of firm earnings is taken by non-contractual financial payments: dividend payments and stock buybacks. Even though, in theory, equity financing does not create any contractual payment obligations, firms now have to meet the financial markets' demands for these payments and provide satisfactory returns. Otherwise, management risks losing its position/autonomy and the firm may face a takeover threat, a withdrawal of financing or difficulty in raising funds for new projects.

Total financial payments including gross interest payments, dividend payments, and stock buybacks now consume, on average, more than 80 percent of the NFC internal funds (Figure 9.5). It is important to note that despite a decline in interest payments, total financial payments ratio has stayed high in the 2000s. In effect, this forces firms to finance their operations externally, and use debt, not equity, since firms are buying back their stocks, and hence contribute to

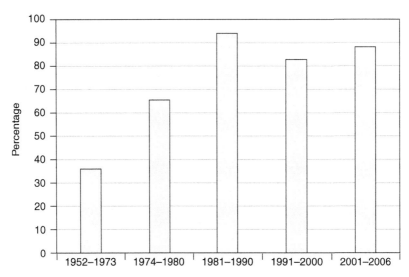

Figure 9.5 NFC total financial payments as a percentage of internal funds (source: Flow of Funds Accounts, Tables F.102 and National Income and Product Accounts Table 7.10–11).

Note
Internal funds equal to total internal funds with inventory valuation adjustment plus net dividends.

increased indebtedness. In the event of an earnings crisis, firms would not be able to meet, at the very least, some of these payments. Non-contractual financial payments may be the first to be cut, however this may have larger implications through their effect on the price of shares and shareholder earnings and further complicate the situation for the firm. Hence, financialization, through NFC financial payments, ties the credit market and stock market in a new way. This is likely to increase the fragility of the NFCs in particular and the financial system in general. In this new configuration, the interactions between downturns in asset markets, credit market contraction, investment and financial payments become all the more important. At a time of earnings crisis, the NFCs now face the danger of not being able to meet either contractual (interest) or non-contractual (dividends and stock buybacks) financial payments, each of which implies further instability.

Financial incomes and fragility

Another complication introduced by financialization is that a sizeable portion of the NFC earnings now comes from financial sources. Interest and dividend incomes make up on average more than 25 percent of the NFC internal funds during the 1981–2006 period (Figure 9.6).[8] This change in the NFC earnings structure has three interesting implications for financial fragility. First, increasing financial investments can support the real incomes when they are in the form

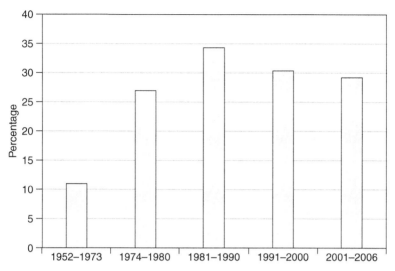

Figure 9.6 NFC financial income as a percentage of internal funds (source: Flow of Funds Accounts, Tables F.102 and National Income and Product Accounts Table 7.10–7.11).

Note
Internal funds equal to total internal funds with inventory valuation adjustment plus net dividends.

of credit extended to the firm's customers. In this case, firms can use the financial resources available to them to fend off earning problems from their real operations and hence prevent or postpone a profitability crisis that could otherwise set off financial fragility events.

Second, although financial incomes can potentially support earnings, they are inherently more volatile than regular expected gross earnings. For example, even small changes in the interest rates could potentially have large impacts on the financial earnings of the NFCs. Therefore, an extra risk is introduced to the expected earning streams of the NFCs and the prospects of future earnings now depend not only on the product markets but also financial markets. For example, the *Wall Street Journal* reports that, in a version of "carry trade" NFCs add to their profits through borrowing at short-term rates and lending directly or through the purchase of securities at higher long-term rates (Eisinger 2004). As long as the difference between these two rates is high, this is a very profitable trade for NFCs. However, if the short-term rates increase faster than long-term rates a good portion of these earnings would quickly disappear.

Third, the larger share of financial assets on NFC balance sheets makes them more solvent at least at the micro level. NFC debt as a percentage of total financial assets is now at its lowest level (Figure 9.7). As opposed to irreversible real investment, in liquid markets firms can easily convert back to cash to meet their payment obligations. Of course, when all firms attempt to do this in the face of a downturn then a deflation in the financial asset markets would be inevitable.

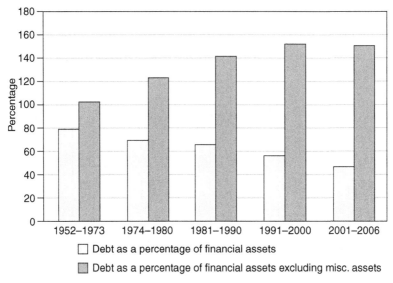

Figure 9.7 NFC debt as a percentage of NFC financial assets (source: Flow of Funds Accounts, Tables B.102).

Moreover, using debt to finance financial investments also creates the risk of maturity mismatch – a situation where assets are long term and liabilities are short term. This creates two potential points of fragility: rollover risk (that maturing debts will not be refinanced and the debtor will have to pay the obligation) and interest rate risk (that the structure of interest rates change against the NFCs' financial investments).

The changes in the rate of returns on assets and liabilities, the different maturity structures and different liquidities in financial markets could introduce further risks for the NFCs – risks mostly associated with banks and other financial institutions. However, it is not possible to analyze these risks properly as we do not have detailed data on financial asset holdings of the NFCs where almost half of the NFC assets are classified as miscellaneous (Figure 9.7). One might argue, on the contrary, that the NFCs can use their financial investments in hedging. It is certainly true that leverage makes it cheaper for NFCs to hedge, however it also makes it cheaper to speculate. Although at the macro level we do not have enough data to analyze the degree of hedging and speculation by NFCs, anecdotal evidence suggests that they are certainly involved in the business of financial speculation. For example, in 2006 Sears earned more than half of its third-quarter net income from investments in financial derivatives: "These derivatives known as 'total-return swaps' are agreements that take on the big risks of highly leveraged investments in equities or other assets without actually buying them or assuming debt to purchase them" (Covert and McWilliams 2006).

In short, the involvement of NFCs in financial investments might help them in hedging and increasing their solvency but at the same time introduces new risks to their balance sheets and earning streams. This also brings up another feature of financialization, the inherent non-transparency of these financial involvements.

Non-fundamental uncertainty

Keynes famously declared that the future is fundamentally unknowable. In the age of financialization, however, not only the future but also the past and the present are becoming increasingly unknowable. At the general level, financial dealings have become more and more complicated. For example, Partnoy (2003) shows that financial engineering reached to a point where they are now inherently non-transparent. Not only the general public but even the top executives of the financial institutions do not have a clear understanding of these complex financial dealings. Although evidence suggests that NFCs are involved in many complicated financial ventures, the extent of these investments is unknown. The hazards of this new type of uncertainty is likely to manifest itself during times of financial distress when markets in complex financial assets become illiquid and firms cannot even value the assets on their balance sheets. As a *Wall Street Journal* article written in the aftermath of the mortgage crisis of 2007 puts it "large parts of American financial markets have become a hall of mirrors" (Pulliam *et al.* 2007).

Added to this is the conscious deception introduced by fraudulent earnings reports, which unraveled at the end of the 1990s' boom with famous examples of Enron and WorldCom. In the case of Enron, the extent of debt was hidden by creating off balance sheet instruments, while WorldCom executives manipulated earnings information. Forced by financial markets to provide high returns to shareholders, many NFCs constrained by product markets, chose to use financial engineering where major restructurings and changes of ownership were used to present favorable earning statements (Froud *et al.* 2000: 109). Obfuscation of earning information delivered by companies became a standard practice (Parenteau 2005: 128–31). As Crotty (2005: 100) points out "destructive competition in product markets in the past quarter of a century has severely constrained the ability of NFCs to earn high profits and cash flow, yet financial markets demand ever-rising earnings to support ever-rising stock prices" and "given conditions in product markets, nothing but massive fraud and deception could possibly have kept stock prices from falling after 1997" (p. 101). Therefore, the very forces of financialization with its incentive and reward structure, opportunities it presents, and complicated financial instruments make NFCs' financial dealings unknowable, which unavoidably introduces further risks into the system. This also shows that the financial markets do not necessarily act as an external disciplinary force since most of these dealings are to satisfy the financial markets' inflated stock price demands.

Concluding remarks

Financialization has increased the potential fragility of the NFCs in various ways. High indebtedness and the changes in the institutional framework cause NFCs to devote an increasing share of earnings to financial payments. This could have significant implications if firms were to face an earnings crisis. Furthermore, a larger share of these earnings now comes from financial sources, which are inherently more volatile and make the firm earnings dependent not only on product markets but also financial markets. Financial investments of the NFCs might decrease fragility by enabling hedging and by supporting their real income. However, financial investments also bring in new risks, such as a potential asset–liability mismatch and increased risks due to easy speculation. Furthermore, the transformation of the institutional framework makes NFCs more susceptible to wild inflows and outflows of financial capital. On the one hand, impatient financial markets can now withdraw credit at the sign of first weakness, and on the other hand they can finance an overexpansion, as seen in the NASDAQ boom of the 1990s. Added to all these is the non-transparency of most financial dealings that potentially increases the uncertainty for investors and managers alike.

Two caveats are in order. First, one needs to be careful with the argument that financialization increases potential instability and fragility, as it runs the danger of concluding a certain crisis ahead. While an increase in financial fragility certainly makes a widespread crisis more likely, adjustments and structural changes by the NFCs as well as policy interventions to avert a crisis can also be expected. In the face of increased fragility and crisis-proneness of the system, significant changes can occur in the coming years. However, we can only wait and see if these adjustments will be abrupt and devastating or slow and extended. Second, the data analyzed in this chapter are at the aggregate level. Although aggregate analysis is quite valuable in depicting macroeconomic tendencies, it implicitly assumes either that the whole sector is one giant firm or it is composed of representative firms all responding in the same way to any change. Further studies at firm and/or industry levels would contribute to a more detailed and precise understanding of how financialization affects the fragility of NFCs.

Notes

1　This created what Crotty (2005) called a "neoliberal paradox."
2　See Crotty (2005) for a detailed exposition of the "neoliberal paradox" and financialization.
3　For example, Crotty (2007) points out that US banks increased their exposure to risk, while Dodd (2005) discusses the role of derivatives markets as the sources of vulnerability in financial markets.
4　See Orhangazi (2008a) for an analysis of the effects of financialization on NFC investment demand.
5　See Parenteau (2005) for a discussion of the investor dynamics behind the boom.
6　See Minsky (1986, especially chapters 8 and 9) for a succinct description of financial fragility. Marx referred to the similar situation as "oversensitivity." See Crotty (1986) for a discussion of parallels and differences of Minsky's approach to Marxian crisis theories and the importance of integrating the strengths of both theories.
7　A hedge unit is able to meet its payments with cash receipts; a speculative unit has difficulty in meeting some payments; and a Ponzi unit must borrow to meet its current interest payments.
8　This ratio increases if one includes capital gains in the financial incomes as well (Krippner 2005). See Orhangazi (2008b) for causes and consequences of the increased involvement of NFCs in financial investments.

References

Covert, J. and McWilliams, G. (2006) "At Sears, Investing – Not Retail – Drive Profit," *Wall Street Journal*, November 17, C1.

Crotty, J. (1986) "Marx, Keynes and Minsky on the Instability of the Capitalist Growth Process and the Nature of Government Economic Policy," in S. Helburn and D. Bramhal (eds.) *Marx, Schumpeter, Keynes: A Centenary Celebration of Dissent*, 297–326, Brooklyn: Sharpe.

—— (2005) "The Neoliberal Paradox: The Impact of Destructive Product Market Competition and 'Modern' Financial Markets on Non-financial Corporation Performance in the Neoliberal Era," in G. Epstein (ed.) *Financialization and the World Economy*, 77–110, Northampton, MA: Edward Elgar.

—— (2007) "If Financial Market Competition is so Intense, Why are Financial Firm Profits so High? Reflections on the Current 'Golden Age' of Finance," Political Economy Research Institute Working Paper No. 134, University of Massachusetts.

Dodd, R. (2005) "Derivatives Markets: Sources of Vulnerability in US Financial Markets," in G. Epstein (ed.) *Financialization and the World Economy*, 149–180, Northampton, MA: Edward Elgar.

Dumenil, G. and Levy, D. (2005) "Costs and Benefits of Neoliberalism: A Class Analysis," in G. Epstein (ed.) *Financialization and the World Economy*, 17–45, Northampton, MA: Edward Elgar.

Eisinger, J. (2004) "Interest Rates, Corporate Profits," *Wall Street Journal*, February 9, C1.

Feng, H., Froud, J., Johal, S., Haslam, C. and Williams, K. (2001) "A New Business Model? The Capital Market and the New Economy," *Economy and Society*, 30(4): 467–503.

Froud, J., Johal, S. and William, K. (2002) "Financialization and the Coupon Pool," *Capital and Class*, 78: 119–51.

Krippner, G. (2005) "The Financialization of the American Economy," *Socio-Economic Review*, 3(2): 173–208.

Lazonick, W. and O'Sullivan, M. (2000) "Maximizing Shareholder Value: A New Ideology for Corporate Governance," *Economy and Society*, 29(1): 13–35.

Minsky, H. (1986) *Stabilizing an Unstable Economy.* New Haven: Yale University Press.

Mitchell, M. and Mulherin, H. (1996) "The Impact of Industry Shocks on Takeover and Restructuring Activity," *Journal of Financial Economics*: 193–229.

Orhangazi, O. (2008a) "Financialization and Capital Accumulation in the Nonfinancial Corporate Sector: A Theoretical and Empirical Investigation on the US Economy, 1973–2003," *Cambridge Journal of Economics*, 32(6): 863–86.

—— (2008b) *Financialization and the US Economy.* Northampton, MA: Edward Elgar.

Parenteau, R. (2005) "The Late 1990s US Bubble: Financialization in the Extreme," in G. Epstein (ed.) *Financialization and the World Economy*, 111–48, Northampton, MA: Edward Elgar.

Partnoy, F. (2003) *Infectious Greed: How Deceit and Risk Corrupted the Financial Markets.* New York: Times Books.

Plender, J. (2001) "Falling from Grace," *Financial Times*, March 27, 20.

Pulliam, S., Smith, R. and Siconolfi, M. (2007) "US Investors Face an Age of Murky Pricing," *Wall Street Journal*, October 12, A1.

10 Marx, Minsky and Crotty on crises in capitalism

Fred Moseley

The relation between the theories of Marx and Minsky has been a topic of interest among heterodox economists in recent years (Crotty (1986, 1990), Pollin (1983, 1997), Dymski and Pollin (1992), Wolfson (1994) and Arnon (1994)). Crotty has argued that Minsky's theory of financial crises is compatible with Marx's theory of crises, but Minsky's theory is one-sided and focuses almost entirely on the financial sector of the economy, and ignores the real sector. Therefore, Crotty argues that Minsky's theory of financial crises should be combined with Marx's theory of crises in the real sector, in order to provide a more comprehensive theory of crises in capitalism.

This chapter explores further the compatibility – of lack thereof – of Marx's theory and Minsky's theory, by means of an examination of Crotty's 1986 paper. The first section discusses the theories of crises presented by Marx and Minsky, and the second section discusses the conclusions of these two theories regarding the effectiveness of government policies to overcome capitalism's tendency toward crises.

Crises and profit

Financial crises

Crotty emphasizes that Minsky's theory of crises focuses almost entirely on the financial sector of the economy. During a period of expansion, "boom euphoria" develops which results in increased risk-taking and higher debt levels for both firms and financial institutions. In Minsky's words, the economy moves from a "robust" financial structure to a "fragile" financial structure. The downturn is usually initiated by an increase of interest rates, which forces over-extended debtors to sell illiquid assets to meet their current debt obligations, which in turn leads to falling asset prices and often to a debt-deflation recession or depression. On the positive side, the bankruptcies during the depression reduce debt levels and help restore a robust financial structure for the beginning of the next expansion.

Minsky's theory can also explain secular trends. The central bank may intervene as lender-of-last-resort and seek to avoid a debt-deflation crisis. However, to the extent that the central bank is successful in these interventions, the restoration of a robust financial structure is aborted, and the economy emerges from the recession with a still fragile financial structure. As a result, the economy becomes more financially fragile over time, inflation increases, and the end result is stagflation.

Crotty argues that this Minskian theory of financial crises is fully compatible with Marx's theory of crises. Marx did not present a full and comprehensive theory of the role of the financial sector, but his various discussions on this topic are very similar to Minsky's theory. As Crotty (1985) demonstrated, Marx suggested that a period of expansion inevitably produces an expansion of business debt, which drives the expansion further to even greater heights. However, this boom-induced increased debt also makes the economy more vulnerable to a downturn, which eventually comes. When the downturn comes, it is worse than it otherwise would have been and often turns into a financial panic and depression. In broad outlines, this is very similar to Minsky's theory (although of course much less detailed and complete).

Real crises and profit

However, the main problem with Minsky's theory, according to Crotty, is that it focuses almost entirely on the financial sector and ignores the real sector. According to Minsky's theory, the real sector cannot be a source of crises and instability. This conclusion follows from Minsky's theory of profit, which Crotty criticizes. Minsky's theory of profit is actually Kalecki's theory of profit, which Minsky accepts in full. According to Kalecki's theory, profit (P) is determined by the sum of investment spending (I) and the government budget deficit ($G - T$) (in a simple model in which all saving comes from profit, and no foreign trade):

$$P = I + (G - T) \tag{1}$$

Kalecki treats this equation as an equilibrium condition, and assumes that it is always satisfied, so that the macroeconomy is assumed to be always in equilibrium. Crotty argues that such a "super equilibrium" theory does not allow for instability arising in the real sector.[1]

Furthermore, Minsky's (Kalecki's) theory assumes a constant profit share of income (i.e. a constant "mark-up"), which is determined by the degree of monopoly. Since the profit share remains constant, a crisis cannot be caused by a declining profit share leading to a decline of investment. Minsky emphasizes this point – that a decline of investment can never be initiated by a prior decline of profit – and argues instead that an initial decline of investment induces a subsequent decline in the amount of profit ("investment calls the tune, and profits dance accordingly").

Crotty argues that Minsky's (Kalecki's) constant mark-up theory of profit is clearly unsatisfactory because it is contradicted by a substantial body of empirical evidence that suggests that there is significant cyclical variation in the profit share, and that the profit share also generally declines well before the end of cyclical expansions and substantially earlier than investment spending. Furthermore, it is well known that there was a very significant secular decline in the share of profit and the rate of profit in the US econmy from the early postwar period to the mid-1970s, which also contradicts Minsky's (Kalecki's) theory of profit.

Therefore, Crotty argues that Minsky's theory of crises in the financial sector should be supplemented with Marx's theory of crises in the real sector, and in particular with Marx's theory of profit and the falling rate of profit. Crotty discusses the following factors as determinants of the rate of profit, according to Marx's theory: the cost of inputs (especially wages); the type of technology; labor discipline and effort; and the aggregate demand for output. Crotty argues that in an expansion, these factors will generally change in ways that have a negative effect on the rate of profit – especially increasing wages. The decline of the rate of profit causes investment spending to decline and leads to a general recession. Combined with the high levels of debt built up during the expansion, a lower rate of profit makes it even more difficult for firms to meet their debt obligations, and forces many firms into bankruptcy, and the economy into depression. Therefore, according to Marx's theory, the falling rate of profit in the real sector is a source of crises and instability in capitalist economies, which is even more important and more fundamental than the instability originating in the financial sector, as emphasized by Minsky.

I am in broad agreement with Crotty's evaluation of Minsky's theory of crises – that Minsky's theory of financial crisis is compatible with Marx's theory, and is a valuable framework for analyzing financial crises, but it needs to be supplemented with Marx's theory of crises in the real sector, caused primarily by a falling rate of profit. I also agree with much of Crotty's interpretation of Marx's theory of crises, especially his emphasis on the rate of profit as the key variable in Marx's theory. However, I would put more emphasis on labor-saving technological change (i.e. increasing composition of capital), rather than rising wages, as the main cause of the falling rate of profit, according to Marx's theory. And I would also prefer to analyze Marx's theory of the rate of profit explicitly in terms of the key determinants of the rate of profit – the rate of surplus-value (RS) and the composition of capital (CC). Algebraically:

$$RP = S/C = (S/V)/(C/V) = RS/CC \qquad (2)$$

Thus the rate of profit varies directly with the rate of surplus-value and inversely with the composition of capital. Implicitly, Crotty emphasizes a decline in the rate of surplus-value as the main cause of the falling rate of profit. This is a possible cause of the falling rate of profit, but Marx himself emphasized an increase in the composition of capital as the main cause of the falling rate of profit.

This difference has important implications for the necessary conditions for restoration of the rate of profit and the recovery of the economy from a crisis. If higher wages and a declining rate of surplus-value cause the falling rate of profit, then wage cuts and an increasing rate of surplus-value should suffice to restore the rate of profit. On the other hand, if labor-saving technological change and an increasing composition of capital cause the falling rate of profit, then wage cuts by themselves are not likely to be enough to fully restore the rate of profit. Instead, what is required in addition is a reduction in the composition of capital, i.e. a "devaluation of capital" (the numerator in the composition of capital), brought about by widespread bankruptcies of capitalist firms. In stark terms, the necessary condition for a full recovery of the rate of profit is a prior depression. (Bankruptcies also wipe out much of the debt, and thus also help to restore the financial stability of the economy, as Minsky emphasizes.)[2]

I am also in broad agreement with Crotty's critique of Minsky's theory of profit – that it is a "super-equilibrium" theory with no room for instability and that it is contradicted by the empirical evidence of cyclical and secular variations in the profit share. However, Crotty does not clearly and explicitly present Marx's own theory of profit. Crotty's discussion is entirely in terms of the share of profit and the rate of profit, not the amount of profit. Marx himself first presented his theory of the amount of surplus-value in Chapter 7 of Volume 1 of *Capital*, and then derived his theory of the rate of surplus-value in the rest of Volume 1 and his theory of the rate of profit in Part 3 of Volume 3. According to Marx's theory, the amount of surplus-value depends on the amount of surplus labor, which in turn depends on four key variables: the length of the working day (WD) (positive), the intensity of labor (INT) (positive), the real wage (RW) (negative), and the productivity of labor (PR) (positive). Algebraically:

$$S = f(SL) = f(WD^+, INT^+, RW^-, PR^+) \tag{3}$$

On the basis of this theory of profit, Marx's theory is able to explain the following very important phenomena in the history of all capitalist nations: conflicts over the length of the working day, conflicts over the intensity of labor, conflicts over wages, and inherent technological change. Crotty mentions the real wage, the productivity of labor, and the "discipline" of labor as determinants of the rate of profit, but he does not state explicitly the Marxian variable of the intensity of labor, and he does not mention the length of the working day as a determinant of the rate of profit.

Marx's theory provides the basis for an even stronger critique of Minsky's theory of profit. Minsky's theory assumes that the total amount of profit is determined by investment spending and the government deficit (and the balance of trade), and that the share of profit is determined by the degree of monopoly. Thus, according to Minsky's theory, the amount and the share of profit are *independent* of the length of the working day, the intensity of labor, the real wage, and the productivity of labor. Therefore, Minsky's theory is unable to explain the important phenomena just mentioned, and thus has considerably less explanatory power than Marx's theory. Crotty emphasizes that class conflict is missing in Minsky's theory, but he does not make clear that the absence of class conflict in Minsky's theory follows from his theory of profit, just as the centrality of class conflict in Marx's theory follows from Marx's theory of surplus-value.

Therefore, this is one important sense in which Marx's theory and Minsky's theory are not compatible – they have entirely different theories of profit.

Effectiveness of government crisis intervention policies

Crotty also argues that, since Minsky's theory ignores class conflict in general, it also ignores class conflict over government economic policies in particular. Crotty discusses Reagonomics and industrial policy as examples of class conflict over government policies. However, Crotty does not discuss the important question of the likely *effectiveness* of government policies, i.e. the ability of government policies to resolve and overcome capitalism's tendency toward crises, both real and financial. According to Minsky's theory, there are two types of government policies which virtually guarantee that a major debt-deflation depression ("it") could never happen again:

1   expansionary fiscal policy, which (according to Equation 1 above) increases profit, and thus "sets a floor" under profit in a downturn; and
2   Central Bank intervention as lender of last resort, which prevents a financial crisis from spreading, as discussed above.

The following will examine each of these two types of crisis intervention policies in turn, from the Marxian perspective discussed above.

Expansionary fiscal policy

Crotty does not explicitly discuss the likely effectiveness of expansionary fiscal policy in resolving a profitability crisis in the real sector. But this is a crucial question which should be thoroughly examined. The following analysis is based largely on Paul Mattick's pioneering extension of Marx's theory to this important question in *Marx and Keynes: The Limits of the Mixed Economy* (1969).

In order to analyze the ability of expansionary fiscal policy to overcome a profitability crisis in the real sector, assume the following scenario: during a period of expansion, the rate of profit falls and the level of business debt rises. Eventually these two trends cause a downturn – investment falls, delinquencies and bankruptcies rise, and output and employment contract. As output and employment contract, the amount of profit falls further, below the already-too-low level at the peak of the expansion.

Now assume that the government increases its spending in order to stop the downturn and revive the economy, and that this increased government spending is financed by borrowing (selling bonds). Assume further (to begin with) that the money supply remains constant, i.e. that the expansionary fiscal policy is not accompanied by expansionary monetary policy (the case of "accommodating" monetary policy will be considered below).

The first question is whether the increase of government spending will result in an overall increase of aggregate demand and output. The answer to this question depends on whether the money borrowed and spent by the government would or would not have otherwise been spent in some other way – either as investment spending or as consumer spending. If the money borrowed by the government would have been spent, either as *I* or as *C*, then the increase of government spending would not increase overall aggregate demand (again assuming no increase in the money supply), and thus would presumably have little or no effect on aggregate output and employment. On the other hand, if at least part of the money borrowed by the government would *not* have been otherwise spent (i.e. would have been "hoarded" due to the downturn), then the increase of government spending would increase aggregate demand, and would presumably also increase aggregate output and employment. As output and employment increase due to the increased government spending, the amount of profit would also increase, compared to the low point of the contraction reached prior to the increase of government spending.

However, this increase in the amount of profit due to the increase of government spending only (partially) reverses the decline of profit that resulted from the downturn from the peak of the expansion. It does not necessarily increase the amount and the rate of profit at the peak of the expansion, which caused the downturn in the first place, because it was too low. I call the rate of profit at the peak of the expansion the "full employment rate of profit." According to Marx's theory, the increase of government spending increases the "full employment rate of profit" *if and only if* either:

1   capital is devalued and the composition of capital is reduced; or/and
2   the amount and rate of surplus-value at full employment is increased.[3]

The devaluation of capital requires widespread bankruptcies, and the increase of government spending does not result in bankruptcies. Indeed, by stabilizing demand and the economy, the increase of government spending probably would allow some firms to *avoid bankruptcy*. This is good for the economy in the short-run, but according to Marx's theory, bad in the long-run, because it postpones the adjustments that are necessary (painful though they may be) in order to restore the rate of profit.

The amount and rate of surplus-value at full employment depend on the variables in Equation 3 above: the length of the working day, the intensity of labor, the real wage, and the productivity of labor. None of these variables are affected much, if at all, by an increase of government spending.

Another way of looking at this is that the total amount of surplus-value in the economy as a whole (S) depends on the total amount of surplus labor (SL) [$S = f(SL)$], which in turn depends on the product of the surplus-value produced by an average worker (SL_i) times the number of workers employed (n) [$SL = n\ SL_i$], and the surplus-value produced per worker depends on the four independent variables in Equation 3 above [$SL_i = f(WD, INT, RW, PR)$].

An increase of government spending could affect the number of workers employed, and thus could affect the total amount of surplus labor and surplus-value;

but it has little or no effect on the determinants of SL_i, and thus little or no effect on SL_i itself. And these increases of n, SL and S only reverse prior declines in these variables from the "full employment rate of profit" at the peak of the expansion. Since it does not affect the "full employment SL_i," it does not affect the total amount of surplus-value that the economy is capable of producing at full employment. The "full employment rate of profit" would still be insufficient to maintain and continue the expansion, as before.

Although an increase of government spending does not increase the "full employment rate of profit," Minsky is correct that the increase of government spending does "set a floor under profit," at least temporarily. The decline of profit resulting from the downturn is stopped and to some extent reversed. This "floor on profit" would presumably enable some firms to meet their debt obligations and avoid bankruptcy, which would reduce the severity of the downturn. However, once again, by avoiding bankruptcy, the "floor under profit" postpones the devaluation of capital which is necessary in order to restore the "full employment rate of profit;" it does not make the devaluation of capital unnecessary.

Next relax the assumption of constant money supply, and assume instead that at least part of the increase of government spending is financed ultimately by printing money. In this case, the increase of government spending would always increase aggregate demand, and thus would always lead to some recovery in the economy, i.e. to some increase in output and employment and profit. But again, these increases of output and profit only reverse the prior declines in these variables during the downturn; they do not solve the fundamental problem of insufficient profitability at full employment. According to Marx's theory, this fundamental problem can be solved only if capital is devalued or if the "full employment rate of surplus-value" is increased. This combination of expansionary fiscal policy and expansionary monetary policy might lead to a small increase in the rate of surplus-value by increasing the rate of inflation and reducing real wages. But this effect is likely to be small in the short run.

Therefore, Marx's theory implies very different conclusions than Minsky's theory with respect to the ability of expansionary fiscal policy to solve a profitability crisis in the real sector, at least in the short-run (see pp. 000–000 for a consideration of the long-run). Minsky's theory implies that expansionary fiscal policy leads to higher profit and would always solve any profit problems that might exist. Marx's theory, on the other hand, concludes that expansionary fiscal policy would lead only to short-run increases in output and profit, and would not solve the fundamental problem of insufficient profitability at full employment.

Central Bank intervention as lender of last resort

Minsky argues that Central Bank intervention as lender of last resort can always in principle stop a financial crisis (assuming the intervention is appropriate and timely). However, Minsky also argues that there is an undesirable side-effect of such successful intervention – there is much less debt liquidation, so that the financial structure of the economy continues to be fragile.

Marx's theory would agree with this conclusion, and would add another undesirable side-effect to successful lender-of-last-resort intervention – it does not resolve the profitability crisis in the real sector. What is necessary to restore the rate of profit in the real sector, as discussed above, is to increase the rate of surplus-value and reduce the composition of capital (and reduce unproductive labor). Central Bank intervention as lender of last resort accomplishes none of these necessary adjustments. To the contrary, lender-of-last-resort intervention stops the bankruptcies from happening, and thereby inhibits the restoration of the rate of profit. Lender-of-last-resort intervention is even less successful in the long run than Minsky thought.

Therefore, we can see from this Marxian perspective that bankruptcies in depressions are a necessary element of the adjustment process (i.e are "functional") for two reasons:

1   bankruptcies partially eliminate debt, which restores financial stability, as emphasized in Minsky's theory; and
2   bankruptcies devalue capital, which restores the rate of profit, as emphasized in Marx's theory.

The two theories combined imply that Central Bank intervention as lender of last resort, although it can stop a spreading financial crisis and spreading bankruptcies, precisely because it stops the bankruptcies, it inhibits the adjustments that are necessary in order to restore the rate of profit and to restore financial stability, which would make possible another extended period of growth and prosperity.

Longer-run effects

Although government intervention policies do not directly increase the "full employment rate of profit" in the short-run, they may do so indirectly in the long-run in the following way: the government intervention policies would presumably stabilize the economy and "put a floor under profit," as discussed above. The economy could then remain in such a state of "contained crisis" or stagnation for many years, perhaps even decades, with slower growth and higher unemployment. The higher unemployment would put continual downward pressure on wages. In addition, inflation might also increase, as another way for firms to restore their rate of profit, especially if the expansionary fiscal policy is accompanied by expansionary monetary policy. The net result would be constant or declining real wages, so that any increase in productivity during these years would increase the "full employment rate of surplus-value" and thereby also increasing the "full employment rate of profit."

Something like this seems to have happened in the past several decades in the US economy. Government intervention policies have prevented a major depression from happening and have "put a floor under the economy," but they have also resulted in a long period of "stagflation." Three decades of slower growth and higher unemployment have resulted in little or no increase in real wages over this entire period,[4] while productivity increases have been continual, first at slow rates through the mid-1990s, and then at faster rates since then. This combination has produced a very significant increase in the rate of surplus-value over this period (it has roughly doubled from approximately 1.5 to approximately 3.0).

Indeed, the rate of surplus-value has increased so much over these decades that as of today (2007), the rate of profit seems to have almost fully recovered from its decline and restored to its early postwar levels. (I refer here to the "conventional rate of profit" on the total capital invested, including unproductive capital, which declined approximately 50 percent from the early postwar period to the mid-1970s). Therefore, although the government intervention policies of this period did not directly increase the "full employment rate of profit" in the short-run, these policies were successful in stabilizing the economy at slower rates of growth and higher rates of unemployment than normal, which provided the conditions for a slow increase of the rate of surplus-value over many years, which eventually restored the "full employment rate of profit."

This almost complete recovery of the "full employment rate of profit," without a serious depression and devaluation of capital, might seem to contradict Marx's theory of the falling rate of profit. It is certainly not what Marx expected, but it can be explained on the basis of Marx's theory. Even though the decline of the rate of profit was not caused by a decline in the rate of surplus-value, but instead was caused by increases in the composition of capital and unproductive labor, 30 years of stagnant real wages and increasing rate of surplus-value have finally been enough to offset these causes of the prior decline of the rate of profit. Therefore, 30 years of stagnant real wages appears to be a viable alternative to bankruptcies and deep depression as a means of restoring the rate of profit, at least in this case. But it takes a long time (as of ten years ago, the rate of profit was still approximately 25 percent below its early postwar peak). Marx's theory provides an explanation of why the restoration of the rate of profit has taken so long – because the rate of surplus-value had to overcome these prior and continuing increases in the composition of capital and unproductive labor. At the very least, the decline of the rate of profit and its slow recovery can be explained much better by Marx's theory than by Minsky's theory, which provides no explanation at all of these all-important trends.

Conclusion

I agree with Crotty's conclusion that both Marx's theory and Minsky's theory have important roles to play in developing a comprehensive radical theory of capitalist crises. The main role of Marx's theory is to provide a theory of profit in the real sector, and a theory of the tendency of the rate of profit to fall, as the main cause of crises in the real sector. The main role of Minsky's theory is to provide a theory of the tendency toward financial fragility in the financial sector, as an additional cause of instability in capitalist economies. Such a combination of Marx's theory and Minsky's theory would provided a comprehensive theory of crises and instability in capitalist economies, as due to internal causes, which is much superior to mainstream theories, which generally assume that capitalism is inherently stable, and that crises and instability are caused only be external, accidental causes.

Minsky's theory of financial fragility seems to be especially relevant to the current situation in the US economy. The Marxian problem of the falling rate of profit seems to have been more or less solved by the past 30 years of stagnant real wages and increasing rate of surplus-value. So the crucial question for the present time is whether the Minskian problem of financial fragility has also been solved, or perhaps has gotten worse. A thorough examination of this crucial question would seem to be a top priority for future research.

Notes

1 Lavoie and Seccareccia (2001) point out that Kalecki's theory of profit, which Minsky seems to accept, contradicts Minsky's theory of increasing financial fragility during an expansion. Even if individual firms increase their debt in order to increase investment, the increased investment results on the macroeconomic level in an equivalent increase of profit, and thus there is no increase in the aggregate debt/profit ratio. Lavoie and Seccareccia conclude from this contradiction that Minsky's theory of financial fragility should be rejected. I conclude, to the contrary, that Minsky's (i.e. Kalecki's) theory of profit should be rejected.

2 It should also be noted that Marx's theory of the falling rate of profit in Part 3 of Volume 3 of *Capital* is at a high level of abstraction; in particular, it is in terms of productive capital and productive labor only. Unproductive labor – labor employed in circulation and supervisory activities, which although entirely necessary in capitalist economies and which allow individual firms to collect profit, nonetheless (according to Marx's theory) produce no additional value for the economy as a whole – is abstracted from. I, and others, have extended Marx's theory to the "conventional" rate of profit on the total capital invested, which also includes unproductive capital invested in unproductive activities. The main new point in this extension of Marx's theory is that the conventional rate of profit depends, not only on the composition of capital and the rate of surplus-value (as in Marx's theory of the falling rate of profit), but also depends on the ratio of the wages of unproductive labor to the wages of productive labor (inversely), which in turn depends primarily on the ratio of unproductive labor to productive labor (directly). If these ratios increase, then a greater share of the total surplus-value that is produced by productive labor must be used to pay the wages of unproductive labor, and a smaller share is left over as the profit of capitalists, so that the conventional rate of profit declines. In this case, a restoration of the conventional rate of profit would require, not only an increase in the rate of surplus-value and a decrease in the composition of capital, but also a reduction in the ratio of unproductive labor to productive labor.

3 The Marxian theory of the "conventional rate of profit" (on the total capital invested, including unproductive capital, discussed above in footnote 2) suggests in addition that the "conventional rate of profit" could be increased by a reduction in the ratio of unproductive labor to productive labor. Expansionary fiscal policy does not accomplish this necessary adjustment either.

4 The long period of stagnation of real wages has also been caused by "globalization," the essence of which is to move production to low-wage areas of the world, and also by the entry of China and India into the capitalist world economy, with their huge labor forces. The combined effect of these two changes has been to roughly double the labor

force of the capitalist world, and thus to greatly increase the global "reserve army," which has exerted (and continues to exert) strong downward pressure on wages in the US and other advanced countries.

References

Arnon, A. (1994) "Marx, Minsky, and Monetary Economics," in R. Pollin and G. Dymski (eds.) *New Perspectives in Monetary Macroeconomics: Essays in the Tradition of Hyman P. Minsky*, Ann Arbor: University of Michigan Press.

Crotty, J. (1985) "The Centrality of Money, Credit and Financial Intermediation in Marx's Crisis Theory," in S. Resnick and R. Wolff (eds.) *Rethinking Marxism*, New York: Automedia.

—— (1986) "Marx, Keynes, and Minsky on the Instability of the Capitalist Growth Process and the Nature of Government Economic Policy," in D. Bramhall and S. Helburn (eds.) *Marx Keynes, and Schumpeter: A Centenary Celebration of Dissent*, Armonk: M. E. Sharpe.

—— (1990) "Owner-Management Conflict and Financial Theories of Investment Demand: A Critical Assessment of Keynes, Tobin, and Minsky," *Journal of Post Keynesian Economics*, 12(4): 519–42.

Dymski, G. and Pollin, R. (1992) "Hyman Minsky as Hedgehog: The Power of the Wall Street Paradigm," in S. Fazzari, and D. Papadimitriou (eds.) *Financial Conditions and Macroeconomic Performance: Essays in Honor of Hyman Minsky*, Armonk: M. E. Sharpe.

Lavoie, M. and Seccareccia, M. (2001) "Minsky's Financial Fragility Hypothesis: A Missing Marcoeconomic Link?" in R. Bellfiore and P. Ferri (eds.) *Financial Fragility in the Capitalist Economy*, Northampton, MA: Elgar Publishers.

Mattick, P. (1969) *Marx and Keynes: The Limits of the Mixed Economy*, Boston: Porter Sargent.

Pollin, R. (1983) "A Theory of Financial Instability," *Monthly Review*, 35(December): 44–51.

—— (1997) "The Relevance of Hyman Minsky," *Challenge*: 75–94.

Wolfson, M. (1994) "The Financial System and the Social Structure of Accumulation," in D. M. Kotz, T. McDonough and M. Reich (eds.) *Social Structures of Accumulation: The Political Economy of Growth and Crisis*, Armonk: M. E. Sharpe.

11 Labor demand under strategic competition and the cyclical profit squeeze

Michele I. Naples[1]

The late-expansion profit squeeze analyzed by Boddy and Crotty (1974, 1975, 1976) derives in part from wage increases (Crotty and Rapping (1975)). As unemployment falls cyclically, wages rise due to workers' improved bargaining power, eroding profits. At some point a sufficient profit squeeze induces companies to contract, and a downturn ensues. The subsequent recession restores workers' economic insecurity, real wages slide, and renewed profitability leads to repeated expansion.

In the course of the expansion, labor demand is treated as relatively autonomous from the wage. Wages rise as the economy grows, yet output and employment continue to expand. This is inconsistent with models of perfect or imperfect competition which assume an inverse relationship between wages and employment due to diminishing returns.

This chapter suggests that the Boddy–Crotty theory of labor demand rests on a different approach, Strategic Competition (Naples (1998), Fazzari (Chapter 7)), which has Institutionalist and Post-Keynesian as well as Marxian roots. Strategic Competition is based on several non-Neoclassical assumptions. Firms face constant short-run returns to labor. Companies make strategic choices and satisfice in a world of uncertainty rather than following short-run profit-maximizing algorithms. They hire people for their potential; actual services elicited in the workplace are not specified in labor contracts.[2]

This chapter identifies flaws in existing theories of labor demand. It develops the Strategic Competition theory of wage determination in the absence of diminishing returns and short-run profit maximization. The conditions likely to generate no, positive, or negative feedbacks of higher wages on profitability are explored, then cyclically situated.

Constructing the demand for labor

Many heterodox analyses of labor demand incorporate Neoclassical assumptions. Efficiency-wage models of labor-effort extraction often assume both diminishing returns to labor and short-run profit maximization (Ash (2005)). Proposals for living wages defend against critics' claims that higher wages will reduce labor demand, implicitly responding to Neoclassical labor-market analyses (Pollin and Luce (1998)). Yet, the dependence of jobs on wages stands on shaky ground.

Short-run returns to labor

In the Neoclassical view, diminishing returns to labor derive from the equipment and space becoming crowded with additional employees.[3] Consequently marginal productive efficiency, i.e. output relative to labor-services rendered, declines as hiring expands.

This claim belies the empirical evidence since the 1930s that companies operate under short-run constant or increasing returns to labor (Blinder *et al.* (1998); Crotty (2001); citations in Johnston (1960); citations in Miller (2001)). This section elaborates on the empirical and analytical source of short-run constant or increasing returns.

Even if capital is fixed in the macroeconomic short run, there are several ways utilization can increase without crowding the workplace. Capital is often divisible in use: a store has many cash registers, a fast-food restaurant has several grills, and a large office has hundreds of desktop computers. And empty work-stations do not enhance workers' productivity. Companies typically have on hand more plant and equipment than are fully utilized (Steindl (1976); Dean (1951)), precisely because planned excess capacity promotes responsiveness to a sudden burst of demand without causing unit-cost increases. Companies often consciously choose to set up several smaller-capacity pieces of equipment rather than one large one to facilitate such flexibility (Andrews (1949)).

Let f represent the percent of an hour a piece of equipment is actually in use. Some machines are designed to be shared by several users in turn (e.g. photocopiers), and the extent of their utilization will be picked up by f. Some machines are used to provide direct services to customers, and will have a higher f when business is brisk, for any given employment level (e.g. cash registers); others have specialized uses and their f will depend on company demand patterns (e.g. sorting machines for large orders).

Capital can also be used by different employees at different times of day. By adding overtime, shifts and weekend work, the workplace's hours of operation can vary daily, weekly or monthly. Define h as the share of potential hours (24/day, 168/week, 61,320/year) the company is operating; changes in h change the extent of capital utilization without necessarily changing the capital-labor ratio for each worker (Andrews (1949)).

Finally, the speed of the machine can sometimes be varied, independent of f or h (Dean (1951)).[4] A stove's temperature is raised to cook chickens faster during dinner hours at a fast-food or superstore take-out, or a hydroelectric dam is adjusted to generate more electricity when demand increases. Speed (s) is measured in proportion to the machine's maximum potential speed.

Then capital utilization is a (row) vector, $\mathbf{\mu}$, whose elements depend on these determinants:

$$\mu_i = f_i * h_i * s_i \tag{1}$$

which is a pure number. Productive efficiency (*PE*), i.e. output per labor-services rendered (*LS*), will be

$$PE = q/LS = f(\mu \, K/LS) \tag{2}$$

where capital stock K is a column vector of various kinds of equipment, plant, and inventories, and its product with μ determines the flow of physical capital services (Naples (1988)). Note that if μ_i and *LS* change proportionately, their ratio will be unchanged, and employment increases will not cause diminishing productivity.

While limited capital may be used more intensively if more workers are hired, it may also be used more intensively by the same workers if *s* increases. If one piece of capital equipment lies idle while another is in use, hourly *f* averages 50 percent. Doubling a company's workforce and doubling *f* will keep *PE* constant. Even if frequency and speed were at workable maxima, it would be irrational for a company to crowd this worksite rather than expanding *h* by adding overtime, shift-work and weekend work,[5] or by reopening a site idled by recession.

When companies choose to expand employment, neither *PE* nor AP_L[6] should fall. Instead the business maintains the staffing ratio designed for its equipment (e.g. one person per desktop computer), and expands by varying capital utilization. Average and marginal productive efficiency, and *ceteris paribus*, productivity, are equal

$$AP_L = MP_L \tag{3}$$

and constant as the firm expands (Eichner (1987)).

The absence of diminishing returns makes sense of the profit-squeeze analysis of the expansion. If productivity is uniform, the marginal worker's unit labor cost is the same as the inframarginal worker's, so there is no productivity or cost constraint on increased hiring in economic booms without wage reductions.

Short-run profit maximization vs. satisficing and long-run goals

However, constant labor productivity raises questions about profit maximization, often used to close analytical economic models. In short-run labor-market models, imposing profit maximization means de facto assuming that companies maximize their profits in the short run, since these are the only profits under consideration.

Equation 3 implies that short-run profit maximization is not a viable business option.[7] If marginal and average productivities are equal, then so are marginal and average variable unit costs. Short-run profit maximization would imply that price would be set equal to marginal cost, or in this case, that the wage would be set equal to the value of the marginal product of labor. But since the 1930s (Aslanbeigui and Naples (1997)), economists have concluded that when price is no greater than average variable cost, the business could not cover any of its fixed costs and would therefore shut down. By extension, wage setting in accordance with short-run profit maximization under constant labor productivity implies that workers would take home their entire average product (including what would otherwise cover overhead costs and profits), so all businesses would be at their shutdown points.

It is more reasonable that corporations with long time horizons, as well as small businesses that hope to survive the next downturn, will make strategic decisions instead of maximizing (Eichner (1987: 360); Shapiro and Sawyer (2003: 364)). They may choose to sacrifice short-run profits if doing so advances their long-run strategic goal, such as maintaining market share, introducing a new product, infiltrating a new market, etc. Many business Institutionalists suggest that companies choose to "satisfice" (Simon (1979)) or obtain "a reasonable profit" (Dean (1951: 460)) rather than maximizing in a dynamic and changing environment. There is no perfect foresight, and information is costly. It would be irrational to maximize on the basis of what turn out to be faulty premises.

The offer wage

Forgoing the assumptions of short-run profit-maximization and diminishing returns in the theory of the demand for labor means that productivity offers inadequate guidance for company wage decisions, even at the micro level. Institutionalists argue that a company's wage offer for each job is determined by administrative criteria, such as managerial or fiduciary responsibilities, and that potential productivity is embodied in the job rather than the person (Thurow (1998)). Certain key wages serve as reference for other wages relying on similar skills and technology in or across industries. Occupational wages vary by firm in accordance with its particular market niche and management culture, including with respect to women, minorities and immigrants.

In the heterodox tradition, the chronic presence of unemployed or underemployed competitors gives all employers significant labor-market power vis-à-vis workers in setting wages (Boddy and Crotty (1975)). Management consultants like Dean (1951) see all companies as having some degree of market power in their local output market, if only by virtue of location; by extension, they would in their local labor market as well.

If different companies have different degrees of labor-market power, they may offer different wages. Case studies of occupations and locales have observed that despite competitive pressures, wages tended to fall in a "range of indeterminacy" rather than conforming to a uniform market wage (Lester (1952); Dunlop (1998)).

Wage determination has intricacies not captured by simple models, as the compensation-management literature attests (Henderson (2005)). Nevertheless, this discussion of labor-market power suggests an expanded interpretation of the Post-Keynesian mark-up and an avenue for constructing the Strategic Competition theory of the wage offer.

In the standard formulation, prices are interpreted as marked up on unit labor costs (*ULC*) and unit materials and energy costs (*UMEC*) (Shapiro and Sawyer (2003)):

$$P = (ULC + UMEC)*(1 + m) \qquad (4)$$

where the mark-up, *m*, covers overhead and profits. We can replace *ULC* with W/AP_L, and rewrite this equation as

$$P = \frac{W}{AP_L}*(1 + \alpha) \qquad (5)$$

for an expanded mark-up, α, that covers non-labor variable costs as well, following Goldstein (1999). Traditionally the mark-up is understood to reflect the extent of overhead, the company's profit-rate target, and its degree of output-market power (Eichner (1987: 375–81)).

It is illustrative to reframe this equation with wages as the dependent variable:

$$W = \frac{P*AP_L}{1 + \alpha} \qquad (6)$$

For strategically competitive concerns, the wage depends on labor productivity and output price as mediated by the mark-up on unit labor costs, α. The above Institutionalist labor discussion suggests that a host of industry and company-specific factors, including racial and gender criteria, may also be captured by α. Then α is a measure of our ignorance, a crucial factor in setting wages that cannot be known without applied industry-based research, namely, a historical, Institutionalist approach.

The effect of wages on labor demand under strategic competition: three cases

It is nevertheless possible to explore possible relationships between the wage and employment demanded analytically. Three cases will be considered: independence, positive relationship and negative relationship. It will later be argued that each holds sway under particular cyclical conditions.

Case 1   Wage-neutral labor demand: Keynesian–Cross

Constant returns to labor imply constant average variable costs; therefore average total costs decline steadily as employment increases. Under Strategic Competition, there is no rising-cost constraint on expanding employment in response to higher demand as there would be in Neoclassical theory.

Then labor-hours hired depends not on the wage, but on the demand for the firm's product (q_D), given worker productivity,

$$L_D = \frac{q_D}{AP_L} \tag{7}$$

Changes in company sales will shift labor demand without the mediation of price (namely, the wage rate), and company demand for labor is vertical.

In this view, output demand affects labor demand through a quantity-quantity mechanism: a higher quantity of sales leads to a higher level of employment. This microfoundation arguably underpins the Keynesian–Cross Aggregate Expenditure model. Aggregating labor demand across companies and industries, any shift in aggregate expenditure (AE) calls forth an equal change in GDP and a proportionate change in employment without reference to the price level. So aggregate employment demanded (N_D) is

$$N_D = \frac{AE}{AP_L} \tag{8}$$

In Boddy and Crotty's (1975) and Goldstein's (1996) story of economic recovery businesses expand in response to increases in aggregate expenditure. There is no appeal to wage changes in these characterizations of economic recovery, employment expands in direct response to greater effective demand for output, which is exogenous to the wage–employment relationship.

Case 2 *Positive wage–employment relationship: wage-induced consumption*

Some Radicals argue for a positive feedback of increased wages on consumption and therefore employment demand (Sherman (1997)). Followers of Kalecki (1971: 28), such as Lavoie (1998), expect wage increases to affect aggregate expenditure directly, causing employment increases. Keynes (1964) too foresaw a negative impact on consumer spending from lowering wages. Early advocates of union rights and minimum-wage laws shared this perspective (Kaufman (1993)), expecting wage-stabilization/wage increases to stabilize/expand employment.

This macro argument would not change Equation 7. Individual companies would hire in response to their sales, which are not likely to change appreciably by paying their workers more. But it suggests a fallacy of composition in extrapolating directly to Equation 8, if in the aggregate workers do purchase more when wages rise, pulling employment up.

If higher wages raise consumption and therefore employment offered, the macroeconomic demand for labor would be upward sloping, despite the vertical microeconomic demand. This is not a trajectory of possible equilibrium points, but a causal model whereby employment offered depends on the wage as mediated by the consumption function and aggregate expenditure. Unlike the Keynesian–Cross model, where consumption depends on GDP, in this Kaleckian formulation, wages drive consumption and therefore employment.

Case 3 Negative wage–employment relationship: cost-induced profit squeeze

Boddy and Crotty (1975) attribute the late-expansion profit squeeze in part to rising wages. Goldstein (1996) has emphasized that this cyclical argument holds even when real wages are trending downward, as in recent years. The increased unit labor costs are not fully passed on in higher prices, and profitability declines. Rising costs eventually push workers out of jobs via their deleterious effect on profits, even if productivity is constant.

Equation 7, the company's demand for labor, is replaced with a more complex causal model:

$$L_D = g\left(\frac{q_D}{AP_L}, F\right),\qquad(9)$$

for some measure of company financial health, F. This measure is itself a composite of profit performance in the recent past, debt and interest rates, as well as current profitability. Beyond some threshold level of F, L_D responds directly to lower F even if the first term is rising. Equation 7 becomes a special case of Equation 7′, which begs the question of when $g_2 \neq 0$.

Some have suggested that companies can pass on cost increases, bypassing any cyclical profit squeeze (Epstein (1991)). Nevertheless extensive empirical research confirms procyclical real wages (see citations in Goldstein (1996: 88); Lavoie (1998: 109)). This suggests that administered pricing prevails rather than Neoclassical marginal-cost pricing. Under the former, it is industry's practice "to change prices infrequently and to attempt to … refrain from major price increases in periods of rising demand" (Dean (1951: 457)). This avoids losing customers to substitute goods, preserves client loyalty and prevents a longer-run loss in sales (Shapiro and Sawyer (2003); Lee (1998: 212–14)). The press of competition, e.g. from imports (Goldstein (1996: 84, 88)), or simply the uneven experience or knowledge of others' wage increases constrains company mark-ups and permits real wages to rise.

The late-expansion vulnerability of profits rests on the particular form competition takes in expansions. Competitive pressures on companies to cut costs are mitigated by the benefit of the growing economy for profits (Goldstein (2006)). Dean (1951) argues that the focus of competition in the boom is to expand markets and market share; it is in the contraction as the pie shrinks that cost-cutting becomes crucial. Those companies that do not engage in product innovation and create new markets for themselves in expansions will not survive recessions any more than successful expanders who do not cut costs in downturns (Crotty (2000)). This suggests that rather than conceiving of competition as attenuating in the late-expansion, the unique shape competition takes is what creates the potential for the late-expansion profit squeeze.

In Case 3, wage increases impair profitability. Some level of F serves as the tipping point beyond which further wage increases lead to layoffs (Equation 7).[8]

The context for each macroeconomic wage–employment case

The macroeconomic demand for labor depends on factors that vary cyclically. The cyclical sensitivity of consumer spending and of profits to wage changes will be taken up in turn.

The sensitivity of consumer spending to wage changes

For several reasons, current wage changes may have little impact on aggregate expenditure. Until consumers know that their income change is permanent, they are not likely to spend any extra money earned (Goldstein (1999: 79)). Workers in cyclically sensitive industries, such as construction and manufacturing, are familiar with the pattern of tight labor markets and rising wages in the boom, and scarce jobs in the recession, and are unlikely to treat cyclical wage increases as if they were somehow on a new higher-income trajectory.

Workers are also uncertain about inflation. A nominal wage increase may or may not translate into higher real purchasing power. In recent decades inflation has tended to erode real household income. Even union cost-of-living clauses are only partial adjustments. Uncertainty about inflation will reduce any tendency to spend wage gains.

This suggests that a feedback from wage increases to higher aggregate expenditures is not automatic but contingent, and more likely if perceived as permanent and real. We cannot draw a positively sloped macroeconomic demand for labor; it is more accurate to treat the aggregate demand for labor as vertical and *AE* as exogenous.

The effect on profits of wage gains

Assume that, despite these caveats, sustained wage increases do at some point promote higher consumer spending as Kaleckians and some Post-Keynesians believe. Such an expansion of sales will tend to raise profits, *ceteris paribus*. Unlike Neoclassical models, where companies only produce until marginal cost equals marginal benefit and then stop expanding, Post-Keynesians argue it is in companies' interest to produce as much as they can sell (Eichner (1987)). Abstracting from changes in unit labor costs, as demand expands companies gain higher profits from two sources: high unit profits as overhead costs are spread over more items so average total costs decline, and higher total profits from increased sales.

To clarify, the profit rate (Π) may be expressed in terms of the profit margin, Π_m:

$$\Pi = \frac{\Pi_m q}{(W/AP_L + UMEC)q + (P_K K + OLC)},$$ (10)

where OLC represents overhead labor costs and $\mathbf{P}_K$ is a row vector of historic capital-good prices. If current labor and material costs are small relative to fixed-capital and overhead-labor costs, then from Equation 5 and a scalar measure of aggregate capacity utilization, $\upsilon = q/q_p$ (potential output),

$$\Pi \approx \frac{\Pi_m}{\mathbf{P}_K\mathbf{K} + OLC/(\upsilon^*q_p)} = \frac{\upsilon^*\Pi_m}{(\mathbf{P}_K\mathbf{K} + OLC)/q_p}. \tag{11}$$

The denominator represents the capital intensity of production, the extent of employee surveillance, and of overhead labor. The numerator on the right differentiates the positive impact of increased sales on the profit rate via υ from the negative impact of a lower profit margin from rising labor costs.

It is tempting to conclude that the issue is whether increased demand (through rising υ) outweighs rising costs (through falling Π_m). However, high demand does not directly translate to higher capacity utilization, which also depends on its denominator, the extent of capacity. Given the procyclical behavior of investment, allowing for some time between initial investment spending in the early expansion and final plant opening, capital grows in the latter portion of the economic expansion.[9] But this implies that the same proportionate increase in AE during the late expansion will have less impact on υ than it would have had earlier, because simultaneously the denominator of υ is expanding due to the expanded capital stock. Since investment lags the cycle, this expanded-capacity effect will likely extend into the onset of recession, reducing υ even faster than AE falls, and exacerbating the crisis phase. It means that the likelihood that a profit squeeze from rising unit labor costs would dominate any induced-consumption effects is greatest in the very phase of the cycle when induced consumption is most likely due to sustained wage increases – the late expansion. Case 2 is not very probable.

Summary: the cyclical pattern for the wage–employment relationship

The effect of wage changes on the macroeconomic demand for labor depends on the phase of the business cycle. In the early expansion, Case 1 dominates, as companies hire more workers in response to higher sales without attending to wages. Unemployment is still high and fear of job loss prevents workers from pressing for higher wages. At the same time, constant returns and administered prices means companies respond to higher aggregate expenditure by increased labor demand, without any prior wage change.

As the expansion proceeds, economic insecurity is mitigated by employment growth. Workers as individuals and as groups have an improved bargaining position to negotiate higher wages. This pattern is consistent with either Case 1 or Case 2, since these wage increases do not hurt employment demand – employment responds directly to AE. Whether wage increases have also promoted higher consumption, capital utilization and therefore profitability is an empirical question. It depends on both the consumption–wage link, and the timing of the opening and operation of new facilities and equipment. In this phase, the expansion of effective demand plus any increased consumption spillovers from higher wages dominate profit-squeeze effects.

The late expansion (from peak profitability to the cycle peak – Boddy and Crotty (1975)) is by definition the period where the profit-squeeze overwhelms any benefits from expanding demand. The analysis presented here shows that part of the reason for this change is the very acceleration of spending in the earlier period: new capital has been brought into production, and as capacity expands, utilization drops. While the economy continues to expand, labor demand fits into Case 1 or 2). Once companies reach their tipping point, the demand for labor shifts back, not because of declining AE, but worsening financial circumstances. This is initially Case 3, but as F worsens and AE falls, we return to Case 1 in the downward direction.

Conclusion

This chapter has illustrated the Strategic Competition theory of employment demand under the cyclical profit squeeze. Constant returns to labor prevail, given companies' practice of varying utilization by changing hours of operation, machine speed and frequency of use of machines in lieu of crowding the workplace. Short-run profit-maximization is not a viable assumption under constant returns, and strategic companies will satisfice and pursue long-run profit strategies rather than maximizing short-run profits. Together these motivated the relative autonomy of wage-setting from company employment decisions, driven by expected sales. Wages are not determinate a priori but are historically contingent, requiring empirical research to close the labor-market model.

The dependence of the wage–employment relationship on cyclical factors provides the microeconomic foundation for the late-expansion profit-squeeze. Even allowing for the Kaleckian case that a higher wage may lead to higher consumption (an empirical question), profits will nevertheless be squeezed once new capacity begins operation later in the expansion. The three cases outlined above expose the labor-market underpinnings implicit in Boddy and Crotty's (1975) macro story.

Notes

1 Thanks especially to Nahid Aslanbeigui, Jim Crotty, Jon Goldstein, Teresa Ghilarducci, Margaret Andrews, Fred Lee, Al Campbell, Gil Skillman, my students, and Rebellious Macroeconomics conference participants for helpful feedback.
2 This assumption underpins the late-expansion productivity slowdown (Naples (1998)).
3 Joan Robinson (1953) observed that adjusting output by adding more workers to equipment requires redesigning the production process with every hire.
4 Dean's *Managerial Economics* rewrote graduate MBA economics from an Institutionalist perspective; it dominated the postwar textbook market through the 1950s and 1960s.

5 Whether night-time or weekend work pays a premium depends on the industry and locale. Some sectors require weekend work without premium pay in alternating shifts (e.g. nursing homes, public libraries). In others, night work is less desirable entry-level work while daytime slots are prized and pay more.

6 $AP_L = PE*LP*LI$, where LP is labor performance per effort exerted, and LI is labor intensity, or hourly effort (Naples (1998)).

7 Crotty (2001) makes a similar argument for core industries with excess capacity. In companies with significant scale economies, marginal costs lie far below average total costs and rise slowly if at all, which also obviates marginal-cost pricing.

8 Goldstein (1996: 68) observed the seeming delay of the profit-squeeze in recent expansions. Alternatively, the profit peak may have more rapidly led to a downturn due to greater financial fragility with high debt overhangs, or proactive Fed intervention.

9 Crotty and Rapping (1975: 796) suggested that late-expansion investment in labor-saving techniques will not come online until early in the next expansion. In conversation at the conference, Ray Boddy reported that metal-working supervisors often let new equipment sit idle rather than miss production goals, given a likely learning curve and needed adjustments. Keynes (1964), however, saw the advent of additional capital assets of a particular type in the boom as explaining downward sloping marginal efficiency of capital. Arguably new office buildings or equipment (desktop computers, forklifts) will take less time to be put into operation than new manufacturing processes; an office complex can be built, furnished and opened in one year.

Sherman's (1997) view that late-expansion stagnant growth of capacity utilization reflected limited demand did not perceive this likely supply-side impact.

References

Andrews, P. W. S. (1949) *Manufacturing Business*. London: Macmillan.

Ash, M. (2005) "Disciplinary Unemployment as a Public Good, or the Importance of the Committee to Manage the Common Affairs of the Whole Bourgeoisie," *Review of Radical Political Economics*, 37(4): 471–5.

Aslanbeigui, N. and Naples, M. I. (1997) "Scissors or Horizon: Neoclassical Debates about Returns to Scale, Costs, and Long-Run Supply 1926–1942," *Southern Economic Journal*, 64(2): 517–30.

Blinder, A. S., Canetti, E. R. D., Lebow, D. E. and Rudd, J. B. (1998) *Asking About Prices; A New Approach to Understanding Price Stickiness*. New York: Russell Sage Foundation.

Boddy, R. and Crotty, J. R. (1974) "Class Conflict, Keynesian Policies, and the Business Cycle," *Monthly Review*, 26(5): 1–17.

—— (1975) "Class Conflict and Macro-Policy: The Political Business Cycle," *Review of Radical Political Economics*, 7(1): 1–19.

—— (1976) "Wages, Prices and the Profit Squeeze," *Review of Radical Political Economics*, 8(2): 63–7.

Crotty, J. R. (2000) "Structural Contradictions of the Global Neoliberal Regime," *Review of Radical Political Economics* (Summer).

—— (2001) "Core industries, Coercive Competition and the Structural Contradictions of Global Neo-liberalism," Working Paper, University of Massachusetts-Amherst.

Crotty, J. R and Rapping, L. A. (1975) "The 1975 Report of the President's Council of Economic Advisors: A Radical Critique," *American Economic Review*, 65(5): 791–811.

Dean, J. (1951) *Managerial Economics*. Englewood Cliffs: Prentice Hall.

Dunlop, J. T. (1998) "Industrial Relations Theory," *Advances in Industrial and Labor Relations*, 8: 15–24.

Eichner, A. S. (1987) *The Macrodynamics of Advanced Market Economies*. Armonk: M. E. Sharpe.

Epstein, G. (1991) "Profit Squeeze, Rentier Squeeze and Macroeconomic Policy Under Fixed and Flexible Exchange Rates," *Economies et Sociétés*, 25(111 & 12): 219–57.

Goldstein, Jonathan P. (1996) "The Empirical Relevance of the Cyclical Profit Squeeze: A Reassertion," *Review of Radical Political Economics*, 28(4).

—— (1999) "The Simple Analytics and Empirics of the Cyclical Profit Squeeze and Cyclical Underconsumption Theories: Clearing the Air," *Review of Radical Political Economics* (Spring).

—— (2006) "Marxian Microfoundations: Contribution or Detour?" *Review of Radical Political Economics*, 38(4): 569–94.

Henderson, R. I. (2005) *Compensation Management in a Knowledge-Based World*. Upper Saddle River: Prentice Hall.

Johnston, J. (1960) *Statistical Cost Analysis*. New York: McGraw-Hill.

Kalecki, M. (1971) *Selected Essays on the Dynamics of the Capitalist Economy*. Cambridge: Cambridge University Press.

Kaufman, B. E. (1993) *The Origins and Evolution of the Field of Industrial Relations in the United States*. Ithaca: ILR Press.

Keynes, J. M. (1964) *The General Theory of Employment, Interest and Money*. New York: Harcourt, Brace and World.

Lavoie, M. (1998) "Simple Comparative Statics of Class Conflict in Kaleckian and Marxist Short-run Models," *Review of Radical Political Economics*, 39(4): 101–13.

Lee, F. S. (1998) *Post Keynesian Price Theory*. Cambridge: Cambridge University Press.

Lester, R. A. (1952) "A Range Theory of Wage Differentials," *Industrial and Labor Relations Review*, 5(4): 483–500.

Miller, R. A. (2001) "Firms' Cost Functions: A Reconstruction," *Review of Industrial Organization*, 18(2): 183–200.

Naples, M. I. (1988) "Industrial Conflict, the Quality of Worklife and the Productivity Slowdown in US Manufacturing," *Eastern Economic Journal*, 14(2): 157–66.

—— (1998) "Technical and Social Determinants of Productivity Growth in Bituminous Coal Mining, 1955–1980," *Eastern Economic Journal*, 24(3): 325–42.

Pollin, R. and Luce, S. (1998) *The Living Wage: Building a Fair Economy*. New York: New Press.

Robinson, J. (1953–4) "The Production Function and the Theory of Capital," *The Review of Economic Studies*, 21(2): 81–106.

Shapiro, N. and Sawyer, M. (2003) "Post-Keynesian Price Theory," *Journal of Post-Keynesian Economics*, 25(3): 355–65.

Sherman, H. (1997) "Theories of Cyclical Profit Squeeze; A Comment on Jonathan Goldstein, 'The Empirical Relevance of the Cyclical Profit Squeeze: A Reassertion'," *Review of Radical Political Economics*, 29(1).

Simon, H. (1979) "Rational Decision Making in Business Organizations," *American Economic Review*, 69(4): 493–513.

Steindl, J. (1976) *Maturity and Stagnation in American Capitalism*. New York: Monthly Review Press.

Thurow, L. C. (1998) "Wage Dispersion: Who Done It?" *Journal of Post Keynesian Economics*, 21(1): 25–37.

Part III

The macrodynamics of the neoliberal regime

12 Cyclical labor shares under Keynesian and neoliberal regimes[1]

Raford Boddy

Introduction

It has become increasingly accepted by heterodox economists that in the era of the Keynesian compromise, the depletion of the reserve army increased labor share, reduced the rate of profit and directly or through its impact on policy served as an integral cause of the cyclical downturns. In the era of neoliberalism, do the economic and political weaknesses of labor mean that nexus no longer operates?

In this chapter I provide a framework to understand cyclical labor shares based on reserve army theory and the influence of capacity utilization on the ability of firms to markup or pass along unit labor costs increases as price increases. While it builds on the work of colleagues it better handles the shift of labor shares from early expansion to late expansion and comes closer to a unified theory of labor share over the cycle. I then use this model to explore how the shift from the Keynesian compromise to neoliberalism has changed the relationship of cyclical labor share to the underlying determinants of capacity utilization and unemployment.

It will be no surprise that the relationship of labor share to capacity utilization and unemployment has shifted between the two regimes. What may be more surprising is that the functional forms linking labor share to capacity utilization and unemployment have remained largely intact.

Modeling cyclical labor share

The typical decomposition shows labor share as WL/PQ, where W is the nominal wage; L is labor paid for; P is an implicit deflator; Q is a real index of value added. Labor share can be written as:

$$WL/PQ = (W/P)(Q/L)^{-1} \tag{1}$$

Within the business cycle, the implicit deflator of a sector's product, P, is likely to differ from the CPI for urban workers. Correspondingly, the product real wage W/P will diverge from the purchasing power real wage W/CPI.

The inverse of labor share can be written as the mark up of the nominal price P to unit labor cost WL/Q.

$$PQ/WL = P/(WL/Q) \tag{2}$$

When the emphasis is on the relationship of the two broad classes of capital and labor the determination of the labor share is often expressed through Equation 1 as the outcome of bilateral negotiation (class struggle) between capital and labor over the product real wage given labor productivity. Where product market mediation is primary, the markup model in Equation 2 comes to the fore and the struggle or bargaining between labor and capital is brought in indirectly. Since it is strictly a matter of algebraic decomposition it does not really matter if the explanation of labor share is framed as the result of bilateral negotiation or the inverse of labor share is explained as the markup over unit labor costs.

I begin with three well-known explanations of labor share or its inverse. The overhead labor-wages lag hypothesis long identified with Sherman (1972, 1997) makes labor share a function of capacity utilization. The depletion of the reserve army theory hypothesis closely identified with Boddy and Crotty (1975) makes labor share a function of unemployment. The markup theories of Goldstein (1986, 1996) make the inverse of labor share a function of unemployment and capacity utilization. Since Goldstein's views on the impact of unemployment are along the lines of Boddy and Crotty, it is his theory on the impact of capacity utilization that is of concern here. I begin with Boddy and Crotty on the role of unemployment and then turn to the contributions of Goldstein and Sherman on the role of capacity utilization.

Unemployment and the strength of labor

Boddy and Crotty focused on the increase in labor share in the second part of the expansion as the outcome of the rising strength of labor. Declining rates of unemployment increase labor share by increasing product real wages for given levels of labor productivity. According to Boddy and Crotty the depletion of the reserve army can also directly affect labor productivity.

Although Boddy and Crotty (1975) carried out the analysis in the Burns–Mitchell NBER cyclical stages framework and not with econometrics, we argued – presciently for my purposes in the present chapter – that the confidence of labor would depend both on the level of unemployment and on the change of unemployment. Most workers are not directly affected by bouts of unemployment. Their confidence should be high when the rate of unemployment is low but confidence should also be affected positively if the rate of unemployment is decreasing. Based on the above arguments, I assume that the change in labor share depends on both the rate of change of unemployment and its level. It is crucial to understand the implications of the inclusion of the level of unemployment as a determinant of the change in labor share. Suppose that the rate of unemployment is extremely low but unchanging. In the absence of the level of unemployment the prediction would be that labor share would remain constant. With the inclusion of the level of unemployment the prediction becomes that labor share would continue to rise.

Capacity utilization and the strength of capital

Goldstein (1996) argues that the degree of product market competition falls as the level of capacity utilization rises. The robustness of the economy reduces cut-throat competition. If capacity utilization changes the markup of price to marginal cost at all, it makes sense that the markup would increase as capacity utilization increases. With domestic production high relative to capacity, buyers have less demand substitutes. Assuming short-run constant returns to scale the markup ratio is also the ratio of revenue to average variable costs.

Because markups and product price elasticities of demand are framed for gross revenue it will be important to understand their implications for value added. Assume that materials inputs are proportionate to real output and the degree of monopoly is the same for final goods and the intermediate inputs. The markup of value added over labor cost will be the same as price over full unit costs. Hall (1986) shows that in general the value added markup overstates the gross output markup with the overstatement increasing in the ratio of materials cost to total revenue. The goal here is not to ascertain the gross output markup but to ascertain how business conditions affect labor share of value added. Goldstein's markup theory implies that the inverse of labor share will increase as capacity utilization increases. Labor share as a proportion of value added will fall as capacity utilization increases.

The overhead labor-wages lag hypothesis of Sherman (1997) also links declining labor share to increasing capacity utilization. Causation runs initially from a collapse in aggregate demand to a collapse in capacity utilization to a collapse in labor productivity due to overhead or hoarded labor, and finally to an increase in labor share in the face of a lag in real wages. In the ensuing recovery demand increases, capacity utilization increases, labor productivity increases, real wages remain relatively quiescent and labor share decreases. With overhead labor this decrease in labor share can occur in the presence of a constant markup over variable production labor costs. In the absence of overhead labor, labor share will only decrease if the markup increases as capacity utilization increases. In either case the change in labor share depends negatively on the change in capacity utilization. The markup hypothesis of Goldstein and the overhead labor–wages lag theory of Sherman have exactly the same implications. The change in labor share depends negatively on the change in capacity utilization.

According to Boddy and Crotty the change in labor share is a function of both the *change* and the *level* of the rate of unemployment. According to Goldstein and Sherman the change in labor share is a function of the *change* in capacity utilization. The two conditioning variables – unemployment and capacity utilization – enter in an asymmetric fashion. The model is then

$$\Delta s_t = \alpha_1 \Delta c_t + \beta_1 \Delta u_{t-1} + \beta_2(u_{t-1} - U) + v_t \tag{3}$$

where, s_t is labor share; c_t is capacity utilization rate; u_t is the rate of unemployment; U is the unemployment threshold and v_t is a random error term.

Instead of positing a generalized lag structure, I have chosen to illustrate the empirically determined lag found in this study. The specific lags shown in Equation 3 are not part of the hypothesis.

The threshold U enters as an unknown parameter in Equation 3. Separating and collecting the terms involving the threshold, the regression becomes,

$$\Delta s_t = S + \alpha_1 \Delta c_t + \beta_1 \Delta u_{t-1} + \beta_2 u_{t-1} + v_t \tag{4}$$

where the intercept $S = -(\beta_2 U)$. The point estimate of the threshold $U = -S/\beta_2$.

In Equation 3 and therefore Equation 4 labor share is expressed directly in terms of its determinant variables. An alternative approach is to explain product real wage and labor productivity as a function of capacity utilization and unemployment and then combine the two explanations into an explanation of labor share. From Equation 1:

$$\mathrm{dlog}\,(WL/PQ) = \mathrm{dlog}\,(W/P) - \mathrm{dlog}\,(Q/L) \tag{5}$$

Boddy and Crotty hypothesized that labor productivity depended on the unemployment rate. Perhaps labor productivity depends only on capacity utilization. From Equation 5, it is clear that in explaining labor share it does not matter if the determining variable works through labor productivity or through the product real wage. The resulting equation comparable to Equation 4 for the same determining variables is:

$$\mathrm{dlog}\,s_t = \pounds + \alpha_1 \mathrm{dlog}\,c_t + \beta_1 \mathrm{dlog}\,u_{t-1} + \beta_2 u_{t-1} + v_t \tag{6}$$

I have made estimates of Equation 4 and Equation 6. Because the variables have little or no trend, the goodness of fit for the arithmetic differences of Equation 4 and the log differences of Equation 6 are very similar. Because it is easier to interpret the arithmetic changes, the estimates for the two regimes presented in this chapter are based on Equation 4.

Estimates for Keynesian and neoliberal regimes

The estimates of this chapter are for labor share out of gross value added in the nonfinancial corporate business sector (NFC). Others such as Weisskopf (1979) have worked with the labor share out of NFC net value added. The labor share out of net value added fits better in Weisskopf's framework for the decomposition of the rate of profit on net capital stocks. I believe that cyclically the labor share out of gross valued added is a better measure of what is "up for grabs" in bilateral bargaining and that profits gross of depreciation allowances are a better measure cyclically of what is important to capital.

I present in Table 12.1 estimates of the labor share for an interval of the Keynesian compromise, for a connecting transition period, and for an interval of the still continuing neoliberal era. Two key elements of the Keynesian compromise were the active use of Keynesian policy and the fixed exchange rates of Bretton Woods. Both of these were unraveling by 1972. For the neoliberal era two key elements have been flexible exchange rates and the adoption of a monetary policy predicated on inflation stability. The monetary policy was not in place until the appointment of Volcker as Chair of the Fed in August 1979. In Table 12.1 each regime and the intervening transition are dated from trough quarter to trough quarter. Of the nine complete cycles starting in 1949:4, cycles I–IV fall in the Keynesian period, cycles V and VI in the transition interval, and cycles VII–IX in the neoliberal period. Bakir and Campbell (2006) suggest a somewhat similar demarcation of the regimes. They date the economic regime change beginning in the early 1970s and "full neoliberalism" commencing with cycle VIII in 1982:4.

The estimates in column (1) for the Keynesian regime show as hypothesized by Goldstein (1996) and Sherman (1997) that changes in capacity utilization negatively affect the change in labor share. As hypothesized by Boddy and Crotty (1975) both the change in unemployment and the level of unemployment here lagged one period negatively affect the change in labor share. Decreases in unemployment and low unemployment both increase labor share. All three variables are significant at the usual levels. Turning to the column (3) estimates for the neoliberal regime we find the same pattern as for the Keynesian compromise. Although the coefficients have fallen roughly by half for both the change in

Table 12.1 Labor share over Keynesian and neoliberal regimes

Variable	(1) Keynesian 1949:4 1970:4	(2) Transition 1970:4 1980:3	(3) Neoliberal 1980:3 2001:4
Intercept	0.93 (.33)	0.67 (0.61)	0.53 (0.29)
Change in capacity utilization	−0.21 (0.04)	−0.18 (0.06)	−0.12 (0.07)
Change in unemployment rate, one period lag	−0.52 (0.18)	−1.54 (0.28)	−0.08 (0.23)
Unemployment rate one period lag	−0.18 (0.07)	−0.08 (0.10)	−0.09 (0.04)
Unemployment threshold	5.2%	7.9%	6.0%
Adjusted R-square	0.43	0.50	0.09
Durbin-Watson	2.17	1.97	2.07

Sources: labor share for the nonfinancial corporate sector is the ratio of two quarterly Bureau of Economic Analysis NIPA series for Compensation of Employees and Gross Value Added (Table 1.14). Capacity utilization is the Federal Reserve series for capacity utilization for manufacturing on a quarterly basis (Table B0004.S). Unemployment is Bureau of Labor Statistics unemployment rate for civilian population 16 years and over on a quarterly basis (Series ID LNS14000000).

Note
Dependent variable is change in labor share.

capacity utilization and the level of unemployment they remain significant. The coefficient for change in the rate of unemployment falls precipitously and is non-significant. What really falls between the two regimes is the adjusted R-square. Whether one is a proponent of the reserve army hypothesis or the overhead labor-wages lag (markup) hypothesis or both, the outcome of the policies of the neoliberal regime has been to diminish the combined effects. The functional form has remained intact. As we shall see the functional form with its diminished values has implications for both the length of the business cycle and what brings the cycle to its end in the neoliberal era.

As shown in Equation 3 the impact of the level of lagged unemployment operates through its deviation from threshold unemployment U. When the level of unemployment is below threshold it drives labor share up. For the Keynesian regime the point estimate of the unemployment threshold U is 5.2 percent. For the neoliberal regime it is 6.0 percent. The relative gap between the thresholds for the two regimes is in the expected direction but one should not read very much into the individual threshold magnitudes. The threshold $U = -S/\beta_2$ is a non-linear function of the regression coefficients of Equation 4. Staiger *et al.* (1997) note that confidence intervals for such threshold variables require Monte Carlo techniques and the confidence intervals can be quite wide. In the comparison of the two regimes it is the response of the change in labor share to the level of unemployment and the other two variables that is most important and not "confidence" in the individual unemployment threshold values.

The estimates of Table 12.1 are by ordinary least squares (OLS). For unbiased estimates OLS requires that the error terms are not correlated with the independent explanatory variables. There are two reasons that it is not likely to be the case. In the specification of a larger model contemporaneous changes in capacity utilization would be an endogenous variable. Also, the measure of capacity utilization has manufacturing output in its numerator. At the same level of aggregation, output per unit of capacity explains output per worker which in turn partly explains labor share. The explanatory variable is correlated with the disturbance term. Typically one tries to obtain consistent estimates by choosing instrumental variables correlated with the explanatory variables but not correlated with the disturbance term. Although military expenditure is a good instrument for the Keynesian period, I have found no instruments that work over both regimes. As Moore (1977) states, business cycles are "Partly Exogenous, Mostly Endogenous." Strong instrumental variables for this model may be hard to come by.

How do the estimates of Table 12.1 compare to the estimates of other colleagues? The most directly comparable estimates are those of Hahnel and Sherman (1982) and Sherman and Kolk (1996). Both of these studies assume that the level of labor share depends on the level of capacity utilization and the level of unemployment. Hahnel and Sherman work in first differences to eliminate trends in variables. Sherman and Kolk do not. In first differences their model is a subset of Equation 4 which underlies the estimates of Table 12.1. The estimates of Table 12.1 imply that their model is a misspecification of Equation

4. The misspecification is fundamental. Their model makes little differentiation between what happens in the early part of the expansion and the later part of the expansion. So long as capacity utilization is increasing and unemployment is falling it makes no difference in their model if we are in the early part of the recovery or the last part of the expansion. The model behind Table 12.1 implies a fundamental change in the relationship between labor share, capacity and unemployment between the early expansion and the late expansion. As evidenced by the estimates for the Keynesian regime, high and stable levels of capacity utilization and low unemployment not only meant a high labor share it meant an increasing labor share. In the neoliberal regime that implication is certainly less strong, but it remains.

Having included them, I will make a brief comment on the estimates of column (2) of Table 12.1 for the transition period. On the surface they too make a case for the importance of capacity utilization and unemployment – measured by R-square seemingly the best case of all. I think that case is spurious. Lucas (1976) is generally correct that coefficients which record the responses of economic agents are influenced by the policies faced by those agents. This should especially be, and has been the case as shown in Table 12.1, when the policy changes are so large as to constitute regime change. When the policies are generally coherent as they were in the Keynesian regime and are now once again in the neoliberal regime there can be a coherent interpretation of the coefficients. My sense is that was not the case for the transition period. The transitional decade was a period of inconsistent and incoherent policies. That is why it is correctly treated as a transition period.

Labor productivity and real wages in the neoliberal era

The Bureau of Labor Statistics (BLS) publishes a quarterly series on labor productivity (1992 = 100) for NFC that is consistent with the NFC series on labor share out of gross value added that has been used in this chapter. Knowing labor share and labor productivity it is straightforward through Equation 1 to derive a quarterly series of the implied product real wage for NFC (1992 = 100). I show, in Figures 12.1 and 12.2, the relative movements of the product real wage and labor productivity for the two major neoliberal expansions. For each expansion, the beginning value of labor productivity is "normed" to be equal to the beginning value of the product real wage. (The actual gaps between the two indexes at the beginning of each expansion are quite small.) The scale on the vertical axis is the index of the product real wage (1992 = 100).

In addition to tracing out the movements of labor productivity and product real wage one can also read the movements of labor share in Figures 12.1 and 12.2. To compare the labor share at a particular quarter to the beginning labor share one takes the ratio of the product real wage to labor productivity. When the product real wage is below labor productivity the corresponding labor share is below the labor share at the beginning of the expansion. When the normed indexes of labor productivity and product real wage converge, the labor share is

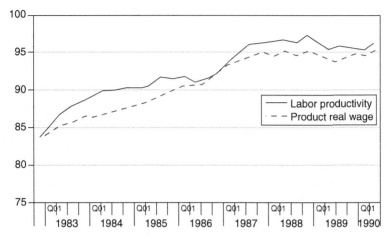

Figure 12.1 1980's neoliberal expansion.

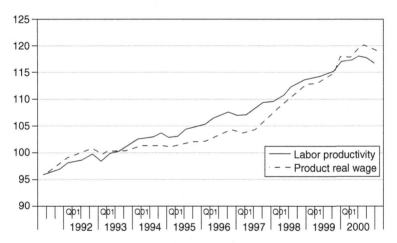

Figure 12.2 1990's neoliberal expansion.

again equal to the labor share at the beginning of that expansion. Within each expansion the spatial gap between the two lines is a good representation of the movements in labor share. Since the vertical axis in Figure 12.2 is compressed almost twice as much as in Figure 12.1, it is not the case that a larger spatial gap in Figure 12.1 compared to the spatial gap in Figure 12.2 translates to a larger change in labor share. The maximum change in labor share in the 1990s is roughly twice the maximum change in the 1980s.

For the expansion beginning 1982:4 labor productivity flattens out by 1986 and then grows until two years before the end of the expansion. For the expansion as a whole the average annual exponential rate of growth of labor productivity is 1.7 percent. From its cyclical nadir in 1984:2 labor share increased from

65 percent to 67 percent in 1986:2. From 1986:2 to the end of the expansion it falls to 66 percent. Starting at an unemployment rate of 10.7 percent at the beginning of the expansion, the rate of unemployment does not go below 6 percent until the third quarter of 1987. The rate of capacity utilization does not go above 80 until the first quarter of 1987. This cycle ended more from Greenspan's concern about the impact of the large increase in debt related to the savings and loan debacle on the stability of the monetary system than it did from any push by labor.

For the expansion of the 1990s, labor productivity increased to the second quarter before the end of the expansion. For the expansion as a whole labor productivity increased at 2.2 percent per year. Labor share fell until 1997:2 only to recover to its initial share value before the end of the expansion. From its low of 64 percent, labor share increased to 68 percent. This turnaround in labor share implies a 9 percent decline in profit share. Unlike in the expansion of the 1980s where unemployment never fell below 5 percent for more than one quarter, unemployment was below 5 percent from the second quarter of 1997 and averaged below 4 percent for the last year of the expansion, 2000. Unemployment had not been below 4 percent in the past 30 years. Capacity utilization, however, was held in check in the period after 1997 by imports of finished goods. The NFC firms had no pricing power. From 1997 to 2000 the NFC gross value added deflator increased less than three-quarters of 1 percent per year. The idea that flexible exchange rates make it possible for firms to pass on unit labor cost and thereby maintain share is clearly not supported by the movement in labor share from 1997–2000.

What happened? There appears to be several things that interacted to mislead the neoliberal policy-makers – particularly the Fed. From 1997:1 to 2000:1 the average annual increase in the implicit GDP deflator was less than 1.5 percent. In the absence of significant inflation, there was an understandable pressure from a Democratic president to increase output and decrease unemployment. Even though it was known that money wages were rising, price movements which were held down by imports did not appear to justify a contractionary monetary response. Greenspan also appeared to hesitate to sop up asset bubble inflation. The low unemployment and the increasing labor share materially reduced profits and did much more to contribute to the break of the bubble than any belated actions of Greenspan. One difference from the expansions of the Keynesian period, and it is an important one, is that the expansion meandered along at a snail's pace in terms of real GDP growth for a much longer time before the neoliberal policy-makers mistakenly laid the foundation for the large increase in labor share and the drop in the profit rate. It's a mistake that they appear in no hurry to repeat.

What happened to the real wage, particularly for the crucial period 1997–2000 when labor share strongly squeezed the profit share? The real wage and the product real wage are linked by the identity

$$W/CPI = (P/CPI)\,(W/P) \tag{7}$$

where the CPI is for urban workers.

On a year over year basis from 1997–2000 the product real wage for the NFC increased 4.3 percent per year. The NFC value added deflator increased only 0.5 percent per year. The CPI increased 2.2 percent per year. The implied real wage for the NFC therefore increased 2.6 percent per year. A comparable calculation for the nonfarm business sector shows a real wage increase of 3.0 percent per year over the same period. Over the average cycle we can expect labor productivity and the real wage in the business sector as a whole to grow at approximately the same rate. For a narrower sector such as the NFC, the labor productivity of the sector affects the real wage only insofar as it affects the product real wage in Equation 7. And that takes us back to the key role of labor share.

Conclusion

A properly specified model linking labor share to capacity utilization and unemployment helps to explain the complex movements of labor share over the cycle – especially the shift from early expansion to late expansion. When applied to the Keynesian and neoliberal regimes, it shows that labor share was much more responsive to capacity utilization and unemployment in the Keynesian period than it has been in the neoliberal period. Still the functional form has remained intact. Based on that functional form and the movements of labor productivity and product real wage we can conclude that unemployment in the 1980s never got sufficiently low to play anything more than a minor role in the end of that long expansion. During the expansion of the 1990s the decrease in unemployment, and its low level, contributed integrally to the decline in the rate of profit and the end of that expansion.

Note

1 I am grateful for discussions with my colleague Tia Hilmer on cointegrated processes. My colleague Bill Carter has shared his insights as to what was happening in the second halves of the two long neoliberal expansions of the 1980s and 1990s.

References

Bakir, E. and Campbell, A. (2006) "The Effect of Neoliberalism on the Fall in the Rate of Profit in Business Cycles," *Review of Radical Political Economics*, 38(3): 365–73.

Boddy, R. and Crotty, J. (1975) "Class Conflict and Macro-Policy: The Political Business Cycle," *Review of Radical Political Economics*, 7(Spring): 1–19.

Goldstein, J. P. (1986) "Mark-up Pricing over the Business Cycle: The Microfoundations of the Variable Mark-up," *Southern Economics Journal*, 53(1): 233–46.

—— (1996) "The Empirical Relevance of the Cyclical Profit Squeeze: A Reassertion," *Review of Radical Political Economics*, 28(4): 55–92.

Hahnel, R. and Sherman, H. J. (1982) "Income Distribution and the Business Cycle: Three Competing Hypotheses," *Journal of Economic Issues*, XVI(1): 49–73.

Hall, R. (1986) "Market Structure and Macroeconomic Fluctuations," *Brookings Papers on Economic Activity*, 2: 285–322.

Lucas, R. E. Jr. (1976) "Econometric Policy Evaluation: A Critique," *Carnegie Rochester Conference Series on Public Policy*, Amsterdam: North-Holland: 19–46.

Moore, G. H. (1977) "Business Cycles: Partly Exogenous, Mostly Endogenous," *Social Science Quarterly*, 58(1): 96–103.

Sherman, H. (1972) *Radical Political Economy.* New York: Basic Books.

—— (1997) "Theories of Cyclical Profit Squeeze," *Review of Radical Political Economics*, 29(1): 139–46.

Sherman, H. and Kolk, D. X. (1996) *Business Cycles and Forecasting.* Boston: Addison Wesley.

Staiger, D., Stock, J. H. and Watson, M. W. (1997) "The NAIRU, Unemployment and Monetary Policy," *Journal of Economic Perspectives*, 11(1): 33–49.

Weisskopf, T. E. (1979) "Marxian Crisis Theory and the Rate of Profit in the Postwar U.S. Economy," *Cambridge Journal of Economics*, 3(4): 341–78.

13 Economic crises and institutional structures

A comparison of regulated and neoliberal capitalism in the USA

David M. Kotz

Introduction[1]

Several analysts have suggested that the dominant cause of capitalist economic crises depends on the institutional structure of capitalism at a particular time and place (Wright, 1979; Wolfson, 2003; Kotz, 2008). Some have suggested that the highly regulated form of capitalism in the post-World War II decades was particularly vulnerable to the reserve army (or profit squeeze) crisis tendency, while in today's neoliberal form of capitalism over-production relative to demand is the main cause of periodic economic crises (Wolfson, 2003; Kotz, 2008).

In the reserve army crisis tendency, economic expansion drives the unemployment rate to a low level, increasing workers' bargaining power so that the real wage rises faster than labor productivity, resulting in a decline in the profit share and the rate of profit, setting off an economic crisis (Marx, 1967: Chapter 25; Sweezy, 1942: Chapter 9). This crisis tendency may be associated with regulated capitalism because its institutions tend to promote workers' bargaining power.[2] By contrast, under neoliberal capitalism workers have little bargaining power, making that crisis scenario unlikely. Instead, various features of neoliberal capitalism should produce expansions in which production outruns demand (Crotty, 2000; Wolfson, 2003; Kotz, 2008).

The literature cited above makes a strong theoretical case for such a connection between crisis tendencies and institutional structures. However, those claims have not been subjected to a comparative empirical analysis for the regulated and neoliberal institutional forms of capitalism. This chapter offers such an empirical analysis. The second section develops a methodology for identifying which crisis tendency or tendencies are responsible for an economic crisis (or recession). The third section applies that methodology to data for the US economy in the eras of regulated and neoliberal capitalism. The final section offers concluding comments.

Empirical identification of crisis tendencies

The reserve army crisis tendency, and its expected connection to regulated capitalism, is relatively straightforward. However, both the problem of over-production, and its connection to neoliberal capitalism, are more complex. We can identify three possible sources of over-production in a neoliberal institutional structure.

The first is known as underconsumption, a crisis tendency associated with capital having the upper hand in wage bargaining. Because of the limited bargaining power of labor in neoliberal capitalism, real wages tend to increase very slowly or even decline during economic expansions. If the real wage stagnates or declines while labor productivity increases during an expansion, the share of profit in total income should rise, creating a potential realization problem. Unless accumulation or some type of unproductive spending (such as state spending or capitalist consumption) rises rapidly to absorb the rapidly rising profit-component of the value of output, production will outrun demand, leading to a crisis.[3]

A second type of over-production crisis tendency, called over-investment, can be associated with a neoliberal institutional structure, stemming from the nature of competition. In contrast to the co-respective behavior toward one another by large corporations in the regulated capitalist era, in the neoliberal era capital–capital relations are characterized by unrestrained competition including frequent price-cutting. Some analysts have argued that the unrestrained competition of neoliberal capitalism leads to excessive investment, as rival firms battle for survival by trying to raise their market share. This in turn leads to excessive creation of productive capacity, resulting in underuse of capacity.[4] Growing idle capacity eventually causes a downturn in investment, which sets off the crisis.

A third type of over-production crisis tendency in neoliberal capitalism stems from asset bubbles. Economic expansions in neoliberal capitalism tend to produce asset bubbles.[5] This happens because rapidly rising profits, and rapidly rising personal income of wealthy households, create a pool of funds seeking investment that exceeds the available profitable productive investment opportunities. As a result, the excess investable funds find their way into the purchase of assets, which tends to raise asset prices, eventually setting off a speculative rise in asset prices – that is, an asset bubble. As paper wealth increases, both consumption and investment are stimulated, tending to rise at a rate out of line with increases in ordinary income. Investment may be so overstimulated that productive capacity rises faster than demand, as the euphoria and elevated expectations induced by the bubble affect corporate decision-makers who form an exaggerated estimate of future returns to investment. Once the bubble bursts, and consumption and investment return to levels in line with ordinary income, a large overhang of excess productive capacity is revealed, which may depress the incentive to invest for a lengthy period.

How can the above four crisis tendencies be empirically identified? Weisskopf (1979) developed a methodology in which the average rate of profit is expressed as the product of several factors, each of which is interpreted as reflecting a particular crisis tendency. He used this approach to determine which of several possible crisis tendencies, including the reserve army effect and underconsumption, was the operative one in the US economy from 1949–75. This chapter follows an approach similar to that of Weisskopf (1979), although with some differences.[6]

Most Marxist analysts have considered the rate of profit to be the key factor in economic crises.[7] In the typical economic expansion, the rate of profit reaches a peak and then declines prior to the crisis, as will be shown in the following section. This pattern is consistent with the view that a declining profit rate eventually sets off the crisis. The central role of the profit rate is due to its impact on capital accumulation, which is believed to be sensitive to changes in the rate of profit. In the US national income and product accounts, investment is the closest approximation to the Marxist concept of capital accumulation. In the nine recessions since 1949 in the USA, real gross private domestic investment declined in the first year of each one, by an average of 7.6 percent (US Bureau of Economic Analysis, 2006).

Since we are interested in the rate of profit as a determinant of business investment, we use the following narrow definition of the rate of profit:

$$r = \frac{R}{NW}$$

where r = rate of profit; R = after-tax profit (after payment of interest); NW =net worth (at market value). The rate of profit is for the nonfinancial corporate business sector of the US economy.[8]

The rate of profit as defined above can be expressed as the product of four variables:

$$r = \frac{R}{Y} \times \frac{Y}{TA} \times \frac{TA}{A} \times \frac{A}{NW} \tag{1}$$

where Y is net output or income; TA is tangible assets (at market value); A is total assets (at market value).

The first ratio in Equation 1, R/Y, is the profit share of income. The second, Y/TA, is the ratio of output to tangible assets, whose variation over short periods of time indicates mainly changes in the degree of utilization of the stock of means of production.[9] The third and fourth ratios in Equation 1, TA/A and A/NW, can be shown to reflect the share of financial assets in total assets and the degree of leverage respectively. Since these two variables were not found to play a significant role in our analysis of movements of the rate of profit during the period under study, they have been omitted from the analysis in this chapter.[10]

This kind of analysis of the determinants of the rate of profit is based on an identity, which cannot explain causation. However, it can be used for a kind of accounting procedure. The sum of the percentage changes in the four right-hand variables must add up approximately to the percentage decline in r.[11] Suppose the rate of profit declines by 10 percent over a period. If R/Y declined by 5 percent over that period, one can say that the decline in R/Y directly accounted for half of the decline in r.

The first ratio above, R/Y, can be further analyzed as follows:

$$\frac{R}{Y} = 1 - \frac{W}{Y} - \frac{T}{Y} - \frac{i}{Y} \tag{2}$$

where W = employee compensation (including employer-paid benefits); T = taxes on profits plus indirect taxes; i = interest paid. Like Equation 1, Equation 2 is an identity, since total output is divided up on the income side among profits, wages, taxes and interest.[12]

The relation expressed in Equation 2 is an additive identity rather than a multiplicative identity. For an additive identity, the sum of the absolute changes in the right-side variables over a period exactly equals the absolute change in the left-side variable. Hence, the most useful way to analyze the change in the profit share is using the concept of "contribution," where the contribution to the change in the profit share of each variable on the right side of Equation 2 is the absolute change in that variable over the period divided by the absolute change in the profit share, expressed as a percentage. The sum of the contributions of the right-side variables is exactly 100 percent, apart from rounding errors, since there are no interaction terms for additive equations.

Since Equation 2 is an identity, strictly speaking the contribution of each right-side variable to the change in the profit share represents a kind of accounting rather than necessarily a cause. If the change in the wage share contributes 80 percent of the change in the profit share over a period, that means that, had the wage share remained unchanged over that period while the other right-side variables had changed as they actually did, then the change in the profit share would have been smaller by 80 percent over that period.

The wage share can be expressed as a function of three underlying variables: the real wage, output per worker and the ratio of the consumer price index to the output price deflator:

$$\frac{W}{Y} = \frac{w_R \times \left(\frac{CPI}{P_Y}\right)}{\frac{Y_R}{N}} \tag{3}$$

where w_R =real wage per worker (nominal employee compensation per worker deflated by the CPI); CPI =consumer price index; Py =price index for the output of the nonfinancial corporate business sector; Y_R =real output of the nonfinancial corporate business sector (deflated by Py); N =number of full-time equivalent workers.

Equation 3, which is also an identity, shows that the relation between the real wage and output per worker does not uniquely account for the change in the wage share. The wage share can rise even if the real wage rises no faster than output per worker, if the ratio CPI/Py is rising. The ratio CPI/Py enters Equation 3 to reflect the assumption that workers are concerned with their real wage (their money wage deflated by the CPI), not their product wage (their money wage deflated by Py), since they do not consume a representative basket of goods drawn from the output of the nonfinancial business sector. The goods covered by the two price indexes, CPI and Py, differ in a number of ways including that consumers purchase imported consumer goods, which are not in the basket for computing the output price index, and they do not purchase capital goods, which are in the basket for computing the output price index.[13]

How can the four crisis tendencies cited above be identified in the movement of the determinants of the profit rate? Consider the relation between capital and labor as they struggle over wages and profits. We assume that labor is concerned, first of all, with its real wage. The real wage depends on the movement of the money wage relative to the consumer price index. A rising real wage is made possible by rising real output per worker (or, as it is often called, labor productivity). Some trade unions cite the rate of increase in labor productivity in setting a target for real wage growth, arguing that labor's real reward should rise as fast as real output per worker. The extent of workers' bargaining power might be indicated by the relation between real wage growth and labor productivity growth. If the real wage rises faster than productivity growth, labor is getting the upper hand over capital, while if the real wage rises more slowly than productivity growth, capital has the upper hand.

However, capital is concerned with the wage share, which directly affects the rate of profit. As Equation 3 shows, the wage share depends on a three-way relation between the real wage, real output per worker, and the ratio of the consumer price index to the output price index. The wage share is determined both by capital's relation with labor, indicated by the relation between the real wage and real output per worker, and by capital's pricing power, which affects the denominator of the price index ratio. Capital's pricing power is affected by the adequacy of total demand in relation to output.

In light of the above considerations, we will identify the four crisis tendencies in relation to the movement of the determinants of the profit rate as follows:

1   Reserve Army Effect: we will regard this crisis tendency as indicated by a decline in the profit rate prior to a recession that stems from a rise in the wage share which, in turn, results from the real wage rising faster than output per worker.

2   Underconsumption: we will consider the underconsumption crisis tendency to be indicated by the joint occurrence of a declining Y/TA and a rising profit share prior to a recession. The concept of underconsumption is based on a rising profit share as the cause of the realization problem, so a rising profit share must be part of the evidence for underconsumption. The evidence that the rising profit share is causing a crisis due to underconsumption would be confirmed by a declining Y/TA. The crisis would be set off by the declining Y/TA outweighing the rising R/Y in Equation 1, causing r to fall.

3   Over-Investment: we will consider the over-investment crisis tendency to be indicated by the following two movements in the profit rate determinants resulting in a decline in the rate of profit prior to a recession:

    a   declining Y/TA;

    b   declining R/Y due to a rising ratio CPI/Py while the real wage is rising no faster than output per worker.

The former indicates reducing real output relative to capacity in response to a demand shortfall, while the latter indicates the effect of the demand shortfall being exhibited by an inability by capital to raise output prices fast enough to prevent the profit share from falling despite the lack of power by labor to increase the real wage faster than productivity growth. That is, we are assuming that the shortfall of demand relative to output resulting from over-investment would cause both a quantity effect and a price effect.

4   Asset Bubble Effects: an asset bubble has two effects, described above, that are relevant here. First, the speculative bubble tends to cause exaggerated expectations of future profitability, which lead to excessive investment. This would produce the same movement of the determinants of the profit rate as are caused by the over-investment crisis tendency. Second, the prolonged elevated levels of both consumption and investment set off by an asset bubble are likely to cause, once the bubble bursts, a long-lasting decline in investment. Hence, the indication that this crisis tendency is the operative one is a combination of:

a   the presence of an asset bubble during the expansion;
b   the same profit rate determinant movements prior to the recession described under the over-investment crisis tendency above; and
c   a prolonged decline in investment following the collapse of the bubble.

Table 13.1 summarizes the empirical identification of each of our four crisis tendencies, as described above.

Evidence about crisis tendencies during the two periods

We regard the regulated capitalist institutional structure in the USA as having been established by 1948 and lasting until 1973 (Kotz, 2003). After a period of transition involving intense class conflict and macroeconomic instability, the

Table 13.1 Empirical identification scheme for the four crisis tendencies

	Reserve army	Underconsumption	Over-investment	Asset bubble effects
Rate of profit	↓	↓	↓	↓
Profit share	↓	↑	↓	↓
Capacity use		↓	↓	↓
Wage share	↑	↓	↑	↑
Real wage/ productivity	↑	↓	↓	↓
Long decline in investment*	no	no	no	yes

Notes
* Prolonged decline in nonresidential fixed investment following the business cycle peak.
  Arrow indicates increase or decrease in variable named at start of row prior to the recession.

neoliberal institutional structure was established by around the end of 1982 and continues through the present.

Figure 13.1 shows the movements of the profit rate in the USA during 1949–2005 in relation to the expansions and recessions of that period.[14] There were nine complete expansions during this period: 1949–1953, 1954–1957, 1958–1960, 1961–1969, 1970–1973, 1975–1979, 1980–1981, 1982–1990 and 1991–2000.[15] We will analyze the late-expansion profit rate declines for the five expansions during the regulated capitalist era (through 1973) and the two late expansions of the neoliberal era (1982–1990 and 1991–2000).

Figure 13.1 shows that, with two exceptions (1949–1953 and 1980–1981), the rate of profit rose in the early part of each expansion and fell in the later part of the expansion. In the 1949–1953 expansion the rate of profit fell continuously from the start of the expansion, due to effects of Korean War taxes (see below, p. 183). In the one-year-long expansion of 1980–1981, the profit rate rose up to the peak of the expansion, only falling after the peak. That brief expansion, which took place amidst the instability of the transition period, was cut short by the Fed's shift to a very tight monetary policy.

Table 13.2 shows the movement of the first two determinants of the profit rate, based on equation (1), during the late-expansion profit rate declines for each of our seven cases. Column 1 shows the percentage change in the profit rate in each period. The late-expansion decline in the profit rate ranged from 9.99 percent in 1972–1973 to 46.49 percent in 1997–2000.

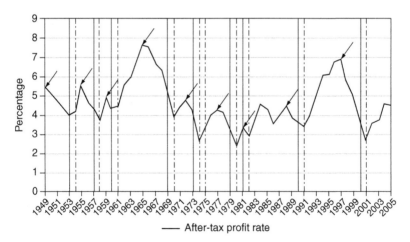

Figure 13.1 The after-tax rate of profit of the nonfinancial corporate business sector in relation to business cycle expansions and contractions, 1949–2005 (source: US Bureau of Economic Analysis, 2006, Table 1.14; US Federal Reserve System, 2006, Flow of Funds, Z.1 Statistical Release).

Key
Solid vertical line indicates last year of business expansion. Dotted vertical line indicates recession year. Arrow indicates peak of profit rate prior to its decline in late expansion.

Table 13.2 Factors affecting the decline in the rate of profit

Percentage change in variable

Period of r decline	(1) r	(2) R/Y	(3) Y/TA
1949–1953	−25.85	−34.26	13.02
1955–1957	−21.07	−15.44	−7.99
1959–1960	−10.55	−10.12	−0.48
1965–1969	−31.90	−34.42	0.15
1972–1973	−9.99	−11.25	3.06
1988–1990	−21.42	−20.51	−2.09
1997–2000	−46.49	−37.76	−4.30

Source: US Bureau of Economic Analysis, 2006, Table 1.14; US Federal Reserve System, 2006, Flow of Funds, Z.1 Statistical Release.

Notes
r: rate of profit.
R/Y: share of profit in income (output).
Y/TA: ratio of output (income) to tangible assets.

Column 2 shows the percentage change in the profit share in each period. Note that a decline in the profit share directly accounts for all or most of the decline in the profit rate in every period. Column 3 shows the percentage change in the ratio of output to tangible assets, which is our measure of changes in capacity utilization. This variable contributed significantly to the decline in the rate of profit in three late expansions: 1955–1957 when it directly accounted for 37.9 percent of the profit rate decline; 1988–1990 when it directly accounted for 9.8 percent of the profit rate decline, and 1997–2000 when it directly accounted for 9.2 percent of the profit rate decline.

Table 13.3 shows the contributions to the decline in the profit share during the seven late expansions from changes in the shares of wages, taxes and interest payments, based on equation (2). A rise in the wage share contributed all, or most, of the profit share decline in every period. However, there are three expansions in which one or both of the other two variables made a significant contribution to the profit share decline. In 1949–1953 a rising tax share contributed almost half of the decline in the profit share, as special Korean War taxes cut into after-tax profits. In 1972–1973 rising taxes and rising interest payments together contributed almost one-third of the profit share decline. And in 1988–1990 the contribution of rising interest payments to the decline in the profit share was almost as great as that of the rising wage share.

Table 13.4 shows the changes in the real wage, output per worker and the price ratio *CPI/Py* for each of the periods, based on Equation 3. Table 13.4 shows that the real wage rose faster than output per worker in every late expansion of the regulated capitalist era. During that period the ratio *CPI/Py* rose in four out of five late expansions but at less than 1 percent per year in each case. For the two late expansions of the neoliberal era, output per worker rose faster (or fell more slowly) than the real wage. The rising wage share in 1988–1990

Table 13.3 Contributions to the decline in the profit share of income

Contribution of variable to decrease in R/Y *(as percentage)*

Period of r decline	(1) W/Y	(2) T/Y	(3) i/Y
1949–1953	52.3	47.6	−2.1
1955–1957	155.8	−66.9	11.5
1959–1960	130.4	−39.9	7.5
1965–1969	92.5	−14.4	21.7
1972–1973	65.7	17.6	15.0
1988–1990	68.3	−16.1	57.7
1997–2000	97.6	−22.0	23.4

Source: US Bureau of Economic Analysis, 2006, Table 1.14.

Notes
1 A positive sign indicates that the change in the variable tended to reduce R/Y. A negative sign indicates that the change in the variable tended to increase R/Y.
2 The sum of the contributions to the change in R/Y may not exactly equal 100.0% due to the omission of business transfer payments and due to rounding errors.

Definitions of variables:
r: rate of profit.
R/Y: share of profit in income (output).
W/Y: share of wages in income.
T/Y: share of taxes in income.
i/Y: share of interest in income.

Table 13.4 Factors affecting the rise in the wage share of income

Annual percentage change in variable

Period of r decline	W/Y	w_R	Y_R/N	CPI/Py
1949–1953	0.81	4.56	4.29	0.54
1955–1957	1.88	3.13	0.46	−0.75
1959–1960	1.92	2.28	1.33	0.97
1965–1969	1.47	2.55	1.61	0.53
1972–1973	0.82	1.02	0.61	0.41
1988–1990	0.78	−1.64	−0.55	1.89
1997–2000	1.77	2.76	2.85	1.86

Source: US Bureau of Economic Analysis, 2006, Tables 1.14, 1.15, 6.5B; US Bureau of Labor Statistics, 2006.

Notes
The change in variables is shown as an *annual* percentage rate of change.

Definitions of variables:
r: rate of profit.
W/Y: share of wages in income.
w_R: real wage.
Y_R/N: real output per full-time equivalent worker.
CPI/Py: Ratio of consumer price index to output price index.

and 1997–2000 was entirely due to an approximately 2 percent per year increase in *CPI/Py* in each case.[16]

Table 13.5 summarizes our findings. The five late expansions during the regulated capitalist period all fit the characteristics of the reserve army crisis tendency, with one minor qualification: the 1970–1973 expansion was followed by a long depression in investment.[17] In all five late expansions the real wage rose faster than labor productivity, leading to a rising wage share, a falling profit share and a falling rate of profit. Thus, our expectation regarding which crisis tendency would be acting in the regulated capitalist era has been substantially confirmed by the data.

In the two late expansions of the neoliberal era, labor productivity rose faster than the real wage. Hence, neither of these expansions fits the requirements for the reserve army crisis tendency. Also, in neither of these expansions are the

Table 13.5 Identifying crisis tendencies in the late expansions

Period	Rate of profit	Profit share	Capacity use	Wage share	Real wage/ productivity	Long decline in investment*	Crisis tendency
1949–1953	↓	↓	↑	↑	↑	No	Reserve army
1955–1957	↓	↓	↓	↑	↑	No	Reserve army
1959–1960	↓	↓	↓	↑	↑	No	Reserve army
1965–1969	↓	↓	↑	↑	↑	No	Reserve army
1972–1973	↓	↓	↑	↑	↑	Yes[a]	Reserve army+
1988–1990	↓	↓	↓	↑	↓	No	Over-investment
1997–2000	↓	↓	↓	↑	↓	Yes[b]	Over-investment; bubble effects

Notes

* Prolonged decline in nonresidential fixed investment following the business cycle peak.

+ The long decline in investment does not fit the identification scheme for the reserve army crisis tendency.

a Nonresidential fixed investment required 4 years to return to 1973 level.

b Nonresidential fixed investment required 6 years to return to 2000 level.

Arrow indicates increase or decrease in variable at top of column during period shown at start of row.

data consistent with the underconsumption crisis tendency. In neither case did declining capacity use outweigh a rising profit share, resulting in a declining profit rate.

Both of the late expansions of the neoliberal era show the characteristics associated with the over-investment crisis tendency. That is, the rate of profit and the profit share declined, capacity use declined, the wage share rose and labor productivity rose faster than the real wage (with the rise in the ratio CPI/Py accounting for all of the increase in the wage share).

In addition, the expansion of 1991–2000 shows the features of the asset bubble effects crisis tendency. There was a huge asset bubble in the stock market during 1995–2000, which burst in the late summer of 2000. There followed a large and long-lasting depression in nonresidential fixed investment following the business cycle peak. It is also noteworthy that our measure of capacity use, Y/TA, declined every year during the three-year long period of profit rate decline.[18]

Concluding comments

We found that all five economic expansions during the regulated capitalist era in the USA showed evidence of the reserve army crisis tendency. The two expansions of the neoliberal era both showed evidence of the over-investment crisis tendency, while the second expansion of that era also showed evidence of the asset bubble effects crisis tendency.[19]

Thus, this study suggests that the operative crisis tendency, or tendencies, are affected by the institutional structure of capitalism in a given period. When the institutional structure undergoes a major change, as has happened periodically in capitalist history, the dominant crisis tendency also changes.

A caution about the methodology of this study is in order. The crisis tendencies under consideration in this chapter all derive from an analysis of capitalism at a relatively high level of abstraction. Some important features of an actual capitalist system are omitted from the theoretical analysis, including specific interventions by the state in the economy. However, the empirical data used in the chapter are undoubtedly affected by state interventions as well as by underlying crisis tendencies. Thus, the inferences from the data presented in this chapter must be treated cautiously, with awareness that it is possible that factors left out of the analysis might have affected the data and the inferences from the data.

Notes

1 Research assistance was provided by Hwok-Aun Lee.
2 Boddy and Crotty (1975) present a case that this crisis mechanism played an important role in the US economy, with data from the era of regulated capitalism. Weisskopf (1979) found this crisis mechanism to be the main one operating in that period.
3 Sweezy (1942: Chapter 10) and Wright (1979) present models of the underconsumption crisis tendency.
4 See Crotty (2000). Brenner (1999) presents a theory of competition-driven over-

investment as a general crisis tendency of capitalism rather than one specific to its neoliberal form.

5 The 1980s expansion produced a bubble in commercial buildings in some sections of the USA, the 1990s expansion gave rise to the great stock market bubble of 1995–2000, and the expansion since 2001 produced a massive housing bubble (Kotz, 2008). The 1920s, which was the last period prior to the New Deal in which the USA had a liberal institutional structure, also saw huge bubbles in both real estate and securities.

6 Bakir and Campbell (2006) extended Weisskopf's (1979) methodology to 2001. Their results have some similarities to the findings in this chapter, although differences in definitions and data sources from those used in this chapter led to some differences in results.

7 Some advocates of the underconsumption crisis tendency do not emphasize the role of a decline in the profit rate in setting off a crisis. An example is Sweezy (1942).

8 Weisskopf (1979) also used data on the nonfinancial corporate business sector. The reasons for using data on the nonfinancial corporate business sector, along with other technical details, are given in an appendix available from the author, at dmkotz@ econs.umass.edu.

9 The ratio Y/TA is also affected by changes in the organic composition of capital, since Y/TA is equal to Y/W times W/TA where W is aggregate wages. W/TA is a measure of the reciprocal of the organic composition of capital although using US national income account data rather than labor value data. However, the organic composition of capital is unlikely to vary much during the short periods of time that we will be analyzing.

10 A longer version of this chapter, which includes the variables TA/A and A/NW, is available from the author on request at dmkotz@econs.umass.edu.

11 In general the sum will not be exactly equal to the percentage change in r because changes in the interaction terms among the right-hand variables also contribute to the change in r.

12 The variable W includes compensation of all employees, not just production workers. One component of nonfinancial corporate sector income is omitted here, namely business transfer payments. These are very small relative to total output (around 1 percent).

13 There are also technical differences between the two price indexes.

14 The variables in Figure 13.1 and in all the tables are based on annual data. This figure starts with 1949 since our interest is in the profit dynamics during the economic expansions of the two eras, and the first expansion of the regulated capitalist era started following the 1949 recession.

15 Business Cycle turning points are from the National Bureau of Economic Research (2006).

16 Bakir and Campbell (2006) found a similar, although not identical, pattern to that found in Table 13.4.

17 The macroeconomic instability after 1973, following the demise of regulated capitalism, is the likely explanation for the long depression in investment after 1973.

18 During the transition period, the 1977–1979 late expansion fit the characteristics of the over-investment crisis tendency, while none of the four crisis tendencies was found in the 1980–1981 expansion (which appeared to end as a result of very tight monetary policy).

19 It is too soon to evaluate the expansion that began in 2002, which is continuing at this time. However, it has been strongly influenced by an asset bubble in housing (Kotz, 2008).

References

Bakir, E. and Campbell, A. (2006) "The Effect of Neoliberalism on the Fall in the Rate of Profit in Business Cycles," *Review of Radical Political Economics*, 38(3) Summer: 365–73.

Boddy, R. and Crotty, J. R. (1975) "Class Conflict and Macro-Policy: The Political Business Cycle," *Review of Radical Political Economics*, 7(1): 1–19.

Brenner, R. (1999). *Turbulence in the World Economy*. London: Verso Press.

Crotty, James. R. (2000) "Structural Contradictions of the Global Neoliberal Regime," *Review of Radical Political Economics*, 32(3) summer: 361–8.

Kotz, D. M. (2003) "Neoliberalism and the Social Structure of Accumulation Theory of Long-Run Capital Accumulation," *Review of Radical Political Economics*, 35(3) Summer: 263–70.

—— (2008) "Contradictions of Economic Growth in the Neoliberal Era: Accumulation and Crisis in the Contemporary U.S. Economy," *Review of Radical Political Economics*, 40(2) Spring: 174–88

Marx, K. (1967) *Capital*, volume I. New York: International Publishers.

National Bureau of Economic Research (2006) *U.S. Business Cycle Expansions and Contractions*. Available at www.nber.org/cycles.html (last accessed December 2, 2006).

Sweezy, P. M. (1942) *Theory of Capitalist Development*. New York: Monthly Review Press.

U.S. Bureau of Economic Analysis (2006) *National Income and Product Accounts*. Available at www.bea.gov/bea/dn/nipaweb/index.asp (last accessed November 16, 2006).

U.S. Bureau of Labor Statistics (2006) *Consumer Price Index*. Available at www.bls.gov/cpi/home.htm (last accessed November 29, 2006).

U.S. Federal Reserve System (2006) Available at www.federalreserve.gov/datadownload/ (last accessed November 20, 2006).

Weisskopf, T. E. (1979) "Marxian Crisis Theory and the Rate of Profit in the Postwar U.S. Economy," *Cambridge Journal of Economics*, 3(4) December: 341–78.

Wolfson, M. (2003) "Neoliberalism and the Social Structure of Accumulation," *Review of Radical Political Economics*, 35(3) Summer: 255–62.

Wright, E. O. (1979) "Historical Transformations of Capitalist Crisis Tendencies," in *Class, Crisis and the State*. London: New Left Books.

14 Historically contingent, institutionally specific

Class struggles and American employer exceptionalism in the age of neoliberal globalization

Michael G. Hillard and Richard McIntyre

Introduction and overview

Since the 1970s the capitalist/employer classes of the OECD nations have been on the offensive in trying to "liberalize" their economies. This has involved changes in tax, industrial and welfare policies, as well as labor market policy, which is our focus. In terms of labor markets and labor relations, employers and their organizations have sought to roll back the common "restrictions" imposed by organized labor and collective bargaining agreements, typically on wages, hours, holidays and managerial hiring/firing provisions.

The advanced nation where liberalization has had singular success is the United States.[1] In this chapter we argue that this new US Exceptionalism is the contingent result of unique patterns of capitalist and working class formation, as well as the peculiarities of US politics.

Capitalists in the United States have sought to gut the New Deal welfare state, and especially to roll back the presence and effect of organized labor in order to lower wages, erode employer and state-provided benefits, and increase both the intensity and extent of labor performed by the typical worker and household. German, French and Scandinavian employers also pursued these objectives in the 1980s and 1990s, but working-class political strength, evidenced in the ability of trade unions to impose costly strikes and in the enduring political support for social-welfare and labor-market regulatory regimes, defended in both normal politics and in mass action, largely rebuffed these offensives (Thelan 2001; Moss 1998).

Whereas US wages declined significantly during the period between the early 1970s and mid 1990s, wages continued to climb in most OECD countries, with manufacturing workers in other countries closing a considerable gap with the United States during that period and in a some cases exceeding the United States by 2000. This is true despite the leap in US productivity growth in the 1990s. American workers increased annual workloads considerably, while those in Western Europe and Japan saw annual hours worked dropping by 200–400 hours per year (Mishel *et al.* 2005) While trade union density declined in most (though not all) of the OECD countries, the drop was most severe in the United States and in fact the variance of trade union density increased. Less tangibly, capitalists and their allies gained ideological hegemony as they did nowhere else outside the Central Bank of Sweden, which awarded the Nobel Prize in economics to a series of Chicago School economists in this period.

A variety of comparative analysts have attributed these differences to the distinctive institutional histories of the advanced capitalist nations (Hall and Soskice 2001; Streeck and Yamamura 2002). Attention to such difference is both the strength and weakness of the Institutional/Keynesian version of heterodox economics. It is a strength in that this approach allows us to think seriously about historical change in a way that neoclassical economics simply does not, but it also means that concepts must always be revised for new situations, and no abstract description of capitalist economies can ever be sufficient.

Our own standpoint is both Institutional and Marxian and thus in some ways parallels James Crotty's attempt to develop the complementary analytical strengths of the Keynesian and Marxian traditions (Crotty 1990). It was Keynes himself who pointed out the affinities between his own work and Institutional thought, in a letter written to John R. Commons in 1927. More recently, Crotty wrote:

> Keynes's theory is – as it ought to be – institutionally specific and historically contingent. In *The General Theory* and elsewhere Keynes made evident his belief that no all-purpose, institutionally abstract macromodel can adequately capture the processes and outcomes of distinct phases or stages of capitalist development: qualitative change in institutions, in class structure or in agent constitution or motivation requires a qualitatively distinct version of his theory.
>
> (Crotty 1990: 161)

This is the approach taken in what we see as the best recent labor history, e.g. the work of Ira Katznelson, Sean Wilentz, Elizabeth Fones-Wolf, and Bruce Laurie, among others. (Katznelson 1990; Wilentz 1984; Fones-Wolf 1994; Laurie 1989; Tomlins 1985). Working-class formation is seen as "the emergence of a relatively cohesive working class, self-conscious of its position in the social structure and willing and capable of acting to affect it" (Katznelson 1990: 11). Institutional and geographical considerations, as well as cultural ones, mediate between structural class position and action as a class. There is no "standard" story of class formation because the conflict between capital and labor is everywhere mediated differently.

This has produced some surprising results in labor history. For instance, in the period before World War I it was Germany that was most truly exceptional, where specific conditions (especially political repression of the Social Democrats in the late nineteenth century) produced a class-conscious, Marxist working-class movement. We think a similar approach can produce novel results in interpreting the recent past and the current conjuncture.

All capitalisms are not equal. The new comparative political economy has been largely concerned with demonstrating that the more socially embedded economies in the German-speaking countries and Scandinavia can perform at least as well as the so-called liberal economies of the UK and the United States. Our issue is a different one. We want to know why divergence developed between the liberal economies and the social economies, especially in the period between 1973 and 1989. Specifically, why has the capitalist class offensive been uniquely successful in the United States?

We extend recent institutionalist comparative analysis by arguing for the continuing relevance of class formation, class struggle and the particular relative autonomy of the state in explaining this divergence. During the third quarter of the twentieth century, the gap between the institutional character of the United States, UK and Western Europe was greatly narrowed. The US labor movement posted major and seemingly permanent gains and "corporatist" policy arrangements abounded in both the economy and in the larger imagination, so much so that into the early 1980s leading American industrial relations scholars imagined that the United States was converging with the German-speaking and Scandinavian nations (Kerr 1984). Meanwhile, in Germany an Anglo-style reliance on collective bargaining rather than society wide co-determination was imposed by the postwar occupation pushing the German model of labor relations closer to the American one, at least in its New Deal version (Jacoby 2001).

The divergence of the United States versus other OECD nations emerged during the 1970s and 1980s. The full-scale frontal attack on unionized workers, labor protections and rights, and rapid structural shift to a non-unionized, low wage/limited benefits path in the United States under Reagan caught many by surprise. The divergence since the 1980s is a *historically contingent* result, one that turned on the ability or inability of working classes in the respective countries to defend themselves, and the relative ability of capitalist classes to organize and mount their attack. The latter, in turn, is partly explained by the greater opportunities for capitalists in the American political system after the mid-1970s.

That the US capitalist class won almost complete victory while the capitalist classes in Germany and France did not is due to a complex set of factors, many of which lie outside labor relations themselves. While acknowledging this complexity and the interaction of the labor relations systems with other economic and non-economic processes, in this chapter we focus narrowly on labor relations and politics. It is our purpose to explore what has made the United States unique/distinct, i.e. – why has capital been able to so thoroughly rout Labor and erode the "New Deal state"?

Here we must directly confront the bogeyman of "American Exceptionalism." According to the Commons school, because of individualist values, a permeable class structure with greater class mobility, universal manhood suffrage predating the Industrial Revolution, and a disinterest in socialist and Marxian politics, US workers "chose" a conservative, pro-capitalist politics with its distinctive "business unionism." The labor historians of the 1960s and 1970s challenged this in a variety of ways, and more recent work allows us to state a clear and (to us anyway) convincing alternative to the American Exceptionalism story. First, given that there is no "typical" process of class formation, the US story is specific but it can't be exceptional by definition. Second, and more important here, the absolute resistance of capitalists and the state provides a compelling materialist explanation for the prevalence of business unionism. US labor has been as and sometimes more radical than that elsewhere. The repressive agency of US capitalists, and the weakness of the state as an autonomous and mediating force has limited working-class formation, cut off radicalism as a viable alternative, and given US capitalists even greater incentive to repress labor. The values and ideology of US employers, the unique combination of a weak state and very large corporations, and disorganized capital (so that wages could not be taken out of competition) led US employers to be fiercely and successfully anti-labor.

This, and not the supposed preferences of US workers, led to conservative, job control unionism. US industries followed the employer association path typical of Europe in bituminous coal, apparel, construction and metal-working, but the bulk of the US manufacturing workforce was in much larger firms, and even in the decentralized industries, open shop anti-unionism was well represented. The outcome of class struggles, especially those of the late 1880s and early 1890s, not innate conservatism, shaped the dominance and resilience of the labor movement's conservative tendencies. It was not a lack of class consciousness or willingness to embrace class objectives that most distinguished the US labor movement's leaders, but a recognition of their distinct and unfavorable context.

A class struggle approach to labor relations (and to the broader question of the differences between "varieties" of capitalism) involves empirically analyzing *both capitalist and working-class formation*. Capitalist-class formation (CCF) includes both the particular agencies of employer classes, vis-à-vis their workers, the state, and society generally, and institutional configurations that shape/define "corporate governance" and relations between capital and state. Class struggle history cannot be understood by looking at WCF in isolation for CCF.

The US capitalist class was more virulent in its opposition to working-class movements, unionism or social-democratic state regulation or income support including during the New Deal period. Business accommodation with the CIO and the New Deal was thin, opportunistic and extremely short-lived.

Distinct patterns of capitalist-class formation and agency – the *real* "American exceptionalism"[2]

Whether one considers the pre-New Deal era, the New Deal era, or the post-New Deal era in US history, the hostile, repressive and consistently aggressive agency of US capitalists, and the impact this had on the efficacy of US working-class movements and institutions, makes the United States stand out, not necessarily (or only) the barriers to class working-class solidarity and radicalism.

This repressive tendency came to the full fore between 1886, beginning with

Haymarket, and ending with suppression of the national Pullman/American Railway Union strike of 1894. As Wilentz notes:

> Haymarket was only the symbolic beginning of what may someday be recognized as the most intense (and probably the most violent) counteroffensive ever waged against any country's workers ... 1886–1894 was a decisive turning point for organized labor ... It could ... be seen as a decisive period of change that, nevertheless, may have had continuities with earlier events, producing a spectrum of ideas and strategies that lasted well into the twentieth century, with radical syndicalism and socialism among them.

Wilentz concludes (along with Laurie) that:

> Looking at the major episodes in American labor history between 1886 and 1894, it is hard to avoid concluding that the major political reality in these years was the extraordinary repression visited upon organized workers by employers' associations, with the cooperation of the courts, state legislatures, and, increasingly, the federal government.
>
> (Wilentz 1984: 15)

As Laurie says, the latter events "reflected and reinforced prudential unionism." In short, Laurie argues, AF of L leaders came to their "limited" horizons/ strategy through tactical experience – i.e. witnessing and experiencing the working-class disasters of this period. For them, mass working-class militancy – usually involving a broader swath of "the masses" that included what were seen as unworthy elements (notably those living in unstable bachelor communities and lacking the discipline that leading intact and "proper" petty bourgeois/ patriarchal families brought) – inevitably failed as it brought on heavy repression by employers and especially the state. Such class-wide solidarity and mass militancy thus was sensibly to be avoided. When Homestead unfolded in the summer of 1892, Gompers was sympathetic and provided limited support to the strike effort. But:

> Homestead was different. The federation had tussled with individual employers ever since its inception, but seldom with a corporation and none on the scale of Carnegie. Homestead, its first collision with really big business, provided a sobering baptism that confirmed apprehensions over taking on basic industry. The price was simply too high.
>
> (Laurie 1989: 203)

Thus, it was not a lack of class consciousness or willingness to embrace class objectives that most distinguished the US labor movement's leaders, but a recognition of their distinct and unfavorable context. The conservatism of the US working class is historically contingent and institutionally specific.

The Great Depression reignited working class insurgency, and the failure of the "first New Deal" – capital's version of how to solve the depression via government sponsored cartelization under the National Recovery Act – led directly to a New Deal state that imposed corporatism on US capital, i.e. state-sponsored support for an industrial relations system based on collective bargaining (under the 1935 Wagner Act), and a tax-supported national social welfare system that included significant labor market regulation (especially the 1938 Fair Labor Standards Act).[3]

We agree with Lichtenstein and other that there never was a "capital–labor accord." Some leading capitalists made peace with the New Deal state and CIO unions, but this "accord" was thin, opportunistic and, from the point of view of capitalist agency, very short-lived. Business desired only short-term and effective state intervention, and experienced or feared that neither was the case. Once there was a hint of recovery in 1934 and 1935, New Deal supporters like Du Pont quickly reneged on their support, and began support for efforts like the American Liberty League that propagandized against it. "Like a drunk rescued from the gutter, suggested Robert LaFollette, business resented both the implication that they had needed any help and the fact that their rescuer had found them in such a degraded condition" (Gordon 1994: 286).

Beginning with the 1937 court-packing incident through the debate over Taft-Hartley in the early postwar period, the class anxiety of the old petty bourgeois stratum and small capitalists came to focus on statism ("creeping socialism") as the greatest threat to American society. This anxiety was stoked by conservatives and business leaders and growing anti-communism. The lynchpin of this defense against establishing a union and state-friendly social democratic corporatism was the "solid South." When Operation Dixie failed, it meant that the New Deal state and industrial relations system were permanently unstable, and gave impetus to erosion through capital flight and political conservatism that accelerated in the 1970s but remained present through the early post World War II era.

The capitalisms that emerged from World War II embedded market processes within a system of constraints, involving both regulation and state ownership, that was meant to improve on what (was perceived to have) failed in the interwar period – unfettered market capitalism. To some degree class conflict was shifted into the state apparatuses through this embedding. The neoliberal project has focused on disembedding capitalism, though it has proceeded in different ways and at different rates across countries.

The growth of the postwar period masked continued struggles. Recent historical scholarship has demonstrated to our satisfaction that the capital–labor "accord" was, at least in the United States, largely an illusion. Capitalists had lost so much ground relative both to labor and to the state in the 1930s and 1940s that the "accord" was the best they could do at the time, but embedded liberalism was never accepted and the economic crisis of the 1970s provided both an opportunity for a capitalist comeback and a real threat in that proposals to *extend* the power of labor and the regulatory state were on the table in North and South America and in Europe (McIntyre and Hilland 2008). The capitalist backlash has been interpreted as an ideological project and as a "political project to re-establish the conditions for capital accumulation and to restore the power of economic elites" (Harvey 2005: 19). In practice it is the latter that has been most important.

The capitalist/employer class in the United States and their allies drew on both historical convention and new forms of organization in this struggle. Rather than a contingent and institutionally specific result of repression, they interpreted working-class conservatism as normal and the New Deal as abnormal. When the opportunity for a comeback presented itself in the 1970s, capitalists and employers went through a process of class formation – moving from a class position to building institutions and attitudes necessary for action – that culminated in a particularly successful disembedding of the economy. This process of class formation included the growth of the Chamber of Commerce from 60,000 members in 1972 to more than a quarter of a million a year later, the movement of the National Association of Manufacturers to Washington, DC and the formation of the Business Roundtable, both also in 1972, and the establishment of the Heritage Foundation the next year, increased corporate backing for the American Enterprise Institute as well as corporate backing for the NBER (National Bureau of Economic Research) and the growing importance of right wing foundation such as Olin and Scaife (Blyth 2002: 126–201).

Ironically, campaign finance reform, by limiting contributions to $5,000, encouraged firm and industry based political action committees to work together, helping to build "alliances based on class rather than particular interests" (Harvey 2005: 49). According to Thomas Edsall, "During the 1970s, the political wing of the corporate sector staged one of the most remarkable campaigns in the pursuit of power in recent history" (cited in Harvey 2005: 54).

This has not led to a restoration of the pre-New Deal system but to a new constellation of capitalist power and privilege involving the extension of capitalist control in the workplace, the re-commodification of labor, a fusion of ownership and management, a heightened role for finance, and both a deepening and widening of transnational capitalist alliances. Despite common patterns and international ties, this process was quite different in the United States than even in the UK, the other country in which neoliberalism has largely succeeded. The absence of a Christian right as an ally, the survival of traditional "British" levers of class power and privilege, and the existence of a Labour Party which in the 1970s actually, and later at least nominally, opposed full on neoliberalism, meant that while privatization and monetarism succeeded, and the back of radical labor broken, the welfare state could not (and need not) be dismantled.

In a sense, it was the unusual strength and not the weakness of the Left in the post World War II period that led to successful neoliberalism in the US. The adversarial relationship between employers and workers, and between business and the regulatory state, combined with a welfare state and tax system that were truly redistributive, meant that when prosperity moved large numbers of Americans out of poverty and even out of the working class, neoliberals could appeal to real material dissatisfaction with the liberal Left in their project of restoring class power. Such an opportunity did not exist in France or Germany, where right-wing governments prevailed and where economic policy was organized around a perceived national interest (reconstruction in Germany and industrialization in France) rather than adversarial politics.

The capitalist-class formation argument is persuasive to us in explaining the change in labor relations, but it needs to be qualified in certain ways as a comprehensive explanation for neoliberal success. Support for large and regressive tax cuts were not universally supported by the new pro-business lobbies, nor did they push hard for cutting means-tested welfare spending. They did support deregulation, but so did key figures of the liberal Left including Stephen Breyer, Edward Kennedy and Ralph Nader. But in labor policy US employers spoke with one voice. Combined with the peculiarities of US working-class formation then, it was capitalist-class formation and strength that explains much of the successful liberalization of US labor markets.[4]

The economic crisis of the 1970s and the weakening of the party system after Watergate created an opening for entrepreneurial politicians and demagogues to mobilize financial and economic resources around issues which no particular social group had previously been pushing: "the autonomous incentives of politicians within a changed institutional setting contributed an independent causal effect to the outcome" (Prasad 2006: 23). This enabled a swing away from regulated and redistributional capitalism in a country that had actually gone much farther in regulating (though without government ownership) and redistributing in an adversarial sense than had Continental Europe.

Reagan and his allies were able to channel the dissatisfaction with economic outcomes in the 1970s in ways that resonated with conventional US wisdom but also played on the prosperity that embedded liberalism had produced. Exaggerating resentment against unions and targeted welfare programs, taking advantage of the fact that the pain of taxation was much more visible than the benefits, and papering over the contradiction between capitalist growth (and its attendant creative destruction) and "family values," movement conservatives captured much of the state and the ideological apparatuses in a coup that was simply unavailable to capitalists in France and Germany. Encouraging a coalition of better off workers and lower level managers against the poor, they were able to paint the United States' adversarial labor relations system as an obstacle to growth. Greater "flexibility" in employment relations appealed not just to employers but to those workers who had not been part of the New Deal system, or who were ejected from it in the structural crisis of the 1970s. It was not terribly difficult for the entrepreneurs and demagogues of the New Right to create a common sense in which freedom and liberty in the labor market were good for everyone, unemployment is always voluntary, and removing welfare support is good for the poor.

To sum up then, neoliberalism succeeded in the United States due to successful capitalist-class formation and working class weakness in an adversarial political environment in which the political "reforms" of the late 1960s and early 1970s had created a candidate-centered (rather than party-centered) political system. These political reforms had the effect of increasing state responsiveness to societal demands and made state actors dependent on non-poor majorities for votes and funding, leaving them less able to protect the interest of workers and the poor. Giving "power to the people" turned out to be giving power to those who wanted to restore capitalist class privilege.

Conclusion

We conclude on a reserved note, with a hint of optimism leavened by the daunting degree of prevailing US business hegemony and what this means to any serious political or policy challenge to the current sway of neoliberalism. The swing in the United States was large; another swing is, at least theoretically, possible. The effects of the Iraq invasion on working-class attitudes need to be carefully watched (Silver 2003: Chapter 4). The current reaction against "free trade" is also a sign that change is afoot. We should always be careful to watch what we hope for. Political reform and the pursuit of individual rights in employment in the 1960s and 1970s both had the perverse effect of undermining collective sources of working-class power. While beyond our scope here, they were the perverse and unintended consequences of legitimate activism that impacted political culture and institutions in a manner that, in the end, gave impetus to capitalist class political agency (Lichtenstein 2002; Prasad 2006).

We argue here and elsewhere that social progress in capitalist society has been the result of working-class formation which in alliance with other classes AND with state actors, forces change on capitalists. The regress of the last generation – social decline through free market economics – in the United States is due to the capitalist class getting organized and fully capturing the state and the ideological apparatuses. A complex, and to us, highly contingent and conjunctural set of developments produced and abetted this development. Belief in the capital–labor accord encouraged some on the Left to look for a new bargain with capitalists as the way out of the crisis. It is much more important, in our view, to remind people of the possibility and historic reality of working-class radicalism in the United States, to kindle that radicalism and abet its viability and efficacy, as those "experts" including heterodox economists seek, among other things, to split capitalists from their unnatural allies. Such a development could be an essential and forceful precondition to challenging that neoliberalism that now produces macro-instability and a decline in the fortunes of working peoples throughout the world. Drawing historical lessons from nations who have fared well, or poorly, or both – as many have in the volume – is a starting point.

Notes

1 Arguably labor relations have shifted even more in the United Kingdom than in the United States, and certainly privatization there had more far-reaching effects than did deregulation in the United States. Still, trade union density remains relatively high (ETUI-REHS, 2007. "European Level Representation." www.worker-participation.eu/

national_industrial_relations/across_europe/european_level_representation) as does social spending relative to GDP (Adema and Ladaique 2005)).

2 This section relies heavily on Jacoby (1991), Laurie (1989), Lichtenstein (2002), and Wilentz (1984).

3 Finegold and Scocpal (1984) show how when the capital-sponsored NRA failed in late 1934, business's hegemony over policy-making imploded. This magnified the already-existing loss of business legitimacy that the Depression created, opening the way for a coalition of Congressional and Executive branch leaders, representing northern urban, working-class, union-based movement, in effect seized control of national policy-making. This permitted a one-time imposition of values and policies alien to US capitalists. See also Gordon (1994).

4 The French case provides another example of why both capitalist class and working class formation as well as the nature of the state are important. Here, while labor suffered a similar decline in organized strength, capital has historically been quite disorganized leaving much of the economy to a state apparatus for which "relative autonomy" does not quite capture the freedom of movement. "Support state services" has a popular resonance in France that is not true in the United States.

References

Adema, W. and M. Ladaique. 2005. "Net Social Expenditure, 2005 Edition – More Comprehensive Measures of Social Support." *OECD Social, Employment and Migration Working Papers, No. 29* (Paris: OECD).

Blyth, Mark. 2002. *Great Transformations: Economic Ideas and Political Change in the Twentieth Century* (Cambridge: Cambridge University Press).

Bowles, S., D. Gordon and T. Weisskopf. 1985. *Beyond the Wasteland: A Democratic Alternative to Economic Decline* (New York: Anchor Press).

Bowles S., D. Gordon and T. Weisskopf. 1990. *After the Wasteland: A Democratic Economic at the Year 2000* (New York: M. E. Sharpe).

Crotty, James. 1990. "Keynes on the Stages of Development of the Capitalist Economy: The Institutional Foundation of Keynes's Methodology." *Journal of Economic Issues* 24(3): 761–80.

Finegold, Kenneth and Theda Scocpol. 1984. "State, Party, and Industry," in C. Bright and S. Harding, eds., *Statemaking and Social Movements: Essays in Time and Theory* (Ann Arbor: University of Michigan Press), pp. 159–92.

Fones-Wolf, Elizabeth. 1994. *Selling Free Enterprise: The Business Assault on Labor And Liberalism: 1945-1960* (Urbana: University of Illinois Press).

Gordon, Colin. 1994. *New Deals: Business, Labor, and Politics in America, 1920-1935* (Cambridge: Cambridge University Press).

Hall, Peter and David Soskice, eds. 2001. *Varieties of Capitalism: The Institutional Foundations of Comparative Advantage* (New York: Oxford University Press).

Harvey, David. 2005. *A Brief History of Neoliberalism* (New York: Oxford University Press).

Jacoby, Sanford. 1991. "American Exceptionalism Revisited: The Importance of Management," in S. Jacoby, ed., *Masters to Managers: Historical and Comparative Perspectives on American Employers* (New York: Columbia University Press), pp. 173–200.

Jacoby, Sanford. 1997. *Modern Manors: Welfare Capitalism Since the New Deal* (Princeton: Princeton University Press).

Jacoby, Wade. 2001. *Imitation and Politics: Redesigning Modern Germany* (Ithaca: Cornell University Press).

Katznelson, Ira. 1990. "Working Class Formation: Constructing Cases and Comparisons," in Ira and Zlberg, eds., *Working Class Formation: Nineteenth Century Patterns in Western Europe and the United States* (Princeton: Princeton University Press), pp. 3–41.

Kerr, Clark. 1984. "Perspectives on Industrial Relations Research – Thirty Six Years Later." *Proceedings of the 36th Meeting of Annual Meeting of the IRRA* (Madison: IRRA).

Kochan, Thomas, Harry Katz and Robert McKersie. 1986. *The Transformation of American Industrial Relations* (Ithaca: ILR/Cornell University Press).

Laurie, Bruce. 1989. *Artisans into Workers: Labor in Nineteenth Century America* (New York: The Noonday Press).

Lichtenstein, Nelson. 2002. *State of the Union: A Century of American Labor* (Princeton: Princeton University Press)

McIntyre, Richard and Michael Hillard. 2008. "The Limited Capital Labor Accord': May it Rest in Peace?" *Review of Radical Political Economics*, 40: 1, 244–9.

Mishel, L., J. Bernstein and S. Allegreto. 2005. *State of Working America: 2004/2005* (Ithaca: ILR Press).

Moss, B. 1998. "The French Strike and Social Divide: The End of Consensus Politics?" in M. Schain, M. Kesselman and H. Chapman, eds., *A Century of Organized Labor in France: A Union Movement for the 21st Century?* (New York: St. Martin's).

Prasad, Monica. 2006. *The Politics of Free Markets: The Rise of Neoliberal Economic Policies in Britain, France, Germany, and the United States* (Chicago: University of Chicago Press).

Silver, Beverly. 2003. *Forces of Labor: Workers Movements and Globalization Since 1870* (Cambridge: Cambridge University Press).

Streeck, W. and K. Yamamura, eds. 2001. *The Origins of Nonliberal Capitalism: Germany and Japan in Comparison* (Ithaca: Cornell University Press).

Thelan, Kathleen. 2001. "Varieties of Labor Politics in the Developed Democracies," in Peter Hall and David Soskice, eds., *Varieties of Capitalism: The Institutional Foundations of Comparative Advantage* (New York: Oxford University Press).

Tomlins, Christopher. 1985. *The State and the Unions: Labor Relations, Law and the Organized Labor Movement in America, 1880-1960* (Cambridge: Cambridge University Press).

Wilentz, Sean. 1984. "Against Exceptionalism: Class Consciousness and the American Labor Movement," *International Labor and Working Class History* 26(Fall): 1–26.

15 Unequal exchange reconsidered in our age of globalization

Makoto Itoh

In our age of globalization, capitalism has reduced social control of various markets, and reveals the fundamental workings of capitalist economies with contemporary features. Neoliberalism has become the dominant ideology upon the basis of neoclassical economics. Despite the neoliberal belief in the fair and rational efficiency of free competitive market order, contemporary capitalist market economy has actually destabilized the economic life of the majority of working people, and widely polarized income and wealth inequality both internationally and domestically.

We are thus thrown back to theoretical issues on how to understand the basic nature and workings of capitalist market economy as a frame of reference for these tendencies. Among others this chapter focuses on the theory of international unequal exchange as a possible basic frame of reference for a global polarization of income and wealth in our age. It relates to the recognition that "Rapid development by poor and middle income countries cannot take place under the Neoliberal rules of the game" (Crotty 2003), and attempts to supplement a theoretical foundation for this perspective.

Classic theories

D. Ricardo

Ricardo's theory of comparative costs still remains as a powerful origin of theories of international trade. In his *Principles of Political Economy and Taxation*, Ricardo denies the direct applicability of labor theory of value by saying "The same rule which regulates the relative value of commodities in one country, does not regulate the relative value of the commodities exchanged between two or more countries" (Ricardo 1817: 133). This is because capital and population would not easily move across borders by following higher profits, unlike the case between different local areas within a country.

The famous numerical example of international trade between Portugal and England follows. Namely, a quantity of wine, say 3,000 bottles, which Portugal shall give in exchange for the cloth, say of 1,000 yards, of England, is not determined by the respective quantities of labor devoted to production of each. In

England, to produce the cloth requires 100 men for one year, and to produce the wine might require 120 men a year. England finds it her interest to import wine by exportation of the cloth in this case, as she can obtain more wine (and/or cloth) by concentrating in production of cloth. In Portugal, to produce the wine requires 80 men a year, and to produce the cloth 90 men a year. It is advantageous also for Portugal to export the wine in exchange for the cloth, as she can obtain more cloth (and/or wine) than producing it domestically. Thus, unequal exchange between 100 men's labor in England and 80 men's labor in Portugal is performed, with a desirable result for both countries.

What happens if Portugal exports to England not just wine but also cloth, as she can produce the same quantity of cloth by less amount of labor than in England? Then, according to Ricardo, England has to pay specie money to Portugal without being paid for her export. As the quantity of money reduces in England, prices of commodities are depressed down, while prices in Portugal rises up as specie money flows in. At some point, as a result of these changes in price levels, England is able to export cloth with a relative cost advantage in comparison with wine production, so as to restore the international distribution of money as well as the international trade advantage for both countries. This logic is the specie flow mechanism, based upon the quantity theory of money. At equilibrium, the relative (exchange) value of specie money in terms of commodity (labor) values would be smaller in Portugal than in England.

Ricardo, who purified the Classical school's labor theory of value thus did not mechanically apply it to the international trade. He in fact assumed an unequal international exchange of labor, and left a series of interesting issues in his theories of comparative costs and the specie flow mechanism. Is the labor theory of value irrelevant to the theoretical analysis of international trade? What does determine the terms of international trade? How do we count labor costs in different countries? How to understand the relative value of money (or different price levels) in different countries in the world? Does Ricardo's theory prove advantage of free trade in general? These served as a touchstone for different approaches of different subsequent schools.

For instance, F. List (1841) opposed Ricardo's argument for free trade, criticizing it as representing just the interests of the most advanced national economy with the absolute advantage of a strong industrial exporting power, and advocated protective tariffs as well as industrial policies for developing countries. His approach founded the German historical school by emphasizing the roles of the state, social institutions and national spirit for the development of a successful national economic system.

In basic theories of value, Ricardo's theory on foreign trade was one of the crucial points where the objective labor theory of value was generally abandoned by neoclassical economics. Ricardo did not explain exactly what determines the exchange ratio of cloth and wine in his example. So far as the exchange rate between cloth and wine (P_c/P_w) is within the range of $100/120 < (P_c/P_w) < 90/80$, Ricardo's theory of mutual advantage (in terms of use-values) for both countries remains. J. S. Mill (1848) mediated a shift away from the labor theory of value by emphasizing the role of reciprocal demand equality in determination of international exchange ratios. The neoclassical marginalist school followed this shift, and the theory of comparative costs is recast into the Heckscher–Ohlin–Samuelson type of law of factor productions, depending upon the notion of opportunity costs.

K. Marx

Marx and his followers, in contrast, attempted to maintain the labor theory of value and to demonstrate the existence of an international unequal exchange of labor. However, Marx did not treat foreign trade fully, which together with state and world market were mostly neglected in *Capital*. This reflected the order of his work plan in the latter half of his life, when he concentrated on capital, landed property and wage labor and was unable to get to these other topics (Itoh 1988: 3–2). His references to the international trade therefore remained incomplete, not yet linked with his critique of Ricardo's quantity theory of money, and have consequently remained a source of debate.

For example, Marx argues that, even according to Ricardo's theory that three days of labor in one country can be exchanged against one of another country, an unequal exchange of labor becomes a possibility:

> Here the law of value undergoes essential modification. The relationship between labor days of different countries may be similar to that existing between skilled, complex labor and unskilled, simple labor within a country. In this case, the richer country exploits the poorer one, even where the latter gains by the exchange.
>
> (Marx 1861–1863 [1972] (3): 105–6)

Thus he clearly recognizes a theoretical possibility for, on the one hand, unequal exchange of labor, and exploitation, and on the other mutual gains by the comparative advantage effect through international trade.

In *Capital* Volume I, Chapter 22's discussion of "national differences in wages", this recognition is deepened and gains some complexity. According to Marx, the average intensity of labor changes from country to country. The more intense national labor, as compared with less intense, produces in the same time more value, which expresses itself in more money. A further modification of the law of value comes from the fact that national labor, which is more productive, counts as more intensive, so long as its products are not compelled by competition to lower the selling price to the level of their value.

The double modifications of law of value relating to international comparison of intensity and productivity of labor in different countries are easily understandable, when production of the same commodity of an industry (or the same composition of commodities by the bundle of industries) is compared. Marx seems to assume this case, for he assumes here piece-rate wages as a measure of intensity and productivity of labor.

In contrast, it is impossible logically to compare intensity and productivity of labor across different industries producing different use-values, as different use-values are incommensurable in themselves. Their commensurability as commodities is given either by prices as their form of value or by amounts of embodied labor time as their substance of value. So long as international trade tends to form an international division of labor among different countries, it is not easy to compare intensity and productivity of labor among these countries independent from prices in the world market.

It is remarkable that Marx consciously avoids such a logical complexity in comparing labor intensity and productivity between different industries here, and carefully concentrates on piece-rate wages as a measure of them. His main intention was to show that the law of labor value need not be abandoned in the case of international trade, but needed modifications by national degrees of intensity and productivity of labor.

A series of problems were left behind. Is this argument persuasive in understanding unequal exchange or exploitation of labor in international trade? How to understand the law of international values? Can national differences in relative values of money (converse of price levels) be explicated in this line of argument?

As a whole, however, Marx's *Capital* concentrated to the basic logic of motion of capitalist economy and did not pay much attention to unequal international exchange, by assuming that an advanced capitalist country shows the future image of later developing countries.

In studying basic logic of motion of capitalist economy in a country, we can indeed theoretically abstract from foreign trade. Because "foreign trade only replaces domestic articles by those of other use or natural form, without affecting value-ratios," so long as normal annual reproduction on a given scale goes on (Marx 1875 [1978]: 546). It is as if some domestic capital was shifted to production of such imported articles from that of domestic products for export. In so far as such foreign trade realizes Ricardo's comparative advantage effect, and reduces the necessary labor costs to obtain foreign products in comparison to the labor costs to produce them domestically, it would mostly contribute to a rise in the rate of surplus-value and profit rate, just as would a rise in productivity in domestic industries.

V. I. Lenin

After Marx, Lenin (1917) presented a stages theory of capitalist development in his study of *Imperialism: The Highest Stage of Capitalism* at a more concrete level that was distinct from, but based upon, the basic principles of capitalist economy like Marx's *Capital*. Historical changes of key industries, the characters of dominant capital, leading countries, economic policies and structures of world market are all concretely considered. The latter half, items of Marx's planned life's work, namely the state, foreign trade and world market, are thus introduced at this level of stages theory of capitalist development.

Comparing the stage of imperialism with that of liberalism, Lenin contrasted the characteristics of these two stages as follows: "Typical of the old capitalism, when free competition had undivided sway, was the export of *goods*. Typical of the latest stage of capitalism, when monopolies rule, is the export of *capital*" (Lenin 1917: 72). It was important for Lenin to emphasize this as an economic foundation for imperialist colonial policies among great powers, necessitating the world war, and the resultant social crisis which induced a new strong ground for socialist revolution.

At the same time, Lenin underlined that the export of capital became "a solid basis for imperialist oppression and exploitation of most of countries" for a handful of rich countries (1917: 75). On the other hand, the aspect of unequal exchange in foreign trade as a possible source of international exploitation, as well as its correlation with the export of capital, tended to be neglected in Lenin's formulation of imperialism.

Japanese debates on international values

Japan has been the site of a series of international value controversies since World War II. Eight representative essays in the controversy were collected in E. Kinoshita's edited book (1960). This controversy went back to the classic international trade theories that preceded Lenin, and attempted to re-examine Ricardo's foreign trade theory from the view of Marx's labor theory of value, by rejecting J. S. Mill's guide to step away from it. The following are the key arguments ventured in this debate.

First, according to T. Nawa, international comparisons of national labor productivity are possible if one examines the same common key industry. Higher productivity in the key industry in an advanced country enables it to obtain gold money in the world market more than its equivalent labor value, and thus reduces the relative value of gold money against whole national labor of that country.

This argument is in a sense in accord with Marx's treatment of the international comparison of intensity or productivity of labor, as we have seen. Though it may imply unequal international exchange of labor, it could not explain the case of international trade between countries with different key industries. Can we assume the same common key industry among various countries in the world market? It is also not clear how and why higher productivity in a key industry in an advanced country is extended to the whole national labor in the form of relatively low value of money.

Second, in M. Hirase's opinion, Marx's theory of market value, where capitals with exceptionally superior productivity can obtain extra surplus-value as if they realized more intensive labor, should be applied to international values. Then exporters would send commodities from a country with lower costs of production to another with higher costs in every industry, in contrast to Ricardo's theory of comparative costs. The result is a realization of equal exchange of value, if not equal exchange of physical labor time. Or, in K. Akamatsu's view,

Marx's theory of complex labor and simple labor should be applied to the Ricardo's foreign trade theory, where exports from both countries are in accord with their domestic value. Then, equal, not unequal, exchange of value and labor must be realized so long as labor to produce wine in Portugal is complex labor to be counted 100/80 times of simple labor to produce cloth in England.

Although these interpretations intended to apply some aspects of Marx's value theory to Ricardo's model of comparative cost, the result negated Marx's view that saw exploitation of the poorer country by the richer through unequal exchange of labor.

Against these arguments, E. Kinoshita emphasized that international unequal exchange of labor is realized due to difference in national labor productivity even among countries with equal intensity and complexity of labor. According to him, higher national productive power of a country brings about, and is represented by, a relatively lower national value of gold money. When the national value of money is no longer matched with national productive power, it is expressed in a trade imbalance to be readjusted through international reallocation of gold money.

Kinoshita also regarded the modification of the law of value as a sort of equal exchange of values as if these values were produced by complex and simple labor. On this point, his position becomes unclear if it really enables us to see international unequal exchange in terms of simple labor. In addition, he seems to assume a Ricardian quantity theory of money. He also has difficulty in defining national productivity independent from relative price levels (inverse of relative national value of money) or the trade balance of a country. Thus he had to confess that this controversy left unsolved even the main issues on international value.

This controversy in Japan reflected, in my view, an actual national concern of that early postwar period. Lenin's notion of imperialism with colonial policy based on export of capital was already remote from the national reality. International trade seemed far more important, along with the dollar shortage problem that plagued the Japanese economy's recovery. The need to strengthen key industries and create national productive power in order to catch up with the US economy dominated national concern.

At that time, international unequal exchange of labor with the third world countries in relation with international capital investment had not yet become a major concern. At the same time, Marxian value theory itself still had various problems to be solved. The distinction and relationship between the forms and the substance of value, such as prices of production and substance of value as embodied abstract human labor in commodities, as well as theoretical issues on complex labor, still needed to be further developed. The concept of international value itself resultantly had to remain problematic and ambiguous. A gravitational center of prices of commodities from advanced countries, as a form of values, which are sold for more money than those from less advanced countries, tended to be directly regarded as containing more labor substance, as if they were products of complex or intensified labor. The issue of unequal exchange of labor is thus obscured in one way or another.

In retrospect, Marx's basic theories of both market value and complex (skilled) labor themselves left serious difficulty by unrealistically assuming the expenditure of a greater amount of labor as if it were performed by intensive labor. As I argued elsewhere (Itoh 1988: 6–3, 7–2), these theories should be approached differently by presupposing a social foundation of economic democracy in which any concrete useful labor (including complex labor or labor under exceptionally advanced conditions of production) is considered the expenditure of a basically equal human capability to perform various works as abstract human labor. This in turn permits these labors to be simply counted by their social contribution of common physical time. This is true even if some wage laborers require more education and training costs, because this aspect belongs to a separate issue concerning how to define the value of labor power. This point has been a potential theoretical ground, in my belief, to solve the related issues in the long-standing three major controversies: the transformation problem, the socialist economic calculation, and the question of international values. Such a way of treating human labor is not just imaginary but already experienced in many cases of LETS (local exchange and trading system) or local money practices.

Unequal exchange in dependency theories

A. Emmanuel (1972) presented a new theory of international unequal exchange by applying Marx's theory of prices of production. His theory served as a basis for the dependency school, which underlined the continuous structural economic difficulty on the part of third world countries even after the political liberation from the old imperialist colonial system. The logic of unequal exchange between the center and the periphery in the world market seemed essential in this context.

According to Marx, so long as capital and labor are free to move across industries, so as to equalize profit rates and wage rates, the price of production is determined by cost price ($c + v$, where c designates constant capital invested in means of production, while v represents variable capital invested in labor power, i.e. the source of surplus-value m) plus average profit (r). Then, the price of production of a commodity which is produced in an industry with an organic composition of capital (c/v) higher than the social average must be greater than the substance of value ($c + v + m$) embodied in the commodity. The reverse must be true for the price of production of a commodity which is produced by an industry with a capital composition lower than average. Unequal exchange of labor value is then realized, and transfers a part of surplus value from the latter type to the former type of industry under the system of prices of production.

Emmanuel called this sort of commodity exchange "a primary form of non-equivalence" in international trade, where advanced countries tend to have industries with higher composition of capital than peripheral developing countries. In addition, there is more important international unequal exchange, or "nonequivalence in strict sense," according to Emmanuel, so long as there is a big gap in wage rates or in the rates of surplus value (m/v) between the center and the periphery. The unequal wage rates or the rates of surplus value are hardly equalized internationally, as mobility of labor power, unlike that of capital, is generally narrowly limited due to political and social restrictions on immigration.

In Emmanuel's numerical example, the wage rate in a central country A is assumed to be 10 times as high as in a peripheral country B. Intensity of labor in A is twice as much as in B (though difference in intensity of labor seems unessential to Emmanuel's theory – Itoh). Then, when the value of labor power to produce the same value product ($v + m$), say 120, is 100 in A, the value of labor power is just 20 in B. While the rate of surplus value in A is 20 percent, that rate in B must be 500 percent. In so far as international trade between these countries is performed under the system of prices of production ($c + v + r$) so as to equalize the rates of profit, apparently a larger scale of transfer of surplus value from B to A must occur in addition to the primary form of nonequivalence.

This model was regarded in the dependency school as a good reason why underdevelopment in the third world countries had to be deepened economically even in the era of neocolonialism. It was presented by opposing the presupposition of international immobility of capital in Ricardo's theory of foreign trade. Export of capital, which Lenin emphasized as a ground for political imperialism, is here structurally combined with the function of international trade of commodities to exploit developing countries in the age of neocolonial economic imperialism.

Shaikh (1980) followed this model and sharply criticized Ricardo's harmonious model of foreign trade together with its basis in the quantity theory of money. If Portugal in Ricardo's numerical example continues to export both wine and cloth to England, by lending money capital, the specie flow mechanism in accord with the quantity theory of money would not work. Then, England may succumb to chronic trade deficit and mounting debt. Shaikh applied this case to the difficulties of current peripheral developing countries with absolute disadvantage, falling in both chronic trade deficit and cumulative international borrowing.

Emmanuel's model contradicted Marx's inclination to see a higher rate of surplus value in more advanced capitalist countries than in less developed countries, reflecting a higher intensity and productivity of labor (e.g. Marx 1867 [1977]: 702). Marx's view on this point must reflect the severely exploitative work conditions in contemporary advanced countries like England.

However, in the period of high economic growth in the post-World War II era until 1973, the so-called Fordist regime of capital accumulation shared the fruits of increased productivity corporately between capital and labor in advanced capitalist countries. It seemed to endorse Emmanuel's view to see lower rates of exploitation in the center, compared with increasing misery in the periphery.

S. Amin (1973) reinforced Emmanuel's theory of unequal exchange by asserting that at least three-quarters of exports from the third world countries are now produced in "super-modern capitalist sectors," with physically equal labor productivity as in the advanced countries where labor time embodied in them is commensurable with labor time in advanced countries.

In our age of globalization

Emmanuel's model of unequal exchange presupposed a big gap in the wage rates between the center and periphery, and left it further to be analyzed. As Marx stated, "the determination of the value of labor-power contains a historical and moral (i.e. social – Itoh) element" (Marx 1867 [1976]: 275). In peripheral countries, reproduction of labor power is widely related with various non-capitalist modes of production and the roles of non-market labor, as Amin (1973) and Wallerstein (1995) noticed. The especially increasing economic difficulty of peasant families in agricultural villages under the pressure of capitalist money economy generally tends to serve as a broad source of cheap labor in the form of "constant latent surplus population" (Marx 1867 [1976]: 796).

In so far as the wide gap in wages between the central and the peripheral countries is an essential source of international unequal exchange and exploitation, differences in social structures and institutions for capital accumulation – including labor laws, industrial policies, educational systems and the roles of trade unions – between the center and the periphery of the world capitalism must be important in this context. In this regard, the approach of the social structure of accumulation school must be encouraged and further applied to the international political economy.

There is indeed a vicious cycle of socio-economic factors in peripheral countries, such as excessive competitive pressure among peasants to sell their products and idle labor power, low wages, cutting down of cost prices of products, higher relative value of world money (e.g. the dollar), cheaper costs of reproduction of labor power, poor conditions of living, and insufficient levels of education. Apparently these factors, which form again circularly, are both the cause and result of international unequal exchange or exploitation of labor in relation with central advanced countries.

The labor theory of value need not be a straightforward simple price theory, especially in the field of international political economy. It still enables us to see a wide room for international unequal exchange or exploitation of labor through forms of value, as prices that are determined actually by including such socio-economic factors as exemplified above. They are decisive particularly on the determination of nationally different levels of wages.

It is noteworthy, however, that unequal exchange in our age of globalization does not work to maintain just a static relationship between stagnant peripheral disadvantageous countries and wealthy advanced countries. Unlike in the initial image of unequal exchange by Emmanuel and other dependency theorists, the third world has become very much diversified, and split into at least three groups.

The first group is oil-producing countries. Most countries in the UAE, for example, gained a huge amount of oil money as a sort of global ground rent by widely and repeatedly elevating oil prices since 1973, a development which served as an important source of globalization of financial transactions through recycling of oil money. The second is the least-among-less-developed countries

(LLDCs), such as those in most parts of Africa. The disadvantage of unequal exchange remained there just as hard as in the initial image of the dependency school, and was rather deepened by repetitive rises in oil price and cumulative international debt.

The third group is a herd of developing countries with higher growth rates. In particular, most Asian countries have joined this group one after another and shown remarkable vitality. Even after the first oil shock, Asian NIEs (Korea, Taiwan, Hong Kong and Singapore) have maintained high annual growth rates – nearly 10 percent, and ASEAN countries (Malaysia, Thailand, Indonesia and the Philippines) have followed. China, with the largest population in the world, has now joined them and grown annually around 10 percent since 1978, and more recently India, with the second largest population, began to grow at nearly the same rate.

It is apparent that new information technologies have facilitated many capitalist corporations in the advanced countries to invest in these Asian countries so as to utilize favorable socio-political conditions of production. Against "the Neoliberal rules of the game," strong industrial policies, such as to supply infrastructure to special economic zones, or to keep stable financial conditions including a fixed exchange rate with the dollar, also clearly worked for inducing foreign capital investment and industrialization in these countries. Export of capital in our age in this regard does not one-sidedly colonize and exploit developing countries, unlike in the age of Lenin. International unequal exchange of labor, especially upon the ground of relatively low levels of wage rates, must remain exploitative of these developing countries too. However, combined with an effect of inflow of multinationals' direct investment from advanced countries, unequal exchange in our age does not have the effect of being just as oppressive and preventive of economic growth of developing countries as it once may have.

Ricardo's argument, as Marx underlined, that international unequal exchange of labor may realize an advantageous effect to either of the participant countries, has actually resurfaced for this group of developing countries in a certain historical context of our age. The advantageous effect in this argument relates to the increase in nationally obtainable amounts of use-values, which are distinct from unequal exchange of labor as the substance of value. However, such an effect should not be taken as evidence to support Ricardian free trade principles or neoliberal rules, as it is realized *ex facto* through positive industrial policies.

At the same time, the advantageous international unequal exchange no longer guarantees relatively high and stable economic growth for the advanced countries, unlike in the preceding phase of capitalism until 1973. In the restructuring process through the continuous economic crises and depressions, neoliberal globalization in our age has accelerated de-industrialization and induced instability of economic life and worsening work conditions among the majority of working people in the advanced countries under competitive pressure from those industrializing developing countries with lower wages. It is as if the globalization of the capitalist economy with international unequal exchange in our age is causing a reaction where the global polarization of economic life is internalized by the central advanced countries.

Our recognition of continuous international unequal exchange in this regard should be utilized not just to underline an opposite economic interest between the advanced and the developing countries, but also to clarify the common pressure and difficulties of working people in both sides of them under dominant neoliberal globalization of world capitalism. It must imply a common need at least to amend the neoliberal globalization policy tide for the sake of great majority of working people in the world.

References

Amin, S. (1973) *L'échange Inégal et la Loi de la Valeur*. Paris: Anthropos.

Crotty, J. (2003) "Core Industries, Coercive Competition and the Structual Contradictions of Global Neoliberalism," in Phelps, N. and Raines, P. (eds.) *The New Competition for Inward Investment*. Aldershot: Edward Elgar.

Emmanuel A. (1972) *Unequal Exchange*, translated by B. Pearce. New York and London: Monthly Review Press.

Itoh, M. (1988) *The Basic Theory of Caitalism*. London: Macmillan.

Kinoshita, E. (ed.) (1960) *Controversy on International Value* (in Japanese). Tokyo: Kobundo.

Lenin, V. I. (1917 [1965]) *Imperialism; the Highest Stage of Capitalism*. Peking: Foreign Languages Press.

List, F. (1841 [1885]) *The National System of Political Economy*, translated by S. S. Lloyd. London: Longmans.

Marx, K. (1861–3 [1969]) *Theories of Surplus-Value*, translated by E. Burus, R. Simpson and J. Cohen, 3 vols. London: Lawrence & Wishart.

Marx, K. (1867, 1875, 1894 [1976, 1978, 1981]), *Capital*, translated by B. Fowes and D. Fernbach, vols 1, 2 and 3. Harmondsworth: Penguin.

Mill, J. S. (1848 [1921]) *Principles of Political Economy*, edited by W. J. Ashley. London: Longmans, Green.

Ricardo, D. (1817 [1951]) *On the Principles of Political Economy and Taxation*, in *The Works and Correspondence of David Ricardo*, edited by P. Sraffa, vol. 1. Cambridge: Cambridge University Press.

Shaikh, A. (1980) "The Laws of International Exchange," in Nell, E. D. (ed.) *Growth, Profits and Property*. Cambridge; Cambridge University Press.

Wallerstein, I. (1995) *Historical Capitalism with Capitalist Civilization*. London: Verso.

16 From capital controls and miraculous growth to financial globalization and the financial crisis in Korea

Kang-Kook Lee

Introduction

Mainstream economists and international organizations have argued that financial liberalization and opening encourage economic growth in developing countries. They emphasize gains from financial globalization such as more investment and higher economic efficiency. However, this argument is seriously flawed both in theory and reality. Financial markets always suffer from market failures, and there is no empirical evidence to support the growth effect of financial globalization.

Heterodox perspectives including the Post-Keynesian view have wisely pointed out that effective capital controls could spur economic growth; the success of the developmental states of East Asia in achieving rapid economic development since the 1960s supports this contention. Conversely, capital account liberalization may destabilize the economy, as shown by the recent series of financial crises in those nations who liberalized, including some of these developmental states who had previously succeeded by deploying capital controls.

Korea presents the most telling case in this respect. The Korean economy was a paragon of the "East Asian Miracle" for its rapid economic growth after the 1960s. Strong and effective capital controls of the developmental government, in combination with industrial policy and domestic financial control, contributed to this success. However, selective financial opening in the 1990s led to the financial crisis, and the economic performance has been disappointing after extensive post-crisis economic restructuring and financial opening. This chapter examines the interesting experience of capital controls, liberalization and economic performance in Korea. I briefly review hot debates on capital controls, liberalization and economic growth in the second section. Then, I investigate how capital controls in Korea were successful in encouraging economic growth in the third section. In the fourth section, I present a historical analysis of financial opening and the financial crisis in the 1990s, and post-crisis changes in Korea.

Capital controls, liberalization and economic growth

It is strongly argued that an integrated global financial market enhances efficiency in capital allocation, reduces the cost of investment and disciplines national governments. Developing countries are said to grow faster with financial globalization and international capital movements for these reasons (Rogoff et al., 2004).[1] However, when financial markets reek with market failures due to information problems and investors' herd behaviors, there is no guarantee for such benefits to be realized. Rather, financial opening could generate instability, as seen in many financial crises related to self-fulfilling expectations and contagion effects (Stiglitz, 2000). Though mainstream economists advocate opening financial markets with a view to promoting prosperity, they still underestimate problems associated with open international financial markets. The East Asian financial crisis had the effect of making many economists more skeptical about benefits of financial opening, and led some to call for better regulation.

Heterodox economists understand capital controls and liberalization in relation to a broader context of economic management. They argue that capital controls could help governments to introduce full employment and egalitarian policies as shown in the experience of the "golden age," when capital controls and Keynesian macroeconomic policy were adopted together in advanced countries. But financial globalization gave difficulty in macroeconomic management to national governments, which lost policy autonomy under the open capital market (Crotty, 1989). This perspective also asserts that capital controls, if effectively adopted under a proper development strategy, can contribute to economic development in developing countries (Crotty and Epstein, 1996).[2] In fact, the experience of East Asia clearly demonstrates that capital controls could promote economic growth and mismanaged capital account liberalization brought about the financial crisis.

Proper capital controls may spur growth through several channels. First, controls can stabilize the economy by checking capital flight and regulating volatile capital movements. Also, they allow manipulating of the terms of trade for international trade, thereby boosting export and economic growth. Adequate management of foreign capital and regulation of foreign direct investment (FDI) are necessary to encouragement of productive investment and spillover effects. But if controls are to be successful they should be incorporated into a broad development strategy of capable governments. Only "developmental states" with strong capacity can execute capital controls effectively, and encourage the productive use of foreign capital with industrial policy and financial control (Lee, 2004). Of course, the change of political economy tends to bring about capital decontrols and liberalization, which finally result in economic instability and financial crises in many countries.

Having said that, it comes as no surprise that there is no consensus in debates on capital account liberalization and economic growth. Actually, empirical studies do not find strong evidence that capital account liberalization spurs economic growth (Kose et al., 2006).[3] Considering limitations of cross-country regressions, it would be more desirable to examine a specific historical experience to show the relationship between capital controls, liberalization and growth, which I will turn to in the next section.

Economic miracle with capital controls in Korea

The developmental state and state-led economic development

It is now well known that rapid economic development in Korea was guided by the government that strongly intervened into the economy from the early 1960s (Amsden, 1989). Opposite to neoclassical arguments, the role of the state was crucial in Korea's growth, represented by selective promotion of industry, credit allocation programs, various measures for trade protection, and capital controls. The key to this successful intervention was a specific institutional structure of the government, called the developmental state, that had a characteristic of embedded autonomy and high capacity (Evans, 1995). The state in Korea had relatively strong autonomy because no powerful economic interest groups existed, in contrast with Latin American captured states. Another important feature was a close government–business relationship with cooperation and discipline. This mitigated information problems and limited unproductive rent-seeking. Furthermore, the Korean government had highly capable officials due to the long history of the bureaucracy system and efforts for internal reform. It was strongly development-oriented, different from other developing governments that attempted to maximize their own revenues.

The Korean government established a state-led financial system on the basis of this institutional structure, in which the government allocated financial resources to priority industries and firms in line with industrial policy. The major industrial policy purpose was export promotion in the 1960s and the development of heavy and chemical industries in the 1970s. In the process of industrialization, domestic business groups, called "chaebol" had been strongly supported by the government, with preferential credit, tax break and trade protection. The most important tool the government made use of was providing them with preferential bank loans, which were owned and controlled by the government itself. The share of policy credit in all loans of deposit money banks was higher than 60 percent from 1960 to 1991.

It is crucial to understand that the government support for businesses was wedded with effective discipline over their practices. The government provided preferential credit in return for export performance of firms, thereby creating contingent rents and minimizing rent-seeking. Hence, the development model of Korea was a unique combination of the market and state mechanism. The specific character of the state and the government–business relationship in Korea made this peculiar system function effectively. This system resulted in high and productive investment in the private sector, and thus economic growth for some 30 years.

Strategic globalization and capital controls

External economic policy of the developmental state of Korea was peculiar too. Opposite to the mainstream view that Korea benefited from globalization significantly, the Korean government did not pursue a mere opening of the economy. Rather, it pursued a strategic integration with the global economy by managing openness (Singh, 1994). First, the trade regime was not totally open but used the two-track approach of both export promotion and import substitution. The government effectively protected the domestic market so that domestic companies could grow internationally competitive, while it pushed them to increase exports for the world market (Chang, 1994).

More importantly, the government actively used extensive capital controls, incorporated into the state-controlled financial system (Nembhard, 1996). The Foreign Capital Inducement Act in 1961 legally stipulated capital controls that covered a broad gamut of financial activities, from foreign exchanges and currency restrictions to foreign investment. In 1962, the control over the foreign exchanges was transferred from the central bank to the ministry of finance (MoF) to increase the discretionary power of the government. Current accounts were controlled because imports were strongly regulated, and strict exchange restrictions were applied to all capital outflows until the 1980s. Tight regulations of FDI in Korea for the purpose of making FDI a conduit of advanced technology and managerial expertise for domestic development were well known (Mardon, 1990). The government inspected foreign investment projects rigorously and limited foreigners' ownership of domestic industry.[4] FDI that might compete with domestic firms were not permitted, and regulation measures including the foreign companies' compulsory use of domestically produced parts were introduced.

As a result, FDI played only a minor role in capital formation in Korea in comparison with other developing countries. As shown in Figure 16.1, the share of FDI in total long-term foreign capital and total domestic investment was much lower than other Asian Newly Industrializing Countries (NICs), let alone Latin America (Haggard and Cheng, 1987: 95).

However, foreign loans were not hindered, but rather promoted, by the government which aimed to mobilize foreign capital to complement scarce domestic savings. The government introduced new laws in 1962 and amended them in 1966 to let state-controlled banks guarantee the payment of long-term foreign loans of the private sector. As private businesses did not have credibility to borrow foreign capital, this policy was essential to their procurement of foreign capital. Due to these measures, long-term loans, particularly commercial loans, soared starting from the mid-1960s as shown in Figure 16.1.[5] The Korean government not only encouraged foreign loans but also made hard efforts to promote productive investment of the private sector using these loans. It allowed private businesses to make foreign loans taking the purpose of industrial policy into account, and actively distributed foreign currency loans through the state-controlled banking system for priority industries. Figure 16.2 demonstrates that the share of foreign savings in GDP between 1966 and 1982 was as high as about 5.5 percent, which financed high investment and the trade deficit. Thus, although the government controlled foreign capital strongly and the role of FDI was small, investment and economic growth in Korea banked highly on foreign capital in the early development period.[6]

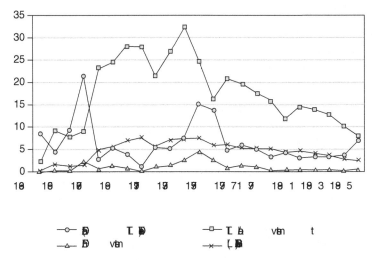

Figure 16.1 Long-term loan and FDI in Korea (source: Economic Planning Board (EPB), Bank of Korea (BOK), Ministry of Finance and Economy (MOFE), arrival base).

Note
LT loan means long-term loan.

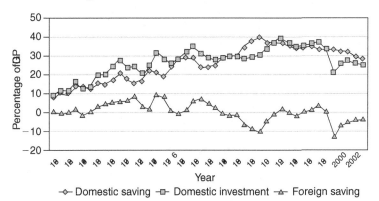

Figure 16.2 Investment and saving in Korea (1960–2002) (source: Bank of Korea (BOK)).

Note
Foreign saving is calculated by domestic investment minus domestic saving.

Capital controls and management of the Korean government were successful and the specific mode of foreign financing contributed to national development significantly. First, controls over capital outflows were highly effective because of the capacity of the government and they helped to contain domestic capital within the economy. Second, efforts to screen and examine foreign capital inflows made contributions to restricting foreign dominance of the economy. Among others, the developmental government successfully mobilized foreign loans and allocated them into priority sectors under the state-led financial system and industrial policy. Capital controls also helped the government to effectively discipline businesses because they relied highly on external finance and foreign capital that was controlled by the government. Hence, capital controls worked as an important element of a development strategy and stimulated productive investment, and thereby promoted economic growth in Korea

From financial opening and globalization to the financial crisis

Financial liberalization and globalizaiton in the 1990s

In Korea, it was not until the early 1990s that the government introduced extensive financial liberalization and opening. Several measures for financial liberalization including privatization of banks and interest rate deregulation were introduced in the 1980s, but the process was gradual and controlled by the government. However, economic development and the change of the financial system and political economy strengthened demands for more liberalization and opening in finance (Lee *et al.*, 2002). In the financial market, non-bank financial institutions (NBFI), less regulated by the government and mainly dominated by chaebols, grew fast, and the capital market also developed rapidly in the 1980s. This change significantly weakened the control of the government over financing of the corporate sector, while it strengthened the power of chaebols against the government. Chaebols that wanted more freedom in their investment and financing requested financial opening to utilize cheaper foreign capital. The government itself began to retreat from the economy after the 1980s, influenced by strong neoliberal ideology, which gained further momentum in the civil government from 1993. There was also external pressure for financial opening from the US government, reflecting the changed international politics and the end of the Cold War.

Against the backdrop of these changes, extensive financial and capital account liberalization were introduced in the early 1990s (Cho, 2000). Domestically, the government introduced significant liberalization of short-term interest rates and deregulation in NBFI sectors, which caused the term structure of domestic loans to be shorter (Cho and McCauley, 2001).[7] Measures for financial opening were also introduced along with the government decision to join the OECD and pressures from domestic and international capital. Capital-market opening for portfolio investment was introduced rather carefully and gradually, and long-term borrowing such as issuing corporate bonds abroad was still regulated in effect.[8] Government maintained regulation because it was concerned about financial instability and the weakening of the government macroeconomic management due to volatile foreign financial capital.

However, deregulation for short-term foreign borrowing by financial institutions and firms was much more extensive (Cho, 2000). The government abolished the ceiling on foreign currency loans of financial institutions and reduced the required ratio of long-term foreign loans in 1993. Furthermore, between 1994 and 1996, 24 finance companies were transformed into merchant banks that dealt in foreign exchanges, and banks were allowed to open 28 new foreign branches.

The government naïvely expected that short-term loans would be automatically rolled over, and the private sector strongly wanted low interest rates available on short-term foreign loans. Despite extensive opening, the financial supervision system was weakening, and was without an effective monitoring structure (Balino and Ubide, 1999). The problem was especially serious for newly licensed merchant banks that were exposed to high risk due to short-term borrowing and risky long-term investment (Lee *et al.*, 2002). The monitoring of internationalized financial business was not effective either, in spite of the rapid expansion of offshore business.

Financial vulnerability and the 1997 financial crisis

The aftermath of this careless financial opening was growing vulnerability and the collapse of the economy. As a consequence of capital account liberalization, foreign capital inflows rose rapidly as shown in Table 16.1. Foreign debt surged from some $44 billion in 1992 to more than $120 billion at the end of 1997, most of which was due to the surge of short-term borrowing of financial institutions and firms.[9]

This foreign borrowing financed the investment boom driven by aggressive investment spending by optimistic chaebols in the early 1990s. It is hard to say

Table 16.1 Foreign debt and net capital inflows into Korea in the 1990s ($ billion)

	1992	1993	1994	1995	1996	1997
Total foreign debt	42.8	43.9	56.8	78.4	104.7	120.8
Long term	24.3	24.7	26.5	33.1	43.7	69.6
Short term	18.5	19.2	30.4	45.3	61.0	51.2
Short term debt/ foreign reserves[a]	–	1.05	1.36	1.54	2.07	5.77
Net capital inflows $(1 + 2 + 3)$	6.99	3.22	10.73	17.22	23.92	6.03
1 Net direct investment	−0.43	−0.75	−1.65	−1.78	−2.34	−1.95
2 Net portfolio investment	5.8	10.0	6.12	11.59	15.18	14.76
3 Other net capital inflows	1.62	−6.05	6.26	7.46	11.08	−6.79
Financial institutions	2.43	1.2	8.98	13.40	14.15	−14.12
Borrowing						
Long-term	1.2	0.08	1.95	1.61	1.53	0.72
Banks	0.9	0.15	2.18	2.03	2.49	0.66
Development institutions	0.08	−0.08	0.01	−0.35	−0.85	−0.01
Merchant banks	0.22	0.01	−0.24	−0.07	−0.11	0.07
Short-term	1.23	1.12	7.03	11.79	12.62	−14.84
Banks	0.7	0.39	5.38	8.52	7.19	−10.31
Development institutions	0.59	0.56	0.78	1.56	2.24	−2.43
Merchant banks	−0.06	0.17	0.87	1.71	3.19	−2.10
Other debts (Trade Credit *et al.*)	2.49	−2.66	4.65	8.05	10.42	18.07

Source: Bank of Korea, *International Balance of Payments* (every year).

Note
a available foreign reserves base.

that the investment boom was overly irrational because there were several factors to explain it, including the temporary export market boom (Crotty and Lee, 2004).[10] But the mode of financing of the Korean economy was problematic and dangerous. For example, the ratio of the foreign debt in all corporate debts rose from 8.6 percent in 1992, to 10 percent in 1994 to 16.4 percent in 1996, owing to the rapid growth of short-term foreign borrowing (Hahm and Mishkin, 2000: 63). Chaebols' higher dependence on short-term and foreign borrowing made their financing structure especially problematic (Lee et al., 2000).[11] Financial institutions also became fragile with excessive risk-taking after liberalization and without good risk management. The share of foreign borrowing in total liabilities in the financial sector rose rapidly from 1.2 percent in 1992 to 10.7 percent in 1996, worsening the term structure and currency mismatch problem (Hahm and Mishkin, 2000). Merchant banks were in the biggest danger since they procured foreign capital mainly in short term and lent it in long term as chaebols' conduit for finance. Therefore, the Korean economy became financially vulnerable due to the significant increase of the short-term foreign debt, following mismanaged financial liberalization and opening.

In 1996, a huge external shock of the export market collapse dealt a severe blow to the Korean economy. Several chaebols started to go bankrupt in the economic recession of early 1997 and this left the financial sector in acute trouble with huge nonperforming loans. As financial institutions, especially troubled merchant banks, struggled to pull back their short-term loans, the crisis spread to the whole economy. Finally, the dangerous structure of foreign debt together with the contagion effect of the Southeast Asian crisis exacerbated foreigners' lack of confidence (Radelet and Sachs, 1998). When they refused a rollover of short-term foreign loans,[12] the Korean economy plunged into a crisis and the government had no choice but to resort to the IMF for the emergency loan in December.

There were serious debates concerning the cause of the East Asian financial crisis. While mainstream economists stress problems of the old development model such as moral hazard and crony capitalism (Borensztein and Lee, 1999; Krueger and Yoo, 2001), heterodox economists emphasize careless financial opening and the problems of the international capital market (Chang, 1998; Crotty and Dymski, 2001). Our investigation points out that mismanaged financial opening, associated with the breakup of the developmental state in the early 1990s, was the most important cause of the crisis in Korea. Capital account liberalization, mainly deregulation of short-term foreign borrowing, without effective regulation was haphazard. The experience of the Korean economy demonstrates that the government must be careful in financial opening and globalization.

Post-crisis restructuring and financial opening

Neoliberal economic restructuring and further financial opening imposed by the IMF after the 1997 financial crisis finally brought down the old development regime in Korea. The Kim government took the position that the crisis was due to inherent inefficiency of the state-led development model and implemented the extensive reform measures (Ministry of Finance and Economy, 1999). As well as restrictive macroeconomic policy, the government introduced the corporate and financial restructuring program, pursuing the Anglo-Saxon style economic model (Crotty and Lee, 2002).[13]

The government also introduced various policies to totally open its capital markets in 1998 even though the main cause of the crisis was careless financial opening. Those measures included eliminating the limit of foreign ownership in the stock market, opening the bond market for foreigners and allowing the hostile merges and aquisitions (M&A) by foreigners. More liberalization of foreign borrowing of the corporate and financial sector and deregulation of outward investment was introduced in 1999. Further deregulation on individuals sending money abroad was adopted in 2001 and the removal of any regulation in foreign exchanges transactions will be introduced soon (Crotty and Lee, 2005). The Korean government has become especially keen about attracting foreign direct investment (FDI). The Roh government announced the plan of "Northeast Asian Business Hub" with several incentives for foreign investors. It finally concluded the Free Trade Agreement with the US, in spite of domestic opposition in 2007, in an attempt to promote inward FDI.

It is certain that this extensive financial opening and restructuring, together with sharp depreciation of the currency, following the crisis increased foreign investment into Korea significantly.[14] Net foreign portfolio investment rose fast from $1.1 billion in 1997 to $4.8 billion in 1999 and $11.3 billion in 2000. FDI inflows recorded a dramatic growth after the crisis, amounting to more than $10 billion in a year, roughly ten times increase from the early 1990s. However, portfolio flows were unstable and the effect of FDI on economic recovery was in question because most of FDI was not productive "greenfield investment" but related to M&A.

All-out financial opening and neoliberal restructuring have actually caused serious concerns about the future of the Korean economy. First, skyrocketing capital inflows have reinforced foreign control of the Korean economy. The foreigners' share in the Korean stock market rose from 14.6 percent in 1997 to some 43 percent in early 2004. While the increase of foreign ownership is expected to provide better management skill and technology, foreigners also exerted a depressing effect on corporate investment with increasing dividends and the threat of hostile M&A. Foreign control and its detrimental effects are the most salient in the financial sector. Many financial institutions were sold to foreigners, who had come to own as much as 65 percent of ownership of commercial banks in late 2004, a dramatic jump after the crisis. Foreign-owned banks were much more reluctant to corporate lending, which depressed financial intermediation and corporate investment. Second, liberalization of international capital movements may give the government more difficulty in managing the economy. The government has already struggled to fight inflationary pressure due to increasing inflows of foreign capital. It is also reported that international capital movements may destabilize the Koran economy and increase the possibility of the currency attack. Therefore, financial opening and the growth strategy dependent on foreign capital would weaken the role of the government significantly and finally enfeeble national development of Korea.[15]

In fact, the economic performance of the post-crisis Korean economy is disappointing in general. As Table 16.2 demonstrates, after the fast recovery in 1999 and 2000, the economy fell in stagnation with a serious decline of investment and domestic consumption. Firms' investment has decreased highly along with the systemic change of the economy as big businesses lowered their debt ratio rapidly and financial institutions have become passive in corporate lending.[16] As Figure 16.2 shows, total domestic investment is now lower than domestic saving and, hence, Korean people have grave concerns about underinvestment and future growth prospects. Besides, income distribution and poverty have worsened so rapidly as to hamper the recovery of domestic consumption (Crotty and Lee, 2002). Worsening distribution is common in developing countries that opened capital accounts and underwent the financial crisis, and Korea is not an exception. In sum, post-crisis Korea became a mediocre economy after neoliberal restructuring and financial opening in stark contrast with the economic miracle with strong and effective capital controls (Crotty and Lee, 2005).

Conclusions

Capital account liberalization has been recommended by many economists and international organizations as one of the most important development policies to developing countries. However, this study suggests that its growth effect is ambiguous, and developing countries should be careful about financial opening considering its negative impacts on the economy. It is highly feasible for developing countries to achieve economic growth based on capital controls when the developmental government adopts an effective growth strategy as heterodox economists such as Crotty have argued.

I have investigated the experience of the Korean economy in view of the success of capital controls and the failure of financial opening. Korea achieved rapid economic growth, called the "East Asian miracle" for several decades under the intervention of the developmental state into the economy. The government made successful efforts to manage foreign capital and limit foreign control of the domestic economy in order to promote national economic development, by establishing the capital controls regime that was an element of a broad development strategy. However, mismanaged financial and capital account liberalization in the early 1990s, reflecting the demise of the developmental state and the change of the political economy, made the economy financially vulnerable. The surge of short-term foreign borrowing and foreign debt after this financial opening coupled with the external shock finally led to the financial crisis in 1997. The Korean government introduced neoliberal economic restructuring and extensive financial opening following the crisis. But the post-crisis Korean economy that has pursued financial globalization has been suffering from lower

Table 16.2 Economic performance in Korea after the 1997 crisis

	1993–1997	1998	1999	2000	2001	2002	2003	2004	2005
Real GDP growth	7.1	−6.7	9.5	8.5	3.8	7.0	3.1	4.6	4.0
Consumption growth	6.5	−10.6	9.7	7.1	4.9	7.6	−0.3	0.2	3.4
Fixed investment growth	12.3	−22.9	8.3	12.2	−0.2	6.6	4.0	1.9	2.3
Total investment/GDP	37.1	25.2	29.3	31.1	29.4	29.1	30.1	30.4	30.2
Total saving/GDP	36.1	37.5	35.3	33.7	31.7	31.3	32.8	34.9	33.0
Net export/GDP	−1.1	12.9	6.7	3.1	2.3	1.4	2.3	4.3	2.5
Manufacturing ordinary profitability	2.2	−1.8	1.7	1.3	0.4	4.7	4.7	7.8	6.5
Debt ratio in manufacturing	319.5	303.0	214.7	210.6	182.2	135.4	123.4	104.2	100.9
Top 20% income/bottom 20% income	4.49	5.44	5.49	5.32	5.36	5.18	5.22	5.41	5.43

Source: Bank of Korea, Ministry of Finance and Economy.

Note
Average value for 1993–1997.

growth and worsening distribution. In particular, there are serious concerns about the foreign control of the economy and higher economic instability along with the rapid increase of foreign capital inflows.

This case study about Korea from the historical and institutional viewpoint supports the heterodox argument about capital controls, liberalization and growth. The experience of capital controls and growth in Korea points to the importance of efforts to manage foreign capital for national development and the active role of the state in economic development. Besides, Korea's experience of financial globalization and the crisis demonstrates the danger of careless financial opening and its detrimental effects. Other developing economies should learn crucial lessons from the historical experience of successful capital controls and problematic financial opening in Korea.

Notes

1 According to them, capital controls only introduce distortions and inefficiency. They are also ineffective because in most cases private capital can evade these controls.
2 In particular, they underscore political will and the feasibility of controls in practice. Recent studies report that capital controls were rather successful in Chile and Malaysia in the 1990s (IMF, 2000).
3 Many empirical studies report different results, depending on different specifications, samples and periods. Some even report that capital controls can promote growth under several contexts associated with East Asian developmental states (Lee and Jayadev, 2005).
4 Only joint ventures between foreign and domestic capital were permitted and moreover it was compulsory for foreign investors to resell their share after some years.
5 The ratio of payment guarantee on foreign borrowings to total deposit money bank loans jumped from 11 percent in 1965 to 71 percent in 1967 and 94 percent in 1970. The average amount of long-term loans rose from $124 million in the 1960s to $1.2 billion in the 1970s. That of foreign direct investment (FDI) also increased from $6 million to $82 million but its share in total foreign capital flows was still significantly lower than that of long-term loans.
6 This high dependence on foreign loan aggravated the foreign debt problem later in the early 1980s, but the crisis was overcome thanks to the political support from the United States and Japan, and the huge trade surplus in the late 1980s.
7 Interest rates on short-term bills such as CP (commercial paper) were formally liberalized in 1991, and were completely liberalized in 1993–1994, while bank interest rates and corporate bond rates continued to be controlled through moral suasion or administrative guidance despite formal liberalization.
8 The government allowed foreigners to own shares of Korean firms in 1992 with the ceiling of 10 percent for groups and 3 percent for individuals. The ceiling for groups was raised to 12 percent in December 1994, 18 percent in April 1996, 20 percent in October 1996, and was still 26 percent in November 1997 before the crisis.
9 Of course, the change in the international financial markets with the backdrop of high growth in East Asia and low interest rates in developed countries was another factor that in increased capital inflows.
10 Crotty and Lee (2004) argue that the argument to emphasize inefficiency of the Korean economy due to crony capitalism and moral hazard does not have empirical ground. Their investigation reports that profitability of the Korean corporate sector was rather high before the crisis both historically and internationally and there is hardly any evidence for serious inefficiency enough to cause the collapse of the economy in 1997.

11 The top 30 chaebols' dependence on external finance increased from 58.8 percent in 1994 to 77.6 percent in 1996 and the share of short-term borrowing rose from 47.7 percent to 63.6 percent over the same period.

12 In 1997, the rollover rate of commercial banks fell from 106.3 percent in June to 85.8 percent in September, 58.8 percent in November and mere 32.2 percent in December.

13 The post-crisis restructuring program covered rapid reduction of the debt ratio of Korean conglomerates, called "chaebol," streamlining of their corporate structure and the shutdown of many financial institutions with resolution of nonperforming loans. The government also introduced measures to strengthen the role of capital markets and labor market flexibilization.

14 Only foreign capital could afford to buy the assets chaebols were forced to sell, corporate-cum-financial opening naturally increased foreign capital inflows partly through a fire sale.

15 A report by Bank of Korea also indicates negative effects of speculative foreign capital such as private equity funds, including potential economic instability, threatening of the management rights, and repressing investment (BOK, 2005).

16 The debt ratio of the manufacturing sector of Korea is now even lower than that of the United States and Japan. The high debt model of the Korean economy appears to finally have come to an end.

References

Amsden, A. (1989) *Asia's Next Giant: South Korea and Late Industrialization*. New York: Oxford University Press.

Balino, T. J. T. and Ubide, A. (1999) "The Korean Financial Crisis of 1997 – A Strategy of Financial Sector Reform," IMF Working Paper, WP/99/28.

Bank of Korea (BOK) (2005) "Problems of Speculative Foreign Capital and Policy Agenda," 3. (Korean). Finance and Economy Institute.

Borensztein E. R. and Lee, J W. (1999) "Credit Allocation and Financial Crisis in Korea," IMF Working Paper, WP/99/20.

Chang H.-J. (1994) *The Political Economy of Industrial Policy*. London and Basingstoke: Macmillan.

—— (1998) "Korea: The Misunderstood Crisis," *World Development*, 26(8).

Cho, Y. J. (2000) "Financial Crisis in Korea: A Consequence of Unbalanced Liberalization?" Presented at World Bank conference.

Cho, Y. J. and McCauley, R. (2001) "Liberalising the Capital Account without Losing Balance: Lessons from Korea," BIS papers. No. 15.

Crotty, J. (1989) "The Limits of Keynesian Macroeconomic Policy in the Age of the Global Marketplace," in A. MacEwan and W. K. Tabb (eds.) *Instability and Change in the World Economy*, 82–100, New York: Monthly Review Press.

Crotty, J. and Dymski, G. (2001) "Can the Global Neoliberal Regime Survive Victory in Asia?" in P. Arestis and M. Sawyer (eds.) *Money, Finance and Capitalist Development*. Northampton, MA: Edward Elgar.

Crotty, J. and Epstein, G. (1996) "In Defense of Capital Control," *Socialist Register*.

Crotty, J. and Lee, K.-K. (2002) "A Political-economic Analysis of the Failure of Neo-liberal Restructuring in Post-crisis Korea," *Cambridge Journal of Economics* 26(5).

—— (2004) "Was the IMF's Imposition of Economic Regime Change Justified? A Critique of the IMF's Economic and Political Role in Korea During and After the Crisis," PERI (Political Economy Research Institute) Working Paper, No. 77.

—— (2005) "From East Asian 'Miracle' to Neoliberal 'Mediocrity': The Effects of Liberalization and Financial Opening on the Post-Crisis Korean Economy," *Global Economic Review*, 34(4).

Evans, P. B. (1995) *Embedded Autonomy: States and Industrial Transformation.* Princeton: Princeton Unviersity Press.

Haggard, S. and Cheng, T.-J. (1987) "State and Foreign Capital in the East Asian NICs," in F. C. Deyo (ed.) *The Political Economy of the New Asian Industrialism.* Ithaca: Cornell University Press.

Hahm, J. and Mishkin, F. S. (2000) "Causes of the Korean Financial Crisis: Lessons for Policy," NBER Working Paper, No. 7483.

IMF (2000) *Country Experiences with the Use and Liberalization of Capital Controls.*

Kose, A. M., Prasad, E., Rogoff, K. and Wei, S.-J. (2006) "Financial Globalization: A Reappraisal," IMF Working Paper, WP/06/189.

Krueger, A. and Yoo, J. H. (2001) "Chaebol Capitalism and the Currency-Financial Crisis in Korea." Presented at NBER conference, 2001.

Lee, C. H., Lee, K. and Lee, K.-K. (2002). "*Chaebol*, Financial Liberalization, and Economic Crisis: Transformation of Quasi-Internal Organization in Korea," *Asian Economic Journal*, 16(2).

Lee, K.-K. (2004) "Economic Growth with Capital Controls: Focusing on the Experience of South Korea in the 1960s," *Social Systems Studies*, 9.

Lee, K.-K. and Jayadev, A. (2005) "The Effects of Capital Account Liberalization on Growth and the Labor Share of Income: Reviewing and Extending the Cross-Country Evidence," in G. Epstein (ed.) *Capital Flight and Capital Controls in Developing Countries.* Northampton, MA: Edward Elgar.

Mardon, R. (1990) "The State and the Effective Control of Foreign Capital: The Case of South Korea," *World Politics*, 43.

Ministry of Finance and Economy (1999) *Djnomics: a New Foundation for the Korean Economy*, published for Korea Development Institute (KDI).

Nembhard, J. G. (1996) *Capital Control, Financial Regulation and Industrial Policy in South Korea and Brazil.* Westport: Praeger.

Radelet, S. and Sachs, J. (1998) "The East Asian Financial Crisis: Diagnosis, Remedies, Prospects," *Brookings Papers on Economic Activity*, 1.

Rogoff, K., Kose, M. A., Prasad, E. and Wei, S.-J. (2004) "Effects of Financial Globalization on Developing Countries: Some Empirical Evidences," IMF Occasional Paper, No. 220.

Singh, A. (1994) "Openness and the Market Friendly Approach to Development: Learning and the Right Lessons from Development Experience," *World Development*, 22(12).

Stiglitz, J. (2000) "Capital Market Liberalization, Economic Growth, and Instability," *World Development*, 28(6).

Part IV
Heterodox macroeoconomic policy

17 Keynes' bourgeois socialism

Soo Haeng Kim

Introduction

John Maynard Keynes was very much influenced by the two world wars, the Bolshevik Revolution, fascism, and the severe inter-war depressions of the world capitalist economy. These events led him to discredit the cosmopolitan and non-interventionist principles of market economies and urged him to find ways of safeguarding capitalism from the attacks by socialism and fascism. According to Keynes, high levels of unemployment and income inequality were the two "outstanding faults" (Keynes 1936: 372) of capitalism, which the state had to solve in order to defend capitalism.

While he introduced a rationale for state intervention in market economies and proposed economic policies that he thought would save capitalism, he also propagated a "bourgeois socialist" politics that sought to change the existing material conditions for the betterment of the working class without altering the capital–labor relations. In this chapter I trace the development of, and also critique, Keynes' analysis of capitalism and economic policy proposals. In particular, I am much concerned with Keynesians' tendency to fall into the trap of a bourgeois utopianism, a state fetishism and an apologetics for capital (see Kim and Park 2007; Kim and Cho 1999).

Capitalism's tendency toward secular stagnation?

According to Schumpeter (1946), even before writing "Economic Consequences of the Peace" (1919) and "A Revision of the Treaty" (1922), Keynes had a socio-economic vision of capitalism called the secular stagnation thesis, a thesis later shared by Paul Baran, Paul Sweezy and the Monthly Review School. The vision presumed that the spirit of private enterprise was flagging, investment opportunities were vanishing and bourgeois saving habits had, therefore, lost their social function. This vision was theorized in *The General Theory* (1936) through the concepts of propensity to consume, liquidity preference, marginal efficiency of investment and others. Baran and Sweezy (1966) also pointed out that "the vision of capitalism as a system always in imminent danger of falling into a state of stagnation ... permeates and, in a certain sense, dominates *The General Theory*."

The secular stagnation thesis in either Keynes' or Sweezy's version, however, does not seem to be satisfactorily postulated. First, in deriving the secular stagnation tendency, Keynes mainly depended on the psychological traits of consumers, speculators and entrepreneurs. In particular, Keynes emphasized the entrepreneurs' expectation of the future as the most important element in deciding the volume of effective demand. It was because Keynes acknowledged that higher liquidity preference followed a fall in marginal efficiency of investment (1936: 316). In a nutshell the entrepreneurs' optimism raises investment and increases consumption by leading to the hiring of more workers. Then, what determines entrepreneurs' optimism or pessimism about the future? This question was not answered by Keynes. Whether it is determined by their animal spirit or sunspots may not produce any difference (Sutcliffe 1977). If we assume, like Marx, that competition among capitals forces capitalists to invest to their utmost, the current, not future, rate of profit may determine the volume of investment. This simple formula by Marx allows us to evade the maze of the illogically changing psychologies (see Crotty 2002).

Second, the secular stagnation thesis seems to emphasize the prior existence of markets for commodities before deciding investment. If the markets for producers' or consumers' goods do not exist a priori, capitalists may not invest in either industry. This logic contradicts the fact that capitalists' investment, i.e. buying means of production and employing workers, creates the markets for producers' and consumers' goods. Although supply and demand are separated in time, space and person, capital's valorization drive in supply-side initiates to disturb and re-establish the balance between supply and demand. In the totality comprising production, exchange, distribution and consumption, Marx points out that production, not consumption, is the most important determinant moment.

Third, the secular stagnation thesis does not mention anything about technological developments or innovations which may expedite a long-term prosperity. Thus, Keynes's short-run static theory is not adequate for explaining secular stagnation.

Fourth, Sweezy and Baran's development of Keynes' secular stagnation thesis is full of errors (Sweezy and Baran 1966). Their "tendency of the economic surplus to rise" (TSR) can not be compared with Marx's "tendency of the rate of profit to fall" (TRPF). For example, if monopolies appropriate some incomes from their buyers, it will raise their economic surplus but not change Marx's profit (surplus-value) created in the labor process. Their thesis that military expenditures maintain economic prosperity by absorbing or wasting the rising economic surplus reflects nothing but the simple fact that the government enriches the military–industrial–academic complex by means of levying higher taxes on the wider population. The war efforts through the military–industrial–academic complex are not a necessary means of wasting the rising economic surplus for maintenance of prosperity but a means of valorizing the war-related capitals. And the economic prosperity mentioned above does not take account of so many awful negative effects of the war such as killings of human beings, destruction of culture and civilization, heightening hatred and insecurity, and the psychiatric syndromes of war veterans and others.

Although Keynes' secular stagnation thesis was postulated very poorly, it nonetheless fulfilled its ideological role in arguing for the state's intervention in market economies. This ideological success was mainly due to the particular real situation of severe long-term depression. In this sense Keynes' secular stagnation thesis occupies the same theoretical and ideological status as Adam Smith's fantastic "invisible hand" thesis, though the latter succeeded in the state's retreat from mercantilist interventions.

Keynes' characterization of the state

This section revisits Keynes' vision of state intervention, and identifies its inherent naiveté and elitism, especially with regard to the influence of class forces on the state. From the secular stagnation thesis, Keynes identified "the outstanding faults of the capitalist economic society" as being "its failure for full employment and its arbitrary and inequitable distribution of wealth and income" (1936: 372). These "outstanding faults," Keynes argued, must be solved in order to save capitalism from extinction. Then, who will undertake this mission? The consumers, the speculators and the entrepreneurs – the members of capitalist society – cannot solve the "faults," because the faults are the "fruits" of their pursuit of private interests amidst "risk, uncertainty and ignorance" of the future. Here the state enters the stage. According to Keynes, the state can be independent of the psychology and behavior of the members of the capitalist society; for instance the state "is in a position to calculate the marginal efficiency of capital-goods on long views and on the basis of the general social advantage" (1936: 164). As Keynes thinks the state is the defender of the social or public interests, the state should eliminate unemployment and income inequality.

Many criticized Keynes' conception of the state as a neutral third party. For example, Sweezy said:

> Perhaps most striking of all [examples of the insularity and comparative narrowness of the Keynesian approach] is Keynes's habit of treating the state as a *dues ex machina* to be invoked whenever his human actors, behaving according to the rules of the capitalist game, get themselves into a dilemma from which there is apparently no escape. Naturally, this Olympian interventionist resolves everything in a manner satisfactory to the author and presumably to the audience. The only trouble is – as every Marxist knows – that the state is not a god but one of the actors who has a part to play just like all the other actors.
>
> (Sweezy 1946)

And Singh also criticized Keynes:

> [Keynes] assumes a State which is not only above the class interests of the conflicting groups – the laborers and the capitalists – but is in the general interest of society as a whole. This assumption is wholly unreal. The class

affiliation of the modern State is so vital that it can only work in the interest of the capitalist class. Dobb (1950) says: "once economic theory is allowed to employ the dues ex-machina of an impartial State, a classless State, all miracles can be demonstrated, even without the aid of algebra. One might dismiss such attempts as harmless pastimes, were it not that ideas ... can not only disseminate the opium of false hopes, but in the cold war of today more dangerous illusions about the grim realities of present-day capitalism."

(Singh 1954)

Why did Keynes dismiss the class nature of the state? It is simply because he intended to mystify the nature of the state. His firm conviction that "ideas" have bigger influences on the state bureaucrats and politicians than vested interests contradicts his ardent plea that the state should reduce unemployment in order to "defend capitalist system" itself. And his equally firm belief that the "impartial" educated elite should control the state organs contradicts his revelation that "the *class* war will find me on the side of the educated *bourgeoisie*" (Keynes 1925).

By emphasizing the impartial elite's leadership in the state, Keynes thought that even an undemocratic bourgeois government would be efficient. Harrod said:

Keynes presupposed that the government of Britain was and would continue to be in the hands of an intellectual aristocracy using the method of persuasion. Keynes tended till the end to think of the really important decisions being reached by a small group of intelligent people, like the group that fashioned the Bretton Woods plan.

(Harrod 1972: 226)

And Keynes said:

I believe that in the future, more than ever, questions about the economic framework of society will be far and away the most important political issues. I believe that the right solution will involve intellectual and scientific elements which must be above the heads of the vast mass of more or less illiterate voters.

(Keynes 1925)

The form of government Keynes preferred is exactly the "club government" that ruled Britain for the first two-thirds of the twentieth-century (Moran 2003). Moran explained:

The club government had three striking features. First, its operations were oligarchic, informal, and secretive. Second, it was highly pervasive. In other words, it was not just practiced in the core of the metropolitan governing machine in Whitehall.... It also shaped government in the overlapping spheres of self-regulation and the vast, labyrinthine world of quasi-government. Third, it was anachronistic, and deliberately so. The institutions and the ideology of the club system were the product of the Victorian era, and of the threats that confronted governing elites in that first industrial nation. But the system survived as a deliberate anachronism, because in the twentieth century it protected elites from more modern forces: from the threats posed by the new world of formal democracy, and from an empowered and often frightening working class.

(Moran 2003: 4)

If small elites rule the government through exchanging informal and tacit knowledge with autonomy from public scrutiny, it would be much easier for the vested interests to influence the government. As the club government was not impartial and efficient, it "had a rich history of policy disaster in Britain in the first two-thirds of the 20th century" (Moran 2003: 172).

Keynes would have been closer to the mark had he acknowledged the following: as far as the capitalist state is concerned, it aims to maintain and strengthen the bases of capitalism, i.e. private ownership of capital and capital's valorization drive. How the state can achieve this depends on the particular situations in which capitals are valorizing themselves. When large-scale unemployment threatens to topple the capitalist system itself, the state needs to reduce or eliminate unemployment. Conversely, when the working-class militancy simply obstructs capital's valorization, the state may use restrictive fiscal and monetary policies to create unemployment and weaken the power of workers. In other words, the reduction or elimination of unemployment is sometimes, but certainly not always the state's mission. During the Thatcher and Reagan periods, the state adopted monetarist squeeze policies to make financially weak companies bankrupt and to reduce the social welfare system in order to increase unemployment and to weaken the power of the working class. Even if the state is under the control of an intellectual aristocracy like Keynes imagined, the state will have to maintain capitalist order and have to facilitate capital's valorization, which involves class conflict between capital and labor.

Economic policies suggested by Keynes

Keynes suggested several state policies. In order to reduce capitalists' uncertainty, ignorance and fear of the future, the state should deliberately control "currency and credit," and collect and publish factual information on the business world (Keynes 1926). The state should impose high income taxes on estates and on the personal incomes of the wealthy classes. By means of an increase in the money supply and commodity prices, the state should reduce real wages as an inducement to investment. More radically, by monetary and credit policies the state should lower the rate of interest towards "that point relative to the schedule of marginal efficiency of capital at which there is full employment" (1936: 375). These policies should lead to the "euthanasia of the rentier and consequently the euthanasia of the cumulative oppressive power of the capitalist to exploit the scarcity-value of capital" (1936: 376). Furthermore, the state should undertake to control and direct the flow of saving and investment, i.e. to "organize" and "socialize" investment, "with a view to a progressive decline in the marginal efficiency of capital" (1936: 325).

These policies would lead to the end-situation in which

> profit and interest are reduced to zero, and in which the full employment would be permanently maintained and the inequalities in income disappeared or would be sharply reduced, and in which money would be reduced to a mere accounting unit, and thus all reasons for preferring money would disappear.
>
> (Negri 1988: 32)

What Keynes in fact showed was a "bourgeois socialism" which, Marx and Engels pointed out in the "Manifesto of the Communist Party," would change existing material conditions for the betterment of the working class, without altering the capitalist relations of production (Gillman 1955). As Keynes, however, did not think through these policy commendations seriously, either as to their practical feasibility or as to their probable impact on the business cycle (Gillman 1955), in his policy suggestions we can see his bourgeois utopianism, mystification of the state and apologetics for capital.

Keynes did not understand that the valorization of capital is the motive power of the capitalist economy and that the valorizing process involves contradictions and struggles between the two fundamental classes, capitalists and workers, and among various factions of the dominant class, i.e. industrial, commercial and financial capitalists. Keynes' conception of capital is exactly the same as that of the neoclassicists. He lacks Marx's viewpoint:

> As a capitalist, he is only capital personified. His soul is the soul of capital. But capital has one sole driving force, the drive to valorize itself, to create surplus-value…. Capital is dead labor which, vampire-like, lives only by sucking living labor, and lives more, the more labor it sucks.
>
> (Marx 1976: 342)

Let us pay more attention to the mysterious "socialization of investment" (see Pollin 1997; Whyman 2006). In the *General Theory*, Keynes said:

> Furthermore, it seems unlikely that the influence of the banking policy on the rate of interest will be sufficient by itself to determine an optimum rate of investment. I conceive, therefore, that a somewhat comprehensive socialization of investment will prove the only means of securing an approximation to full employment; though this need not exclude all manner of compromises and of devices by which public authority will co-operate with private initiative.
>
> (1936: 378)

Here it is difficult to understand the exact concept of the "socialization of investment." But in other places he offer a more concrete vision. For example, in the "End of Laissez-faire" (1926), Keynes said:

> I believe that some coordinated act of intelligent judgment is required as to the scale on which it is desirable that the community as a whole should save, the scale on which these savings should go abroad in the form of foreign investments, and whether the present organization of the investment market distributes savings along the most nationally productive channels. I do not think that these matters could be left entirely to the chances of private judgment and private profits, as they are at present.
>
> (Keynes 1926)

From here we glean some elements of socialization; namely that the scale and direction of investment are determined in the societal level, not at the private enterprise level, and that "socialized" investment is not for private profits but for social interests. Also, in the "End of Laissez-faire", Keynes uses as illustrations of social-interest augmenting institutions the examples of semi-autonomous bodies within the state such as universities, the Bank of England, the Port of London Authority, the railway companies, as well as joint stock companies. He said about joint stock companies:

> But more interesting than these [semi-autonomous bodies within the state] is the trend of joint stock institutions, when they have reached a certain age and size, to approximate to the status of public corporations rather than that of individualistic private enterprise. One of the most interesting and unnoticed developments of recent decades has been the tendency of big enterprise to socialize itself.
>
> (Keynes 1926)

Keynes' vision of the socialization of investment thus contained the following elements: the scale and direction of investments are determined by the policies of the state and its organs; public works (which he demanded as a cure for the massive unemployment); investments made by the semi-autonomous organs within the state; and investments made by the joint stock companies in which ownership and management of capital are separated. Therefore, the socialization of investment does not necessarily rely on the heavy public works financed by government deficits, because Keynes said: "If the State is able to determine the aggregate amount of resources devoted to augmenting the instruments and the basic rate of reward to those who own them, it will have accomplished all that is necessary" (1936: 378). This socialization of investment can be compared with and distinguished from Marx's "socialization of production." According to Marx, as division of labor within a factory and social division of labor develops, labor assumes more social character than individual or private character, while capital reveals more social character as common ownership by shareholders surpasses individual or private ownership of capital. Thus, the contradiction between the social character of production and the private character of appropriation leads to the final situation: "The knell of capitalist private property sounds" (1976: 929).

It is evident that Keynes mistook the increasing social character of capital for the gradual loss of capital's power of domination and exploitation. In particular, his conception of the joint stock company is in line with James Burnham's managerial revolution, in which "the general stability and reputation of the institution are the more considered by the management than the maximum of profit for the shareholders" (Keynes 1926). But as the joint stock company "offers an individual capitalist [a big shareholder] an absolute command over the capital and property of others [other shareholders], within certain limits, and, through this, command over other people's labor" (1981: 570), the expropriation of small and medium capitalists takes "the antithetical form of the appropriation of social property by a few" in the joint stock company (1981: 571). Valorization of capital still remains the basic aim of the joint stock company. Of course, Marx recognizes that the joint stock company "presents itself prima facie as a mere point of transition to a new form of production" (1981: 569). His reasoning is:

> the contradiction between the general social power into which capital has developed and the private power of the individual capitalists over these social conditions of production develops ever more blatantly, while this development also contains the solution to this situation, in that it simultaneously raises the conditions of production into general, communal, social condition.
>
> (1981: 373)

Keynes tried to mystify the nature of capital and the relationship of domination–exploitation and to prescribe the deceptive and apologetic "New Jerusalem." Seymour Harris said: "Keynes would indeed try to preserve capitalism by ridding it of its parasitic elements: excess savings, high rates of interest, the hereditary principle and its debilitating effect on capitalism, the preference of the future over the present" (Harris 1947: 544). Dobb also characterizes Keynes as follows: "He [Keynes] thought he could separate the parasitic elements of capitalism from capitalism itself in order to save the life-blood of the system from exhaustion" (Dobb 1950). Keynes' mention of "New Jerusalem" was based on his intention to set aside the fear for the future and to reconstruct capitalism amidst the increasing power of the working class. Or, in Negri's words:

> where the relationship between the classes has become dynamic, any attempt to create a new equilibrium is bound to be insecure and unstable. Therefore, [Keynes] introduced the State as the restorer of an equilibrium and allowed it to use violence, direct and indirect, to defend the mystified general interests or public good.
>
> (Negri 1988: 33–5)

Keynes and the welfare state

Joan Robinson once pointed out that one of the reasons why Keynes failed was "to allow budget deficit as a prophylactic against recessions, the main consequence of which was the hypertrophy of the military-industrial complex in the USA" (Robinson 1979). It is true that when Keynes explained how building mansions and pyramids or paying men to dig holes in the ground will maintain employment and the real national income, he added: "It is not reasonable, however, that a sensible community should be content to remain dependent on such fortuitous and often wasteful mitigations when once we understand the influences upon which effective demand depends" (1936: 220). Nevertheless, Keynes did not support the social welfare system with the same enthusiasm that he exuded for his theory of effective demand. He was, importantly, a proponent of reducing income inequality. The *General Theory* refuted the principal argument favoring income inequality, namely that such inequality is essential if the substantial volume of saving necessary for investments is to be maintained. Grahl (1983) called Keynes "the Liberal Revolutionary," because he believed Keynes consequently laid the foundation for the welfare state. Welfare state is used as "shorthand for the State's activities in four broad areas: cash benefits; health care; education; and food, housing and other welfare services" (Barr 2004: 21). But while he may have helped to obviate a classic rationale for not expanding the state, in fact Keynes did not actively join or contribute efforts to devise and build the British welfare state. "Keynes was not an egalitarian socialist; he was a liberal who accepted an intellectual aristocracy as a necessary and desirable part of the good society" (Vaizey 1969).

Recently, Maria Marcuzzo insisted that

> there is a widespread tendency to portray Keynes as the founding father of the welfare state and to claim that Keynesian revolution provided the justification for the need of a large public sector in the economy ... there are scant grounds for these claims.
>
> (Marcuzzo 2006)

The grounds for her insistence seem to be solid. The policy message in the *General Theory* is to sustain the level of investment, but this should be interpreted more in the sense of "stabilizing business confidence" (Bateman 1996: 148) than as a plea for debt-financed public works (Kregel 1985). Evidently, therefore, Keynes' involvement in the design of the two milestones of the welfare state in Britain, i.e. national social insurance and full employment policy, was rather limited. On substantive issues Keynes was not in favor of high taxes to pay for social benefits and pension, the costs of which ought to be borne out by employers.

Conclusion

In this chapter I tried to dig out the foundation of Keynes' "bourgeois socialism;" namely his bourgeois utopianism, mystification of the state and apologetics for capital. As an elite intellectual aristocrat operating in a historical juncture where fighting against Marxism and fascism were paramount for those sharing his class background and political orientation, he propagated a vision of dramatic policy shifts to save capitalism, but they left intact and in no way questioned, acknowledged or proposed changing capitalist class relations. His biographer, Professor Skidelsky, informed us of the then prevailing atmosphere at the University of Cambridge.

> Keynes's conviction that Washington [the New Deals], not Moscow, was the economic laboratory of the world was not widely shared in Cambridge [in England]. Anthony Blunt, returning in October 1934 from a year in Rome to a fellowship at Trinity College, found that "all my friends ... almost all the intellectual and bright young undergraduates who had come up to Cambridge ... had suddenly become Marxists under the impact of Hitler coming to power". Marxism was embraced by the "brightest and the best" as the cure for war, fascism and unemployment. Membership of the University's Socialist Society and Labour Club, both Marxist-dominated, rose to about 1,000 – a fifth of the undergraduate total – by the time of the Spanish Civil War [1936]. Marxism invaded and captured the Apostles [Cambridge Conversazione Society], the citadel of Keynes's Cambridge.
>
> (Skidelsky 2004: 514)

In conclusion, this chapter does not share Schumpeter's opinion that "the attempts to Keynesify Marx or to Marxify Keynes" would be fruitful (1954: 885).

References

Barr, N. (2004) *The Economics of the Welfare State*, 4th edition, Oxford: Oxford University Press.

Bateman, B. (1996) *Keynes's Uncertain Revolution*, Ann Arbor: University of Michigan Press.

Crotty, J. (2002) "Why Do Global Markets Suffer From Chronic Excess Capacity? Insights from Keynes, Schumpeter and Marx," Political Economic Research Institute (UMASS).

Dobb, M. (1950) "Full Employment and Capitalism," *Modern Quarterly*, 5(2).

Gillman, J. M. (1955) "An Evaluation of John Maynard Keynes," *Science and Society*, 19(2).

Grahl, J. (1983) "The Liberal Revolutionary," *Marxism Today*, June.

Harrod, R. (1972) *The Life of John Maynard Keynes*, London: Penguin Books.

Harris, S. E. (ed.) (1947) *The New Economics: Keynes' Influence on Theory and Public Policy*, New York: A. A. Knopf.

Keynes, J. M. (1925) "Am I a Liberal?" *CWK* IX.
—— (1926) "The End of Laissez-faire," *CWK* IX.
—— (1936) "The General Theory of Employment, Interest and Money," *CWK* VII.
Kim, S. and Cho, B. (1999) "The South Korean Economic Crisis: Contrasting Interpretations and an Alternative for Economic Reform," *Studies in Political Economy*, 60.
Kim, S. and Park, S.-H. (2007) "A Critical Appraisal of the Park Chung Hee System," in H. Martin, S. Jeong and R. Westra (eds.) *Marxist Perspectives on South Korea in the Global Economy*, Aldershot: Ashgate.
Kregel, J. (1985) "Budget Deficit, Stabilization Policy and Liquidity Preference: Keynes's Post-War Policy Proposals," in F. Vicarelli (ed.) *Keynes's Relevance Today*, London: Macmillan.
Marcuzzo, M. C. (2006) "Keynes and the Welfare State," mimeo. Available at www.uniroma1.it/marcuzzo/homepage.htm.
Marx, K. (1976) *Capital*, Vol. I, Harmondsworth: Penguin.
—— (1981) *Capital*, Vol. III, Harmondsworth: Penguin.
Moran, M. (2003) *The British Regulatory State: High Modernism and Hyper-Innovation*, Oxford: Oxford University Press.
Negri, A. (1988) *Revolution Retrieved: Selected Writings on Marx, Keynes, Capitalist Crisis and New Social Subjects, 1967–83*, London: Red Books.
Pollin, R. (1997) "'Socialization of Investment' and 'Euthanasia of the Rentier': The Relevance of Keynesian Policy Ideas for the Contemporary US Economy," in Arestis Philip and Malcolm Sawyer (eds.) *The Relevance of Keynesian Economic Policies Today*, London: Macmillan.
Robinson, J. (1979) "Has Keynes Failed?" *Annals of Public and Co-operative Economy*, 50(1).
Schumpeter, J. (1946) "John Maynard Keynes 1883–1946," *American Economic Review*, 36.
—— (1954) *A History of Economic Analysis*, Oxford: Oxford University Press.
Singh, V. B. (1954) "Keynesian Economics in Relation to Underdeveloped Countries," *Science and Society*, 18(3).
Skidelsky, R. (2004) *John Maynard Keynes 1883~1946: Economist, Philosopher, Statesman*, London: Pan Books.
Sutcliffe, B. (1977) "Keynesianism and the Stabilisation of Capitalist Economies," in F. Green and P. Nore (eds.) *Economics: An Anti-Text*, London: Macmillan.
Sweezy, P. M. (1946) "John Maynard Keynes," *Science and Society*, 10.
Sweezy, P. M. and Baran, P. A. (1966) *Monopoly Capital: an Essay on the American Economic and Social Order*, New York: Monthly Review Press.
Vaizey, J. (1969) "Keynes," *Irish Banking Review*, June.
Vicarelli, F. (ed.) (1985) *Keynes's Relevance Today*, London: Macmillan.
Whyman, P. (2006) "Post-Keynesianism, Socialisation of Investment and Swedish Wage-earner Funds," *Cambridge Journal of Economics*, 30.

18 The case of capital controls revisited

Gerald Epstein[1]

Introduction

The degree of international capital mobility is an expression of the power of capital over labor and society. Mechanisms to control the degree of capital mobility are therefore weapons in the political struggle for a more humane and sustainable economic and social life.

The heterodoxy has long been critical of capital mobility and has considered capital controls, but a tension has existed between different analyzes. At one level, Marx tended to argue that capital mobility, as a reflection of the power of capital, was a juggernaut that would wash over the globe, bringing capital to every corner of the world, eventually increasing both the forces of production and the class struggle that would ultimately bring about its own demise. Barriers against capital mobility might be able to dam its advance temporarily, but eventually, capital would break them down, and continue to roam the globe, unfettered (Marx and Engels, 1998).[2]

Keynes, on the other hand, believed that capital controls and government control over important aspects of social investment, could tame capitalism, even bringing about the euthanasia of the rentier. As we discuss in more detail below, Keynes believed national capitalism, protected by capital controls, was possible, at least in the UK and other large countries.

After the 1970s, with the rise of neoliberalism and the decline of the social democratic movement following World War II – when capital controls were widespread and the power of capital was subdued by social forces in many parts of the world – we once again face this tension. Marx's prediction of the juggernaut of capital with its expression in the hyper-mobility of capital seems to have trumped Keynes' hope for controlled capital, and more progressive national capitalisms. In this world of neoliberalism, financialization and globalization, are capital controls simply passe? Or, even in this situation, is there still a case that can be made for capital controls? And, what do the answers to these questions tell us about the relevance of the work of Marx and Keynes to contemporary debates about international capital mobility and economic dynamics? These are the questions this chapter addresses.

In making my argument I distinguish between the *technical* or *policy aspects* of capital controls on the one hand, and the *transformative* aspects of capital controls on the other. By "technical" I mean the ability of capital controls to facilitate one or another economic policy that might have more or less important impacts on economic growth, employment generation and income distribution. These impacts can be very important for the quality of life of workers and citizens and therefore are of major significance. Still, those hoping for a more profound change in the structure of society and economy may be more interested in the transformative aspects of capital controls: the degree to which capital controls are able to help shift political and social power away from capital and toward society, thereby making feasible a more dramatic change in the overall structure of the political economy which leads to a more egalitarian and sustainable – and, possibly, socialist order.

Below, I argue that, in contrast to the claims of much mainstream analysis, capital controls have been very successful and, indeed, can continue to be very successful in the technical sense. Moreover, looking over the last century, we see that capital controls have been crucial to virtually all transformative economic change. Nonetheless, more recently, left-leaning governments who have presumably wanted to undertake major transformative policies, have not tended to adopt capital controls. I briefly explore the reasons for this choice in recent years and attempt to understand the implications of this change for the prospects of fundamental political and economic change in contemporary capitalism.

The rest of the chapter is structured as follows. In the next section, I discuss in somewhat more detail Keynes' views of the importance of capital controls and Marx's views on the possibility of economic reform. Here I also develop further the distinction between the technical and the transformative aspects of capital controls. The third section briefly discusses the technical case for capital controls and the fourth section discusses in more detail the transformative aspects of capital controls, exploring the difficulties involved in transformative projects, focusing on the role that capital controls can and have in fact played. The final section briefly concludes.

On the nature of capital controls and economic reform according to Keynes, Crotty and Marx

Crotty (1983) described in great detail Keynes' strong support for capital controls. Unearthing key passages from a variety of Keynes' writings, Crotty showed that in a period spanning the 1930s and into the 1940s – virtually up to the time of his death – Keynes was very skeptical that nations could achieve full employment and social transformation as long as they were integrated into a world of highly mobile capital. He therefore thought that controlling international capital mobility was a requirement for both bringing about better macroeconomic management and achieving social transformation.

Crotty began by showing that Keynes understood that capital mobility posed a significant problem for Keynes' proposal that the rate of return on capital be driven close to zero, bringing about the euthanasia of the rentier.

Crotty acknowledges that, by the 1940s, Keynes became more accepting of an internationally integrated British economy, but argues forcefully that Keynes continued to place a high degree of importance on the necessity to control international capital flows. Wrote Keynes in 1941: "I share the view that central control of capital movements, both inward and outward, should be a permanent feature of the post-war system" (1980: 52). "When it became clear that the U.S. did not share his view on this issue, he insisted that strict capital controls be permitted in the new international monetary order in those countries which chose to adopt them." According to Crotty, Keynes argued here as he had before that "the free flow of capital among countries would make successful domestic planning for full employment in any country impossible" (Crotty, 1983: 62).

As Crotty shows, as late as 1942, in a letter to Roy Harrod, an ardent opponent of capital controls, Keynes remains a strong advocate of capital controls:

> I disagree most strongly with your view that the control of capital movements may very possibly be unnecessary.... I see no reason to feel confidence that the more stable condition [of the post-war era] will remove the more dangerous movements [of capital]. These are likely to be caused by political issues. Surely in the post-war years there is hardly a country in which we ought not to expect keen political discussions affecting the position of the wealthier classes and the treatment of private property. If so, there will be a number of people constantly taking fright because they think the degree of leftism in one country for the time being looks to be greater then somewhere else.

Keynes goes on even more emphatically to state the case to Harrod:

> you overlook the most fundamental long-run theoretical reason. Freedom of capital movement is an essential part of the old *laissez-fare* system and assumes that it is right and desirable to have an equalization of interest rates in all parts of the world.... In my view the whole management of the domestic economy depends upon being free to have the appropriate rate of interest without reference to the rates prevailing elsewhere in the world. Capital control is a corollary to this.
>
> (1980: 148–9)

In terms of the distinction between the *technical* or policy role of capital controls, and the *transformative role* of controls, clearly Keynes had both in mind. In the quote just reproduced, Keynes says that "whole management of the domestic economy" depends on capital controls, where management presumably refers to the policy or technical role. But for Keynes, the more important role was the transformative one. Keynes' emphasis on social experimentation and protecting the possibility of bringing about the "euthanasia of the rentier" signaled truly transformative projects, designed to bring about a profoundly changed economy. Keynes made it clear that capital controls were a prerequisite for protecting the desired experimentation, presumably undertaken by a "leftist government," which inevitably would call into question the prerogatives of the wealthy and powerful.[3]

Marx on the technical and transformative roles of capital controls

Marx too seemed to have had this distinction in mind in terms of talking about political and economic transformation. Though I failed to find a direct quote from Marx on this issue with respect to capital controls per se, Marx did seem to make such a distinction in his writing on another important area of class struggle: unions.[4] First, Marx chided those who claimed that trade union attempts violated some abstract law of economics:

> As soon as workers learn ... that the degree of intensity of the competition amongst themselves depends wholly on the pressure of the reserve army; as soon as, by setting up trade unions they try to organize planned co-operation between the employed and the unemployed in order to weaken the ruinous effects of this natural law of capitalist production on their class, so soon does capital and its sycophant, political economy, cry out at the infringement of the "eternal" and so to speak "sacred" law of supply and demand.
>
> (Marx, 1865)

Marx appeared to argue that only the transformative role was worth trying to implement. One quote along these lines relevant to trade unions, is as follows:

> Trades Unions work well as centers of resistance against the encroachments of capital. They fail partially from an injudicious use of their power. They fail generally from limiting themselves to a guerilla war against the effects of the existing system, instead of simultaneously trying to change it, instead of using their organized forces as a lever for the final emancipation of the working class that is to say the ultimate abolition of the wages system.
>
> (Marx, 1865)

At times the line between the technical role and the transformative role of capital controls is somewhat blurry. Sometimes, goals which seem somewhat technical in nature, or policy goals that are short term, may in fact entail much more profound social transformations. This point comes through powerfully when we consider one of Keynes' key goals, namely, the attainment of full employment. Kalecki pointed this out in his famous and profound paper "Political Aspects of Full Employment" published in 1943. Kalecki argued that maintaining full employment for a long period of time under capitalism would require a major transformation in the social relations of production, leading to a major redistribution of power from capital to labor. If true, this suggests that while capital controls designed to bring about and maintain full employment might, at first, appear to be a purely technical or policy role, in fact, over time, they would become truly transformative. This point has an affinity with the concept of "revolutionary reforms" well known from political and socialist theory.

Andrew Glyn (1986) recognized this point. In line with Keynes' argument, Glyn argued that for Britain to adopt a full employment policy, it would need to put on capital and exchange controls. Glyn then went on to describe in great detail how such controls could work and what the costs and benefits of these controls would be. In doing so, he made it clear both that such controls would be a major undertaking with some costs, but that they could also be feasible and effective. One of the best papers ever written on capital controls, Glyn's *New Left Review* piece appears to agree with Kalecki that full employment is both a technical and a transformative reform and that capital controls on behalf of full employment play both of these roles as well.

In Crotty and Epstein (1996) we expanded on Keynes' argument for the role of capital controls in defending social experimentation. Whereas Keynes, Kalecki and Glyn were discussing a situation in which the advocates of social experimentation had the political power to implement experimentation, we were concerned also with the situation in which the "progressive's" hold on power is somewhat more tenuous and in which labor and other progressive forces would need the cooperation of capital in order to make progressive changes. As such, we focused on the issue of how labor and social forces could enhance their bargaining power vis-à-vis capital in order to bring about more progressive economic and social transformation.

With this in mind, we argued that implementing capital controls, or in some cases, simply the *threat of imposing capital controls*, are a useful weapon for labor and society to get capital to come to the bargaining table and cooperate with attempts at social transformation, or experimentation as Keynes put it. In South Korea, for example, capital controls were used partly in this way. Of course, the capacity to implement controls are necessary in this case, in case capital refuses to cooperate and begins to flee. In short, our point was to emphasize the strategic aspects of controls in the class struggle and to emphasize the role of controls as a weapon in the class struggle, just as capital recognizes that capital flight is among the most powerful weapons in its arsenal (see, for example, Bronfenbrenner, 1997). But, empty threats of controls will only lead to capital flight, so social forces threatening controls must have sufficient bargaining power to begin with to use such a ploy.

Moreover, it should be obvious that capital controls of a transformative nature will not be considered without the strong presence of progressive political forces. At the same time, even capitalist interests with no transformative agenda may well chose to impose capital controls for technical reasons, for example, in a financial crisis when they have little or no choice. But, unintended consequences do occur and by altering the relative power of capital and labor, even in this case, capital controls might have a stronger political impact that initially intended. But for that to happen, progressive social forces would have to seize the time.

On the technical aspects of capital controls

Capital controls, exchange controls, or more generally *capital management techniques*, historically have been widely used in many countries and, despite the march of neoliberalism, are more widely used today than commonly admitted. All countries, including the United States, have some type of capital controls; in the United States, they involve scrutiny of inward foreign direct investments on so-called "national security grounds." On outflows, they likewise involve "national security" considerations in terms of sanctions against particular countries, or export constraints on the FDI associated with certain military technology. Increasingly, calls are going out for closer official scrutiny of inflows of so-called "sovereign wealth funds," which would be a type of capital control on inward investment. Many countries have controls on foreign ownership in particular sectors, including natural resources, media and banking. And numerous countries have controls – on the books, at least – that apply to inflows and outflows of other types of capital.

Still, with the rise of neoliberalism and the aggressive push by capitalist enforcement agencies such as the IMF, many countries have been increasingly liberalizing their capital accounts, so that the global capital accounts are much more liberalized now than they were at the height of the so-called "golden age" of the 1950s and 1960s.

The technical case for capital controls

The technical case for capital controls is strong and has been well described by many, including Grabel (2005; Ocampo, 2002; and Epstein *et al.*, 2005). Capital controls or capital management techniques can give policy space for more expansionary macroeconomic policy (Rodrik and Kaplan on Malaysia; Pollin *et al.* and Epstein on alternative policy for South Africa); they can help governments channel credit to socially and economically productive sectors (see Nembhard, 1996, on South Korea, for example; Epstein, 2007, on postwar experiences in Europe and Japan;) they can help maintain a competitive exchange rate and thereby help export-led growth (Frenkel and Rapetti, 2008, on Argentina; McCauley, 2006, on China and Singapore;); can insulate economies from financial contagion (see Epstein *et al.* on China during the Asian financial crisis); and they can prevent the currency from becoming internationalized and thereby retain more control over monetary, credit policy and the exchange rate (McCauley on Singapore and other Asian countries).

Though many economists still doubt the efficacy of capital controls in this technical sense, I believe the technical case for them is very strong. In this sense, Marx was at least partially wrong and Keynes was right. Capital controls – barriers to the movement of capital and some restrictions on the prerogatives of capital are feasible even in the long run, and even when capitalism is at its height of power.

But, what about the transformative case for capital controls? Was Marx's view of the juggernaut power of capital more correct here? Or, as Marx sometimes implied, can the implementation of capital controls play a more transformative role if the political will, the organization of class forces and the strategic political acumen exist?

Capital controls and political – economic transformation

Ultimately, Crotty, Keynes and Marx are more interested in the transformative possibilities of capital controls. For Marx, capital controls are only truly important in the long run in so far as they help to facilitate a complete transformation of capitalism. As we saw, Keynes thought they would allow countries to engage in experimentation to develop institutions, including more state control over investment, that can bring about full employment, the euthanasia of the rentier and other socially more progressive outcomes. For Crotty, at a minimum, they could help bring capital to the bargaining table and allow workers and governments to pursue more progressive agendas and, ultimately, could help bring about the transition to socialism. To be clear: for neither Crotty nor Keynes are capital controls a *sufficient* condition for these outcomes. But, the argument is that they are a *necessary* condition, still a very strong claim.

Are capital controls a *necessary condition* for transformative change in modern capitalism? Another way to put the question is this: have major (at least somewhat progressive) social transformations occurred under capitalism in the absence of capital controls?

With respect to the issue of "necessity," I believe the evidence shows that – at least so far – Keynes and Crotty are correct. To illustrate this, in what follows, I offer a very brief, and therefore superficial, survey of this vast historical landscape.[5]

Of course, after the Russian Revolution, the Soviet Union was closed off from the free flow of capital. With the Chinese revolution, Mao and his government also closed off China from market-determined capital flows. When China began to open up to capital flows with Deng Xiao Ping, these flows were managed carefully by the state; they were not market-determined flows. Strong capital controls remain in place in China to date.

In the 1930s, due to the collapse of the global economy, market-determined capital flows came to a virtual standstill and this was reinforced during the war, when most countries had very strong capital controls in place. Of course, under Schact, Germany had strong controls in place, though one can hardly call Nazi Germany's transformation progressive. But limitations on capital flows also supported the New Deal in the United States. Major transformations continued to occur in the US economy during World War II, again behind the protection of a destroyed global financial system. Following World War II, social democratic regimes came to power in many European countries with strong credit allocation policies protected by capital controls. In Latin America, virtually all the import substitution industrialization policies were supported by capital controls of various kinds. Cuba, of course, by choice and necessity, has strong controls over capital.

The Asian tigers were all transformed behind protective capital controls or capital management techniques of various kinds, with the possible exception of Malaysia, though they did impose controls at key points. Perhaps South Korea had the most elaborate and well developed sets of controls, but Taiwan's were also important. Even capitalist Singapore had effective controls that helped maintain a competitive exchange rate and helped with credit allocation. India, too, has long had an elaborate set of capital controls and though they have been somewhat liberalized the structure remains in place today.

It is difficult, if not impossible, to find counter-examples of major social and economic transformations from the modern era that have taken place *without* capital controls. It seems that, as Keynes and Crotty have argued, capital controls are in fact a necessary condition for a progressive transformation.

But are we now witnessing a change in this pattern?

Recent history

This picture gets murkier when we look at recent history, say of the last 20 years. When we look at cases where political changes have led to the promise of major progressive social transformation, we find that capital controls have not been widely used. Nor, to be sure, has major social transformation occurred.

There are a number of examples where progressive forces came into power promising major social transformation but there are serious doubts about whether such transformations have occurred. We can start with the overthrow of apartheid in South Africa, where the African National Congress (ANC) has adopted a mostly neoliberal economic policy and has mostly abandoned capital controls. Likewise, in Brazil with Lula's election, we again have seen a largely neoliberal set of policies in the macroeconomic sphere and commitments to open capital markets; in the new leftist states of Latin America, we mostly see very open capital markets with a few key exceptions: Argentina initially used capital controls to manage its transition, but these were quickly removed. On the other hand, Venezuela has implemented stricter capital controls in support of transformative policies.

For the most part, leftist governments are coming to power promoting more radical economic transformations, but without imposing capital controls. Can transformation be successful there? In the world of "high-tech" derivatives, could these countries implement more stringent controls to help facilitate transformational change if they wanted to, or would the costs simply be too high? Another possibility is the Gramscian point about ideological hegemony. Have these governments been hoodwinked by the IMF and the neoclassical propaganda that tells them that they will be severely punished if the try to interfere with the prerogatives of capital?

My answer is that there is some of both going on most cases. That is, there can be severe short-run costs associated with going against the juggernaut of financial globalization as Marx suggested, but – and this is where the "hoodwinking" comes in – the costs needn't be as large and the benefits as small as the neoliberal ideological consensus would have us believe.

The "lessons" of Mitterand's France and Mexico's economic failures in the early 1980s are often seen as demonstrating the "futility" of capital controls, that nations on a transformative mission cannot stand up to the mighty power of the financial markets.

Let us take the French case first (see Lombard, 1995, for an excellent discussion). Socialist Francois Mitterrand was elected in May 1981 on a platform of completely overhauling of French society and substantially redistributing income (Lombard, 1995: 359). Mitterand initiated a program consisting of four initiatives: income redistribution; expansion of the public sector; labor legislation to reduce unemployment; and nationalization of major enterprises (Lombard, 1995: 360). Unsurprisingly, French capital was spooked by this program and initiated a great deal of capital flight. The French government instituted capital controls to limit capital flight, but within a year or so, the government relented and greatly cut back on the program. Critics have used this episode to argue that the program could not have worked because of the constraints of global capitalism, including international capital mobility. This program was especially problematic, according to many observers, because the French government was trying to expand at a time when much of Europe was entering a recession, thereby imposing balance of payments problems on the French economy.

Lombard, and others,[6] by contrast, argue that the key problem was that the government was committed to maintaining a fixed exchange rate in the European Monetary System framework, which placed a major constraint on its monetary and fiscal policy. Moreoever, the capital controls that were imposed were not strongly enforced. Thus it was the external constraint that undermined the program but the program was not strongly followed to begin with. Stronger measures to deal with these external constraints were possible – such as exchange rate depreciations and stricter capital controls – but for largely political reasons, were not implemented.

The Mexican case presents somewhat similar lessons.[7] For several decades prior to the Mexican Debt Crisis of 1982, developmentalist economic thinking had dominated the economics profession and economic policy advice in Mexico. This included support for capital controls and strong regulation of the financial sector. Just prior to the debt crisis, and in the early stages as it unfolded, were crucial moments in which transformative policy ran directly head-on with an economic crisis and powerful neoliberal pressures coming both from within Mexico, led by, among others, foreign-trained economists, and from without, primarily from US bankers, economists, policy-makers such as Paul Volcker at the Federal Reserve and the IMF. Mexican economists, many of whom trained at or were influenced by economists from Cambridge, UK, pushed for an expansionary macroeconomic policy, nationalized banking system, industrial policy and strong financial regulation, all supported by strong exchange and capital controls. In the end, they lost out to the neoliberal side in a fierce political struggle within the government and supported by outside actors.

The Mexican heterodox economists were fighting from a weak position because Mexico was on the verge of bankruptcy. Moreover, they had almost run out of foreign exchange reserves, partly as a result of massive capital flight. Still, despite this weakened position, many observers believe the Mexican government could still have followed an alternative path, including defaulting on foreign loans, possibly by joining forces with other debtor countries. Capital controls, as envisaged by the architects of this policy, was a crucial component of this alternative path. In the end, this was not the path chosen, but many believe that that it could have been.

What lessons do we draw from the French and Mexican cases? They are certainly consistent with the argument that capital controls are necessary for a transformative path in the simple sense that controls were not implemented and major transformation did not occur. But this is hardly helpful in a positive sense. In my view, they do NOT demonstrate that such controls are impossible in the new environment. They suggest that they are difficult, may be costly in the short run and require strong social forces, political and strategic savvy to carry off, as Marx suggested.

Conclusion

So what lessons on transformative change and the role of capital controls in the current environment are we left with? It seems that past experience does vindicate the notion that capital controls must be a central component of this change, as argued by Keynes and Crotty. This has worked most dramatically when the global financial system has collapsed or countries have been frozen out of financial flows so countries could transform themselves without the hindrance of foreign capital (say during and after the great depression and World War II or in the wake of communist revolutions). But this has also occurred when, for a variety of political, economic and cultural reasons, countries have chosen to go or remain behind strong capital control barriers as a way to develop (e.g. in the cases of South Korea, Taiwan, Singapore and post-Deng China). But as Marx suggests, the juggernaut forces of capital are strong and while the transformative role is not impossible, it is difficult to implement and can impose short-run costs that raise opposition and undermine the long-run project.

Paradoxically, this cost curve is an inverted U-shaped function of the degree of net-liabilities incurred from interactions with the global economy. At very low levels of integration, where the country has borrowed little from the global economy, there are few losses from closing off. Similarly, at the other end, where the country has borrowed an excessive amount (such as the case of Mexico in 1982 and Argentina in the 1990s) the costs of default and closing off the financial sector are relatively small. As we saw, Mexico chose not to close off while Argentina chose to put up barriers and default, at least temporarily. In the middle, where countries have borrowed a moderate amount from the global financial markets and can expand such interactions, the short-term costs of imposing strict capital controls and engaging in serious transformative policies may be higher, though, of course, the long-run benefits might be great as well. To do this, the party in power must be willing and able, being supported by a strong coalition, to institute broader institutional change. In particular, getting the government institutions and quasi-public institutions much more involved in credit allocation to help socialize investment, as Keynes argued, is key. Without these substitute institutions, simply instituting capital controls is likely to impose costs, without delivering the transformational benefits.

Notes

1 The author thanks James Crotty and Michael Hillard for extensive comments on the current paper and James Crotty, Ilene Grabel, Arjun Jayadev, Kang-Kook Lee, Robert McCauley and K. S. Jomo, who have contributed enormously to my thinking on capital controls over the years.
2 As is so often the case, Marx had a more nuanced view of the possibility for reform than this, one that we explore more fully below.
3 Of course, Keynes was no Marxist, or even socialist. But as Crotty, among others, has forcefully argued, Keynes' arguments for the socialization of investment and the eutha-nasia of the rentier call for major changes in capitalism that radically constrain some of its central features.
4 I am indebted to James Crotty for help with this point.
5 In this whirlwind survey I draw on Epstein *et al.*, 2005; Epstein, 2007; Nembhard 1996; Helleiner, 1994; Helleiner 2005 and the references cited therein.
6 See the references in Lombard (1995).
7 For fascinating accounts of this history on which I have liberally drawn see Ros, 1987, and Babb, 2001, especially Chapter 7, pp. 178–9.

References

Babb, S. (2001) *Managing Mexico*. Princeton: Princeton University Press.
Bronfenbrenner, K. (1997) "The Effects of Plant Closing or Threat of Plant Closing on the Right of Workers to Organize," Report to Department of Labor.
Crotty, J. (1983) "Review: Keynes and Capital Flight," *Journal of Economic Literature*, 21(1) March: 56–65.
Crotty, J. and Epstein, G. (1996) "In Defense of Capital Controls," *Socialist Register*: 118–49.
Epstein, G. (2007) "Central Banks as Agents of Development," in Ha-Joon Chang (ed.), *Institutional Change and Economic Development*, United Nations University and Anthem Press.
Epstein, G., Grabel, I., and Jomo, K. S. (2005) "Capital Management Techniques in Developing Countries," in Gerald Epstein (ed.), *Capital Flight and Capital Controls in Developing Countries*, Northampton, MA: Edward Elgar.
Frenkel, R. and Rapetti, M. (2008) "Five Years of Competitive and Stable Real Exchange Rate in Argentina, 2002–2007," *International Review of Applied Economics*, 22(2): 215–26.
Glyn, A. (1986) "Capital Flight and Exchange Controls," *New Left Review*, I/155, January–February.
Grabel, I. (2005) "Averting Crisis? Assessing Measures to Manage Financial Integration in Emerging Economies," in Gerald Epstein (ed.), *Financialization and the World Economy*, Northampton, MA: Edward Elgar.
Helleiner, E. (1994) *States and the Reemergence of Global Finance: From Bretton Woods to the 1990's*, Ithaca: Cornell University Press.

—— (2005) "Regulating Capital Flight," in Gerald Epstein (ed.), *Capital Flight and Capital Controls in Developing Countries*, 289–300, Cheltenham, UK and Northampton, MA: Edward Elgar.

Keynes, J. M. (1980) *The Collected Writings of John Maynard Keynes, Vol. 25, Activities, 1940–1944: Shaping the Post-War World, The Clearing Union.* Ed. Donald Moggridge, London: Macmillan and Cambridge University Press.

Lombard, M. (1995) "A Re-examination of the Reasons for the Failure of Expansionary Keynesian Policies in France, 1981–1983," *Cambridge Journal of Economics*, 19(2): 359–72.

McCauley, R. N. (2006) "Understanding Monetary Policy in Malaysia and Thailand: Objectives Instruments and Independence," BIS Papers, No. 31.

Marx, Karl. (1865) *Wages, Prices and Profit*, available at www.marxists.org/archive/marx/works/1865/value-price-profit/ch03.htm#c13.

—— (1968) *Das Kapital*, Moscow: International Publishers, ch. 25.

Marx, K. and Engels, F. (1998) *The Communist Manifesto*, New York: Penguin. Available at www.marxists.org/archive/marx/works/1848/communist-manifesto/index.htm.

Nembhard, J. G. (1996) *Capital Control, Financial Policy and Industrial Policy In South Korea and Brazil*, New York: Praeger Press.

Ocampo, J. A. (2002) "Capital-Account and Counter-Cyclical Prudential Regulations in Developing Countries," UNU/WIDER Discussion Paper, August.

Ros, J. (1987) "Mexico from the Oil Boom to the Debt Crisis: An Analysis of Policy Responses to External Shocks, 1978–85," in R. Thorp and L. Whitehead (eds.), *Latin American Debt and the Adjustment Crisis*, 68–116, Pittsburg: University of Pittsburg Press.

19 Neo-liberal finance and third world (mal)development

Ilene Grabel

Introduction[1]

The Mexican crisis of 1994–1995 signaled the beginning of a wave of financial crises across the developing world that continues to this day. Former International Monetary Fund (IMF) Managing Director Michel Camdessus had it right when he dubbed the Mexican debacle the "first financial crisis of the twenty-first century" (cited in Boughton, 2001). The most serious and perhaps surprising of these took place in the East Asian "miracle economies," economies that were hailed as such right up until they imploded. It was followed by severe financial instability in Turkey, Brazil, Poland, Russia and Argentina.

Though each of these crises was marked by unique characteristics, each occurred in the fragile environment fueled by speculative booms made possible by misguided programs of internal and external financial liberalization. What Camdessus did not understand was that the neo-liberal financial regime that his institution promotes to this day induces the very turbulence that he lamented at the time of the Mexican crisis. Indeed, as I will argue below, policymakers in the developing world now face even greater pressures to conform to the neo-liberal model because the Fund's traditional advocacy for it has been reinforced by the new commitment to policy coherence and by interlocking commitments to liberalize that are embodied in bi- and multi-lateral trade and investment agreements.

I have three chief objectives in this chapter. First, I argue that neo-liberal financial reform remains inappropriate for developing countries. The neo-liberal financial model introduces several types of risks to developing countries, encourages a pattern of what I have earlier termed "speculation-led economic development" (Grabel, 1995), promotes economic stagnation and aggravates problems of economic inequality, and shifts power and resources to domestic and foreign financiers. Second, I argue that advocacy for the neo-liberal financial model continues unabated despite signs that some mainstream economists (even those conducting research for the IMF) have acknowledged its shortcomings since the Asian crisis. Third, I argue that the IMF's traditional advocacy has been amplified by the "cross conditionality" that stems from a particular understanding of policy coherence and from provisions in recent trade and investment agreements.

Risk, power and stagnation in a neo-liberal economy

Over the last quarter century, neo-liberal economists have pressed for radical reform of all sectors of developing economies. A centerpiece of neo-liberal reform over this period is financial reform that entails promoting market over state mediation of internal and external financial flows.

Neo-liberal financial reform introduces five distinct, interrelated risks to developing economies. The realization of these risks (and the interaction thereof) is at the root of the currency and financial crises that have occurred in the developing world over the last 13 years. I term these risks currency, flight, fragility, contagion and sovereignty risk. It is also the case that neo-liberal financial reform induces stagnation, aggravates problems of income and wealth inequality and promotes the creation of a speculation-led rather than a production-led economy.

Currency risk

Currency risk refers to the possibility that a country's currency may experience a precipitous decline in value following investors' decisions to sell their holdings. This risk is an attribute of any type of exchange rate regime, provided the government maintains full currency convertibility. That floating exchange rates introduce currency risk is rather obvious. But as Friedman emphasized in 1953, and as events in Asia and Argentina have underscored, pegging a currency does not eliminate currency risk.

Developing economies confront much more severe currency risk than do wealthier economies for two reasons. First, governments in developing economies are unlikely to hold sufficient reserves to protect the value of their currency should they confront a generalized investor exit. Second, developing economy governments are rarely able to orchestrate multi-lateral currency rescues or pool official reserves as wealthier countries are frequently able to do (though some policymakers in Asia are moving toward pooling arrangements, see below, pp. 257–8).

Flight risk

Flight risk refers to the likelihood that holders of liquid financial assets will seek to sell their holdings en masse, thereby causing significant declines in asset values and increasing ambient risk in the macroeconomy. By acting on fears of capital losses, investors create a self-fulfilling prophecy. To the extent that declining asset values have spillover effects to other sectors, the realization of flight risk can aggravate currency risk and render the economy vulnerable to a financial crisis. If, for instance, stock portfolios serve as loan collateral, an investor flight from the equity market can induce bank distress, as was the case in East Asia.

Flight risk is severe in developing economies because investors in this context are less confident about the integrity of the information they receive, and they perceive there to be greater political and economic risks. Moreover, since investors tend to see developing economies in an undifferentiated fashion, these countries are more vulnerable to generalized investor exits.

Flight risk is most severe when governments fail to restrict capital inflows that are subject to rapid reversal. The elimination of capital controls in many developing economies in the neo-liberal era has meant that policymakers have no means to reduce the risks associated with capital flight.

Fragility risk

Fragility risk refers to the vulnerability of an economy's private and public borrowers to internal or external shocks that jeopardize their ability to meet current obligations. Fragility risk arises in a number of ways. First, borrowers might finance long-term obligations with short-term credit, causing "maturity mismatch." Second, borrowers might contract debts that are repayable in foreign currency, causing "locational mismatch." Third, if much of the economy's private investment is financed with capital that is highly reversible, then the economy is vulnerable to fragility risk. Fourth and finally, fragility risk is introduced whenever actors finance their projects with risky, off-balance sheet instruments, such as derivatives.

Fragility risk is, to some extent, unavoidable. But the degree to which the decisions of actors induce fragility risk depends very much on whether the institutional and regulatory climate allows or even encourages the adoption of risky strategies. If regulatory bodies do not coordinate the volume, allocation and/or prudence of lending and investing decisions, then there will exist no mechanisms to dampen maturity or locational mismatches, or the impulse to overborrow, overlend or overinvest. Financial integration magnifies the possibilities for over-exuberance (and introduces currency-induced fragility) by providing domestic agents with access to external finance.

Contagion risk

Contagion risk refers to the threat that a country will fall victim to financial and macroeconomic instability that originates elsewhere. While financial integration is the carrier of contagion risk, its severity depends on the extent of currency, flight and fragility risk in the economy. Countries can reduce their contagion risk by managing their degree of financial integration and by reducing their vulnerability to currency, flight and fragility risks.

Sovereignty risk

Sovereignty risk refers to the danger that a government will face constraints on its ability to pursue independent economic and social policies once it confronts a financial crisis. The constraint on policy autonomy can be introduced for numerous reasons.

First, governments may be forced to pursue contractionary macroeconomic policies during financial crises in order to slow investor flight. While speculators are not dictating policy per se, governments may find their ability to pursue expansionary policy severely constrained when they seek to reverse investor flight. Second and more directly, developing economies face constraints on their sovereignty when they receive external assistance from powerful actors. Speaking practically, bailouts have been widely conditioned on the acceleration of neo-liberal reform.

Although sovereignty risk stems from the structural position of developing economies in the world economy, this does not imply that this risk is unmanageable. Measures that constrain currency, flight, fragility and contagion risk render financial crisis less likely (or reduce its severity should it occur), and thereby buttress policy sovereignty vis-à-vis speculators and external actors.

Risk interactions

These distinct risks are deeply interrelated. The realization of currency risk can induce investor flight, and inaugurate a vicious cycle of further currency decline, flight and increased fragility. Should these circumstances develop into a full-fledged crisis, policy sovereignty is compromised. In this context, other countries may face contagion. The severity of the contagion risk depends in turn on the degree of financial integration, the degree to which investors can and do herd out of developing economies, and the extent to which countries constrain currency, flight and contagion risks.

These risk interactions capture well the dynamics of currency and financial crises in the neo-liberal era (on Korea, see Crotty, 1983; Crotty and Epstein, 1996; Crotty and Lee, 2002, 2005a, 2005b, 2006 and Grabel, 1996, 1999). I am not, however, proposing a strict temporal model of risk interaction. Analytically, the key point is that the construction of neo-liberal financial systems in developing countries introduces the constellation of risks presented here. The weight of each risk varies from country to country. The precise triggering mechanism is ultimately unimportant and usually unpredictable. Similarly, the particular characteristics of an individual country (e.g. the level of corruption) do not themselves induce a vulnerability to crisis. Vulnerability to currency and financial crisis is created instead by the specific and interacting risks of the neo-liberal financial model.

The creation of a speculation-led economy

Neo-liberal financial reform increases the opportunities for investors to secure project financing (more easily and/or more cheaply) and to trade assets. In nearly all cases, neo-liberal financial reform has induced a speculative bubble in commercial real estate and land development and stock prices, and an environment wherein overlending, overborrowing and overinvesting is the norm. In this type of environment, "productive" activities (like manufacturing or infrastructure projects) simply cannot compete because they rarely offer the opportunity for massive capital gain associated with speculation. To the extent that productive activities are nevertheless undertaken, they often take on the characteristics of speculative activities. For example, instead of producing energy, a utility company might become involved in trading energy futures. Even productive activities become risky and volatile in a neo-liberal environment because these activities are financed by short-term loans or highly reversible capital flows. These financing strategies exacerbate the susceptibility of businesses to changes in interest rates or investor whims.

Stagnation and inequality

Neo-liberal financial reform heightens the stagnationist tendencies and inequalities in wealth, income and power that are an inherent feature of developing and, indeed, all capitalist economies (see citations above in relation to Korea). This is the case for several reasons. First, by increasing ambient risk in the economy, neo-liberal finance discourages productive activities that are central to employment and long-term income and economic growth in developing countries. Second, by creating a miniscule class of rich financiers, neo-liberal financial reform widens existing disparities in income, wealth and political power. Third, neo-liberal finance increases the mobility and hence the power of capital vis-à-vis labor. The bargaining power of labor is weakened in an environment where capital can relocate easily in search of an ever cheaper and more compliant workforce and a less regulated business environment. Fourth and finally, the majority of the population bears the devastating human costs of the recession, curtailment of government spending and deterioration in living standards that follow the collapse of speculative bubbles and attendant financial crises. One can look at the situation of just about any developing country following neo-liberal financial reform to find evidence of stagnation in the productive sector and a widening of political and economic inequality.

Has the economics profession learned anything from the failures of neo-liberal finance?

It is interesting that, faced with cumulative evidence of policy failure and the human misery associated with these crises, economists in the academic and policy community ultimately seem to have learned something, particularly from the events in Asia. Granted, some were slow learners. The slow learners did quite well for a while in the various cottage industries that sprung up after each crisis. They shared with wide audiences the serious problems that they came to see as deeply rooted and pervasive, albeit somehow also undetected by international investors and policymakers who extolled the virtues of the model economies. Here I refer to those that gave crisis post-mortems that focused on the role of corruption, cronyism and malfeasance, on misguided programs of government intervention, on nostalgic attachments to pegged exchange rates, and on inadequate information about the true conditions of firms and governments in crisis-afflicted countries.

The informational inadequacy crowd had perhaps the biggest reach in the policy world. Their views dominated the agenda at the Group of Seven's Halifax Summit of 1995 and the Rey Committee that was later formed. The informational inadequacy constituency was influential in other practical ways as well. They promoted a variety of early warning systems, such as the widely known one developed by Goldstein *et al.* (2000); they were prime movers behind the IMF's creation of a Special Data Dissemination Standard, the Reports on the Observance of Standards and Codes, and the Financial Sector Assessment Program; and they drove Basel II efforts to incorporate assessments by private bond rating agencies in the global financial architecture.[2]

But ultimately, even the slow learners came to acknowledge – at least to an extent – that there was something to be learned from countries like India, China, Chile, Colombia and Malaysia, all of which were able to weather this period of turbulence successfully (e.g. Ariyoshi *et al.*, 2000). Among these experiences, the most important drivers of a change in conventional wisdom were Malaysia's deployment of temporary, stringent capital controls, Chile's use of market-friendly capital controls that were adjusted in response to changing market conditions and identified channels of evasion, and China and India's gradualist approach to financial integration and liberalization (Crotty and Epstein, 1996; Grabel, 2003b; Epstein *et al.*, 2004). With a few exceptions (notably, prominent academics Edwards (1999) and McKinnon with Huw Pill (1998)[3]), the new conventional wisdom can be inelegantly stated in the following way:

> Unrestrained financial liberalization, especially concerning international private capital flows, can aggravate or induce macroeconomic vulnerabilities that often culminate in crisis. Therefore, subject to "numerous and customary caveats," temporary, market-friendly controls over international capital movements can play an important role in mitigating the risk of financial crises in developing countries.

Notably, a widely cited report by an IMF team issued in 2003 (Prasad *et al.*, 2003) received a great deal of attention for reaching these startling findings. There have been other studies by neoclassical or otherwise high profile economists that have reached complementary conclusions. For example, Bhagwati's (1998) work is notable in this connection, as is that by Eichengreen (1999), Rodrik (1999) and Krugman (1998).

Thus, perhaps the most lasting and important effect of this decade of crises is that the center of gravity has largely shifted away from an unequivocal, fundamentalist opposition to any interference with the free flow of capital to a kind of tepid, conditional support for some types of capital controls. This shift certainly moves policy discussions in the right direction, but the new, weak consensus is not adequate to the task of preventing an Asian crisis redux.

Why we should not get too excited

There are a couple of reasons why, I think, the new conventional wisdom should not be cause for too much celebration by heterodox economists that are looking for signs that the neo-liberal financial model has finally been exposed and invalidated by recent events.

The first reason has to do with an inconsistency between the policy lessons of these crises and the content of recent bi- and multi-lateral trade and investment agreements.

These agreements codify what is referred to these days with the new buzzword of "policy coherence" – a term that on the face of it seems innocuous and sensible since incoherent policy regimes hardly have much to recommend them. The intuition behind the concept of policy coherence is simple: any individual economic policy – such as free trade – will only yield beneficial outcomes if it is nested in a broader policy environment that is conducive (that is, consistent or coherent) with its objectives. From this perspective, the justification for expanding the scope of trade reform and agreements to new areas over the last decade is that previous efforts to liberalize trade have failed to promote growth because of inconsistencies between trade and other economic and social policies.[4]

But there is a problem here: recent trade and investment agreements have become a new Trojan horse for bringing developing countries in line with fundamentalist and outdated ideals about internal and external financial liberalization (see Grabel, 2007a). Indeed, the bi- and multi-lateral trade and investment agreements go much further in instantiating neo-liberal financial reform and an expansive notion of investor rights than has even the IMF in the recent past or at present. These agreements (such as the US–Chile and US–Singapore Free Trade Agreements, the North American Free Trade Agreement, the Central American–Dominican Free Trade Agreement and all of the bilateral investment treaties that the US has signed of late) establish mechanisms that punish developing countries for taking entirely reasonable actions to prevent or respond to financial crises.[5] Punishment takes the form of legal actions by foreign investors in international dispute settlement bodies against signatories that deploy temporary capital controls of any sort. Examples of prohibited measures would include steps to make foreign capital sticky during times of crisis, temporary suspension of currency convertibility, adjustment in the exchange rate, and a variety of commonplace macroeconomic and social policies that can now be interpreted as being tantamount to expropriation of foreign investment.

These same trade and investment agreements preclude many important types of developmental financial policies; they limit the opportunity for institutional and policy heterogeneity; and they frustrate the right of countries to engage in policy experimentation. All of these are critical components of successful development experiences (as much recent work has shown, for example, Crotty and Epstein, 1995; Rodrik, 2003; Chang and Grabel, 2004; Epstein *et al.*, 2004; Epstein and Grabel, 2006).

For these reasons, these agreements introduce a new kind of dangerous policy incoherence. Financial crises are increasingly likely as a consequence of the outdated ideologies and financial interests that are driving trade and investment agreements. These two steps back come just when IMF researchers and some prominent academic economists seem to have absorbed some key lessons about prevention and defensive policies from 13 years of financial crises.

A second dimension of incoherence is the strange disconnect between IMF research since the East Asian crisis and its own practice when it comes to Article IV negotiations with countries. The latter seem to be moving on a track that is orthogonal to the institution's own research.

The final reason why we should not be satisfied with the new post-crisis policy consensus is that – even were it to be operationalized on the level of policy – it does not go far enough. The new consensus does not endorse the case for increasing substantially the policy space of developing countries when it comes to promoting financial stability. Moreover, it does not place policies that promote financial stability squarely at the center of a policy agenda that harnesses the resources of domestic and international capital markets in the service of economic and human development. Policies that reduce the likelihood of financial crisis or enable countries to respond to crises are necessary co-requisites to other developmental financial policies because they protect the policy space and the achievements of developmental policies. Here I will just note that many heterodox economists have described elsewhere many types of developmental financial policies, such as, programs of credit allocation, tax incentives or quotas aimed at promoting lending to priority projects or groups, development banks, credit guarantee schemes or subsidies that reduce risk premia on medium- and long-term lending, partnerships between informal and formal financial institutions, new institutions to channel credit to underserved populations and regions, asset-based reserve requirements, and employment targeting for central banks (e.g. Chang and Grabel, 2004; Epstein and Grabel, 2006).

Where do we go from here?

Where does all of this leave policymakers and heterodox economists who hope to secure reforms that will protect developing country policy autonomy while insulating their economic and social achievements from new financial crises?

Developing countries need to rethink their participation in trade and investment agreements that constrain their ability to protect themselves from and respond to financial crisis. The costs of these agreements are clear, and the benefits are, at best, negligible insofar as there is no empirical evidence that they actually enhance trade or investment flows to the developing world.[6]

Heterodox economists might also want to capitalize on signs that policymakers in some parts of Asia and South America are discussing alternative mechanisms and institutional frameworks for protecting policy space and for promoting regional financial stability, cooperation and policy dialogue. For instance, the Chiang Mai Initiative agreed to by the Association of Southeast Asian Nations

+3 (ASEAN and China, South Korea and Japan) created a mechanism for swap lines and credits. Other innovations within the region include a reserve pooling arrangement and the Asian Bond Market Initiative.

Within the Americas, it is clear that some countries have begun to turn away from the IMF (e.g. Bolovia, Ecuador, Nicaragua, Argentina and Venezuela) (for details, see Hearn, 2006; MSNBC.com, 2007). Argentina repaid the last of its $9.6 billion in debt to the IMF ahead of schedule (following Venezuela's purchase of about $1.5 billion in Argentine bonds); in the spring of 2007, Venezuela withdrew from the World Bank and the IMF (though it should be noted that the country had no outstanding debts to either institution); Ecuador's President Rafael Correa recently asked the World Bank's representative there to leave; and Nicaraguan President Daniel Ortega announced that he, too, is pursuing the possibility of exiting the Fund. At least some countries may well bolt the Fund in favor of the Bank of the South that has recently been proposed by the Venezuelan President.

However we might debate the costs, benefits and likelihood of success of these initiatives, we must recognize that their currency stems from the increasing awareness today of the serious inadequacies of the Bretton Woods Institutions and the neo-liberal policies that they have so long pursued. This is an important moment to press the case for financial policies in developing countries that promise genuine development and that ameliorate social ills, rather than that conform to an elegant but now thoroughly discredited economic model.

Notes

1 This chapter draws on several of my previous papers, especially (Grabel, 2007a, 2007b, 2003a, 2003b, 1996 and 1995).
2 See Grabel (2004) for a review and a critical assessment of early warning models and other efforts to prevent crisis through the provision of information (aimed at inducing self-correcting market behaviors); Wade (2007) for a critical discussion of programs that focus on standards, surveillance and compliance to promote financial stability; and Sinclair (2005) for a discussion of bond rating agencies and the privatization of authority in global financial goveranance.
3 Forbes (2007) discusses the unintended negative consequences of Chile's capital controls for smaller firms during the 1990s.
4 This intuition is reminiscent of neoclassical theories of policy credibility and of Polanyi's discussion of the rhetorical strategies employed by defenders of neo-liberalism (on both, see Grabel, 2003a).
5 As of this writing, the US–South Korea Free Trade Agreement has not been ratified. But the information available on this agreement at this time suggests that it will carry forward many of controversial provisions embodied in the other agreements listed above, particularly the NAFTA-style protections (embodied in Chapter 11 of the agreement) afforded to foreign investors. I thank Keith Gehring for this point.
6 See citations to empirical literature in Grabel (2007a: fn. 16).

References

Ariyoshi, A., Habermeier, K., Laurens, B., Otker-Robe, I., Canales-Kriljenko, J. and Kirilenko, A. (2000) *County Experience with the Use and Liberalization of Capital Controls*, Washington, DC: IMF.

Bhagwati, J. (1998) "The Capital Myth: The Difference Between Trade in Widgets and Dollars," *Foreign Affairs*, 77(3): 7–12.

Boughton, J. (2001) "Was the Suez the First Financial Crisis of the Twenty-first Century?" *Finance and Development*, 38(3).

Chang, H.-J. and Grabel, I. (2004) *Reclaiming Development: An Alternative Policy Manual*, London and New York: Zed Books.

Crotty, J. (1983) "On Keynes and Capital Flight," *Journal of Economic Literature*, 21(1): 59–65.

—— (2000) "Structural Contradictions of the Global Neoliberal Regime," *Review of Radical Political Economics*, 32(3): 361–8.

—— (2003) "The Neoliberal Paradox: The Impact of Destructive Market Competition and Impatient Finance on Nonfinancial Corporations in the Neoliberal Era," *Review of Radical Political Economics*, 35(3): 271–9.

Crotty, J. and Epstein, G. (1996) "In Defense of Capital Controls," in L. Panitch (ed.) *Are There Alternatives? Socialist Register 1996*, 118–49, London: Merlin Press.

—— (1999) "A Defense of Capital Controls in Light of the Asian Financial Crisis," *Journal of Economic Issues*, 33(2): 427–34.

Crotty, J. and Lee, K. K. (2002) "A Political-Economic Analysis of the Failure of Neoliberal Restructuring in Post-Crisis Korea," *Cambridge Journal of Economics*, 25(5): 667–78.

—— (2005a) "Was Korea's Economy Structurally Deficient in the mid-1990s?: A Critique of the IMF's Justification for Regime Change," Political Economy Research Institute, University of Massachusetts.

—— (2005b) "From East Asian Miracle to Neoliberal Mediocrity," Political Economy Research Institute, University of Massachusetts.

—— (2006) "The Effects of Neoliberal Reforms on the Post-Crisis Korean Economy," *Review of Radical Political Economics*, 38(4): 669–75.

Edwards, S. (1999) "How Effective are Capital Controls," *Journal of Economic Perspectives*, 13(4): 65–84.

Eichengreen, B. (1999) *Toward a New International Financial Architecture*, Washington, DC: Institute for International Economics.

Epstein, G. and Grabel, I. (2006) "Financial Policies for Pro-Poor Growth," prepared for the United Nations Development Programme (UNDP), International Poverty Centre, Global Training Programme on Economic Policies for Growth, Employment and Poverty Reduction. Available at www.peri.umass.edu.

Epstein, G., Grabel, I. and Jomo, K. S. (2004) "Capital Management Techniques In Developing Countries: An Assessment of Experiences from the 1990's and Lessons For the Future," Published as *G24 Discussion Paper No. 27*, March, United Nations, New York and Geneva.

Forbes, K. (2007) "One Cost of the Chilean Capital Controls: Increased Financial Constraints for Smaller Traded Firms," *Journal of International Economics*, 71: 294–323.

Goldstein, M., Kaminsky, G. and Reinhart, C. (2000) *Assessing Financial Vulnerability: An Early Warning System for Emerging Markets*, Washington, DC: Institute for International Economics.

Grabel, I. (1995) "Speculation-led Economic Development: A Post-Keynesian Interpretation of Financial Liberalization in the Third World," *International Review of Applied Economics*, 9(2): 127–49.

—— (1996) "Marketing the Third World: the Contradictions of Portfolio Investment in the Global Economy," *World Development*, 24(11): 1761–76.

—— (1999) "Rejecting Exceptionalism: Reinterpreting the Asian Financial Crises," in J. Michie and J. Grieve Smith (eds.) *Global Instability: The Political Economy of World Economic Governance*, 37–67, London: Routledge.

—— (2003a) "Ideology, Power and the Rise of Independent Monetary Institutions in Emerging Economies," in J. Kirshner (ed.) *Monetary Orders: Ambiguous Economics, Ubiquitous Politics*, 25–52, Ithaca: Cornell University Press.

—— (2003b) "Averting Crisis: Assessing Measures to Manage Financial Integration in Emerging Economies," *Cambridge Journal of Economics*, 27: 317–36.

—— (2004) "Trip Wires and Speed Bumps: Managing Financial Risks and Reducing the Potential for Financial Crises in Developing Economies," Published as *G24 Discussion Paper No. 33*, November, United Nations and Geneva.

—— (2007a) "One Step Forward, Two Steps Back: Policy (In) Coherence and Financial Crises," in B. Muchhala (ed.) *Ten Years After: Revisiting the Asian Financial Crisis*, 95–104, Washington, DC: Wilson Center Press.

—— (2007b) "Policy Coherence or Conformance: The New IMF-World Bank-WTO Rhetoric on Trade and Investment in Developing Countries," *Review of Radical Political Economics*, 39(3): 335–41.

Hearn, K. (2006) "Venezuela Proposes 'Bank of the South,'" *Washington Times* January 13, available at www.washingtontimes.com.

Krugman, P. (1998) "Open letter to Mr. Mahathir," *Fortune*, September 28.

McKinnon, R. and Pill, H. (1998) "International Overborrowing: A Decomposition of Credit and Currency Risks," *World Development*, 26(7): 1267–82.

MSNBC.com (2007) "Chavez: Venezuela to Exit IMF, World Bank," May 1, 2007.

Prasad, E., Rogoff, K., Wei, S. and Kose, M. A. (2003) *Effects of Financial Globalization on Developing Countries: Some Empirical Evidence.* Available at www.imf.org/external/np/res/docs/2003/031703.htm.

Rodrik, Dani (1999) *The New Global Economy and Developing Countries: Making Openness Work*, Washington, DC, Overseas Development Council, Policy essay No. 24.

—— (ed.) (2003) *In Search of Prosperity: Analytical Narratives on Economic Growth*, Princeton: Princeton University Press.

Sinclair, T. (2005) *The New Masters of Capital: American Bond Rating Agencies and the Politics of Creditworthiness*, Ithaca: Cornell University Press.

Wade, R. (2007) "From Liberalize the Market to "Standardize the Market" and Create a "Level Playing Field," in B. Muchhala (ed.) *Ten Years After: Revisiting the Asian Financial Crisis*, 73–94, Washington, DC: Wilson Center Press.

Part V

Conclusion

20 Heterodox macroeconomics and the current global financial crisis

Jonathan P. Goldstein

Introduction

This concluding chapter applies the integrated heterodox macrofoundations developed in this volume to explain the current global financial crisis. I argue that to effectively understand the current global crisis of capitalism requires the integration of various strands of heterodox crisis theory, particularly Keynesian, Marxian and Institutionalist approaches.[1] The chapters in Parts I, II and III of this book, particularly those authored by Goldstein (Chapters 3 and 8), Dymski (Chapter 5), Orhanganzi (Chapter 9), Boddy (Chapter 12) and Kotz (Chapter 13) provide an essential foundation for achieving this goal.

An integrated heterodox view of the current crisis

The world economy is in the grips of a financial crisis that has the potential to rival the Great Depression. Yet, the readily visible financial aspects of the crisis are merely the superficial expression of a deeper crisis that revolves around the nexus of under-consumption, over-investment and financial crises.[2] An integrated heterodox approach is uniquely suited to understanding these interconnected crisis components due to its focus on the interrelations between social classes, the distribution of income, effective demand, Marxian competition, crisis theory, Keynesian uncertainty, financial innovation and fragility, endogenous expectations, and structural and institutional change.

Let us consider the three interrelated crisis mechanisms currently operating. The decline of the Golden Age led to significant changes in the balance of power between social classes. First, industrial capitalists increased their power relative to labor. Second, the absolute rise to power of financial capitalists[3] resulted in the further weakening of labor and the relative weakening of industrial capitalists. This realignment of power resulted in a dramatic shift in the distribution of income against labor in the advanced capitalist economies, documented by Boddy (Chapter 12) and Kotz (Chapter 13), with the possible exception of the Asian economies but only prior to the 1997 East Asian financial crisis. This shift created the basis for a slowly evolving secular under-consumption crisis that would remain dormant until its countervailing tendencies were exhausted.[4]

At first, workers responded to reductions in their real income by transitioning to a two-income-earner household in the early 1980s. After that, the consumption of American families could only be maintained through increasing hours of work, a dependence on increasing levels of debt and most recently by wealth-induced consumption as a result of asset bubbles. When these mechanisms failed to maintain the growth in household consumption, credit, in the form of sub-prime mortgages, was extended to households on the margin of financial stability. This was done in an attempt to increase financial profits, but also had the effect of bolstering overall consumption.

Yet, this manner of sustaining consumption turned out to be far more risky than previous countervailing measures for under-consumption. In this case, financial innovation, in the form of these new mortgages, was more directly aimed at a weakened consumer market rather than an investor market. This qualitative difference in endogenous lending, occurring during the latter stages in the development of a potential under-consumption crisis, made the economy far more susceptible to a deep under-consumption crisis set off by a financial crisis.

At the same time that the potential for an under-consumption problem developed, industrial profit rates recovered slowly or stagnated after their late Golden Age decline. Despite the weakening of labor that supported higher markups, financial firms captured an increasing share of industrial profits (see Orhanganzi (Chapter 9)). International competition, both industrial and financial (see Crotty (2008)), increased as corporate free trade and financial liberalization policies gained favor. Thus, in addition to keeping consumption afloat via debt, the accumulation of industrial capital became heavily debt dependent. Industrial capitalists facing increased international competition found it necessary to defend their illiquid and already underutilized (due to slow growth in consumption) capital at a time when internal funds (profits) were inadequate. This set of outcomes is consistent with Goldstein's (Chapter 8) model of investment. Firms attempted to maintain their competitive position via debt-financed cost-cutting investment and destructive price wars. Thus, a tendency to over-investment emerges (Crotty (2003a, 2003b, 2005)). In order to ease the financing of this survival strategy and to improve the earnings outlook in the eyes of impatient financial markets (Orghangazi (Chapter 9)), industrial firms pursued a low road labor strategy, based on downsizing and wage and benefit concessions, that further weakened consumption demand. Crotty (2003a, 2003b, 2005) has referred to this over-investment/under-consumption dynamic as the Neoliberal paradox.

Simultaneously, now powerful financial interests (Epstein (2005) and Orhanganzi (Chapter 9)) pushed for the deregulation and liberalization of world financial markets. This resulted in intensified financial competition over increased household and firm demand for credit that in turn fed a wave of financial innovation (from junk bonds, securitization, collateralized debt obligations to credit default swaps). In Minskian fashion (Dymski (Chapter 5) and Orhanganzi (Chapter 9)), these financial market developments allowed under-consumption to be temporarily averted and furthered over-investment tendencies that were transmitted via liberalized financial markets to developing economies.

Continued macroeconomic growth now became dependent on a financially fragile debt structure that increasingly relied on consumption propped up by wealth effects induced by asset bubbles. These asset bubbles were internally generated by increases in endogenous credit facilitated by financial innovation. These bubbles were allowed to persist by competition-induced decreases in inflation that allowed monetary authorities to place a greater weight, than previously used, on GDP growth via lower interest rate policies. In the most recent period, such policies fueled both speculative and new demand for homes resulting in rising house prices.

Given the operation of these three crisis tendencies, I now consider how their interaction can result in a deep and prolonged economic downturn. In the above scenario, the reproduction of viable growth has relied heavily on debt-financed consumption and investment, luxury consumption and asset bubbles/wealth effects. Yet the inability to maintain a permanent bubble, despite capitulation by the Fed, sounds the death knell for the countervailing tendencies to the underlying under-consumption/over-invest crisis. While bubbles have popped before and the system has recovered with minor setbacks, it is the increasing dependency on debt and competition-induced and deregulation-inspired increases in the riskiness of financial innovation,[5] that suggests that the most recent burst in the housing price bubble will fully expose the deep-seated contradictions and unsustainable nature of Neoliberal macrodynamics.

In an economy where two-thirds of demand is consumption based, it becomes very difficult to sustain economic growth when consumption is propped up by inordinate levels of debt, asset bubbles and the extension of debt to marginally solvent households. As in the current situation, when an asset bubble that underlies the marginal extension of debt bursts,[6] it is not only the marginal borrowers that are affected. Additionally, the typical over-extended households that have hit their borrowing limits will also be constrained, particularly as the wealth effect that cushioned their expenditures disappears. Finally, when consumption demand collapses, industrial capitalists already laden with excess capacity must shift from an investment strategy geared at meeting the competition to a strategy geared at preserving cash flow. Thus investment also declines.

As the crisis unfolds, a Fischer–Keynes–Minsky debt-deflation mechanism will deepen the severity of the crisis. The widespread distribution of toxic assets and their derivatives that underlie the housing price bubble has resulted in fundamental uncertainty concerning the exposure of firms and institutions to such assets. Additionally, there exists the lack of a full understanding, even by the fundamental players, of the mechanisms of new financial instruments and the shadow banking system. As a result, credit markets have not only contracted during this crisis, but have frozen in a manner reminiscent of a Keynesian liquidity trap. Thus, limited economic activity during the downturn will be further constrained and when the conditions for the profitable accumulation of capital are finally re-established, the credit system may still act as a drag on the system.

This sketch of the current crisis relies heavily on argumentation from heterodox macroeconomic traditions and suggests that an integrated heterodox approach is most suited for developing a holistic understanding of Neoliberal macrodynamics. This approach also highlights a major heterodox proposition concerning the elusive nature of balanced growth (Goldstein (Chapter 3)). When the distribution of income significantly impacts effective demand in contradictory ways,[7] shifts in distribution/accumulation regimes from unbounded versions of wage-led to profit-led to finance-led regimes carry with them the seeds of unsustainable growth. The latter two regimes that engender under-consumption tendencies may take time to overcome countervailing tendencies, but once those defense mechanisms are exhausted, a significant crisis is likely to result. The finance-led regime that allows for debt/credit offsets to under-consumption only results in a deeper decline when a potential financial crisis brings an abrupt end to debt-supported consumption, particularly as debt-deflation erodes the foundations of those supports.

As discussed by Goldstein (Chapter 3), the conditions for balanced growth require bounded social relations, both competitive and industrial relations. These conditions are most likely to obtain in a bounded wage-led regime as experienced during the Golden Age. The Golden Age came to an end when both sets of social relations became unbounded. Given recent experience, the conditions for balanced growth must also exclude incursions from financial capitalists and financial institutions that undermine the bounded nature of these other social relations.

Thus the major policy conclusion from the recent global crisis experience is that the current corporate form of globalization must be replaced with a more balanced and equitable approach to trade – fair trade, where balance is achieved across classes and across countries with different levels of development. Additionally, financial markets must be regulated in the fashion discussed by Epstein (Chapter 18) and Grabel (Chapter 19).

Notes

1 For papers that specifically consider the current crisis using this approach, see Crotty (2003a, 2003b, 2005), Goldstein (2009), Kotz (2008, Chapter 13) and Orhangazi (Chapter 9).

2 Since 1980, the most visible sign of crisis has been a string of financial crises. These include the savings and loan crisis, the housing price bubble of the late 1980s, the stock market crash of 1987, Japan's real estate bubble, the Mexican currency crisis, the Russian currency crisis, the East Asian financial crisis, the dotcom stock market crash and now the sub-prime mortgage/housing bubble debacle. Yet, it would be myopic to ignore the class-based real sector factors underlying these more visible crisis tendencies.

3 The rise to power of financial capitalists is associated with the decline in industrial profit rates at the end of the Golden Age and the intensification of foreign competition and thus the need for firms to investment with diminished internal funds. In addition, the shift in focus of macroeconomic policy from unemployment to inflation, the deregulation of financial markets, the resulting unfettered financial innovation, the opening up of international financial markets and changes in consumer bankruptcy laws all contributed to this rise in power. A burgeoning heterodox literature on financialization has analyzed this transition. See Epstein (2005) and the papers within.

4 Also, see Goldstein (2000) for an analysis of the shift in the distribution of income and the potential and offsetting tendencies for an under-consumption crisis. These counter-vailing tendencies include luxury consumption, exports, a two-income-earner house-hold, debt-led consumption and wealth effects induced by asset bubbles. Under-consumption crises are usually slow to evolve, but when they present them-selves their impact on the economy can be devastating.

The flipside of Boddy's (Chapter 12) demonstration of the weakening of the profit squeeze mechanism is the evolution of an under-consumption tendency. While Kotz (Chapter 13) does not find evidence of under-consumption in the first two cycles of the Neoliberal era, this does not imply that such tendencies lie just beneath the surface. The success of counter-tendencies during the first two cycles underlies this result.

5 Additionally, continued shifts in the distribution of income, further competitive pressures on industrial capitalists and continued low-road labor strategies have played a role.

6 It is not my intention to imply that the bursting of a bubble is exogenous. There are numerous internal reasons, both real and financial, that can lead to the end of an asset bubble. See Crotty (1986) for a discussion.

7 An increase in labor's share of income stimulates consumption in the long-run, while it also dampens investment in the short and long-runs and vice versa.

References

Crotty, J. 1986. "Marx, Keynes and Minsky on the Instability of the Capitalist Growth Process and the Nature of Government Economic Policy," in, *Marx, Keynes and Schumpeter: A Centenary Celebration of* Dissent, eds. D. Bramhall and S. Helburn, 297–326. Armonk: M. E. Sharpe.

—— 2003a. "Core Industries, Coercive Competition and the Structural Contradictions of Global Neoliberalism," in *The New Competition for Inward Investment: Companies, Institutions and Territorial Development*, eds. N. Phelps and P. Raines, 9–37. North-ampton, MA: Edward Elgar.

—— 2003b. "The Neoliberal Paradox: The Impact of Destructive Product Market Com-petition and Impatient Finance on Nonfinancial Corporations in the Neoliberal Era," *Review of Radical Political Economics*, 35(3): 271–9.

—— 2005. "The Neoliberal Paradox: The Impact of Destructive Product Market Com-petition and 'Modern' Financial Markets on Nonfinancial Corporation Performance in the Neoliberal Era," *Financialization and the World Economy*, ed. G. Epstein, 77–110. Cheltenham, UK and Northampton, MA: Edward Elgar.

—— 2008. "If Financial Market Competition Is Intense, Why Are Financial Firm Profits so High? Reflections on the Current 'Golden Age' of Finance," *Competition and Change*, 12(2): 167–83.

Epstein, G. 2005. *Financialization and the World Economy*, Cheltenham, UK and North-ampton, MA: Edward Elgar.

Goldstein, J. P. 2000. "The Global Relevance of Marxian Crisis Theory," in *Political Economy and Contemporary Capitalism: Radical Perspectives on Economic Theory and Policy*, eds. R. Baiman, H. Boushey and D. Saunders, 68–77. Armonk and London: M. E. Sharpe.

—— 2009. "Heterodox Crisis Theory and the Current Global Financial Crisis," *Review of Radical Political Economics*, 41(4).

Kotz, D. M. 2008. "Contradictions of Economic Growth in the Neoliberal Era: Accumu-lation and Crisis in the Contmporary U.S. Economy," *Review of Radical Political Eco-nomics*, 40(2): 174–88.

Index